Daimler-Benz in the Third Reich

Daimler-Benz in the Third Reich

Neil Gregor

Yale University Press
New Haven and London

Set in Goudy by MATS, Southend-on-Sea, Essex
Printed in Great Britain by St. Edmundsbury Press

Library of Congress Cataloging-in-Publication Data

Gregor, Neil, 1969–
    Daimler-Benz in the Third Reich/Neil Gregor.
    Includes bibliographical references and index.
    ISBN 0–300–07243–0
    1. Daimler-Benz Aktiengesellschaft—History. 2. Forced labor—Germany. 3. World War, 1939–1945—Prisoners and prisons, German. 4. Defense Industries—Germany—History—20th century. 5. Industrial mobilization—Germany—History—20th century.
    I. Title.
    HD9743.G48G74   1998
    338.7'6234'0943—dc21   97–34850
                                                                                          CIP

A catalogue record for this book is available from the British Library.

10 9 8 7 6 5 4 3 2 1

All photographs, unless otherwise stated, courtesy Mercedes-Benz Classic Archive, Stuttgart.

For my parents

Contents

Acknowledgments

It is a great pleasure to record the many professional and personal debts that I have incurred during the period in which this project was undertaken. First thanks must go to Jeremy Noakes for his encouragement, advice and engaged criticism before, during and since the period in which the original research for this book was carried out. Beyond this, the Department of History at the University of Exeter provided a supportive and friendly environment in which to carry out the initial research. More recently, I have enjoyed the friendship and support of colleagues in the Department of History at the University of Southampton. Academic life is not without its frustrations, and I owe my colleagues a great deal for their support. Beyond thanking them all for their convivial company and good humour, I am particularly grateful for having been given the space to bring the project to a successful conclusion when I first arrived at Southampton.

Generous financial support was provided by the Economic and Social Research Council. I have been fortunate to benefit from the expertise of librarians and archivists in many institutions in Britain, Germany and the United States – a particular word of thanks is due to Dr Harry Niemann and the staff of the Mercedes-Benz Archive in Stuttgart. Dr Niemann not only gave me unlimited access to the materials contained in the Mercedes-Benz Archive, including much previously unreleased material, but also provided a superb working environment. In addition to the papers I gave at Exeter and Southampton, Hans Mommsen and Hans-Peter Ullmann enabled me to present papers in Bochum and Tübingen respectively. Heidrun Edelmann, George Bernard and Andrew Thorpe commented and made useful suggestions for improvement on all or parts of the manuscript, for which I am grateful and which I hope have benefited the final text. Thanks are also due to Robert Baldock at Yale University Press, not only for his encouragement, but also for allowing me to continue to develop the project in the manner in which I wished.

On a personal level, my thanks go to the many friends who have provided good company, accommodation and other support along the way. Particular mention must be made of Alison Ayres, C.C.C., Marianne Reeve, Neil

Riddell, Holger Schweinfurth, the Cafe Winzig Scooter Club, Kevin Stannard and Russell Thomas.

Two final debts have to be recorded. The first is to Chris Marks, an inspirational teacher who first stimulated my interest in German history and culture; the second, and most important, of my debts is to my parents for their love and support over the years.

N.G.
Southampton, February 1997

Abbreviations

ABB	Amt für Berufserziehung und Betriebsführung der DAF (Office for Vocational Training and Factory Management of the DAF)
AKL	Arbeitskreis Lastwagen (Working Party on Lorry Production)
AOG	Gesetz zur Ordnung der Nationalen Arbeit (Law for the Ordering of National Labour)
AWI	Arbeitswissenschaftliches Institut der DAF (Labour Science Institute of the DAF)
BA (K)	Bundesarchiv Koblenz
BA (P)	Bundesarchiv Abteilung Potsdam
BA-MA	Bundesarchiv-Militärarchiv Freiburg
DAF	Deutsche Arbeitsfront (German Labour Front)
DBAG	Daimler-Benz Aktiengesellschaft (Daimler-Benz Joint Stock Company)
DVP	Deutsche Volkspartei (German People's Party)
FAKRA	Fachnormenauschuss der Kraftfahrzeugindustrie (Automobile Industry Standardisation Committee)
FMO	Flugmotorenwerk Ostmark (Ostmark Aero-Engine Company)
GBK	Generalbevollmächtigte für das Kraftfahrwesen (General Plenipotentiary for the Automobile Industry)
HWA	Heereswaffenamt (Army Weapons Procurement Office)
KdF	Kraft durch Freude (Strength through Joy)
LKdDB	Leistungskampf der Deutschen Betriebe (Achievement Competition of German Business)
LKEM	Lohngruppenkatalog Eisen und Metall (Wages Group Catalogue for the Iron and Metal Industries)
LSA	Landesstrafanstalt (State Prison)
MBAG	Archiv der Mercedes-Benz AG, Stuttgart
NSDAP	Nationalsozialistische Deutsche Arbeiter Partei (National Socialist German Worker's Party)
OKW	Oberkommando der Wehrmacht (Armed Forces High Command)

OT	Organisation Todt
RAM	Reichsarbeitsministerium (Reich Labour Ministry)
RDA	Reichsverband der Deutschen Automobilindustrie (Reich Association of Automobile Producers)
RGBl	Reichsgesetzblatt (Reich Statute Book)
RLM	Reichsluftfahrtministerium (Reich Air Ministry)
RMfBuM	Reichsministerium für Bewaffnung und Munition (Reich Ministry for Weapons and Munitions)
RMfEuL	Reichsministeruim für Ernährung und Landwirtschaft (Reich Ministry for Food and Agriculture)
RMfRuK	Reichsministerium für Rüstung und Kriegsproduktion (Reich Ministry for Armaments and War Production)
RüIn	Rüstungsinspektion (Armaments Inspectorate)
RüKo	Rüstungskommando (Armaments Commando)
RVM	Reichverkehrsministerium (Reich Transport Ministry)
RWM	Reichwirtschaftsministerium (Reich Economics Ministry)
USSBS	United States Strategic Bombing Survey
WiGruFa	Wirtschaftsgruppe Fahrzeugindustrie (Economic Group Vehicle Industry)
WiGuLFZ	Wirtschaftsgruppe Luftfahrtindustrie (Economic Group Aircraft Industry)
WiRüAmt	Wirtschafts- und Rüstungsamt (Economic Armaments Office)

I. Introduction

All societies construct myths about their pasts, and none more so than post-war West Germany. While historians might consciously regard their work – in part, at least – as an exercise in the debunking of popular myths, popular mythologies about the past undoubtedly also influence the type of questions that historians ask. After all, historians are socialized in cultures saturated with myth too, and these cannot fail to influence the assumptions from which they themselves formulate the questions they ask of the past.

Post-war West German culture and historical writing are a case in point here. Above all, the myth of the 'zero hour', the central legitimating myth of the post-war Federal Republic, has undoubtedly exercised a strong influence over the ways in which historians have, until recently, thought about the relationship between the Third Reich and the history of the early Federal Republic. The popular fiction that post-war West German economic success was founded on its industry having been rebuilt from nothing, by dint of the hard labour of its industrious population alone – a fiction underpinned by a culture saturated with visual images of the rubble of 1945, and a fiction mobilized now to legitimate West German resentment at the subsidies paid to support the economy of the new federal states since reunification – has had a significant influence in shaping the work carried out by scholars on the post-war economic boom. In the sphere of economic and social history, the dominant view of post-war reconstruction and recovery largely absorbed the notion of a 'zero hour', with the prosperity of the Federal Republic in the 1950s and 1960s being put down to an 'economic miracle'. An exception was provided by the counter-critique of the hard Left, whose radical anti-capitalism led it to regard the post-war Federal Republic as a restored fascist state – the terrorist murders of prominent industrialists in the 1970s by the RAF (Hans-Martin Schleyer, the top Mercedes-Benz manager who was killed in 1977, is, in fact, a perfect example) is to be seen very much in this context. But the very fact that the exception to the dominant school of thought was rooted in a counter-culture that was strongly inspired by the Marxist-Leninist ideology of the German Democratic Republic hardly assisted its acceptance into either mainstream historical writing or popular opinion. Indeed, Cold War exigencies ensured that western non-German scholarship was, in general, as willing to facilitate the rehabilitation of West Germany by stressing the status of 1945 as a break with the past, as West German writings themselves.

If one looks at the various branches of German industry in the post-war period, the limits of the validity of the notion of a 'zero hour' in the economic sphere become immediately apparent. In heavy industry, it was the same firms that dominated in the post-war period as in the 1920s and 1930s. The same is true of the electrical engineering industry, as the examples of Siemens, AEG and Bosch show. Seen from this viewpoint, the notion of an 'economic miracle' seems indeed to represent less an accurate depiction of historical reality than a comfortable myth allowing West German society to distance itself psychologically and morally from the brutalities of the Third Reich.

Considerations such as these have led historians to begin to focus more closely on the issue of continuity between the Third Reich and the early post-war period. Recently, some historians have attempted to conceptualize the relationship between the National Socialist period and the early period of the Federal Republic by reference to the idea of 'modernization'. The view that the National Socialist regime had a 'modernizing' impact on German society is of direct relevance to an analysis of industry in the German war economy because – implicitly – it suggests that the post-war prosperity of the Federal Republic was primarily the product of developments in the National Socialist period. The main exponent of this line of argument is Rainer Zitelmann, who has not only argued that National Socialism had a modernizing impact on German society, but has also related this directly to what he characterizes as an intentionally modernizing ideology.[1]

Zitelmann argues that by insisting on the value-loaded nature of the concept, historians have only been able to apply the notion of modernization to liberal-democratic western societies, and that its applicability to the phenomenon of National Socialism has been rejected purely on the grounds that the National Socialist regime does not conform to the 'positive' liberal-democratic model. By using modernization as a value-free concept, on the other hand, one that implies neither positive nor negative judgment, Zitelmann argues that it is possible to apply the concept to societies other than liberal-democratic western societies, and thus to divest the word of its normative implications.[2]

1 Zitelmann, R., *Hitler. Selbstverständnis eines Revolutionärs*, 2nd edn., Stuttgart, 1989; Prinz, M. and
   Zitelmann, R. (eds.), *Nationalsozialismus und Modernisierung*, Darmstadt, 1991; Backes, U., Jesse, E.
   and Zitelmann, R. (eds.), *Die Schatten der Vergangenheit. Impulse zur Historisierung des
   Nationalsozialismus*, Frankfurt, 1991. For a critique see Frei, N., 'Wie Modern war der
   Nationalsozialismus?' in: *Geschichte und Gesellschaft* 19 (1993), pp. 367-87. Also Mommsen, H.,
   'Nationalsozialismus als vorgetäuschte Modernisierung' in: Pehle, W. (ed.), *Der Historische Ort des
   Nationalsozialismus*, Frankfurt, 1990, pp. 31–46; Kershaw, I., *The Nazi Dictatorship. Problems and
   Perspectives of Interpretation*, 3rd edn, London, 1993, pp. 202–6.
2 Zitelmann, R., 'Die Totalitäre Seite der Moderne' in: Prinz and Zitelmann (eds.),
   Nationalsozialismus und Modernisierung, p. 3.

Zitelmann's opposition to the tendency to equate the term 'modernization' with 'positive, desirable, good' is undermined not least by his own use of words such as 'progressive' to describe, for example, National Socialist social policy and planning.[3] Even if one accepts the possibility or desirability of using 'modernization' in a value-free manner, the fact remains that if it is to be usefully applied it has to be defined closely. Once the key elements of what one considers to be modernization are defined, however, one has constructed a model – which is therefore, by definition, normative. 'Modernization' cannot be used in anything other than a normative fashion precisely because, if it means anything, it implies that there are common constituent elements in the transformation of all societies. An examination of National Socialism that places those secular trends common to most European industrial societies at the centre of its analysis, however, necessarily marginalizes those aspects of National Socialism by which the peculiarity of the regime is defined and wherein its singularity lies (its genocide policies). The regime's racist ideology and policy and its imperialist expansionism – i.e. its core characteristics – are necessarily relativized by an interpretative framework constructed around 'modernization'.[4] Attempts to apply this concept to specific areas of National Socialist policy are equally problematic. The assertion that National Socialist policy in particular spheres was 'modernizing' in intent or effect is only possible by decontextualizing specific areas and treating them in isolation from the analysis of National Socialist ideology and policy as a whole – the core of which was, in both intent and effect, singularly destructive.[5]

If modernization is an inappropriate way of conceptualizing the relationship between the Third Reich and the Federal Republic, the issue of continuity nonetheless remains. An analysis of the history of one particular company during the war, and of the impact of the regime and the war on that company, offers precisely the chance to point to real, historical, empirically derivable lines of continuity in one specific sphere. As a typical example of a large armaments-producing company in the war and a major company in one of the key sectors of the post-war West German economy, the automotive engineering company Daimler-Benz AG lends itself particularly well to such a study.[6]

This study places the history of Daimler-Benz AG in the Second World

3   Zitelmann, 'Die Totalitäre Seite der Moderne', p. 17.
4   Frei, 'Wie Modern war der Nationalsozialismus?', p. 377.
5   Mason, T., 'The Primacy of Politics – Politics and Economics in National Socialist Germany' in: Turner, H.A. (ed.), *Nazism and the Third Reich*, New York, 1972, pp. 196–7.
6   The history of Daimler-Benz AG in the Third Reich was the subject of two general studies that appeared in the 1980s. The first was a company-sponsored, nominally independent but highly uncritical study produced by a group led by Hans Pohl; the second was essentially a riposte by a group of radical historians led by Karl-Heinz Roth. Both are deeply flawed. The former completely fails to problematize the relationship between big business and the Nazi regime, decontextualizing the development of the company in such a way as to avoid addressing the issue of the complicity of the company in the criminality of the regime; the second, which proceeds from assumptions that are strongly influenced by the Marxist-Leninist historiography of the former GDR, not only greatly

War within a broader continuum, tracing the development of the company from its formation in 1926 through to 1945, and pointing to factors in the company's development in the Third Reich that help to explain the company's successful recovery in the late 1940s and 1950s.[7] It examines how, in the radically changing economic context created by the Depression, the rearmament boom and the war, and in the radically changing political context provided by Weimar and the evolving National Socialist regime, the company pursued core strategies that help account for its ability to emerge from the wreckage of 1945. By focusing on the issue of rationalization policy – defined for the most part broadly as the utilization of capacity, the organization of production and the deployment of labour – within the broader context of the strategy of Daimler-Benz AG, and by assessing how the development of the company was influenced by the conditions of the National Socialist regime and the war economy, it becomes possible to assess the specific impact of the National Socialist regime and the war on (one part of) German industry without reference to the concept of 'modernization'. As rearmament and then the war greatly increased the role of the state in the direction of the economy, an analysis of rationalization involves not only the examination of developments at shop-floor level within the context of company strategy, but also of state-led attempts to reorganize each sector of the economy as a whole in the interests of the military and the regime itself, such as the Schell Programme of the immediate pre-war period and Speer's rationalization drive from 1942 onwards. Where private company strategy and the regime's interventionism came into conflict, the focus here is on assessing how far industry was able to pursue its own interests on the basis of an autonomous strategy within the overall context created by the regime and the war.

In order to assess the impact of the war on the longer-term development of policy at the company, Chapter II provides an analysis of the reception of 'Fordism' by the automobile industry in general and surveys the development

over-states the autonomy of industry vis-à-vis the regime and the extent to which Nazi policy was orchestrated in the interests of big business, but is also deeply unscholarly and polemical. Pohl, H. et al., *Die Daimler-Benz AG in den Jahren 1933 bis 1945*, Stuttgart, 1987; Hamburger Stiftung für Sozialgeschichte (HRG) (ed.), *Das Daimler-Benz Buch. Ein Rüstungskonzern im Tausendjährigen Reich*, Nördlingen, 1987; for a penetrating critique of the latter see Hentschel, V., 'Daimler-Benz im 3. Reich. Zu Inhalt und Methode zweier Bücher zum Gleichen Thema' in: *Vierteljahresheft für Sozial- und Wirtschaftsgeschichte* 75 (1988), pp. 74–100.

7   For an interesting attempt to address the issue of continuity between the war and post-war eras on the basis of a comparison between the British and German experiences see Reich, Simon, *The Fruits of Fascism. Postwar Prosperity in Comparative Perspective* (London, 1991). However, Reich's contention that the Third Reich witnessed the emergence of a culture of protecting domestic companies against foreign competitors, while highly stimulating, is simply not borne out by the evidence at key points. As the case of Daimler-Benz – a company that portrayed itself and was celebrated in the Third Reich as a traditional German company like few others – shows, pragmatic considerations could easily lead to its interests being subordinated to those of American competitors (in this case Opel); similarly, an American company – Ford – was one of the few to gain exemption from having to comply with aspects of the Schell Programme.

of Daimler-Benz in particular in the 1920s and 1930s, establishing the main features of the production processes and the strategies underlying them. It also contains a lengthy discussion of the rearmament process prior to the outbreak of the war, as both the impact of armaments production under National Socialism on the company and the company's changing response to this in the war cannot be understood without reference to the pre-war phase.

An analysis of one company also allows the possibility of addressing open questions on the history of the war economy itself. Since the publication of the results of the United States Strategic Bombing Survey (USSBS), research into the German war economy has essentially centred on the search for an explanation of the causes of the huge difference in output of the armaments economy in the first and second halves of the war.[8] The discussion of the differences in aggregate armaments output – expressed in terms of general indices of production – has traditionally been closely linked to discussion of the extent to which the regime was willing and able to cut back on consumption and consumer production in the first half of the war. The discussion of both the conversion of industrial capacity and the mobilization of the economically active and inactive sectors of the labour force has centred on how far fears for civilian morale, issues of ideology, the option of plunder as an alternative to domestic mobilization and the expectation of imminent final victory prevented the regime from mobilizing the economy for 'total war' until forced to do so by the reverses of the winter of 1941–2. What were in many respects incredible increases in armaments output from March 1942 onwards have usually been attributed to a conversion of capacity from consumer production to military production and a radical reorganization of the management of the war economy under Speer, who centralized control of the economy under the Ministry of Armaments and Munitions, completed the process of transferring control from the military to civilian agencies and instituted a mass rationalization programme.[9] As the key lift-off phase in armaments production coincided with radical changes in the administration of the economy, previous research has paid most attention to developments at the administrative level.

Accepting the conclusion of the USSBS that the years 1939 to 1942 saw only a partial conversion of capacity to armaments production, Alan Milward developed an analysis of the German war economy that argued that the first half of the war was characterized by an intentional policy of 'Blitzkrieg' economics ('Blitzkriegswirtschaft').[10] Milward argued that the concept of

---

8   United States Strategic Bombing Survey (USSBS), *Finished Report No.3. The Effects of Strategic Bombing on the German War Economy*, Washington D.C., 1947.
9   USSBS, *The Effects of Strategic Bombing*; Wagenführ, R., *Die Deutsche Industrie im Kriege 1939 bis 1945*, Berlin, 1963; Milward, A., *The German Economy at War*, London, 1965; Carroll, B., *Design for Total War. Arms and Economics in the Third Reich*, The Hague, 1968.
10 Milward, *The German Economy at War*, pp. 1–54.

'Blitzkrieg' referred not just to military strategy in the narrow sense, but to 'a method of waging war which would avoid the misery which war seemed destined to bring the civilian population.'[11] 'Blitzkrieg' thus referred to a policy of limited economic mobilization, which also allowed rapid switches in priorities between different branches of armaments production according to the strategic requirements of each 'lightning war'.[12] Not only was this system designed to prevent the need for a total mobilization of German industry and labour, it was 'conformable to the ad hoc administrative methods of National Socialism'.[13] Implicit in this final argument is the view that the plethora of party, civilian and military agencies active in the administration of the economy in the first half of the war actively facilitated this process of switching priorities and production programmes.

In fact, it now seems clear that, if anything, 'Blitzkrieg' tactics were less the product of an elaborate overall strategy for the mobilization and management of the war economy, and more a necessary product of failure.[14] Moreover, close analysis of data on Reich finance policy, civilian consumption and labour policy suggests that Hitler was expecting a long war and planned accordingly, and that the regime was mobilizing the economy for 'total war' from 1939 onwards.[15] Richard Overy has shown that the main real and percentage increases in taxation and financing of armaments production occurred in the first half of the war.[16] He also argues that cuts in civilian consumption during the first half of the war were in fact considerable, and that there was a far more substantial mobilization of the workforce – including the female workforce – for the war effort from 1939–1941 than is usually accepted.[17] According to Overy, the German war economy was 'close to full mobilization' in the summer and autumn of 1940.[18] The stagnation of output was not a product of an intentional strategy, but the result of 'mismanagement of the war economy on a very large scale between 1939 to 1941'.[19]

Indeed, far from constituting a highly flexible administrative system allowing a rapid and effective transfer of resources between different sectors, the plethora of self-duplicating and competing military, civilian and party agencies represented more of a barrier than an aid to the effective utilization

11 Ibid., p. 7.
12 Ibid., p. 10.
13 Ibid., p. 8.
14 Mason, T., *Sozialpolitik im Dritten Reich. Arbeiterklasse und Volksgemeinschaft*, Opladen, 1977.
15 See above all the work of Richard Overy: Overy, R. J., 'Hitler's War and the German Economy' in: *Economic History Review* 35 (1982) pp. 272–91; Overy, R. J., 'Mobilisation for Total War in Germany 1939–1941' in: *English Historical Review* 103 (1988), pp. 613–39; Overy, R. J., 'Blitzkriegswirtschaft? Finanzpolitik, Lebensstandard und Arbeitseinsatz in Deutschland 1939–1942' in: *Vierteljahreshefte für Zeitgeschichte* 36 (1988), pp. 379–435.
16 Overy, 'Blitzkriegswirtschaft?', p. 391.
17 Ibid., pp. 414–22.
18 Overy, 'Mobilisation for Total War', p. 625.
19 Ibid., p. 635; Overy, 'Blitzkriegswirtschaft?', p. 433.

of the available resources.[20] The successive erosion of rational-bureaucratic government and administration which was the key characteristic of the internal development of the Nazi polity was such that, even before 1939, the regime was moving away from, not towards, the principle of systematic planning and direction of the economy.[21] Bureaucratic frictions, inter-service rivalries and lack of coordination between various agencies were in themselves a prime cause of the failure to utilize resources effectively, not a result of a conscious policy of not doing so.[22]

Overy's interventions have not attained the status of a new orthodoxy, and it is nonetheless the case that there was potential for a further mobilization of resources and capacity in the first half of the war than that which actually took place. Rolf-Dieter Müller has pointed to policies such as the decentralization of contracts to small and medium sized firms in the first half of the war, rather than the concentration of resources on larger, more efficient plants as evidence of the ideological, political and systemic pressures militating against a fuller – or at least more effective – mobilization. Müller also stresses the extent to which the military victories of the first half of the war undermined any sense of urgency or necessity amongst key sectors of the regime and allowed an indecisive Hitler to avoid having to adjudicate between the rival claims of the civilian and military agencies. Common to both Overy and Müller, however, is the basic assertion that the regime was trying to mobilize the economy for a lengthy 'total' war from the outset.

Inherent in most approaches to the mobilization of the German war economy, with the exception of Müller's analysis, is the tendency to see the responsiveness (or otherwise) of the German economy, measured in terms of indices of output, as a direct indicator of the effectiveness (or otherwise) of the regime's policies. Increases in aggregate output in particular spheres are seen as a direct product of either organizational or administrative changes or of re-allocation of resources between different sectors of the armaments industry. While this is crucial and has to be taken into account when examining the development of one company within the broader context, industry itself tends in this approach to be relegated to the status of being a passive object of the regime's policies. An analysis that focuses more strongly on industry itself, on the impact of the regime's management of the war economy on industry and on the strategies industry attempted to pursue within the overall context

---

20 Müller, R.-D., 'Die Mobilisierung der Deutschen Wirtschaft für Hitlers Kriegsführung' in: Kroener, B. et al., *Organisation und Mobilisierung des Deutschen Machtbereichs. Kriegsverwaltung, Wirtschaft und Personelle Ressourcen 1939–1941*, Stuttgart, 1988 (Militärgeschichtliches Forschungsamt [ed.], *Das Deutsche Reich und der Zweite Weltkrieg*, Band 5.1.), pp. 347–689.
21 Müller, 'Mobilisierung', p. 356; on the general development of the Nazi state see Broszat, M., *The Hitler State*, London, 1981; Rebentisch, D. and Teppe, K. (eds.), *Verwaltung Contra Menschenführung im Staat Hitlers. Studien zur Politisch-Administrativen System*, Göttingen, 1986; Rebentisch, D., *Führerstaat und Verwaltung im Zweiten Weltkrieg*, Stuttgart, 1989.
22 Muller, 'Mobilisierung', pp. 366, 368.

created by the war, allows the possibility of approaching some of the questions raised by previous research on the war economy from a slightly different angle. It is clear that after the defeat of France the regime's attempts to mobilize armaments output conflicted with the expectations of industry that the war would be over soon and therefore pointed to the existence of a separate agenda on the part of industry.[23] It remains the case, however, that we know little about the attitude of industry to the war at various points: how did industrial companies see the situation in March 1940, September 1941, or April 1943? Where did they see their long-term interests and how did they seek to assert them within the changing military, economic and political context of the war? A key feature of the development of the war, seen from the viewpoint of German industry, is that for very significant phases of its course the widely held assumption was that it would be over more or less imminently. Given that industrial companies by their nature plan on the basis of mid- and long-term prognoses, it seems necessary to ask how industry balanced the need to respond to the demands of war production in the short-term – in a situation where armaments production provided its only market and in which it necessarily had to participate and compete – with issues of post-war expectations and long-term strategies that went beyond the war.

Analyses of the German war economy that focus on indices of industrial output also have the disadvantage that they imply a continuous production at shop-floor level, more or less moving at the same level as the overall index in any particular branch. The experience of German industry in the war economy was not, however, characterized by the continuous production of uniform models in long production runs, but by a regular process of complete or partial retooling for the production of changing models or numerous models with different specifications.[24] An analysis of the company's responses to such rapid shifts in production priorities, retooling for different models and changes in design – against the background of a radically changing labour force – allows not only insights into the very real problems for industrial managers caused by the regime's mismanagement, but also the possibility of assessing how far, within the limited room for manoeuvre available, this strategy was a product of war-time considerations on the one hand and post-war projections on the other.

Chapter III provides an overview of the development of the company during the war and attempts to relate the development of the company's strategy to its changing perception of the military situation and to changing political pressures emanating from the regime. In Chapter IV, the development of rationalization policy at two individual plants is traced. Here the focus is on assessing how far state pressures to rationalize production in the aero-engine and lorry sectors were compatible with private company strategy

---

23   Ibid., pp. 491, 496.
24   USSBS, *The Effects of Strategic Bombing*, p. 155.

and, where there was conflict between the two, on examining how this manifested itself at the interface between the pressures from above and those from below.

Any study of rationalization policy in the German war economy has immediately to come to terms with the fact that for crucial phases very little is discernible that one can term 'rationalization' in the sense of rational reorganization based on clear strategic planning and long-term perspectives of the type that occurred in the 1920s and mid-1930s. This is particularly the case for the period 1939 to 1941. In stressing how the failure to rationalise production in the interests of the war economy was not only a product of the regime's inherent organizational shortcomings, but also a consequence of the strategic choice of the company not to pursue such a policy owing to its perception of the war situation as an anomalous one of short duration, it becomes clear that all through the war, industry was pursuing objectives that went beyond it and was planning (as far as possible) for the long-term. While rationalization itself thus inevitably fades from focus in the years 1939 to 1941, the emphasis remains on the extent to which industry's pursuit of a particular course of action with regard to its utilization and organization of capacity was still based upon a rational calculation of its own interests in the context of that particular period. Again, as will be stressed, it was largely rational calculation of private interests that led the company to bridge the growing incompatibility between maximizing armaments output and the fundamental imperative of survival, by increasing collaboration in the brutal exploitation of forced and concentration camp labour both within and without the factory.

Much of the discussion of 'modernization' has been based on the recognition that in some respects developments under National Socialism did indeed go with the grain of longer-term secular trends in German – and European – society.[25] At the centre of much of this discussion has been the issue of industrial social policy, an area in which developments did indeed build on those of the 1920s and, in some respects, prefigure changes in the 1950s. An examination of the relationship between long-term secular trends and intentional modernization on the part of the regime therefore naturally leads to a discussion of the German Labour Front (*Deutsche Arbeitsfront* – DAF), the social policy programmes it developed, and the development of company social policy as practised by industry.[26] In the war, social policy was

25 Frei, 'Wie Modern war der Nationalsozialismus?', p. 378.
26 On the DAF see Schumann, H.-G., *Nationalsozialismus und Gewerkschaftsbewegung. Die Vernichtung der Deutschen Gewerkschaften und der Aufbau der Deutschen Arbeitsfront*, Hannover, 1958; Mason, *Sozialpolitik*, pp. 174–207; Recker, M.-L., *Nationalsozialistische Sozialpolitik im Zweiten Weltkrieg*, Munich, 1985; Mai, G., 'Warum Steht der Deutsche Arbeiter zur Hitler? Zur Rolle der Deutschen Arbeitsfront im Herrschaftssystem des Dritten Reichs' in: *Geschichte und Gesellschaft* 12 (1986), pp. 212–34; Smelser, R., *Robert Ley. Hitler's Labor Front Leader*, Oxford, 1988; Siegel, T., *Leistung und Lohn in der Nationalsozialistischen Ordnung der Arbeit*, Opladen, 1989;

an area of crucial importance owing to the necessity of maintaining and increasing the productivity of labour in the face of acute shortages, and to the need to integrate the new forms of labour that flooded into the factories and into the production processes. An examination of social policy in the war, against the background of state labour policy, forms the basis for Chapter V.[27]

Industrial social policy was an integral part of rationalization policy, whose evolution was directly related to technological and organizational change within the workplace.[28] The recognition that the alienating effects of monotonous work could have a negative influence over productivity in the long run led to the development of company social policy programmes that were essentially compensatory in nature, in that they attempted to counteract the dehumanizing effects of routinized labour by providing leisure activities, canteens and washrooms, and improvements to the work environment to reduce worker stress and fatigue. The realization that a worker's productivity could be influenced not only by purely technical factors but also by external factors such as family and home life underpinned the vision of a 'factory community' whereby all aspects of a worker's life would revolve round the factory, which would provide welfare structures arranged in line with the productivity-orientated goals of the company.[29] The integrative effects of a policy of improving work conditions were combined with a policy of atomization through the use of productivity-based pay and incentive systems that sought not only to improve productivity but to undermine collective attitudes among the workforce in favour of a more individualistic worker type who identified his interests with, rather than against, those of the company.[30]

In its promotion of social policy programmes aimed at raising worker productivity, the DAF was going very much with the grain of the employers' own policies towards their workers in the 1930s – policies which, in the political and legal framework created by the National Socialist seizure of power and the subsequent restructuring of labour relations in the interests of the employers, were much easier to implement than within the Weimar context.[31] The regime's labour legislation of January 1934 implicitly excluded

Freyberg, T. von and Siegel, T., *Industrielle Rationalisierung unter dem Nationalsozialismus*, Frankfurt/M., 1991; Frese, M., *Betriebspolitik im Dritten Reich. Deutsche Arbeitsfront, Unternehmer und Staatsbürokratie im Dritten Reich*, Paderborn, 1991.

27 Werner, W.-F., *Bleib Übrig. Deutsche Arbeiter in der Deutschen Kriegswirtschaft*, Düsseldorf, 1983; Salter, S., 'The Mobilisation of German Labour 1939–1945', unpublished D.Phil., Oxford, 1983; Wysocki, G., *Arbeit für den Krieg*, Braunschweig, 1992.

28 Freyberg and Siegel, *Industrielle Rationalisierung*, pp. 29–60; Homburg, H., *Rationalisierung und Industriearbeit. Das Beispiel des Siemenskonzerns Berlin 1900–1939*, Berlin, 1991, pp. 586–662.

29 Sachse, C., *Betriebliche Sozialpolitik als Familienpolitik in der Weimarer Republik und im National-sozialismus. Mit einer Fallstudie über die Firma Siemens*, Hamburg, 1987; Sachse, C., *Siemens, der Nationalsozialismus und die Moderne Familie. Eine Untersuchung zur Sozialen Rationalisierung in Deutschland*, Hamburg, 1990.

30 Homburg, *Rationalisierung und Industriearbeit*, pp. 584–5.

31 Frese, *Betriebspolitik*, pp. 112–13. On the AOG see Mason, T., 'Zur Entstehung des Gesetzes der Ordnung der Nationalen Arbeit von 20.Januar 1934' in: Mommsen, H. et al. (eds.), *Industrielles*

the DAF from the formulation of labour and social policy; nevertheless, the DAF continually tried to gain institutionalized jurisdiction over the formulation of all areas of labour policy. Its growing interest in social policy as a 'conditioning' process designed to maximize productivity was also reflected in the work of its Labour Science Institute (*Arbeitswissenschaftliche Institut –* AWI) and Office for Vocational Training and Management (*Amt für Berufserziehung und Betriebsführung –* ABB), the latter institute (previously DINTA) having been taken over from heavy industry in 1933.[32] The employers, however, remained suspicious of the DAF and opposed any measures that would set a precedent for outside interference in internal company affairs.[33] The restoration of managerial autonomy had been a key element in the cementing of cooperative relations between business and the regime in 1933–4, and business was equally keen on retaining this autonomy in the face of the DAF's attempts to gain codified influence over industrial social policy. Where companies did institute policies that were in line with those being promoted by the DAF, they were careful to implement them independently and under their own initiative. While the programmes of the DAF were in line with the ideals of modern factory management, caution is necessary in assessing how far it was an active agent in developing these methods and how far industry was, essentially, acting on its own agenda.[34]

The nature of the conflict between the DAF and industry has been the subject of much recent writing. Some historians have tended to stress the importance of conceptual differences between the racist-eugenicist elements of the DAF's programmes and company production-orientated criteria.[35] Others see these issues as secondary compared to more fundamental questions of power, jurisdiction and the retention of autonomy.[36] During the war, issues of both productivity and ideology came to the fore and, set against the background of the overall development of social policy, an analysis of the relationship between Daimler-Benz and the DAF allows an assessment of the significance of these issues on the level of an individual company.

Of particular importance for an analysis of labour policy in the war is the issue of forced foreign labour and prisoner of war and concentration camp labour. With regard to the policy towards the thousands of foreign workers

System und Politische Entwicklung in der Weimarer Republik, Band 1, Düsseldorf, 1977, pp. 322–51; Kranig, A., *Lockung und Zwang. Zur Arbeitsverfassung im Dritten Reich*, Stuttgart, 1984, pp. 38–55; Spohn, W., 'Betriebsgemeinschaft als Innerbetriebliche Herrschaft' in: Sachse et al. (eds.), *Angst, Belohnung, Zucht und Ordnung. Herrschaftsmechanismen im Nationalsozialismus*, Opladen, 1982, pp. 140–70.

32 On the ABB see Frese, *Betriebspolitik*, pp. 252–333.
33 Hachtmann, R., *Industriearbeit im Dritten Reich. Untersuchungen zu den Lohn- und Arbeitsbedingungen in Deutschland 1933–1945*, Göttingen, 1989, p. 212; Salter, 'Mobilisation', pp. 280–3.
34 Hachtmann, *Industriearbeit*, p. 257.
35 Sachse, *Betriebliche Sozialpolitik*; Sachse, *Siemens, der Nationalsozialismus und die Moderne Familie*; Freyberg and Siegel, *Industrielle Rationalisierung*.
36 Frese, *Betriebspolitik*; Hachtmann, *Industriearbeit*.

who flooded into Daimler-Benz's factories from 1941 and especially from the
winter of 1941–2 onwards, the focus is on assessing how policies were
implemented according to the racist hierarchy stipulated by the ideology of
the regime. While the issue of productivity increased in importance as the war
situation worsened, and while brutal physical exploitation gradually gave way
to a more differentiated form of discipline, control and reward for the foreign
workforce, it is argued that these issues were at all times secondary to the
discriminatory racist ideology. By examining how Daimler-Benz developed its
policy towards foreign workers in accordance with the racist principles of the
regime, the processes by which industry colluded in the realization of the Nazi
racial hierarchy within the industrial workplace are traced. Given the radical
discontinuity in the structure of the labour force, represented by the huge
influx of foreign workers, and the unique context within which 'social policy'
towards these workers was discussed, an analysis that places long-term
continuities at the centre of its approach is in many respects highly
problematic. However, a discussion of social policy towards both German and
foreign workers, and its role in raising – or at least maintaining – productivity,
is of relevance to the continuity debate insofar as it allows an assessment of
how far a genuine transformation of the production process was responsible for
the 'Production Miracle' in the second half of the war, and how far some of
this is attributable to a short-term intensification of labour made possible only
by the unique structure of the labour force and the unique political conditions
then prevailing.

An analysis of the history of an industrial company that emphasizes the
active pursuit of an independent strategy on the basis of interests that were not
always completely convergent with those of the political leadership naturally
has to define how much scope industry had for the pursuit of an autonomous
agenda within the context of the Nazi regime, and thus touches on the
broader issue of the relationship of politics and economics in the 'Third
Reich'. Instrumentalist analyses of the history of industry during the National
Socialist period which assert the 'primacy of politics' or the 'primacy of
economics' tend to overemphasise the homogeneity of both German industry
and the regime – both of which contained conflicting interest groups – and the
static nature of what, in fact, was a changing relationship characterized by
partial convergences and divergences of interest at different points in time.
Most attempts to construct a model of the relationship between industry and
the regime and to analyse developments within such a formulaic framework
founder on the diversity of individual experiences and on the lack of
empirically founded research in many areas. Leaving aside the Marxist-
Leninist orthodoxies of the historiography of the GDR, which, despite the
contribution it made to illuminating particular aspects of the history of
industry under National Socialism, nonetheless found little acceptance
outside the GDR in its overall contentions, most scholarship is agreed on the
view that a crucial change in the relationship between big business and the

regime took place in 1936. While often coming from radically different ideological and methodological starting points, much of this research confirms the basic contention of Mason's original intervention on the 'Primacy of Politics'.[37]

Mason's key contention was that 'both the domestic and the foreign policy of the National Socialist government became, from 1936 onward, increasingly independent of the influence of the economic ruling classes, and even in some essential aspects ran contrary to their collective interests'.[38] Most sectors of business had welcomed the apparent restoration of political stability in 1933–4, the destruction of the Left and the rapid economic recovery and creation of armaments contracts, and had experienced a rapid return to profitability which far outweighed occasional frictions over currency shortages or import controls. From the mid-1930s onward, however, there was growing unease within business circles at Hitler's adventurist foreign policy – Peter Hayes characterizes the period 1936-9 as 'the nervous years', even for a company (I. G. Farben) closely associated with the regime in the latter 1930s.[39] Opposition to the autarky policies of the Four Year Plan from export-orientated industries combined with general fears of the damaging impact of forced rearmament on the economy and fears of the consequences of becoming overdependent on state contracts.[40] From 1936 onwards, industry was forced to react in a defensive fashion to assert its interests within an overall set of developments that it regarded with ambivalent unease.

Mason himself argued that the accelerated pace of rearmament from the mid-1930s and the growing proportion of economic activity for which state expenditure accounted radically altered the nature of capitalist competition between individual companies. First, this manifested itself in direct competition for contracts from the state rather than for market share in a free market. Second, as rearmament brought with it shortages of labour, raw materials and foreign currency, companies were forced to compete for allocation of these finite resources, and their ability to produce was thus increasingly dependent on resources allocated or at least regulated by the state.[41] This took place within a far broader process of increased state intervention which, as the example of Daimler-Benz shows, caused huge frictions even with a company that had identified itself strongly with the

37 Mason, 'The Primacy of Politics'; this is a translation of Mason, T., 'Das Primat der Politik – Politik und Wirtschaft im Nationalsozialismus' in: Das Argument 8 (1966), p. 474; for the subsequent discussion Czichon, E., 'Der Primat der Industrie im Kartell der National-sozialistischen Macht' in Das Argument 10 (1968), pp. 168–92; Mason, T., 'Primat der Industrie? Eine Erwiderung' in: Das Argument 10 (1968), pp. 193–209; Eichholtz, D. and Gossweiler, K., 'Noch Einmal: Politik und Wirtschaft 1933–1945' in: Das Argument 10 (1968), pp. 210–27.
38 Mason, 'The Primacy of Politics', p. 176.
39 Hayes, P., Industry and Ideology. IG Farben in the Nazi Era, Cambridge, 1987.
40 Overy, R. J., 'Heavy Industry in the Third Reich: The Reichswerke Crisis' in: War and Economy in the Third Reich, pp. 93–100.
41 Mason, 'The Primacy of Politics', p. 186.

regime from the outset. These factors became even more prominent in the war, when companies had not only to compete for the allocation of resources, but to assert their interests within a radically changing context created by the regime's military expansion.

It was in many respects precisely the desperate pursuit of commercial self-interest that led directly to Daimler-Benz's managers collaborating in the barbarism of the Nazi regime to the extent that they did. Under certain circumstances, pragmatism encouraged barbarism. This may be partly explicable in terms of managerial culture. As an examination of the collusion of managers in the racial policy of the regime suggests, the process of creeping barbarization in the Third Reich is on one level as important as rational choices being made by industrialists in explaining much of what happened during the war. However, the issue is arguably less one of 'why good men do bad' than that of asking how the self-reproduction of capitalism manifested itself in the peculiar circumstances created by a uniquely destructive regime. Down to the end of the war, business complicity in the criminality of the Third Reich was a product primarily of rational choices, and the rationale behind them was a capitalist one. Different managers would not have made substantially different choices, which is why they as individuals receive relatively little attention in this study.

Viewing the firm as a single historical actor is in many ways itself problematic. Both the minutes of the internal company board meetings and the unified face presented to the outside exaggerate the internal cohesion of the company board and the coherence of policy formation. As with any company – as indeed with any body of people – there were divisions in opinion and agenda. Within the board, there were convinced Nazis who wished to use the opportunities offered by the regime to pursue a massive programme of armaments-orientated expansion both in Germany and in occupied Europe. There were also more national-conservative figures, who certainly did not reject the regime in any sense and who were certainly not above adopting Nazi racism if it might benefit the company (Wilhelm Kissel, the chairman of the managerial board from 1926 to 1942, is a case in point here), but who differed from the more fanatical Nazis in their somewhat more cautious view of the firm's interests and prospects. In addition, there were increasingly figures who can be seen as hard-headed technocrats. The fact that this generation of technocratic managers came to the fore in the war – embodied in the replacement of Wilhelm Kissel as chairman of the board in 1942 by Wilhelm Haspel – and that precisely this generation presided over the brutal exploitation of forced workers and concentration camp inmates tells us much about the hard-headed pragmatic pursuit of company self-interest which led to its collusion in Nazi barbarism.

Seeing the firm as a single historical actor is also problematic insofar as on crucial occasions divisions within the board allowed the regime to impose measures on the company after individual actors had acted of their own accord in giving assurances or offers to representatives of the regime without the assent of the board, with which the company was then forced to comply. This was the case with the establishment of a plant at Königsberg, for example. The failure to present a united face to the representatives of the regime was also partly responsible for the company being forced to accept the production of the Opel 3-ton lorry under licence.

However, it would be easy to overstate these divisions and lose sight of the essential fact that this was a company, whose managers operated collectively and on the basis of interests that were essentially corporate, not personal. The fact that industry was pursuing corporate interests that, by the time war broke out at the latest, were only partly convergent with those of the regime, and that within the National Socialist system companies were acting to defend competitive positions against other companies rather than in self-identification with the aims of the regime, does nothing to relativize the complicity of industry in the criminality of the regime. In pursuit of their own interests, companies actively participated in the exploitation of foreign, concentration camp and Jewish labour, in 'Aryanization' policies, and in the exploitation of the occupied territories. Daimler-Benz was no exception here. Without the collaboration of industry, none of these crimes would have been possible. Industry placed its own interests – directly and indirectly, the pursuit of profit – above those of the victims of the regime. As the discussion of the deployment of concentration camp inmates in the dispersal of production from 1943 shows (Chapter VI), the issues of continuity and complicity are most closely linked precisely where industry had abandoned the regime and was acting purely in self-interest.

II. Fusion and Crisis: Daimler-Benz in the 1920s

1. The Reception of Fordism by the German Automobile Industry

While the phrase itself was a novelty in the 1920s, the basic aim underlying the concept of industrial rationalization in the context of an economy organized on capitalist principles – the maximization of private profit – reflected the primary purpose of industrial management since the emergence of the industrial capitalist economy itself. The ongoing process of optimizing the deployment of technology, labour and time and the relationship between all three in any given economic and political situation was in this sense nothing new.[1] It was in the 1920s, however, under the influence of new forms of factory organization and management that had recently been developed in America, that the phrase became associated with an integrated vision of technological, economic and social development which would encompass, and indeed define, the whole of society.[2]

The Fordist-Taylorist paradigm of technical and organizational rationalization, based on mass production techniques first introduced at the Highland Park Factory of Ford Motor Company and on the scientific management of Taylor, Bedaux and others, combined the promise of increased efficiency and profits with a propagandistic vision of social progress. Mass production of standardized goods on special-purpose machinery, operated by unskilled labour

---

1 The definition of the term 'rationalization' is discussed in Reichskuratorium für die Wirtschaftlichkeit (RKW) (ed.), *Handbuch der Rationalisierung*, Berlin, 1930, pp. 1–2; Gramsci, A., 'Americanism and Fordism' in: Hoare, Q. and Nowell, Smith G. (eds.) *Selections from the Prison Notebooks of Antonio Gramsci*, London, 1971, pp. 279–318; for discussions in the historiography see Homburg, *Rationalisierung und Industriearbeit*, pp. 1–15; Freyberg and Siegel, *Industrielle Rationalisierung*, pp. 9–27.

2 Homburg, *Industriearbeit*, pp. 1–2; On developments in the 1920s see Freyberg, T. von, *Industrielle Rationalisierung in der Weimarer Republik*, Frankfurt, 1989. The implications of 'American' production methods were discussed extensively in contemporary engineering and technical journals: in one issue of one journal see Schmidt, K.H., 'Betriebswissenschaftliche Grundlagen für die Einführung der Fließarbeit' in: *Maschinenbau* 4 (1925), 9, pp. 409–15; Michel, E., 'Fließarbeit und ihre Entwicklungsmöglichkeiten', pp. 416–17; Wiedmann, W., 'Die Anwendung der Fließarbeit in Amerika und in England', pp. 425–30.

repeating simple, easy-to-learn functions, combined with the centrally planned integration of the factory's capital goods, labour and materials into a coordinated and flowing production process using the minimum of time, energy and material at each point, would greatly reduce production costs.[3] The lowering of unit costs brought about by mass production and scientific management would translate into lower prices for finished goods. Higher wages, brought about by increased efficiency, would simultaneously increase the purchasing power of the mass of the population. These two factors combined would bring the goods produced into the purchase range of an ever-broadening sector of society, extending downwards the ability to consume and stimulating the demand for further mass-produced goods. The development of mass consumer society was thus a self-perpetuating one in which the demands of capital for increased profits and those of labour for increased consumption would be harmonized.

The 1920s in Germany did indeed see the widespread introduction of 'new labour- or time-saving forms of investment; the introduction of new manufacturing methods based on high technology, as in the chemical industry, the replacement of manual operations by machine-tools; and assembly-line mass production, in which work processes were subdivided into separate tasks performed at a determined speed.'[4] These moves combined the search for improved efficiency and competitiveness within the market with the realization of the disciplining and controlling potential within the factory of a system of production characterized by a relentless flow of goods 'in which the pace of work is usually set not by the worker but by the interlocking and continuously operating mechanical or quasi-mechanical processes.'[5] This disciplining and controlling function was the product of a broader aim of excluding or neutralizing all disruptive influences on the autonomy of management and was as such implicitly political in motivation.[6] The exclusion of all individual or collective external influences on production and management which was integral to the capitalist vision of rationalization represented, behind the propaganda of social progress, an attempt to reinforce a particular set of power relationships both within the factory and in the

3 Nevins, A., Ford. *The Times, the Man, the Company*, New York, 1989; Meyer, S., *The Five Dollar Day. Labor Management and Social Control in the Ford Motor Company*, New York, 1981; Gartman, D., *Auto Slavery. The Labor Process in the American Automobile Industry 1897–1950*, New Brunswick, 1986; Stahlmann, M., *Die Erste Revolution in der Autoindustrie. Management und Arbeitspolitik von 1900 bis 1940*, Frankfurt, 1993, pp. 26–34.
4 Peukert, D., *The Weimar Republic*, London, 1991, p. 113.
5 Brady, R., *The Rationalisation Movement in German Industry. A Study in the Evolution of Economic Planning*, New York, 1933, p. 44; Freyberg, *Industrielle Rationalisierung in der Weimarer Republik*, p. 200.
6 For an interpretation that locates shop-floor developments within a far broader distributional conflict between capital and labour contested by employers' and workers' organizations against the changing political context provided by Kaiserreich, Weimar and the Nazi period see Homburg, *Rationalisierung und Industriearbeit*; also Frese, *Betriebspolitik*, pp. 12–13.

broader political context at a time when capitalism was becoming increasingly crisis-prone.

The ideal-typical model contrasted strongly with the real economic and political situation within which German industry found itself operating after the First World War. Far from witnessing the continuous upward spiral of production, consumption and prosperity, the experience of German industry was conditioned by the problems of demobilization, inflation and hyper-inflation, by fluctuating demand, stagnation and Depression, and by political instability, upheaval and polarization. These problems were particularly reflected in the experience of the automobile industry, which laboured under conditions of 'permanent crisis' in the 1920s.[7] Even in the mid- to late 1920s, genuine stability was never achieved, demand remained weak and profitability elusive.[8]

Perhaps not surprisingly, the automobile industry was one of the first to recognize the potential of the new forms of production being pioneered in America, and, in some way or another, all companies in the sector moved towards a system of management in which, in principle, 'the group producing motors produces one motor in regular tempo in the same time as the group producing rear axles produces one rear axle.'[9] With this went the increasing centralization of the planning of production and a clear tendency thus towards a division of planning and execution, which undermined the autonomy of the master in each workshop in favour of a production process coordinated by new 'work preparation offices'.[10] This was paralleled by an ongoing process of reduction of transportation distances, 'scientific' evaluation of each individual work process, development of forming rather than cutting machine processes to reduce material wastage, changes in component design to allow easier and cheaper production, improvements to storage, and so on.[11] The 1920s also saw widespread moves towards the usage of standardized, interchangeable parts – the pre-condition of mass production – which were produced in volume and increasingly procured from specialist subcontractors, allowing ease of assembly and substantially reducing unit costs.[12] In 1925, one expert noted that 'even today, no automobile manufacturer would consider producing his own carburettors, rather this is taken over by specialist factories.'[13] In 1925, in fact,

7 Blaich, F., 'Die Fehlrationalisierung in der Deutschen Automobilindustrie 1924 – 1929' in: *Tradition – Zeitschrift für Firmengeschichte und Unternehmerbiographie* 18 (1973), p. 18.
8 On the general economic background in the late 1920s see Borchardt, K., 'Economic Causes of the Collapse of the Weimar Republic' in: Borchardt, K., *Perspectives on Modern German Economic History*, Cambridge, 1991, pp. 143–60; James, H., *The German Slump. Politics and Economics 1924–1936*, Oxford, 1986; Kruedener, Jürgen Baron von (ed.), *Economic Crisis and Political Collapse. The Weimar Republic 1924–1933*, Oxford, 1990.
9 RKW (ed.), *Handbuch der Rationalisierung*, p. 206.
10 Stahlmann, *Die Erste Revolution*, pp. 93, 143–153.
11 RKW (ed.), *Handbuch der Rationalisierung*, *passim*.
12 Stahlmann, *Die Erste Revolution*, p. 26.
13 Schmidt, W.H., 'Betriebswissenschaftliche Grundlagen für die Einführung von Fließarbeit' in: *Maschinenbau* 4 (1925), p. 410.

the automobile manufacturers cooperated in the establishment of FAKRA (*Fachnormenausschuss der Kraftfahrzeugindustrie* – Automobile Industry Standardization Committee) which coordinated the gradual introduction of industry-wide norms for many components.[14]

The company that went furthest towards implementing production techniques resembling 'American' methods was Opel,[15] which introduced the first mechanized assembly line in Germany in 1923–4.[16] Opel, however, very much represented one extreme in the German automobile industry, and was unique in the extent to which it had successfully introduced relatively large-scale production of a cheap, standard car meant for a bigger market. The majority of German manufacturers, of which the Mannheim-based Benz & Co. and the Stuttgart-based Daimler Motor Company (the two predecessor firms of Daimler-Benz AG) were fairly typical, produced a much greater range of cars in small series designed to cater for a far more exclusive segment of the market. For these manufacturers and their clients, the car was seen as (and consciously marketed as) a luxury item and status symbol rather than an item of everyday utility.[17] The war had disrupted the gradual expansion of the private market, and the inflationary period had destroyed the purchasing power of those sectors of the middle class which would have formed the social basis for a large-scale increase in car ownership.[18] High maintenance costs, petrol costs and taxes also ensured that the car remained a luxury item few could afford.[19] Most manufacturers concentrated consequently on supplying a broad range of cars to the exclusive end of the market, where there was a limited, but more stable demand.[20]

Not only did most manufacturers produce a relatively large range of cars in small volume, but the demands of the luxury market for new models and new fashions, combined with a culture in which the buyer could dictate individual wishes and specifications, meant that they were constantly changing their products and having to re-tool or adapt existing production lines to provide for them. The uniformity of product which was the precondition of a genuine mass production was thus not given, limiting manufacturers in their ability to introduce such techniques except where they were able to standardise components for all their models. Where they were introduced it was done on

---

14 Edelmann, H. *Vom Luxusgut zum Gebrauchsgegenstand. Die Geschichte der Verbreitung von Personenkraftwagen in Deutschland*, Frankfurt/M., 1989, p. 81; Kugler, A., 'Von der Werkstatt zum Fließband. Etappen der Frühen Automobilproduktion in Deutschland' in: *Geschichte und Gesellschaft* 13 (1987), p. 325; Stahlmann, *Die Erste Revolution*, p. 73.
15 On Opel see Kugler, A., *Arbeitsorganisation und Produktionstechnologie der Adam Opel Werke (von 1900 bis 1929)*, Berlin, 1985; Kugler, 'Von der Werkstatt zum Fließband', pp. 304–39; Stahlmann, *Die Erste Revolution*, pp. 60–76.
16 Hachtmann, *Industriearbeit*, p. 68.
17 Kugler, 'Von der Werkstatt zum Fließband', p. 315.
18 Blaich, 'Fehlrationalisierung', p. 25.
19 Ibid., p. 24; Edelmann, *Vom Luxusgut zum Gebrauchsgegenstand*, pp. 42–7.
20 Blaich, 'Fehlrationalisierung', p. 24.

a limited basis and care was taken to ensure that the benefits of mass production were combined with the necessary flexibility to cope with changing demands and changing designs.

Aware that what demand there was for mass-produced cheap cars was catered for by Opel, the majority of manufacturers continued to produce on a workshop basis, using a far greater proportion of skilled workers than was the case in American factories.[21] The different approaches to production were reflected in the time it took to produce each car – in 1925 it took 400 hours to produce a basic Ford car, while a typical smaller German car took around 5000 hours.[22] This was also reflected in prices – in 1928 Ford's most expensive car, the 3l Model A, cost RM 4800.[23] In 1929 typical cars in the 3l range in Germany, the Adler Standard 8 or the Audi S Zwickau, cost RM 13,300 and RM 11,625 respectively.[24] In Germany, in 1929, you could have any colour you liked, as long as you could pay for it.

2. Rational Production and its limits at Daimler Benz in the 1920s

Unsurprisingly, the majority of German automobile manufacturers were ill-equipped to withstand the economic upheavals of the post-war era, and, in the post-inflationary crisis in the industry, eighty per cent of manufacturers folded.[25] The Daimler Motor Company and Benz & Co. were no exceptions here, experiencing acute difficulties in the post-war period, struggling as they were with the legacy of under-investment in the war and years of producing expensively for a guaranteed market rather than investing in cheaper, more efficient production methods to guarantee long-term profitability. While the inflation had shielded German industry from the impact of immediate post-war readjustment, the post-inflationary crisis revealed the true extent to which it had become uncompetitive and was suffering from excess capacity. In response to the crisis Daimler and Benz, who had previously been fierce competitors, entered into a cooperative partnership in 1924 in an attempt to restore profitability by a coordination of types produced and a standardization of components used by each firm.[26] The failure of this partnership to solve the underlying problem of chronic overcapacity and unprofitable volumes of production led to the full fusion of the two companies in June 1926, resulting

---

21 That new methods introduced in Germany did not necessarily mean de-skilling is shown by the fact that at Opel the proportion of skilled workers (66 per cent in 1929) was actually higher than in the industry as a whole (56.6 per cent in 1929). Stahlmann, *Die Erste Revolution*, p. 72; also Kugler, 'Von der Werkstatt zum Fließband', p. 338.

22 Stahlmann, M., *Die Erste Revolution*, p. 68.

23 Kruk, M. and Lingau, G., *100 Jahre Daimler-Benz. Das Unternehmen*, Mainz, 1986, p. 121.

24 Blaich, 'Fehlrationalisierung', p. 23.

25 Edelmann, *Vom Luxusgut zum Gebrauchsgegenstand*, pp. 60–1.

26 Stahlmann, *Die Erste Revolution*, p. 154.

in the formation of Daimler-Benz AG.[27] Although the initial partnership had proved insufficient and its failure had led to the full fusion, it was nonetheless developments in the period 1924–6 that formed the foundation for the subsequent restructuring.[28]

In line with German company law, the company was run by a managerial board, chaired from 1926 to 1942 by Wilhelm Kissel, with major investment decisions being referred to a supervisory board, which represented shareholders' interests. This was dominated by the banking interests that controlled the capital of Daimler-Benz (Deutsche Bank, Dresdner Bank, Commerzbank), which in turn were dominated by the key shareholder among them, the Deutsche Bank. Deutsche Bank nominated one of its representatives as chairman of the supervisory board – from 1926 to 1942 this was Emil Georg von Stauss.[29] The board of the company from the mid-1920s through to the end of the war comprised, typically, eight members, the eldest of whom, such as Wilhelm Kissel himself, had been born in the mid-1880s. The younger members, especially those who gradually joined the board in the 1930s, were typically born in the 1890s. In terms of age and background these were thus people who were socialized politically in the era of Wilhelmine nationalism and had their formative experiences as engineers and 'middle managers' during the First World War and its immediate aftermath. Although rarely explicitly mentioned, the internalization of the memory – both individually and collectively – of the experience of the First World War and the problems of the post-war period undoubtedly formed the basis for much of the company's response to the pressures created by the National Socialist regime, and, above all, the pressures created by the Second World War itself.

Capitalized with RM 36m of company capital and RM 60m of external capital – the high ratio of the latter to the former being gradually reduced as the company repaid the substantial restructing loan provided by the banks in 1926 – the newly formed company comprised five main plants. Mannheim, Gaggenau (both previously Benz), Untertürkheim and Sindelfingen (previously Daimler) formed the south-west German core of the company thereafter. In addition, the company inherited a plant in Berlin-Marienfelde from Daimler. Following the fusion, the bulk of the company's car production was centred on Untertürkheim; lorry production was centred in Gaggenau (production in Marienfelde was closed down and transferred to Gaggenau); body-work production was concentrated in Sindelfingen.[30] The factory at

27   MBAG Kissel I/1, Minutes of the Supervisory Board Meeting of Daimler and Benz on 1.6.1926. On the fusion see Stahlmann, *Die Erste Revolution*, p. 154; Roth, K.-H., 'Der Weg zum Guten Stern des Dritten Reiches. Schlaglichter auf die Geschichte der Daimler-Benz AG und ihrer Vorläufer (1890–1945)' in: HSG (ed.), *Das Daimler-Benz Buch*, pp. 71–8.
28   MBAG Kissel I/1, Minutes of Meeting No. 15 of the cooperative partnership on 11.5.1926.
29   For a detailed survey of the membership of the company boards, the structure of the company and its decision-making processes see Pohl et al., *Die Daimler-Benz AG*, pp. 15–48.
30   MBAG Kissel I/1, Minutes of the Full Board Meeting on 29.6.1926; Kissel I/2, Minutes of the Full Board Meeting of DBAG on 8.9.1926.

Mannheim continued to produce cars and body-work, and the management and administration of the company were centralized in Untertürkheim.[31] As a result of the fusion, the combined workforce of the company totalled 16,750.[32] By concentrating production lines in one rather than several places, the management intended to establish the preconditions for a rational production that would do away with a situation where both Gaggenau and Marienfelde were each producing at only 50 per cent of capacity in favour of a situation where a cost-effective full utilization of capacity could be achieved.[33] This, combined with a thorough overhaul of the range of vehicles produced, was intended to pave the way for a return to profitability.

Over the course of 1926, the new range of types was developed and gradually introduced, and the restructuring process was initiated. By February 1927 Untertürkheim had begun production of a new 2l car and Mannheim had begun production of a new 3l model.[34] During the winter of 1926–7 the factories more or less completed the reorganization of their production processes.[35] The return of relatively favourable economic conditions enabled a reasonable volume of production, and preparations were made to increase the capacity of Untertürkheim from 200–250 to 500 2l cars per month.[36] Similarly, after reorganization it was intended that the Gaggenau plant should have a capacity of 500 lorries per month, providing the basis for a substantial reduction in unit costs and thus in prices.[37]

Despite the centralization of production of a reduced number of types in each location, however, the volume of production at Daimler-Benz was still insufficient to make the introduction of full serial-flow production on anything like an American scale profitable. On the assembly lines, an extensive division of labour was carried through, together with a limited mechanization of transportation, which resulted in a substantial de-skilling of assembly labour and a reduction in the number of unskilled transport workers deployed.[38] By only assembling the main standard models on the assembly lines and removing the different sub-types for assembly in separate workshops,

31 MBAG Kissel I/1, Minutes of the Full Board Meeting on 29.6.1926. The total workforce in each plant was reduced by 52 per cent in Sindelfingen, 47 per cent in Gaggenau, 46 per cent in Marienfelde, 38 per cent in Mannheim, and 26 per cent in Untertürkheim (MBAG Kissel I/2, Minute No. 1 of the Meeting with the Factory Council on 4.12.1926). This was used by the company to dismiss the least effective or pliable workers. It also used the fusion to get rid of both blue- and white-collar workers deemed to be more prone to illness and absenteeism (MBAG Kissel I/16, Minute No.146 of the Directors' Discussion on 13.9.1926). The fusion was thus used as the pretext for positive and negative selection of workers aimed at obtaining the most productive and compliant workforce possible.
32 Roth, 'Der Weg zum Guten Stern', p. 333.
33 MBAG Kissel I/2, Minutes of the Meeting of the Administration Committee on 18.10.1926.
34 MBAG Kissel I/3, Minutes of the Supervisory Board Meeting of DBAG on 21.2.1927.
35 MBAG Kissel I/2, Minutes of the Meeting of the Working Committee on 28.12.1926.
36 MBAG Kissel I/2, Minutes of the Board Meeting of DBAG on 6.10.1926.
37 MBAG Kissel I/18, Minute No. 175 of the Directors' Discussion on 14 and 15.11.1927.
38 MBAG Kissel I/17, Memorandum, 15.1.1927.

a substantial acceleration of the assembly process was achieved. In the machine workshops, however, where the individual components were produced, the reorganization proceeded differently. Here, the production process was organized according to the principle of group production.[39]

Group production was a system of production developed by a Daimler engineer which had gradually been introduced at Untertürkheim from 1919 onwards.[40] In place of the traditional workshop organization, in which machine-tools were grouped according to machine type (e.g. all the milling machines were grouped together in the milling workshop), machine-tools were reorganized in groups according to the piece they were being used to produce and in the order necessary for the piece to be produced by passing it from one machine-tool to another (i.e. the workshops were divided according to what was being produced).[41] Flow production was thus utilized but confined to the individual workshop. The system of group production greatly reduced transport distances within the factory and, by reducing the number of tasks different machine-tools were used for, also avoided the constant and time-consuming resetting of machinery. As the parts were produced and transported in batches rather than flowing individually into the next workshop, the need for intermediary storage of parts remained. The fact that workshops remained separate from each other, however, meant that the bottlenecks which would be caused in serial-flow production by disruptions to output in one workshop could be confined in this way to the individual workshop concerned. Although group production necessarily meant that the individual machine-tools stood idle for some of the time and were thus under-utilized, this was not as extensive as would have been the case with full-scale mass production, and as such the system represented a balance, utilizing flow production but adapted to the smaller volume of output.[42]

The continued utilization of flexible multi-purpose machine-tools traditionally used in German industry for the bulk of machining operations also meant that production times and unit costs were higher than in America, where highly specialized single-purpose machine-tools could carry out each operation in a fraction of the time and at a fraction of the cost, once a certain volume of production had been achieved.[43] On the other hand, the German

39 Stahlmann, *Die Erste Revolution*, pp. 135–40; Kugler, 'Von der Werkstatt zum Fließband', pp. 329–33; Bellon, B., *Mercedes in Peace and War. German Automobile Workers 1903–1945*, New York, 1990, pp. 160–3.
40 Bellon, *Mercedes in Peace and War*, p. 161.
41 RKW (ed.), *Handbuch der Rationalisierung*, p. 205.
42 Stahlmann, *Die Erste Revolution*, pp. 135–6.
43 The United States Strategic Bombing Survey summarized the difference between American and German production methods thus: 'German machine-tools, type for type, perform the same operations as those of any other country . . . There was, however, a very fundamental difference between Germany and the United States as to the type and utilisation of machine-tools. American industry, designed along mass production lines, has used its machines for the purpose of achieving the highest possible volume of production with the minimum amount of human

production line could consequently be far more easily altered to accommodate changes in the specifications of each piece being produced, and machine-tools could eventually be used to produce something else. While they had been introduced to a limited extent even before the First World War, the relatively small volume of production meant that special-purpose machine-tools, which cost much more and took much longer to reset owing to their complexity, were uneconomic to use in the majority of cases. Thus, the deployment of mainly multi-purpose machinery was more rational. The preference for flexible, multi-purpose machinery also ensured that, despite substantial reorganization in the 1920s, the core of the workforce at Daimler-Benz and in the German automobile industry in general remained highly skilled.

This process of fusion and reorganization and the gradual introduction of new types, which initially sold well, resulted in a short-lived return to moderate profitability. In 1927 the company achieved a turnover of RM 121.4m, compared with RM 68.0m in 1926, and in 1928 and 1929 turnover rose above RM 130.0m.[44] After recording a loss of RM 18.0m in 1926, the company made a moderate gross profit of RM 4.75m in 1927 and gross profits of RM 26.85m and RM 27.76m in 1928 and 1929 respectively.

The return to profitability rested on very shaky foundations, however. The practice of producing a small initial run of a new model, in order to make improvements to the product and the production process before assuming full serial production meant that it took some time before the plants produced at a volume that approached profitable level.[45] The constant process of changing and improving design also militated against a smooth, continuous production. In mid-1928 neither Untertürkheim or Sindelfingen had attained a regular, constant programme.[46] Further problems were caused by poor-quality and irregular supplies from subcontractors, especially at Gaggenau, where unreliable deliveries caused repeated disruptions to production.[47] Firms that continually delivered late lost their contracts, but the regular process of changing subcontractors was in itself also costly and disruptive.[48]

---

effort and skill. This has involved the use of semi-automated machines of a specialised design and limited scope of productive functions which substitute design and precision of function for the skill of the operator ... German industry, on the other hand, partly due to the nature of its market, which was smaller than that of the United States, and the dependence upon foreign trade, and partly due to the relative cheapness of an abundant supply of highly skilled labour has designed its industry along different lines. The machines developed by German machine-tool makers were largely general purpose machine-tools, with a wider range of applicability, and usually lower productivity, and which required a higher degree of skill on the part of the operator.' (USSBS Finished Report No. 2, *The Effects of Strategic Bombing on the German War Economy*, 2nd edn, Washington D.C., 1947 p. 85. See also Freyberg and Siegel, *Industrielle Rationalisierung*, pp. 27–31; pp. 216–21.)

44   Roth, 'Der Weg zum Guten Stern', p. 333.
45   MBAG Kissel I/16, Minutes of the Technical Discussion in Gaggenau, 12.11.1926.
46   MBAG Kissel I/4, Minutes of the Full Board Meeting on 28.6.1928.
47   MBAG Kissel I/17, Minute No. 162 of the Directors' Discussion on 5.4.1927.
48   MBAG Kissel I/17, Minutes of the Discussion of the Material Situation on 27.4.1927.

Furthermore, problems with the initial runs of the new models not only caused costly repair and guarantee work, but also began to generate a reluctance among the public to buy Daimler-Benz models.[49] These problems, combined with the general background of a stagnant economy and low demand, placed strong limits on the extent to which Daimler-Benz was able to increase sales, more fully utilize capacity and enjoy the benefits of efficient, relatively large-scale production which the reorganization had been meant to bring. In 1927, the company was only utilizing 60 per cent of its capacity, and in 1928 only 58 per cent.[50] The capital-intensive nature of automobile production, with its high fixed costs, meant that low capacity utilization kept unit costs high.[51] While some productivity improvements allowed the management to cut prices and thus attempt to stimulate demand, low capacity utilization ensured that the real scope for price cuts was small.[52] Falling average prices for automobiles in the late 1920s were as much the product of a gradual shift in the market towards smaller cars and of intensifying competition as they were of huge productivity improvements.

The late 1920s were marked by a clear, albeit limited tendency towards proportionally greater demand for smaller cars.[53] The board of Daimler-Benz – searching for a new model to utilize its excess capacity and aware that this shift in demand could leave the company stranded in a shrinking market for large cars – considered on several occasions in the period after the fusion whether or not to extend its range downwards and enter into large-scale production of a cheaper car. In 1928, the board made its first overtures to the banks for finance for the introduction of a new 1.6l car at Untertürkheim, which the board believed it could sell at the rate of 1000 units per month.[54] This, together with a monthly production of 600 2l and 100 various larger models at Untertürkheim and 420 larger cars at Mannheim, was calculated as forming the basis for an acceptable level of capacity utilization and a profitable volume of production.

The banks, however, refused to finance the introduction of a smaller model, arguing that sales would not be high enough and that the company would not be able to produce cheaply enough to compete with Opel.[55] Despite the argument of Kissel, the chairman of the board, that there was less competition in this sector of the market than in that in which Daimler-Benz currently competed, and that Opel appealed to a different group of purchasers, the supervisory board demanded that Daimler-Benz compete by cheapening

49 MBAG Kissel I/20, Minutes, 7.1.1930. See also Stahlmann, *Die Erste Revolution*, pp. 173–4.
50 Roth, 'Der Weg zum Guten Stern', p. 333.
51 MBAG Kissel I/17, Minute No. 158 of the Meeting on 9.2.1927.
52 MBAG Kissel I/3, Minutes of the Board Meeting of DBAG on 19 and 20.9.1927; Minutes of the Board Meeting on 22.12.1927.
53 Edelmann, *Vom Luxusgut zum Gebrauchsgegenstand*, p. 129.
54 MBAG Kissel I/4, Minutes of the Full Board Meeting of DBAG on 28.6.1928.
55 MBAG Kissel I/4, Minutes of the Full Board Meeting of DBAG on 16.8.1928.

production of its existing models. In the face of the banks' refusal, the board
was forced to take a different course. In order to broaden the range of cars
produced but retain a profitable level of production of each, Kissel proposed
the construction of new 2.6l and 2.6l luxury models out of the existing 2l
model and the simultaneous production of all of them.[56] Three separate
models could thus be offered while retaining large-scale serial production of
most parts, which would be standard to each model. The chassis and basic
construction of the body would be the same for all three, allowing the
production of uniform items at the rate of several hundred a month. The
production level had been reduced in October 1928 in response to falling
demand and over-production.[57] The production plan adopted would allow a
production level that substantially reduced unit costs and would enable – it
was hoped – a production level of 250 2.6l and 400 2l cars per month.[58]

The adoption of this comparatively large programme, combined with the
introduction of new machine-tools and the replacement of a range of skilled
with semi-skilled functions, allowed the company to achieve a substantial
reduction in production time and cost.[59] Combined with measures to intensify
the labour process, above all ongoing reductions in piece-rates, these enabled
the company to reduce the production time of the 2l car (excluding the body)
from 432 hours in August 1928 to 300 hours in July 1929.[60]

Despite the substantial reductions in production costs brought about by
internal standardization of parts for different models, however, the price of
Daimler-Benz's cars remained high owing to the costs of producing the bodies,
which were one of the most expensive main components of the car. A central
aspect of the management's attempts to return to permanent profitability thus
lay in efforts to reduce production costs at Sindelfingen. While internal
standardization and the modular construction principle allowed the achievement of an acceptable balance between efficient production and product
variety in chassis and engine production, the standardization of body types was
much harder. The largely functional role of the chassis and engine meant that,
apart from technical improvements, the pressure to change design was
minimal, and once a design had proved acceptable the preconditions for a
smooth, continuous production were in principle given. With body production, however, the broad range of models produced, the need constantly to
change them according to public taste and fashion, and the culture of
responding to individual customers' particular wishes meant that a large range
of constantly changing bodies was being produced in small series or even in

56   MBAG Kissel I/4, Minutes of the Board Meeting of DBAG on 24.10.1928.
57   MBAG Kissel I/4, Minutes of the Board Meeting of DBAG on 2.10.1928.
58   MBAG Kissel I/19, Minutes of the Discussion on 4.10.1928.
59   MBAG Kissel I/4, Minutes of the Board Meeting of DBAG on 24.10.1928.
60   BA (P) 80 Ba2 P3245, Response of the Factory Management of Untertürkheim to the 6th report
     of chief Engineer Müller, 3.7.1929.

individual versions.[61] In 1927, for example, the 2l car was built in two main types, but with seven different variations, and, in addition, a large number of individual contracts were accepted.[62]

In the interests of achieving a larger volume of production for each model, the board attempted to decrease gradually the number of variations it built.[63] Demands from the production managers for a reduction in types were, however, always met by the insistence of the sales managers on a wide range of models to meet customers' requirements.[64] As such, the search for a balance between market-orientated variety and production-orientated uniformity manifested itself in a clear cultural conflict within the company. When, in 1926, the supervisory board initially pressured the management to introduce American methods at Sindelfingen based on the usage of sheet-metal parts produced in volume using presses – representing a significant technical advance but also a break with traditional craft techniques – the management refused this on the grounds that the preconditions for mass production at a level that would make the purchase of expensive presses viable were not given.[65] Managerial conservatism and the conscious policy of marketing hand-produced wooden bodies as superior to mass-produced sheet-metal bodies also militated against such a development.

Internal standardization and use of the modular construction principle nonetheless meant that by 1928 the company had reached a volume of production that would allow the mass production of bodies on such a basis, if the policy of responding to individual customers' wishes was abandoned and the management elected to supply only standard bodies.[66] The improvement in the company's financial position, although modest, was now such that it could consider investing in large presses, while continued stagnation in the market increased the imperative to cheapen production. There was still widespread opposition to press techniques from more traditionalist members of the board, who doubted the ability of the company to compete with American manufacturers on this basis and who believed the technique to be

61 MBAG Kissel I/2, Minutes of the Full Board Meeting of DBAG, on 8.9.1926. The impact of changing public taste on the attempt to produce continuously in volume is shown, albeit impressionistically, by the comments of the Sindelfingen management concerning one of Daimler-Benz's many Cabriolet models: 'The C-Cabriolet which is now over two years old – we first displayed it in Baden-Baden in the summer of 1928 – is, because of its straight windscreen, no longer up-to-date. Compared to a modern Cabriolet with its slanted windscreen it looks far too ungainly. We are worried that if we do not adapt to contemporary taste we will, if the C-Cabriolet is kept, get into real difficulties, as the public will demand Cabriolets with slanted windscreens like the ones the other German manufacturers produce.' (MBAG Kissel VI/15, DBAG Sindelfingen to the Board of DBAG, 5.11.1930.)
62 MBAG Kissel I/3, Minutes of the Directors' Discussion on 30.11.1927.
63 MBAG Kissel I/17, Minutes of the Discussion between Messrs. Gross, Kissel, Schippert and Lang on 12.1.1927.
64 MBAG Kissel I/19, Minute No. 199 of the Directors' Discussion on 25.7.1928.
65 MBAG Kissel I/2, Minutes of the Meeting of the Working Committee on 28.12.1926.
66 MBAG Kissel I/4, Minutes of the Board Meeting of DBAG on 24.10.1928.

too complicated. Wilhelm Haspel, one of Sindelfingen's directors (and from 1935 a board member) was, however, able to push through the decision to change from wooden to sheet-metal bodies and with it from traditional wood-shaping techniques (although these did not immediately become totally redundant) to the installation of a press shop. From January 1929, the main panels of the body were produced with presses. At the same time, the Sindelfingen plant was reorganized and two engineers were sent to America to study the techniques.[67] The introduction of presses, the mechanization of transportation, the cumulative integration of more and more processes into an overall flow of production did indeed allow a great reduction in production costs at Sindelfingen.[68] From 1929 to May 1930 the cost of a standard body was reduced from RM 1750 to RM 1100.[69]

3. The Depression Years

The reorganization following the fusion and the introduction of new production and assembly processes in chassis, engine and body manufacturing represented, despite the unfavourable economic climate, a substantial transformation of Daimler-Benz's capacity in the years 1926 to 1929. No sooner had the restructuring process been completed, however, and a relatively stable level of production been achieved, than a new crisis emerged in the face of first a fall and then a virtual collapse in demand. In 1928 and 1929, despite record sales, the management was regularly forced to revise its production figures downwards in order to avoid over-production.[70] The annual seasonal increase in demand in the automobile industry failed to materialize in early 1929.[71] As well as cutting car production, the company was forced to reduce lorry production at Gaggenau by ten per cent in June 1929.[72] As the Depression set in and the decline in demand accelerated, the company began laying off workers in bulk. Substantial reductions in the work force had already taken place at Mannheim between 1928 and 1929, when rationalization measures had meant that the same number of cars could be produced using fewer workers.[73] Car production fell at Untertürkheim from

---

67 MBAG Kissel I/5, Minutes of the Board Meeting of DBAG on 13 and 14.6.1929.
68 Stahlmann, *Die Erste Revolution*, pp. 158–68; Bellon, *Mercedes in Peace and War*, pp. 210–13. On rationalization of the lacquering process in the automobile industry in the late 1920s, for example, see 'Rationalisierung der Lackierverfahren des Automobilbaues der Adlerwerke' in: *Automobiltechnische Zeitschrift* 34 (1931), pp. 601–4.
69 MBAG Kissel I/5, Minutes of the Supervisory Board Meeting on 30.5.1930, reprinted in Roth, K. H. and Schmid, M., *Die Daimler-Benz AG 1918–1948. Schlüsseldokumente zur Konzerngeschichte,* Nördlingen, 1987, p. 74.
70 MBAG Kissel I/4, Minutes of the Board Meeting of DBAG on 2.10.1928.
71 Edelmann, *Vom Luxusgut zum Gebrauchsgegenstand*, p. 129.
72 MBAG Kissel I/20, Minute No. 214 of the Meeting on 26 and 28.8.1929.
73 MBAG Kissel/Finance I, Minutes of 3.2.1928.

5842 in 1929 to 4494 in 1930 and 2872 in 1931.[74] Lorry production fell on a similar scale. The workforce was drastically reduced from a total average of 11,800 in 1929 to 8700 in 1930, with cuts in Gaggenau of 50 per cent.[75] In 1931 it was reduced further, to 6600 by the third quarter of the year.[76] By the final quarter of 1932, it had reached 5600.[77]

As the market tightened, first gradually and then drastically, the need to reduce costs intensified. In part, it was achieved by the further introduction of more efficient machinery which allowed a lowering of production costs.[78] Investment in new machinery fell greatly in the Depression however, from RM 8.9 m in 1928 to RM 1.6 m in 1931.[79] Given the reserve of unemployed workers, moreover, the company was able to use the Depression both to cut wages drastically and above all to push through a massive programme of intensification of labour, which greatly improved productivity and cut production costs with the minimum of new investment and at the expense of the workers.

From 1929 to 1930 the management engaged the services of a rationalization engineer, Müller, to advise on cost-saving measures in all the factories as part of a broader programme of cost-cutting designed to retain profitability with a lower level of turnover. Müller's reports were based on an ongoing examination of individual workshops, individual production processes and machine-tool utilization, factory layout and transportation, and energy and heat efficiency. The reports provide an extensive insight into the way the conditions of the Depression were used to force an intensification of the labour process at Daimler-Benz, which both the workers and the organized labour movement were powerless to oppose.[80]

Some proposals were indeed implemented that resulted in savings through more effective utilization of capacity. A further standardization of parts for as many as possible of Daimler-Benz's engines, chassis and bodies was carried out, and production of these parts was centralized at single plants rather than scattered over different factories, as had hitherto been the case. The automated workshops, which had until this time been located separately in Mannheim and Untertürkheim, for example, were centralized at Unter-türkheim.[81] This process of concentrating production was paralleled by a movement towards returning to self-production of parts that had previously

---

74 *Das Werk Untertürkheim. Stammwerk der Daimler-Benz Aktiengesellschaft. Ein Historischer Überblick*, Stuttgart, 1983, p. 192.
75 MBAG Kissel I/5, Minute No. 10 of the Supervisory Board Meeting on 30.5.1930.
76 MBAG Kissel I/6, Report of the Board for the third Quarter of 1932.
77 MBAG Kissel I/7, Report of the Board for the fourth Quarter of 1932.
78 MBAG Kissel I/20, Minutes of the Directors' Meeting on 18 and 19.7.1929.
79 *Geschäftsbericht der Daimler-Benz AG 1928; Geschäftsbericht der Daimler-Benz AG 1931*.
80 On the effects of rationalization against the background of the Depression on labour and labour politics see Zollitsch, W., *Arbeiterschaft zwischen Weltwirtschaftskrise und Nationalsozialismus*, Göttingen, 1990.
81 BA (P) 80 Ba2 P3245, 5. Report on the Daimler-Benz Factories, 4.5.1929, p. 1.

been produced by subcontractors, in an effort to utilize idle capacity. Like all other automobile manufacturers, Daimler-Benz had extensively adopted a system of subcontracting parts production and buying in standardized parts common to all manufacturers, accepting the consensus view that this was the way production would develop in the future.[82] During the Depression, however, in cases where the company already had all the necessary machines, these could be used to produce parts sometimes at a lower cost than that which would be incurred by paying subcontractors.[83] This was all the more so in situations where specialist producers saw the chance to use their monopoly position to incorporate a huge profit margin into their price, negating the supposed benefits of producing and selling in bulk.[84] In late 1929, the company completely reverted to producing itself all parts for which a new machine did not have to be purchased.[85]

These measures allowed the company to reduce the initial impact of falling production on capacity utilization. However, given the strength of the downturn, they were in themselves marginal in effect. The majority of the measures introduced were designed to reduce costs by accelerating the production process without any organizational changes.

First, the growing reserve of unemployed labour was used by the management to implement a selection of the most productive workers. Less capable or industrious workers were to be sacked in greater numbers than the cuts in production demanded, to allow a selection of more capable replacements from the available reserve of labour.[86] Despite assurances that redundancy would be implemented according to social criteria, the management proceeded purely according to criteria of shop-floor efficiency. Above all, workers who were no longer fully productive owing to age or physical incapacity were replaced by a smaller number of younger and more able workers.[87] Those who retained their jobs still came to feel the impact of their weakened position, however. Developments on the shop floor during the Depression were characterized above all by an ongoing process of 'speed-up'. In numerous departments Müller complained of a 'lack of urgency and tempo on the shop floor'.[88] This was to be remedied by the substantial reduction of the timed piece-rates used to calculate wages.[89] The pace of production in

82 MBAG Kissel I/2, Minutes of the Meeting of the Administration Committee on 18.10.1926.
83 BA (P) 80 Ba2 P3245, 3. Report on the Daimler-Benz Factories, 1.3.1929, p. 8.
84 BA (P) 80 Ba2 P3245, 5. Report on the Daimler-Benz Factories, 4.5.1929, p. 3.
85 MBAG Kissel I/5, Discussion of Works Deliveries on 21.9.1929.
86 MBAG Kissel I/20, Minutes of the Directors' Meeting on 18.12.1929.
87 MBAG Kissel I/20, Minutes of the Meeting of 17 and 18.10.1929.
88 BA (P) 80 Ba2 P3245, Report on the Daimler-Benz Factory in Untertürkheim on 11.1.1929, p. 2.
89 e.g. BA (P) 80 Ba2 P3245, Report on the Daimler-Benz Factories, 1.3.1929; 2. Report on the Daimler-Benz Factory in Untertürkheim on 25.1.1929, p. 10; Report on Daimler-Benz AG Mannheim on 17.8.1929, p. 3.

individual workshops would be increased to such an extent that it was possible to produce the same amount with two-thirds of the existing workforce.[90]

During this period, Daimler-Benz reduced its workforce on an ongoing basis with this in mind. The process manifested itself in sometimes brutal reductions in piece-rates – thus, for example, a cut of 50 per cent was implemented for workers on the polishing machines, meaning effectively that the workers had to produce twice as much in the same period of time, day in, day out to achieve the same levels of earnings as hitherto.[91] This intensification of labour represented a substantial improvement in productivity achieved entirely at the expense of the worker. Similarly, at Mannheim, the times on which piece-rates were calculated were halved in some workshops.[92] Not only were the wages of those workers paid according to timed piece-rates to be reduced, but wages for those paid on an hourly basis were reduced too. From 1929 the employers were continually on the offensive as regards wage levels. The average hourly wages at Untertürkheim fell from 124.6 pf in 1929 to 106.8 pf in 1932 for a skilled worker, and from 82.8 pf in 1929 to 71.5 pf in 1932 for an unskilled worker.[93]

The fall in the index of prices and cost-of-living during the Depression was such that in real terms these cuts in hourly wages did not represent as heavy a blow as the figures in themselves might imply. Indeed, in real terms, hourly wages may have improved slightly – what really affected workers' standards of living (where as they still had a job) was the reduction in the numbers of hours worked per week. However, these developments still illuminate the extent to which the Depression was used to exert strong downward pressure on costs and reduce wage levels. Moreover, the real significance of this is that wages were forced down to a level at which they were more or less held over the 1930s, despite labour shortages, thereby facilitating the accelerated accumulation of capital and profit for investment in this period.

The Depression was used especially to cut the level of so-called 'phantom' piece-rates (*Scheinakkorde*), which were widespread in the Mannheim area.[94] Timed piece-rates had been introduced originally during the inflationary period, when calculating rates according to the time set for each piece to be produced was easier than setting a fixed price for each piece.[95] They also, however, had the advantage that they allowed covert wage increases in times of labour shortage – by manipulation of the results of time-and-motion studies

90 BA (P) 80 Ba2 P3245, Report on the Daimler-Benz AG Mannheim on 17.8.1929, p. 1.
91 BA (P) 80 Ba2 P3245, 5. Report on the Daimler-Benz Factories on 4.5.1929, p. 4.
92 BA (P) 80 Ba2 P3245, 3. Report on the Daimler-Benz Factories, 1.3.1929, p. 5.
93 Roth, 'Der Weg zum Guten Stern', p. 333; for comprehensive details of wage movements at Daimler-Benz see Röhwer, G., 'Die Lohnentwicklung bei Daimler-Benz (Untertürkheim) 1925–1940' in: *1999. Zeitschrift für Sozialgeschichte des 20. und 21. Jahrhunderts* (4) 1989, 1, pp. 52–83.
94 BA (P) 80 Ba2 P3245, Record of the Discussion at the Mannheim Factory on 5.3.1930.
95 BA (P) 80 Ba2 P3245, Memorandum: Calculation, Payments and Wages Contracts, 31.1.1930.

– without renegotiating official wage contracts with the trade unions, which would be difficult to reverse later.[96] Those who performed work usually paid on an hourly basis were for this reason also often paid on the basis of a nominal piece-rate, allowing covert increases in wages for individual segments of the hourly-paid labour force, too, without creating pressure for general increases and without the necessity for renegotiating the contract.

This situation made it all the more easy for the employers to cut wage rates again once labour market conditions allowed it. Although the Daimler-Benz board was keen to avoid causing unnecessary labour unrest and attempted to avoid an overtly confrontational stance, there was very little the workers' representatives could do.[97] This was even more the case as the management intentionally proceeded upon a piecemeal basis, reducing rates workshop by workshop rather than all at once. Even when focusing on the 'phantom' rates, the management lowered them on a gradual basis and deliberately implemented the cuts at a time of seasonally conditioned falling employment to undermine the workers' resolve to defend their wage levels.[98] Finally, when the regional employers' federation tore up its collective agreements with the trade unions, the position of the workforce was undermined even further.[99]

Not only was an intensification of the labour process instituted by reductions in piece-rates, but a higher output was forced from each worker by the practice of having one worker to do the work hitherto performed by two (or more) simultaneously. This occurred in the auxiliary workshops, such as the foundry at Untertürkheim, where it was found that 'to empty the moulding casings one man is sufficient, whereas at the moment two are employed', or in the metal storage rooms, where one man was to be employed sawing metal into the correct lengths where two had previously worked.[100] Similarly, by forcing a greater workload and more regimented tempo on each transport worker, Müller demanded that the number of workers engaged in transportation at Untertürkheim be reduced by 25 per cent.[101] The intensification of the labour process achieved in this way was most extensively applied in the machine shops. In Gaggenau, it was found that in the lathe shop 'each man operates only one machine, even in the numerous cases where the machining of each piece requires lengthy cutting times, and where the man could thus simultaneously operate two or more machines.' It was also

96   BA (P) 80 Ba2 P3245, von der Porten to Müller, 16.2.1930.
97   BA (P) 80 Ba2 P3245, Response of the Factory Management of Untertürkheim to the 6th Report of Engineer Müller, 3.7.1929. That the reductions caused substantial unrest is shown by the response of the factory council, which stressed that the reductions had caused 'great anger and disquiet' even among workers who during many years of employment at Daimler-Benz had never previously complained (MBAG Kissel I/20, Minute No. 6 of the Meeting with the Factory Council on 1.8.1929).
98   BA (P) 80 Ba2 P3245, Minutes of the Discussion at the Mannheim Factory on 5.3.1930.
99   MBAG Kissel I/21, Minute No. 245 of the Meeting on 18.11.1930.
100 BA (P) 80 Ba 2 P3245, Report on the Daimler-Benz Factory in Untertürkheim on 11.1.1929.
101 BA (P) 80 Ba2 P3245, 2. Report on the Daimler-Benz Factory in Untertürkheim on 25.1.1929.

decided that the piece-rates were too high, and that 'it must be possible, by giving the workers more than one machine, and by reducing the piece-rates to a reasonable level, to get by with half as many people.'[102] Similarly, in the milling shop, it was decided that by giving workers more than one machine to operate simultaneously, the number of workers could easily be halved. Where two semi-automated machines were previously operated by each man, it was proposed greatly to reduce piece-rates and give each worker four to operate, which again would effectively force the worker to double output to achieve the same level of pay.[103] Overall, it was argued, the workforce in the machine shops could be reduced by one-third while retaining the same level of output.[104]

Finally, as well as reducing unit labour costs by cutting wages and intensifying the labour process, the management attempted where possible to replace skilled male workers with semi-skilled female workers.[105] These women were cheaper on two accounts: first, because they were less skilled, and second, because they were women. At Untertürkheim, for example, greater employment of women in the production of mouldings in the foundry was recommended, or in the automated lathe shop, where women not only cost two-thirds as much as male workers but were also deemed to be faster workers.[106] Similarly, the company moved towards employing more women in the upholstery workshop in Sindelfingen, which again was deemed to be work to which women were in any case particularly well suited.[107]

The reductions in hourly wages and piece-rates, the expansion of multiple machine operation and the partial feminization of at least some activities all contributed to substantial increases in productivity, gained entirely at the expense of the workforce, which made price reductions in the Depression more possible and allowed the company to retain some competitiveness. Despite the huge cost reduction programme that was initiated, however, Daimler-Benz made a loss of RM 8.55m in 1930. This was followed by a huge loss of RM 13.4m in 1931.[108] In 1931, the supervisory board noted that the cost-cutting measures introduced in 1930 would have led to a substantial profit in 1931, had it been possible to maintain the previous year's turnover, but this had fallen by almost one-third in a single year from RM 99.0m in 1930 to RM 69.0m in 1931.[109]

102 BA (P) 80 Ba2 P3245, Report on the Daimler-Benz AG Factory in Gaggenau on 29.6.1929, p. 2.
103 BA (P) 80 Ba2 P3245, 3. Report on the Daimler-Benz Factories AG on 1.3.29, p. 6.
104 BA (P) 80 Ba2 P3245, Report on the Daimler-Benz AG Factory in Gaggenau on 29.6.1929, p. 4.
105 This reflected partial trends visible in German industry in general during the Depression. See Hachtmann, R., 'Arbeitsmarkt und Arbeitszeit in der Deutschen Industrie 1929–1939' in: *Archiv für Sozialgeschichte* 27 (1987), p. 182.
106 BA (P) 80 Ba2 P3245, Report on the Daimler-Benz Factory in Untertürkheim on 11.1.1929, pp. 1, 9.
107 BA (P) 80 Ba2 P3245, 3. Report on the Daimler-Benz Factories AG on 1.3.1929, p. 6.
108 Roth, 'Der Weg zum Guten Stern', p. 333.
109 MBAG Kissel I/6, Minutes of the Meeting of the Working Committee of DBAG on 1.6.1931.

Not only did the number of cars and lorries sold fall drastically during the Depression, but the economic crisis accelerated the tendency in the market further towards the purchase of cheaper, more economical cars, which had been characteristic of the latter 1920s.[110] The proportion of cars sold in the price bracket over RM 5000 fell from 60 per cent in 1928 to 18 per cent in 1931.[111] While some of this is accounted for by price-cutting, which meant that more models fell into the lower price range than previously, a substantial shift in the structure of the market clearly took place which lasted well beyond the crisis years of 1929–32. In the face of this further shift downwards in the market, the company re-examined the issue of extending its range of models further downwards and producing a smaller, cheaper car. Whereas in 1928 the banks had blocked the move, by 1931 both the board and supervisory board were unanimous in recognizing the necessity of this.[112] In this year the company introduced a new 1.7l car, the smallest it had ever produced.[113] Although still more a medium-sized than a small car, its advanced technical design, basic construction and the fact that it was produced in few variations at a relatively low price – when introduced it cost only RM 4400 – meant that it was ensured a successful introduction.[114] Although in 1932 turnover fell further, Daimler-Benz was able to increase its market share from 6–7 per cent of total sales (in number) to 13–14 per cent in 1932.[115] Like the rest of the German automobile industry, Daimler-Benz still suffered from ruinously low capacity utilization in 1932. In 1932 the industry was working at an average 24 per cent of capacity, compared to an average of 42 per cent for German industry as a whole.[116] Daimler-Benz's capacity utilization had actually bottomed out in 1931, when its factories worked at an average of 23 per cent of capacity, but improved only slightly, to 26 per cent, in 1932.[117] Nonetheless, whereas the total value of cars sold in 1932 was 75 per cent lower than in 1931, at Daimler-Benz the total value was only 12 per cent lower.[118]

Through the further concentration of productive departments in the wake of the initial fusion, through consistent adaptation of production programmes and models to the changing nature of the German market, through huge reductions in the workforce and through a brutal intensification of labour, Daimler-Benz was able to ensure that it was one of the companies in the automobile industry that survived the sharp cyclical downturn of the economic

110   MBAG Kissel I/6, Report to the Supervisory Board on the first Quarter of 1932; Edelmann, Vom Luxusgut zum Gebrauchsgegenstand, pp. 92–9.
111   Stahlmann, Die Erste Revolution, p. 180.
112   MBAG Kissel I/6, Minutes of the Supervisory Board Meeting of 1.6.1931.
113   Stahlmann, Die Erste Revolution, p. 185.
114   Edelmann, Vom Luxusgut zum Gebrauchsgegenstand, p. 140.
115   Geschäftsbericht der Daimler-Benz AG 1931–1932.
116   Edelmann, Vom Luxusgut zum Gebrauchsgegenstand, p. 133.
117   Roth, 'Der Weg zum Guten Stern', p. 333.
118   MBAG Kissel I/6, Report of the Board of Directors for the third Quarter 1932.

crisis and emerged in a strong position relative to other manufact
Despite the continual crisis conditions prevalent in the industry in the 192
Daimler-Benz had made a substantial reorganization of its capacity which, if it
had not been able to utilize it fully in the years 1926 to 1932, provided one of
the major preconditions for the huge expansion of output in the 1930s.

the Reich: Daimler-Benz

1. The Economic Boom

The economic and political climate within which industry had to operate was radically altered by the National Socialist seizure of power. The subsequent rearmament-led economic boom saw a massive expansion of business activity from 1933 onwards, with a correspondingly rapid decline in unemployment, and led to a phase of high profitability and accelerated investment – both of which were greatly facilitated by the continuously low wage levels that the working class, deprived of all means of effective collective action, experienced in the 1930s, even after shortages of labour had led to modest wage increases in some areas. Industrial production more than doubled between 1933 and 1938, while GNP rose from RM 59 billion in 1933 to RM 83 billion in 1936 and RM 130 billion in 1939.[1] Unemployment, which had stood officially at just over six million in January 1933, fell to 3.8 million in January 1934, to 2.9 million in January 1935 and by 1936–37 Germany was reaching full employment again.[2] The substantial shift in economic activity away from consumer goods and towards capital goods and armaments production in the 1930s meant that, despite the continued existence of a reserve of unemployed workers in the mid-1930s, sectoral labour shortages were already occurring in key industries by 1934. These gradually broadened to the point where, in the immediate pre-war years, the German economy suffered from considerable labour shortages.

The automobile industry was one of the first to enjoy the fruits of the economic upturn and, in turn, provided a powerful stimulus to the rest of the economy from 1933 onwards. Although total sales for 1932 were far below those of 1931, the automobile industry was experiencing clear signs of economic recovery from the autumn of 1932 onwards.[3] In January 1933, the industry as a whole produced 2851 cars altogether, compared to 2205 in

---

1 Noakes, J., and Pridham, G. (eds.), *Nazism 1919–1945. Volume 2. State, Economy, Society 1933–1939*, Exeter, 1984, pp. 297–8.
2 Ibid., p. 359.
3 Edelmann, *Vom Luxusgut zum Gebrauchsgegenstand*, p. 162.

January 1932, an increase of 22 per cent.[4] As such, recovery can be said to have been not only tentatively but strongly underway prior to the appointment of Hitler as Chancellor on 30 January 1933. The initial expansion of output and sales owed as much to the release of pent-up demand from the previous four years as it did to factors specifically related to the National Socialist seizure of power or the policies of the new regime.

Nonetheless, the range of tax measures introduced by the regime in the spring of 1933 – which represented the realization of long-held aims of the automobile lobby – were a powerful further stimulus to the recovery of the industry.[5] By the time the initial impact (both financial and psychological) of these measures had faded, a general rearmament-led economic recovery had begun that provided the basis for rapidly expanding sales for the next four years. The Autobahn projects probably did more in the short term to alleviate unemployment than they did directly to stimulate automobile sales, although here, too, their importance should not be underestimated.[6] The road-building programme was nonetheless crucial to the industry, both because it created the illusion of dynamic action to get the economy moving again and thus contributed to revived consumer confidence, and because it asserted the centrality of the automobile to future transport policy.[7]

The combined effect of these impulses was to cause an unprecedented expansion in automobile production in 1933.[8] In 1933 as a whole, 92,610 cars were sold, compared to 42,193 in 1932. Over the next three years, the automobile industry enjoyed a recovery in production far more rapid and extensive than virtually any other branch of industry.[9] In 1934, car production was already much higher than in 1928, and over three times as high as in 1932.[10] In 1936, the German automobile industry produced 244,640 cars.[11] The lorry sector enjoyed a similarly rapid recovery – production in 1933 totalled 12,404 lorries, compared to 8082 in 1932, representing an increase of over 50 per cent.[12] In 1936, after three years of unparalleled growth, production reached 56,779.[13] Thereafter, growth in the sector remained more

4 'Der Aufschwung der Automobilwirtschaft' in: *Die Deutsche Volkswirtschaft*, (1934), 8, p. 240.
5 The full range of the tax measures is discussed in Edelmann, *Vom Luxusgut zum Gebrauchsgegenstand*, pp. 160–2; Overy, R.J., 'Cars, Roads and Economic Recovery in Germany 1932–1938' in: *Economic History Review* 28 (1975), p. 474.
6 Edelmann, *Vom Luxusgut zum Gebrauchsgegenstand*, p. 177.
7 On the Autobahn project see Overy, 'Cars, Roads and Economic Recovery'; Overy, R. J., 'Transportation and Rearmament in the Third Reich' in: *Historical Journal* 16 (1973), pp. 397–401. On measures to stimulate the vehicle industry in 1933 in general see also Blaich, F., *Wirtschaft und Rüstung im Dritten Reich*, Düsseldorf, 1987, pp. 15–17.
8 For sales figures for 1933 see 'Der Aufschwung der Automobilindustrie', p. 240.
9 Overy, 'Cars, Roads and Economic Recovery', p. 475.
10 Langelütke, H., 'Der Aufschwung in der Automobilwirtschaft' in: *Die Deutsche Volkswirtschaft*, 26 (1935), p. 832. In 1934, 147,330 cars were produced, compared to 108,029 in 1928.
11 *Geschäftsbericht der Daimler-Benz AG 1937*
12 'Der Aufschwung der Automobilwirtschaft', p. 240.
13 *Geschäftsbericht der Daimler-Benz AG 1937*

modest, as the regime channelled more and more resources into rearmament under the Four Year Plan. Although production continued to rise in the late 1930s, the German automobile industry was unable to expand production to meet demand, since raw material allocations placed an effective ceiling on output, and in 1939 production of cars actually fell.[14]

The experience of the automobile industry in general was very much mirrored in the development of Daimler-Benz's business in the early years of the National Socialist regime. First signs of a recovery in demand were registered by the board in September 1932, and after January 1933 the company enjoyed a rapid growth in sales, especially after the elections of March 1933.[15] At Untertürkheim, 7617 cars were produced in 1933, 9187 in 1934, and by 1936 the figure had reached 19,924, while, in contrast to the rest of the industry, Daimler-Benz's lorry production actually initially recovered faster.[16] As with the rest of the automobile industry, raw materials allocations limited the growth of production thereafter – the plant produced at a constant level of approximately 26,000 cars in 1937, 1938 and 1939.[17]

The expansion of Daimler-Benz's activity in the 1930s is reflected in the figures for turnover and profits for the period 1926–39:[18]

Turnover of Daimler-Benz AG 1926–39 (Million RM):

1926 68.0	1931 69.0	1936 295.1
1927 121.4	1932 65.0	1937 399.1
1928 130.8	1933 100.9	1938 462.0
1929 130.4	1934 146.8	1939 527.6
1930 99.0	1935 226.1	

Gross Profits of Daimler-Benz AG 1926–39 (Million RM):

1926 – 18.00	1931 – 13.40	1936 + 60.10
1927 + 4.75	1932 – 10.92	1937 + 72.23
1928 + 26.85	1933 + 14.37	1938 + 85.33
1929 + 27.76	1934 + 27.56	1939 + 101.19
1930 – 8.55	1935 + 45.32	

Net Profits of Daimler-Benz AG 1933–9 (Million RM):

1933 + 2.47	1936 + 6.23	1938 + 2.52
1934 + 4.12	1937 + 2.52	1939 + 3.25
1935 + 4.12		

14 Edelmann, *Vom Luxusgut zum Gebrauchsgegenstand*, pp. 196–7.
15 MBAG Kissel I/7, Report of the Board for the fourth Quarter of 1932, 4.3.1933; Report of the Board for the Quarter-Year from 16.12.1932 to 11.3.1933.
16 *Das Werk Untertürkheim*, p. 192.
17 MBAG Statistics, Annual Production of Cars at DBAG 1927–1944.
18 Figures for turnover and profits are given in Roth, 'Der Weg zum Guten Stern', pp. 333–4; Pohl et al., *Die Daimler-Benz AG*, pp. 126, 132.

Investment, which had been low since 1926 and had all but disappeared in the Depression, also rose greatly, as the following figures show:

Investment at Daimler-Benz AG 1932–39 (Million RM):

1932	0.49	1935	20.2	1938	26.8
1933	5.5	1936	22.0	1939	44.0
1934	9.5	1937	23.0		

The huge increases in production were reflected in the very rapid expansion of the workforce from 1933 onwards. By 1934, employment in the automobile industry had already returned almost to the levels of 1928.[19] The number of workers at Daimler-Benz had risen to 6781 by March 1933, compared to 4958 in March 1932, and by the third quarter of 1933 had reached 9369.[20] It thereafter expanded annually to reach 31,995 by the end of 1936, and 35,994 by the end of 1939.[21]

Despite the rapid recovery in the automobile sector at Daimler-Benz, however, the company experienced a clear loss of market share in the first two years of the National Socialist regime. In car sales it fell from 12.9 per cent in 1932 to 9.6 per cent in 1933 and 6.8 per cent in 1934.[22] This was a result of the continued trend towards smaller cars which had been characteristic of the previous years, and of which the greatest beneficiary in the first years of the National Socialist regime was Opel.[23] Over the course of the period 1933–5, the company initially attempted to counter this development by extending its range of models further downwards. In 1933, the board decided to begin production of a 1.3l car, the smallest it had ever produced, intended to compete directly with Opel and the other small car manufacturers.[24] This, according to the intentions of the board, would be cheap enough to produce to allow a volume of production of 1000 per month from late 1933 onwards, and offset the impact of falling market share in the mid-sized car range.[25] The company consistently failed, however, in its attempts to break into the lower end of the market, as design and production problems ensured that only 1513 of these cars were sold in 1935 and just 421 in 1936.[26]

In the face of this failure, the core of the company's car business remained

19 Overy, 'Cars, Roads and Economic Recovery', p. 475.
20 MBAG Kissel I/7, Report of the Board for the Quarter-Year from 16.12.1932 to 11.3.1933; Report of the Board for the Quarter-Year 1.7.1933 to 30.9.1933.
21 Pohl et al., Die Daimler-Benz AG, p. 136.
22 'Der Aufschwung in der Automobilwirtschaft', p. 242; Strohmeyer, H.C., 'Die Deutsche Automobilindustrie im Jahre 1934' in: Die Deutsche Volkswirtschaft, (1935), No. 5, p. 147.
23 Edelmann, Vom Luxusgut zum Gebrauchsgegenstand, p. 166.
24 MBAG Kissel I/7, Minutes of the Board Meeting of DBAG on 28.6.1933; Minutes of the Meeting of the Working Committee of DBAG on 4.7.1933.
25 MBAG Kissel I/7, Minutes of the Board Meeting of DBAG on 25.4.1933.
26 Schley, E., 'Vier Jahre – Das Wunder Deutscher Motorisierung' in: Automobiltechnische Zeitschrift (1937), 3, p. 54.

in the mid-sized sector, for which it continued to produce a broad range in more moderate (though still substantially expanded) volumes. Throughout the 1930s, the company's strategy remained thereafter firmly orientated towards producing a variety of related cars, which it constantly changed and adapted according to fluctuations in demand, but which remained the same in terms of the mid-range market that it was attempting to supply. The basic concept underlying the production range of Daimler-Benz – the balance between diversity of product, uniformity of specification and flexible production methods – remained that of the 1920s. The 1.7l car remained the smallest of the company's models to enjoy large-scale long-term production, and was complemented in the 1930s by a changing range of cars in the 2l–3l range which were evolved out of the 1.7l car.[27] In 1936, 15,141 1.7l cars were sold and 4043 cars in the 2l-3l range, while only 211 large and luxury cars were sold, so the former provided the vast bulk of Daimler-Benz's car production in the mid-1930s.[28]

The decision to remain in the mid-sized range consequent upon the failure to introduce the 1.3l car was confirmed retrospectively for the board as having been the correct one. The structure of the car market was greatly altered in the mid-1930s by the emergence of the National Socialist regime's Volkswagen project. Daimler-Benz and the other private car manufacturers were aware that the appearance of such a cheap mass-produced car on the market would greatly alter the conditions under which the rest of the industry competed.[29] Not only did the Daimler-Benz board realize that it would not itself be able to compete with the Volkswagen in the small car market, confirming the already half-taken decision to abandon the 1.3l car, it was also aware that those manufacturers that had hitherto produced primarily for the lower end of the market (especially Opel and DKW) were drawing the same conclusions and attempting to diversify back into the mid-range. The prospect of the Volkswagen appearing on the market, as Daimler-Benz assumed would happen in 1937, and the growing competition this would inevitably cause among private manufacturers in the mid-range, created additional pressure on the company to strengthen its position in this range in the mid-1930s. Indeed, the emergent intensified competition in the mid-range increased the imperative to reduce production costs and was one of the main stimuli of a further process of rationalization that set in in the mid-1930s.

In part this was achieved by a further substantial redevelopment of the company's cars in the mid-1930s. The 1.7l car was redesigned, and the 2l and 2.9l cars were redeveloped as 2.3l and 3.2l cars respectively.[30] Thus, the effect of the Volkswagen project was not only to force the company to abandon the

27   For example MBAG Kissel I/8, Minutes of the Board Meeting of DBAG on 25.10.1935.
28   Schley, 'Vier Jahre – Das Wunder Deutscher Motorisierung', p. 54.
29   MBAG Kissel I/9, Minutes of the Board Meeting of DBAG on 22.4.1936.
30   MBAG Kissel I/9, Minutes of the Supervisory Board Meeting of DBAG on 8.10.1936.

1.3l car, but also to shift its other products away from the small car market. In addition to this, the company introduced a 2.6l diesel car in 1935. Daimler-Benz also continued to proceed on the principle of standardizing the main components of all its products, so as to allow as large as possible a volume of production despite the changing range it offered. The bodies of the 1.7l car and the various cars in the 2l range were largely standardized, allowing a further reduction of costs and the expanded use of pressed panels for models that were produced in smaller volume.[31] This process was extended to unifying the company's car engines with those used in the smaller lorry designs, allowing the smallest possible number of different engines to be produced.[32]

Until 1935 or 1936 Daimler-Benz, as with the German automobile industry in general, was largely able to cope with expanding demand by utilizing pre-existing capacity which had been idle in the Depression, and by increasing its workforce, and the hours and number of shifts worked. Where necessary, some production lines could be transferred to other factories where there was still available capacity, without the need for any expansion of individual factories or overall capacity. In some departments, limited new investment occurred from 1933 onwards.[33] In the summer of 1934, the increases in car production were such that the press shop at Sindelfingen had to be expanded.[34] However, investment in machinery and machine- tools was limited in the first two or three years of the recovery, as the company still had, by and large, sufficient capacity to increase production without large-scale new investment. In 1933, the company invested RM 5.5m, and in 1934 RM 9.5m, but much of this was taken up by the reactivation of closed-down capacity or by investment in areas other than automobile production – specifically, in expanding into the small but promising armaments market.[35] Investment in new machinery was limited to RM 1.9m in 1933 and RM 3.7m in 1934.[36] Most of this was used to replace worn-out machinery that the company had failed to replace during the Depression. In Gaggenau, for example, no machinery had been purchased for four years by the beginning of 1934.[37]

By the beginning of 1935, however, the economy had expanded to such an extent that the company had more business than it was capable of supplying, leading to a growing backlog of orders. This was especially the case in lorry production, where the Gaggenau plant had a three-month backlog and where monthly orders outstripped monthly capacity.[38] As a result of this, the

31 MBAG Kissel I/10, Minutes of the Board Meeting of DBAG on 11 and 12.3.1937.
32 MBAG Kissel I/24, Minute No. 299 of the Discussion in Gaggenau on 15.4.1936.
33 MBAG Kissel I/7, Minutes of the Meeting of the Working Committee of DBAG on 4.7.1933.
34 MBAG Kissel I/23, Minutes of the Discussion of Program Issues in Friedrichshafen on 10.8.1934.
35 Roth, 'Der Weg zum Guten Stern', p. 335.
36 Geschäftsbericht der Daimler-Benz AG 1933; Geschäftsbericht der Daimler-Beng AG 1934.
37 MBAG Kissel I/8, Minutes of the Board Meeting of DBAG on 16.2.1934.
38 MBAG Kissel I/8, Minutes of the Board Meeting of DBAG on 16.7.1935; on the lorry sector in general see Castorp, C., 'Der Deutsche Kraftfahrzeugabsatz 1935' in: Automobiltechnische Zeitschrift 3 (1936), p. 74.

company undertook an initial expansion of capacity at Gaggenau in the first half of 1935, after which the factory was capable of producing 650 lorries each month.[39] Even after this expansion, the company was unable to keep pace with expanding demand in the lorry sector, and by July 1935 Gaggenau had orders for 2000 lorries waiting to be completed.[40] By September, this backlog had risen to 2500.[41] A further expansion of capacity was thereupon carried out, to 750 lorries per month.[42]

By 1935, the huge backlog of orders produced by the economic boom had created a context in which an accelerated development towards more capital-intensive methods of production could occur. In 1935, investment in lorry production at Gaggenau alone totalled RM 10.7 m.[43] In the car sector, as well, an expansion of investment occurred from 1935–6 onwards, including the wide-spread replacement of older machine-tools and the replacement of belt-drives on machine-tools with more efficient individual electrical motors, which allowed more efficient usage of existing machines.[44] From 1936 onwards the press shop at Sindelfingen was also further expanded and new presses added.[45]

A further impetus towards accelerating the introduction of more capital-intensive production processes was given by developments in the labour market as a result of the rearmament boom.[46] Demographic factors, combined with the impact of reductions in training in the Depression, meant that once the recovery had set it, there was very soon a shortage of skilled workers.[47] Daimler-Benz had reduced the number of its apprentices by roughly one-quarter during the Depression.[48] The rapidity of the economic recovery after 1933 meant that industry did not have time to adjust its apprentice intake in time for it to have any effect on the supply of skilled workers.[49] As an industry that relied on a high proportion of skilled metal-workers, a sector of the workforce that was in short supply by 1934, the automobile industry began to feel this shortfall much sooner than most other industries.[50] Daimler-Benz complained of a shortage of skilled workers in both south-west Germany and Berlin in 1934.[51]

39 MBAG Kissel I/8, Minutes of the Presidium Meeting of DBAG on 3.6.1935.
40 MBAG Kissel I/8, Minutes of the Board Meeting of DBAG on 16.7.1935.
41 MBAG Kissel I/8, Minutes of the Presidium Meeting on 24.9.1935.
42 MBAG Kissel I/8, Minutes of the Supervisory Meeting of DBAG on 24.9.1935.
43 Roth, 'Der Weg zum Guten Stern', p. 335.
44 MBAG Kissel I/9, Main Plant (Untertürkheim) to Hoppe, 18.4.1936; Minutes of the Board Meeting of DBAG on 8.5.1936.
45 MBAG Kissel I/9, Minutes of the Board Meeting of DBAG on 22.4.1936.
46 On the impact of the rearmament boom on the labour market in the 1930s see Mason, Sozialpolitik, pp. 208–37; Hachtmann, Industriearbeit, pp. 37–42, 112–28.
47 Wolsing, T., Untersuchungen zur Berufsausbildung im Dritten Reich, Düsseldorf, 1977, p. 82.
48 MBAG Kissel I/7, Report of the Board for the Quarter-Year from 16.12.1932 to 16.3.1933.
49 Hachtmann, 'Arbeitsmarkt und Arbeitszeit', p. 195.
50 Hachtmann, Industriearbeit, pp. 61–2.
51 MBAG Kissel I/7, Minutes of the Board Meeting of DBAG on 22.2.1934; Minutes of the Board Meeting of DBAG on 20.6.1934.

The result of this was that, despite the large overall reserve of unemployed workers, and despite subsequent controls on labour mobility introduced by the regime, key sectors of the workforce were able to exploit their market position to effect limited wage increases from an early stage onwards. Rising labour costs did indeed encourage the implementation of labour-saving production processes to a limited extent. The defeat of the organized Left in 1933 meant, however, that labour was unable to exploit its renewed strength in the market with much real effectiveness, and labour costs remained low throughout the 1930s. Hourly wages for skilled metal-workers did not reach the levels of 1928 again until 1941.[52] It was thus not so much the price of labour but the complete lack of it that was an additional cause of rationalization measures aimed at reducing the need for skilled labour from the mid-1930s onwards.

Following the restructuring process after the fusion of 1926 and the wage reductions and intensification of labour achieved in the Depression, the mid-1930s thus saw a phase of accelerated implementation of more capital-intensive production processes. The rapid expansion of production and the more-or-less perpetual growth in demand, which by 1935–6 was increasingly outstripping supply, would seem, on the face of it, to have created a context within which rationalization policy had to be formulated but that was markedly different from the fluctuating and stagnant demand of the 1920s. Above all it would seem to have created a context in which the installation of highly productive single-purpose machinery – one of whose advantages was that it allowed greater employment of semi-skilled machine operators – would continued to be accelerated. However, the continued reliance of private industry on the production of a broad range of cars, a policy that the National Socialist Volkswagen project tended to reinforce despite its failure to materialize, together with the traditionally regular changes in product designs and models, meant that the German automobile industry continued to invest primarily in its traditionally preferred multi-purpose machinery. The German machine-tool industry correspondingly continued to supply machines for car manufacturers that allowed an ongoing reduction of production times by the faster and more accurate cutting or shaping of each work-piece, thereby reducing the need for subsequent machining, such as polishing, but that could be easily adapted to meet the annually changing production needs of the automobile manufacturers.[53] The rearmament programme brought with it a strong diversification in production itself, and, if anything, the fact that machine-tools were increasingly being used simultaneously to produce military versions of cars and lorries, or transferred totally into the expanding armaments sector, meant flexibility of capacity was all the more important in the 1930s despite the guaranteed demand in the short term. Even single-purpose machine-tools,

52 Hachtmann, *Industriearbeit*, pp. 104–5.
53 'Neuzeitliche Werkzeugmaschinen im Automobilbau' in: *Automobiltechnische Zeitschrift*, 39 (1936), 22, p. 561.

where they were deployed (such as lathes and polishing or milling machines used exclusively for one component), were designed so that items of different size or specification could easily be worked on them. The underlying strategy of rationalization policy at Daimler-Benz remained one of balancing optimal short-term efficiency with the retention of long-term flexibility of capacity.

By the 1930s, the increasing exactitude of machine-tools and the ongoing reduction of the amount of time needed to machine each individual item meant that the largely manual process of feeding the piece into the machine-tool, fixing it in place, and retrieving it once the operation had been performed came increasingly to account for a proportionately greater amount of the total time taken for the completion of one machining operation. Machine-tools were thus increasingly developed to which appliances could be attached which automatically fed, fixed and removed each individual work-piece before and after each operation, reducing or even removing one of the main elements of manual intervention in the production process. For example, semi-automatic or automatic lathes were introduced which performed the actual cutting operation independently of the machine operator, whose role was reduced to occasionally refilling the magazine of the machine.[54] The practice of developing these appliances and attaching them to multi-purpose machine-tools speeded up the production process and simultaneously removed the need for manual intervention, allowing the achievement of a balance between higher speed, lower cost and the greater deployment of semi-skilled labour on the one hand, and continued flexibility on the other.

In other cases, an important role in reducing production times was played by the deployment of multi-spindle drills, which were able to perform several drilling operations on one or more sides of the same work-piece simultaneously. For example, a 96-spindle drill could be used to drill 96 holes in a crankshaft at the same time, where previously a worker might have drilled 96 holes one after another. The role of the manual worker now consisted in fixing the work-piece in place, bringing the drill-bits to the work-piece and activating the machine. In this way, an operation that might before have taken two or three hours could be performed several times per minute.[55] The volume of production achieved in the 1930s was such that the lengthy initial process of setting the machine was more than offset by the time saved in the long run, while the fact that the holes were drilled by a pre-set machine rather than manually ensured complete uniformity of product and thus interchangeability with all the other items.

Similarly, semi-automated machines were developed and extensively deployed which operated using a revolving magazine that rotated automatically to bring each item in turn to be machined. The operator was

54 Ibid., pp. 562–3.
55 Ibid., p. 567.

again reduced to the role of feeding each item into the magazine every few seconds and retrieving the finished object once the magazine had completed its rotation. As the machine operated automatically, according to a pre-determined speed, the worker had practically no influence over the pace or quality of the work. These machines could also be equipped with revolving tool heads, so that several machining operations could be performed by a machine operated by one semi- or even unskilled worker.[56] However, important as it was that less skilled operators could be deployed on these machines, the workers' scope for influencing the production process was also greatly reduced. The breaking of the workers' ability to resist management by collective action in 1933 was thus complemented by the widespread introduction of machining processes that limited the workers' potential for exercising informal methods of shop-floor control or for engaging in passive resistance by 'go-slow' behaviour.

In many cases, a clear de-skilling of segments of the labour force was caused by the implementation of these production techniques. However, as the production process became more capital-intensive, the savings in skilled machine operators were offset by the need for more and more engineers to install, set, alter and repair machinery, so that the increased deployment of semi-skilled machine operators did not result in a substantial skills dilution within the workforce as a whole. Although the attachment of appliances to multi-purpose machine-tools allowed their operation by less skilled labour, the basic motivation for retaining flexible machine-tools – their applicability to a wide range of tasks – meant that it was necessary to retain a workforce capable of operating them in a wide variety of contexts. By the time the labour shortage was such that the company attempted to accelerate the introduction of single-purpose machinery, import restrictions and currency controls had created a further barrier to their mass deployment (most were imported from the USA), and although Daimler-Benz was able to pressurize the relevant authorities to allow it to import machine-tools on occasion, there clearly was a real restriction on the company's freedom in this respect.[57] Even in 1938, by which time labour shortages were becoming especially acute, 51 per cent of the male workforce in the car production shops at Untertürkheim were skilled workers, while 36 per cent were semi-skilled and only 13 per cent were unskilled.[58] In the engineering and automobile industry as a whole, 53.8 per cent of all workers were skilled in May 1939, compared with 59.3 per cent in October 1928, underlining the fact that rationalization in the metal-working

---

56 Ibid., p. 564.
57 MBAG Kissel II/8, DBAG to Technical Products Regulatory Office, 25.9.1937; DBAG to Economic Group Engineering 13.10.1937.
58 MBAG Kissel VI/1, DBAG Untertürkheim to Reich Office for Economic Expansion, 1.10.1938. If one includes the female workforce, for which no breakdown of skill levels is available, but which can be assumed not to have included skilled workers, the total proportion of skilled workers was 49 per cent.

industries only implied de-skilling to a very limited extent, and that labour-saving capital-intensive production methods were far from synonymous with skills dilution.[59]

2. The Four Year Plan and the Schell Programme

By 1936, the company could euphorically report that the automobile industry had experienced 'uninterrupted expansion for three years'.[60] Production in the industry had reached record levels and the impact of the Depression had long since been overcome. The continuous growth in demand was so great that it seemed on the surface that the automobile industry would be able to expand car and lorry production on an ongoing basis. In both the car and lorry sector, demand was such that the backlog of orders was constantly increasing.[61] However, if prior to 1936 the rearmament boom had provided stimulus for a huge growth in production, from this point onwards the impact of forced rearmament on the German economy began to undermine the automobile industry's ability to capitalize on the growing demand from the consumer and commercial sectors. The forced pace of rearmament was, by 1936, beginning to have a serious impact on Germany's balance of payments situation, a product of the increases in raw materials imports upon which rearmament depended and of increased demand for imports caused by the economic boom generally. Up until this point, the Minister for Economics, Hjalmar Schacht, had been able to alleviate the worst effects of periodic balance of payments problems by currency allocation, import controls and the expansion of bilateral trading agreements; but the trade surplus he was able to engineer in 1935 was followed by a renewed balance of payments crisis which could not be solved with existing means. The outcome of this crisis was the creation of the Four Year Plan, which combined the attempt to achieve economic autarky (for economic and strategic reasons) with the accelerated orientation of the German economy towards raw materials and armaments production through the channelling of investment, capacity and raw materials towards war-related industries. In 1936, investments instituted under the Four Year Plan accounted for 34 per cent of all industrial investment, in 1937 54 per cent, in 1938 53 per cent and in 1939 48 per cent.[62]

The channelling of raw materials towards armaments production by an increasingly dirigiste regime, and the development of direct allocation of quotas by the Four Year Plan authorities, began to limit the amount of

59 See also Hachtmann, *Industriearbeit*, p. 62. The continued prevalence of skilled labour in the workforce at Daimler-Benz is also explained by the fact that one of the most important aspects of rationalization in the period was the mechanization of transportation within the factory, so that if anything, it was unskilled activity that was 'rationalized away' extensively in the 1930s.

60 *Geschäftsbericht der Daimler-Benz AG 1935*.

61 MBAG Kissel I/9, Meeting of the Supervisory Board of DBAG on 18.6.1936.

62 On the Four Year Plan see Petzina, D., *Autarkiepolitik im Dritten Reich*, Stuttgart, 1968.

materials available to the manufacturers to expand their civilian production. The development of foreign exchange shortages and imposition of import restrictions simultaneously limited the potential for resolving these problems by importing materials such as rubber from abroad.[63] The moves towards autarky and partial materials allocation motivated by the needs of rearmament created increasing friction between the regime and an automobile industry that was traditionally strongly orientated towards international trade and that, if it was keen to participate in the rearmament process, still wished to capitalize on the expanding demand in the consumer and commercial sectors which provided the core of its business.

The general unease within business circles in the two to three years immediately prior to the war was compounded in the case of the automobile industry by the programme of enforced type-reduction embarked upon initially within the Economic Group Vehicles Industry (*Wirtschaftsgruppe Fahrzeugindustrie* – WiGruFa) at the behest of the Reich Economics Ministry (RWM) and then under the so-called Schell Programme. During this period, individual manufacturers negotiated first with each other and then with Colonel von Schell with the aim of reducing the number of vehicle types produced by the industry as a whole. However, despite the fact that the manufacturers were all completely opposed to the idea, they failed to act in a unified fashion to defend their common interests. Rather than aiming collectively to find a solution that would protect the autonomy of the industry against the regime, the negotiations tended to act as a forum in which companies competed against each other for private advantage. The fact that individual manufacturers were clearly more inclined to treat the WiGruFa as a forum for pursuing agendas against competitors within the industry, rather than as a means of representing the interests of the sector as a whole against the regime, not only meant that the industry failed to find universally acceptable solutions to the type reduction question of its own accord, but also ensured that the potential for using the WiGruFa as a means of collectively defending entrepreneurial and managerial autonomy against the increasingly interventionist regime was greatly undermined.

Whereas previously competition between companies had been articulated within the market, while the sector as a whole had continued to defend its interests collectively in the political sphere, the growing indirect regulation of production by the regime was leading to a situation in which companies were forced to compete against each other for favourable treatment either within or by the various regulatory agencies. This tendency towards displacement of competition onto the political level brought with it a progressive disintegration of the unity of the employers that had characterized the Weimar period. What resulted was a situation in which each used the various forums

---

63   Edelmann, *Vom Luxusgut zum Gebrauchsgegenstand*, p. 196.

available to pursue short-term competitive interests within the political framework rather than in the marketplace. This manifested itself in rivalry for contracts, raw materials and labour, or, in this case, in attempts to gain preferential treatment for one's own company in the type-reduction programme. The net impact of this disintegration of unity amongst the producers was to increase the dependence of the industry as a whole upon the regime.[64]

The first raw materials problems were created by rubber shortages in 1936 which caused problems in the supply of tyres.[65] In October 1936, the RWM ordered that tyres be allocated to factories at a level that would allow manufacturers to produce for four and a half days per week.[66] In November 1936 the Mannheim and Untertürkheim factories were indeed reduced to working a 38-hour week owing to shortages of material.[67] From November onwards, the automobile industry worked under the assumption that production cuts could be forced on the industry at any point by the raw materials situation.[68] Wehrmacht vehicles were in fact delivered without tyres at some points in 1937.[69]

Even more consternation was aroused by the introduction of a formal system of iron and steel allocation for the automobile industry in May 1937.[70] The basis for quota allocations for civilian production was calculated from the amount used by each firm in the second quarter of 1936, of which three-quarters would be allocated for 1937. In the second quarter of 1936, Daimler-Benz had been producing 2400 to 2500 cars per month and could thus expect, taking into account the limited Wehrmacht orders that the south-west German plants had at this point, allocations sufficient for a maximum monthly production of 2200 cars per month. In the meantime, however, demand was such that the company was capable of producing and selling 4000 cars per month.[71] Similarly, in lorry production, the allocations to Gaggenau would allow a total production for domestic sales of 420 per month against a capacity of 750, despite the fact that the Gaggenau plant had slightly more military orders. The fears of the board were confirmed when the company was allocated 4000 tons of iron and steel per month, whereas to utilize capacity fully 10,000 tons per month were needed.

This shortage was partially alleviated by the ongoing process of substituting

64   See on this subject above all Mason, 'Primacy of Politics', pp. 185–90.
65   MBAG Kissel I/9, Minutes of the Supervisory Board Meeting of DBAG on 18.6.1936.
66   MBAG Kissel I/9, Minutes of the Supervisory Board Meeting of DBAG on 8.10.1936.
67   SOPADE-Bericht 1936 p. 1426 (*Deutschland-Berichte der SOPADE 1933–1940*, Frankfurt/M., 1980, vol. 3.).
68   MBAG Kissel I/9, Minutes of the Board Meeting of DBAG on 24.11.1936.
69   MBAG Kissel I/10, Minutes of the Board Meeting of DBAG on 5.1.1937; Minutes of the Board Meeting of DBAG on 8.4.1937.
70   Kirchberg, P., 'Typisierung in der Deutschen Kraftfahrzeugindustrie und der General-bevollmächtigte für das Kraftfahrwesen' in: *Jahrbuch für Wirtschaftsgeschichte* 10 (1969) 2, p. 129.
71   MBAG Kissel I/10, Minutes of the Board Meeting of DBAG on 26 and 27.5.1937.

materials in short supply with less rare materials, or by substituting domesti-
cally produced materials for imported ones.[72] The shortages also accelerated
the introduction of materials-saving production processes, above all the
replacement of cutting processes with shaping processes that had been taking
place throughout the 1930s. These could only alleviate the problem in a very
marginal way, however, given the size of the shortfall in materials. The main
way in which Daimler-Benz could get extra raw materials allocations, besides
continuously putting direct pressure on the Four Year Plan agencies for
preferential treatment, was to expand its exports, in return for which extra
quotas were allocated.[73] As an exporter of finished goods, the automobile
industry was a particularly good source of foreign currency for the regime, so
that the Four Year Plan agencies introduced a system of additional allocations
in return for increasing exports, forcing the automobile industry to expand its
exports to retain profitable levels of production overall, even though the
exports themselves were, for most companies, not profitable.

From 1936 to 1937 the volume of exports achieved by the automobile
industry rose from RM 75.6m to RM 135.8m as a result of this policy.[74]
Daimler-Benz increased the value of its exports in the same period from RM
28m to RM 45m.[75] By doing so, it was able to avoid making cuts in production
until the war; and although the downturn in the world economy and the
increasingly tense diplomatic situation provided limits to the extent to which
exports could be forced, it was also able to make up any shortfall by
substantially increasing the proportion of capacity devoted to military
production from 1938 onwards. Nonetheless, after rising from 19,924 in 1936
to 25,895 in 1937, primarily as a result of increased exports, car production at
Untertürkheim fell slightly to 25,833 in 1938 and 25,250 in 1939.[76] From
1936–7 onwards, the 'motorization' of German society propagandized by the
National Socialist regime was sacrificed to the far more central aim of
militarization.

While friction between the regime and the automobile industry over raw
materials allocations was tempered by the high levels of production and
profitability guaranteed by the rearmament programme, far greater tension
was created over the related, but potentially far more significant issue of type-
reduction in the industry from 1936 onwards. The raw materials shortages in
1936 led the RWM to call for the reduction of the number of types produced
by the automobile industry.[77] State-led pressure to undertake an industry-wide
rationalization programme was motivated in the short term by the materials

72 On the impact of the raw materials situation in the 1930s on rationalization policy see Freyberg
    and Siegel, *Industrielle Rationalisierung*, pp. 292–95.
73 MBAG Kissel I/10, Minutes of the Board Meeting of DBAG on 26 and 27.5.1937.
74 Edelmann, *Vom Luxusgut zum Gebrauchsgegenstand*, p. 194.
75 Pohl et al., *Die Daimler-Benz AG*, p. 114.
76 *Das Werk Untertürkheim*, p. 192.
77 Kirchberg, 'Typisierung', p. 126; Edelmann, *Vom Luxusgut zum Gebrauchsgegenstand*, p. 198.

issue, but also in the longer term by the desire to standardize types in the interest of military efficiency, and was part of a broader set of interventions from the mid-1930s onwards designed to prepare the automobile industry for eventual war.[78] Within the industry, however, there was very little interest in type-reduction at this point, as business was such that the manufacturers were making large profits without feeling the need for a radical overhaul and the disruption this would bring.[79]

The industry was nevertheless aware of the need for at least an outward gesture of compliance, especially after Hitler himself had called for a reduction of types at the Automobile Exhibition of 1937. The experience of the Volkswagen project had shown that, if industry was not seen to be taking a positive lead on the subject, then the regime would develop a solution that would probably be less in keeping with the interests of private industry and over which it would have far less control. Hagemeier, a member of the board of the Adler Company and chairman of the WiGruFa, the committee of automobile manufacturers within the RWM, warned the other industrialists in a WiGruFa meeting of 7 November 1937 that 'If the industry does not produce adequate proposals itself, then it will inevitably lead to a solution being imposed by decree from above, which will be far more unpleasant in its effects than if we had acted ourselves.'[80]

Kissel was likewise aware that RWM demands would have to be accommodated in some form and argued that the WiGruFa should take up the issue out of a desire to keep it under the control of the private manufacturers.[81] He remained opposed, however, to any solution that would create a precedent for allowing external intervention in decisions that he saw as being the prerogative of the individual manufacturers. At the following meeting of the WiGruFa, on 18 November 1937, Kissel not only expressed opposition to the proposed type reduction programme, but argued that it was unfair to expect the largest manufacturers to cut radically the number of types they produced while the smaller manufacturers remained untouched.[82] If type-reduction was to be carried through, Kissel clearly wanted it to be done in such a way that the smaller companies would bear the brunt of the impact.

Over the following year, negotiations were carried out with a view to constructing a voluntary agreement within the industry to reduce both the number of car types and the number of lorry types.[83] The forum for this was the newly formed Technical Committee of the WiGruFa, which was set up to oversee the standardization process in accordance with the RWM's wishes.

78 Kirchberg, 'Typisierung', p. 125; Edelmann, *Vom Luxusgut zum Gebrauchsgegenstand*, p. 199.
79 Edelmann, *Vom Luxusgut zum Gebrauchsgegenstand*, p. 198.
80 Kirchberg, 'Typisierung', p. 126.
81 MBAG Kissel I/10, Minutes of the Board Meeting of DBAG on 12.11.1937.
82 Kirchberg, 'Typisierung', p. 127.
83 MBAG Kissel I/10, Minutes of the Supervisory Board Meeting of DBAG on 1.12.1937.

Although the industry had succeeded, for the time being, in retaining control over the resolution of the issue, Daimler-Benz was still very sceptical about the work of the Technical Committee and, above all, suspicious of the motives of the representatives of the other companies who were participating. Daimler-Benz did not, at this point, have a representative on the board of the WiGruFa.[84] Neither was it initially planned to involve a Daimler-Benz representative in the work of the Technical Committee.[85] Kissel was clearly aware of the implications of not having a member of the company involved and suspected that it was being intentionally excluded by the other manufacturers, who he feared would use their privileged position within the WiGruFa to force the main impact of the type-reduction process onto Daimler-Benz.

In the end Daimler-Benz was able to secure a place for one of its representatives, Oberbaurat Schmidt, on the Technical Committee.[86] The negotiations took place over the course of 1938. Some companies were willing to make minor concessions, although most offered to drop types that they had been planning to drop anyway, in order to present themselves as cooperating and force other manufacturers to give up models as well. Most of the models that the individual companies offered to drop were the smaller types, for which they already saw no future owing to the expectation that the Volkswagen would corner that market anyway.[87] The process was greatly undermined, however, by the tendency of the manufacturers to use the negotiations to try to force their competitors to drop models that directly competed with their own.[88]

The failure of the attempt to find a voluntary solution within the industry led Göring to appoint Colonel von Schell as General Plenipotentiary for the Automobile Industry (*Generalbevollmächtigte für das Kraftfahrwesen* – GBK), with powers to impose a solution on the industry, on 15 November 1938.

---

84 BA (P) 80 Ba2 P3179, Kissel to Rummel, 18.1.1937.
85 BA (P) 80 Ba2 P3179, Rummel to the Management of DBAG, 16.1.1937.
86 MBAG Kissel/WiGruFa – Circulars and Communiqués 1936–1942, WiGruFa to DBAG, 18.1.1937. The committee was formed of one representative each from Adler, Auto-Union, BMW, Bosch, Büssing-NAG, Daimler-Benz, NSU, Opel, one representative from the components industry and one from the raw materials industry.
87 MBAG Kissel I/10, Minutes of the Board Meeting of DBAG on 12.11.1937.
88 Daimler-Benz, for example, used the negotiations to try to get Opel to give up its 'Admiral' model for this reason. MBAG Kissel I/11, Minutes of the Board Meeting of DBAG on 14.9.1938. Daimler-Benz's own opposition to the process was probably strengthened by the fact that the initial proposals produced by Hagemeier did indeed envisage Daimler-Benz making far more substantial cuts to its car range than the other manufacturers. While Opel was spared any reduction under Hagemeier's proposal, and Auto-Union was to cut its range from nine to seven models, Daimler-Benz would be forced to cut its own number of models from eight to four. Hagemeier's firm, Adler, was to reduce its own number of models from five to four. It seems likely that Hagemeier was using his position to try to undermine the position of Daimler-Benz, one of Adler's direct competitors, while securing the support of other manufacturers by suggesting only minimal restrictions for them. For details of Hagemeier's programme see Kirchberg, 'Typisierung', p. 139.

Schell was ordered by Göring to introduce first a reduction of the number of types of lorry (on 1 December 1938), then also of the number of types of cars and other vehicles (on 2 February 1939).[89] Thereafter, the introduction of new types had to be authorized by the GBK, who was also given powers to reduce the number of types a company produced. According to Schell's programme, the number of lorry types produced by the industry was to be reduced to four models – all lorries hereafter had to be 1½, 3, 4½ or 6½ tons.[90] Egger, chairman of the WiGruFa since April 1938 and a board member of Büssing-NAG, was charged with the renewed task of producing a programme of voluntary reduction by 15 December 1939, now with the additional threat of the GBK to force compliance.[91] Egger urged compliance on the remaining manufacturers, arguing that by so doing the industry could gain the favour of Schell and that it was better to cooperate than to force Schell to use his powers to dictate a solution.

In public, Daimler-Benz declared its full support for the Schell Programme.[92] In private, it remained very sceptical and wary.[93] The company found itself, in fact, in a relatively strong position with regard to the prospect of forced reduction. Its range of products was so diverse that the reduction of turnover brought about by the loss of one model would have a minimal impact, especially as the unsupplied demand in the market would inevitably be compensated by increased sales of other models. The constant process of standardizing its models internally meant that very little would be gained in terms of efficiency by dropping one type. Of the lorry types that Schell had permitted, Daimler-Benz was confident that it would be able to retain its 3 and 4½-ton lorries and possibly its 1½ and 6½-ton lorries as well.[94] In the event, the programme that Schell produced did not seriously disrupt Daimler-Benz's production or generate any conflict with the company. The number of lorry types overall was reduced from 113 to 21, and the number of car types from 52 to 30.[95] The manufacturers had to adapt to this programme by 1 January 1940.[96] Daimler-Benz, however, was able to retain all its car types and most of its lorry types, keeping the 1½-ton, 3-ton and 4½-ton, and losing only the 6½-ton of the permitted types.[97] In addition to the fact that the company's

89   Kirchberg, 'Typisierung', p. 131; Edelmann, Vom Luxusgut zum Gebrauchsgegenstand, p. 200.
90   Kirchberg, 'Typisierung', p. 135.
91   Ibid., p. 133–4.
92   Geschäftsbericht der Daimler-Benz AG für 1938; Geschäftsbericht der Daimler-Benz AG für 1939.
93   MBAG Kissel/WiGruFa – Correspondence 1935–1939, Kissel to Werlin, 30.3.1939.
94   MBAG Kissel I/11, Minutes of the Board Meeting of DBAG on 1.12.1938; Minutes of the Presidium Meeting on 2.12.1938.
95   Kirchberg, 'Typisierung', p. 136; Pohl et al., Die Daimler-Benz AG, p. 64; Schell, A. von, 'Nationalsozialistische Wirtschaftsformen und Kraftfahrzeugindustrie' in: Der Vierjahresplan (1939), p. 1011; also Schell, A. von, 'Neue Wege der Deutschen Motorisierung' in: Der Vierjahresplan (1939), pp. 362–64.
96   Edelmann, Vom Luxusgut zum Gebrauchsgegenstand, p. 201. The outbreak of war, in any case, meant that Schell's initial programme was eventually superseded.
97   'Die Typenbegrenzung in der Kraftfahrzeugindustrie' in: Der Vierjahresplan (1939), p. 530.

internal standardization over the 1930s had put it in a good position, its close contacts with the regime and intensive lobbying of Schell himself undoubtedly helped the company defend its interests very successfully.

Further passive resistance within the industry, including Daimler-Benz, was caused by Schell's attempts to enforce increased standardization of components in 1939. This followed on from the declaration of the RVM (*Reichsverkehrsministerium* – Reich Transport Ministry) of obligatory standards for the industry in 1938, replacing the voluntary basis upon which existing norms had hitherto been recognized.[98] At the same time as enforcing the reduction of vehicle types, Schell ordered Colonel Zuckertort to supervise the acceleration of the standardization of components, again in cooperation with the Technical Committee of the WiGruFa.[99] Once more, the company made public proclamations of support for the work of the GBK, stating that the industry had as much interest in reducing the number of different components as the military. The automobile industry was, in fact, willing to standardize where conditions allowed; and where negotiations were already underway, or where the industry was in favour of further standardization, these were carried out under the auspices of Zuckertort's programme.[100] However, individual firms again tended to oppose specific measures, depending on which of their components did not yet conform to the envisaged norm, and tried to argue for exceptions where their implementation would cause disruption to themselves. Despite his public support, Schmidt tried to ensure that the main role be given to industry and that a procedural format be adopted that would slow down the progress of standardization. Other members of the industry acted similarly, opposing individual measures as 'premature' or 'inappropriate', suggesting the need for industry to resolve the issue itself and attempting to retain autonomy for manufacturers.[101]

In private and in correspondence with other industry figures, Kissel was even more frank in his opposition to the enforced standardization of components, expressing his anger that the regime was willing to impose such conditions upon the automobile industry under such circumstances.[102] He was particularly critical of Egger for allowing military representatives to attend the

98   BA (K) R 13 IV/15, WiGruFa to all Members, 10.3.1938.
99   MBAG Kissel/WiGruFa – Correspondence 1935–1939, Minutes of the 19th Meeting of the Technical Committee of WiGruFa, 29.3.1939.
100 MBAG Kissel/WiGruFa – Circulars and Communiqués 1936–1942, Minutes of the Meeting of 5 and 6.7.1939 concerning Standardization of Components on Cars and Lorries.
101 MBAG Kissel/WiGruFa – Correspondence 1935–1939, Minutes of the 19th Meeting of the Technical Committee of WiGruFa 29.3.1939.
102 MBAG Kissel/WiGruFa – Correspondence 1935–1939, Kissel to Werlin, 30.3.1939. Kissel also heaped scorn on Schell's visit to the USA (MBAG Kissel/WiGruFa – Circulars and Communiqués 1936–1942, Werlin's memorandum of the Meeting of the Council of the Economic Group on 19.5.1939; Kissel/WiGruFa – Correspondence 1935–1939, Kissel to WiGruFa, 17.6.1939).

meetings of the WiGruFa, arguing that this prevented 'open discussion' among the industrialists themselves, and demanding that the WiGruFa represent the interests of private industry more effectively.[103] Kissel's anger at Egger was further fuelled by the fact that he suspected him of using his position as chairman of the WiGruFa to gain exemptions from the regulations for Büssing-NAG with which other companies were forced to comply.[104] In the event, the passive resistance of the industry to Schell's programme forced the postponement of the introduction of the new standards from the original date of 1 July 1940 to 1 April 1941.[105]

While the issue of type-reductions was being addressed in the years prior to the outbreak of war, the backlog of orders in the industry steadily grew. From 1936 onwards, Daimler-Benz was unable to keep pace with the volume of outstanding orders. This was partly a product of continued increases in demand. The backlog in the late 1930s was, however, less a product of real consumer demand outstripping capacity than a result of the gearing of economic policy towards the pursuit of the regime's primary goal – rearmament. The prospect of the Volkswagen appearing strengthened the assumption that private automobile manufacture had reached a virtual plateau in the mid-1930s.

Meanwhile, the ongoing introduction of labour-saving production processes on the one hand and the failure to expand car production substantially from the mid-1930s on the other, meant that relatively fewer and fewer workers were needed on Daimler-Benz's car production lines. At the end of 1936, the board, recognizing the effect forced rearmament was having upon the economy, came to the conclusion that it would no longer be able to maintain both its Untertürkheim and Mannheim factories as pure car-producing plants.[106] Demand in the lorry sector remained very strong, by contrast, owing to the greater element of military production in this sector, and the Gaggenau plant was constantly overloaded. At the end of 1936, the board came to the conclusion that a shift in emphasis was necessary towards the greater production of lorries.

Over the course of the period 1936–9 Mannheim's capacity was thus gradually converted from car to lorry production. In 1937, an initial transfer of some of Mannheim's car production to Untertürkheim was effected, so that

103   MBAG Kissel/WiGruFa-Correspondence 1935–1939, Kissel to Egger, 30.3.1939.
104   MBAG Kissel/WiGruFa-Correspondence 1935–1939, Memorandum on the Handling of the Lorry Types Question, 6.4.1939.
105   MBAG Kissel/WiGruFa-Correspondence (Standardization of Parts 1939–1941), Implementation Regulation No. 6 on the Decree on Type Reduction in the Vehicle Industry of 2.3.1939, 10.7.1939; MBAG Kissel/WiGruFa-Correspondence 1935–1939, Implementation Regulation No. 13 of the Degree on Type Reduction in the Vehicle Industry of 2.3.1939, 19.9.1940.
106   MBAG Kissel I/9, Minutes of the Presidium Meeting of DBAG on 18.6.1936; Minutes of the Board Meeting of DBAG on 24.11.1936. See also Kissel VI/18, Hoppe/Circular concerning production of the 1½- and 2-ton Lorries, 14.10.1936.

Mannheim could begin producing small volumes of 1½- and 2-ton lorries.[107] By mid-1937, however, continually increasing demand in the lorry sector, combined with growing pressure to reduce production costs in the car sector, led the company to follow its initial shift of strategy in late 1936 with a complete restructuring of car and lorry production at Mannheim and Untertürkheim in the two years prior to the outbreak of war.[108]

As part of this process, the car production lines at Untertürkheim, which in the mid-1930s were still structured on the principle of group production, were converted to large-scale serial production methods, facilitated by a further concentration of car production on Untertürkheim.[109] As a result of this, the production time for the 1.7l car was reduced by one-third from 1936 to 1940.[110] At Mannheim, the restructuring was complicated by the uncertainty caused by the WiGruFa negotiations, but in March 1938 it was decided to tool for production of Daimler-Benz's 3-ton lorry, of which 300 were to be produced at Mannheim each month, in addition to the 1½-ton and 2-ton lorries already being produced there.[111] In all, RM 8.2m were invested to increase the capacity of Gaggenau to 930 lorries per month and to re-tool Mannheim for the production of the 3-ton lorry.[112]

The growing volume of contracts – including increasing numbers of military contracts – was such that even this conversion proved insufficient to adapt to the changing situation. In the summer of 1938, the board finally decided to transfer all remaining car production from Mannheim to Untertürkheim, and to convert Mannheim's capacity completely to lorry production. From January 1939, the plant was to be used exclusively for this purpose.[113] The impending loss of the 2-ton model as a result of the WiGruFa negotiations led the board to combine this with a further increase of capacity to 700 3-ton lorries per month rather than the 300 initially envisaged.[114] Over the course of 1939 this re-tooling process was carried out, and was still underway when war broke out in September 1939.

The National Socialist seizure of power and the economic boom of the 1930s had thus created the conditions under which an accelerated transition

---

107 MBAG Kissel I/9, Minutes of the Board Meeting of DBAG on 24.11.1936.
108 MBAG Kissel I/10, Minutes of the Board Meeting of DBAG on 27 and 28.7.1937; Minutes of the Supervisory Board Meeting of DBAG on 1.12.1937.
109 MBAG Kissel I/11, Minutes of the Presidium Meeting of DBAG on 1.3.1938; Kissel I/12, Minutes of the Board Meeting of DBAG on 10.2.1939.
110 *Leistungsbericht der DBAG Zentralverwaltung und Werk Untertürkheim 1940*, p. 216 (reprinted in Roth and Schmid, *Die Daimler-Benz AG 1918–1948*, p. 164 Doc. 60).
111 MBAG Kissel I/25, Minutes of the Meeting regarding Transfer of Omnibus Production from Gaggenau to Sindelfingen 25.3.1938.
112 MBAG Kissel I/25, Minutes of the Meeting of 29.3.1938 regarding Expansion of Lorry Production at Mannheim.
113 MBAG Kissel I/11, Minutes of the Board Meeting of DBAG on 13.7.1938.
114 MBAG Kissel VI/19, Minute concerning Tooling for Production of LGF 3000 Lorries at the Mannheim plant, 12.9.1938.

to more capital-intensive production processes could be instituted as the key element in an ongoing process of rationalization which saw substantial reductions in production times. Despite the great expansion of output, however, the underlying strategy of the company remained that of producing a broad range of mid-sized cars, and rationalization policy was implemented very much with the need to retain the necessary flexibility of capacity to pursue this in mind. The continued preference for general-purpose machine-tools that this naturally entailed meant that, despite the greater volume of production, production processes at Daimler-Benz remained geared towards and dependent upon a highly skilled workforce.

The same rearmament boom that had created the context for this expansion and rationalization of production up until 1936–7 also began, however, to create a ceiling beyond which production could not rise, as the Four Year Plan channelled more and more raw materials and resources towards war-related production. For the automobile industry in particular, the Four Year Plan also brought the unwanted intervention of the Schell Programme, which threatened to undermine seriously the managerial autonomy that the employers believed to have been restored in 1933, and which caused not only considerable friction with the regime, but great uncertainty in the immediate pre-war years. This uncertainty, however, was only part of a broader nervousness with regard to the economic prospects of the Reich and the company strategy to be pursued as a result. Above all, company uncertainty in the late 1930s was fostered by the rearmament programme and its impact on Daimler-Benz, which also has to be examined before the development of the company's strategy and rationalization policy in the war can be understood.

3. Daimler-Benz and Rearmament 1926–39

a) Covert Rearmament 1926–32

From virtually the moment of its formation, Daimler-Benz participated in the covert rearmament programme of the Reichswehr. Both predecessor firms had been major armaments manufacturers in the First World War, and both presided over know-how and capacity that was never fully lost or closed down thereafter. As such, the re-diversification into this area in the late 1920s was not difficult for the company. Daimler-Benz was not one of the companies permitted to produce military goods under the terms of the peace settlement of 1919; given that the Reichswehr had no power (or need) to enforce participation, Daimler-Benz's involvement was obviously voluntary.

The long-term motives of the company and its bankers, the process by which it increased its participation in the rearmament programme, and the relationship between the armaments production of the 1920s and the National Socialist rearmament boom of the 1930s have been the subject of controversy. It is clear that both the supervisory board and the board itself were well disposed towards the covert rearmament of the Reichswehr and the participation of Daimler-Benz in it. Where it did not accept contracts in the 1920s, it acted out of reasons of financial calculation and criteria of profitability, and not out of principle. As such, the inference, from the refusal of the company to participate in tank design in 1927, that Daimler-Benz rejected all participation before the Depression is clearly misleading.[115] However, the evidence linking Daimler-Benz's participation in the rearmament of the Reichswehr to a broader, politically motivated strategy pursued by the banks from 1926 onwards – which, as Karl-Heinz Roth implies, was aimed at bringing a regime to power that would provide Daimler-Benz with the lucrative armaments contracts for which the company had been intended all along –is less conclusive.[116]

It is well established that by the onset of the Depression significant sectors of finance and industry were becoming increasingly antipathetic to parliamentary democracy and saw a resolution of the economic crisis as only being possible in the context of an extra-systemic solution involving the permanent establishment of authoritarian government, the exclusion of the organized Left, the dismantling of Weimar's progressive welfare apparatus and the expansion of armaments production. For a small but influential minority of industrialists this led to direct support for the National Socialist movement prior to the seizure of power.[117] This was one factor of many in the complex set of processes by which the National Socialist regime was established. Figures closely associated with Daimler-Benz, especially with the supervisory board, were also among those who played a role in facilitating links between the Reichswehr and industry in the 1920s, and some were associated with key weapons and munitions manufacturers from the First World War.[118] The chairman of Daimler-Benz's supervisory board himself, Emil Georg von Stauss, was sympathetic to the idea of rearmament and, as a member of the Reichstag faction of the right-wing DVP (German People's Party), was never more than a fair-weather Republican with no political or ideological commitment to the Weimar Republic. Stauss, in fact, became one of the first to establish contact with the National Socialist party after the 1930 election

115   Hansen, E., *Reichswehr und Industrie. Rüstungswirtschaftliche Zusammenarbeit und Wirtschaftliche Mobilmachungsvorbereitungen 1923–32*, Boppard am Rhein, 1978, p. 175.
116   This is the core of Roth's argument. See Roth, 'Der Weg zum Guten Stern', pp. 37–9.
117   Stegmann, D., 'Zum Verhältnis von Grossindustrie und Nationalsozialismus 1930–1933' in: *Archiv für Sozialgeschichte* 13 (1973), pp. 399–482; Turner, H.A., *German Big Business and the Rise of Hitler*, Oxford, 1985; for a summary of the arguments see Geary, D., 'Employers, Workers and the Collapse of the Weimar Republic' in: Kershaw, I. (ed.), *Weimar: Why Did German Democracy Fail?*, London, 1990.
118   von der Porten, the rationalization expert who advised Daimler-Benz during the Depression, was the chairman of the supervisory board of Rheinmetall AG, for example, and Paul von Gontard, a member of the supervisory board of Daimler-Benz, was also a director of the Berlin Karlsruher Industrie-Werke AG (Hansen, *Industrie und Reichswehr*, pp. 167–8). Both had been key military producers in the First World War and both individuals were linked to the 'military-industrial complex', the core of which remained intact in the 1920s.

results, and later gravitated towards the National Socialists himself.[119] Rearmament of the Reichswehr and the contracts for industry this implied were clearly part of the ideological system to which these individuals subscribed and a key component of the interest-group politics they pursued in the Depression.

On the other hand, it seems unlikely, to say the least, that the Deutsche Bank would engineer the fusion of Daimler and Benz in 1926 and keep the new company afloat for years on end for an unforeseeable rearmament boom carried out by a movement that was not only not in power, but that, at the time of the fusion, had no prospect of being so. In 1926, the National Socialist movement was a marginal phenomenon, with a leader who had just come out of prison, and neither the Depression nor the accession to power of the movement could have been predicted by the Deutsche Bank any more than by anybody else at this point. The one-dimensional conspiracy theory that Roth constructs depends upon a great deal of hindsight, and as much concrete evidence exists to contradict it as does to support it.[120]

The participation of Daimler-Benz in the covert rearmament process can probably be characterized as a diversification into a field in which the company had a great deal of residual expertise in the context of an economy that, if relatively stable by the standards of the early 1920s, remained stagnant. The onset of the Depression, especially, and the huge reduction in turnover this brought, greatly increased the willingness of the company to take in military contracts. The shift from democratic to authoritarian government and to a more overtly revisionist foreign policy, moreover, created a situation where participation in covert rearmament offered the likelihood of profits in

119 Turner, *Big Business*, pp. 142–4.
120 Roth contends, for example, that the reason Daimler-Benz did not enter into large-scale production of standard small cars using 'American' production methods was a product of the banks' intention of keeping Daimler-Benz's capacity for future armaments production, which rendered large investment in rationalization measures in car production undesirable (Roth, 'Der Weg zum guten Stern', pp. 42, 80–81). It is clear, however, that on occasion it was precisely the supervisory board that proposed the adoption of 'American' techniques, such as the adoption of press techniques for the production of body panels, and the company board that opposed it. There is also little evidence to suggest that the banks' refusal of capital for the introduction of production of a smaller car in 1928 was motivated by the desire to keep Daimler-Benz's capacity for armaments production. Rather, it was based primarily on the belief that there was not a large enough market for the proposed car for the project to be profitable (MBAG Kissel I/4, Minutes of the Board Meeting of DBAG on 16.8.1928). Finally, if the Deutsche Bank, or Daimler-Benz, could foresee the National Socialist rearmament boom in 1926 (as Roth implies), then it could clearly foresee it all the more clearly in 1931. This leads to the question – why did Daimler-Benz go to such lengths in the Depression to try to sell its Marienfelde plant, which was the main initial beneficiary of large armaments contracts from 1933 onwards? From 1929 to 1931 Daimler-Benz made attempts to sell the plant to the Berlin city authorities, to the Reichsbahn and to the Reichspost, and even considered selling it to Ford (BA [P] 80 Ba 2 P3268, Correspondence concerning the Sale of Marienfelde 1929–1931). It would hardly have tried so hard to sell the plant if it had been simultaneously pursuing a policy of engineering the seizure of power of the National Socialist movement in order to provide the same plant with armaments contracts.

this area in a way that had not previously been the case. There was no great conflict of principle on the issue between the supervisory board and the managerial board. The rapidity with which Daimler-Benz became involved in large-scale production of armaments after 1933 was more a result of the close contacts it developed with the Army Weapons Procurement Office (*Heereswaffenamt* – HWA) in the later 1920s than of a conspiracy between the banks and the National Socialist movement during this period.

It is impossible to ascertain at what point Daimler-Benz began to be involved in the various aspects of the rearmament programme with any degree of certainty, in view of the secrecy with which the whole matter was handled. Initially, the company seemed reluctant to produce prototypes for the army, seeing the huge costs involved as prohibitive in view of the fact that large-scale orders would clearly not be forthcoming in the immediate future. The army was only able to offer contracts for prototypes without any guarantee of future purchases. It also preferred to distribute contracts among several firms, in order to give a wider number experience of producing for the military, rather than give larger, more profitable orders to a few firms. Daimler-Benz, on the other hand, argued in 1926 that it was unacceptable for the military to spread contracts so widely, and, in response to the military's argument that the automobile industries of other countries produced for the armed forces as a matter of course, countered that other countries were not subject to the restrictions of the Treaty of Versailles.[121]

However, soon after Daimler-Benz obviously accepted a contract for the production of military versions of its cars and by 1927, had delivered a small number of all-terrain three-axled cars to the military.[122] In 1928 it worked on an improved model in anticipation of future contracts, and, even before the Depression had begun, the company was placing increasing emphasis on military contracts, seeing the improvements as being 'of greatest importance for our future business'. For this reason it started developing a 3-ton lorry for the military and was already engaged in the design of a military version of a 1½-ton lorry.[123] The company placed 'great emphasis' on production of cars and lorries for the military, which were clearly of particular interest as they could be adapted relatively easily from general commercial vehicles.[124]

In 1926, when most of the treaty restrictions on aero-engine development were lifted, Daimler-Benz began reactivating its expertise in this area. In the same year, the company negotiated with the Marine Office of the Reichswehr

121 MBAG Kissel I/2, Report on the Negotiations with the Army Inspectorate for Weapons and Equipment, 22.11.1926.
122 MBAG Kissel/Public Contracts and Armed Forces Contracts 1928–1935, Public Contracts Department to the Directorate of DBAG Stuttgart-Untertürkheim, 21.5.1928.
123 MBAG Kissel/Public Contracts and Armed Forces Contracts 1928–1935, Public Contracts Department to the Directorate of DBAG, 29.8.1928.
124 MBAG Kissel/Public Contracts and Armed Forces Contracts 1928–1935, Public Contracts Department to the Directorate of DBAG, 1.10.1928.

Ministry over the construction of one air-cooled and one water-cooled prototype aero-engine.[125] The company was also willing to participate in this development, if the work was subsidized, and agreement was reached in principle. It is unclear exactly when Daimler-Benz began this work, but by 1929 the development of large engines specifically for the air force or the navy was underway.[126] By 1931, the company was able to present a 'multi- purpose' aero-engine, ostensibly to the Reich Transport Ministry, but also to the military authorities.[127] In addition, the company was offered a contract to construct a new tank prototype in 1927. After consideration, it apparently decided against accepting the contract.[128] However, the changed political and economic circumstances of the Depression led the company to accept a contract to design a new tank prototype in 1931.[129]

Evidence on individual contracts is very fragmented, but the importance of military contracts to the company during the Depression is underlined by the increasing percentage of its turnover derived from military production in the period prior to 1933. From eight per cent in 1926 and ten per cent in 1927, it rose to 19 per cent in 1932.[130] This was, however, mainly owing to the falling overall turnover of the company and is not evidence of a massively expanding military production in the Depression. The real value of military contracts before 1933 reached a peak in 1929, at about RM 15.6m, and declined in 1930 and 1931 to approximately RM 12m in 1931 and 1932.[131]

b) Rearmament at Marienfelde 1933–39

Measured by the standards of the 1930s, rearmament expenditure in the 1920s had a minimal impact on the German economy, accounting for only one per cent of GNP in 1932. From 1933 onwards, National Socialist rearmament had a radical effect on the German economy, both in terms of its role as the main stimulus of the economic boom and in terms of greatly increasing the proportion of economic activity that was dependent upon state expenditure. This rose from RM 1.9 billion in 1933 (when it accounted for three per cent of GNP) to RM 4.1 billion in 1934 (six per cent of GNP), and rose annually in real terms to RM 17.2 billion in 1938 (17 per cent of GNP). Finally, as a result of the regime's decision to force the pace of rearmament drastically in mid-1938, expenditure rose to RM 30 billion in 1939 (23 per cent of GNP), by which point armaments expenditure was placing the economy as a whole

125   MBAG Kissel I/2, Minutes of the visit of *Ministerialrat* Laudahn, 24.11.1926.
126   MBAG Kissel I/10, Minutes of the Supervisory Board Meeting of DBAG on 1.12.1937.
127   BA (P) 80 Ba2 P3185, DBAG Untertürkheim to Stauss, 2.7.1931.
128   Hansen, *Reichswehr und Industrie*, p. 175, notes a *Waffenstab* (Weapons Staff) document of
        27.7.1928 citing Daimler-Benz's refusal to participate.
129   Hansen, *Reichswehr und Industrie*, p. 175.
130   Roth, 'Der Weg zum Guten Stern', p. 333.
131   Figures calculated according to Roth, 'Der Weg zum Guten Stern', p. 333.

under considerable strain.[132] The board of Daimler-Benz was already aware in 1933 of the greatly increased potential that the National Socialist seizure of power represented for armaments production, and orientated its strategy from the beginning towards large-scale participation in the rearmament programme, emerging as one of the main military producers for the Reich in the 1930s. The proportion of Daimler-Benz's total turnover derived from armaments expenditure rose from 26 per cent in 1933 to 43 per cent in 1936, and to 65 per cent in 1939.[133]

In 1933, the board immediately recognized the need to strengthen its connections with the military, and moved to 'expand the contact between the company and the authorities in such a way as to create a permanent and intense relationship on a broad basis', noting that 'the fortunes of the company demand that all possibilities are exhaustively exploited (*restlos erschöpft*).'[134] As part of this initiative, the company's Public Contracts Department (*Behördenabteilung*), which coordinated the contacts between the company and the HWA, was strengthened (the office itself was situated in the Charlottenburg suburb of Berlin, in the same neighbourhood as the HWA). The board went so far as to reinstate the recently sacked Jakob Werlin, an old acquaintance of Hitler and a committed Nazi, appointing him to the board in 1933 and giving him the express brief of exploiting his contacts with Hitler and the regime for the benefit of the company.[135] Over the next years Werlin intervened directly with Hitler on a number of occasions to gain advantages for the company, and his 'insider' position was very useful to Daimler-Benz for gaining preferential treatment and information. The company also attempted to engage the staff of competitors who were known to have strong links to the regime – an employee of Adler, for example, was approached because he had 'good connections to Reichsminister Göring'.[136]

The main initial consequence of this reorientation was the decision to

---

132 Noakes, J. and Pridham, G. (eds.), *Nazism 1919–1945. Volume 2: State, Economy and Society 1933–1939*, Exeter, 1984, pp. 297–8.

133 Roth, 'Der Weg zum Guten Stern', p. 333.

134 MBAG Kissel I/7, Minutes of the Board Meeting of DBAG on 25.4.1933.

135 On Werlin see Pohl et al., *Die Daimler-Benz AG*, pp. 35–41, although Pohl's attempts to recast Werlin, who was clearly a convinced Nazi, as an ambivalent figure render the treatment problematic.

136 MBAG Kissel I/7, Minutes of the Board Meeting of DBAG on 25.4.1933. The other side of the public 'self-coordination' of the company following the National Socialist seizure of power manifested itself in the dismissal or withdrawal from public positions of employees whose political persuasions rendered them unsuitable. After the March 1933 elections, for example, the board decided that 'Herr Frank A. can no longer represent Daimler-Benz AG in view of his well-known political views' (MBAG Kissel I/7, Minutes of the Board Meeting of DBAG on 15.3.1933). This practice also extended to the company's links with the ideological enemies of the regime – in September 1933, for example, Kissel ensured that all links with a Jewish lawyer who had been representing the company were broken (MBAG Kissel XIII/15, Correspondence with Kissel-Rohde Sept. 1933); similarly, in October 1937 Kissel refused to employ someone on account of his Jewish wife (MBAG Kissel XIII/15, Kissel to Zimmermann/Adlerwerke South Africa, 5.10.1937).

reactivate the Marienfelde plant. Despite the fact that all other Daimler-Benz plants were working at below capacity and that it would have been sounder financially in the short term to keep it closed, the prospect of military contracts and the importance Daimler-Benz attached to establishing a position as a large-scale producer of military goods led it to reopen the plant in 1933.[137] By mid-1934, the plant, which was managed by the board member directly responsible for military production, Wolfgang von Hentig, was already employing 800 workers.[138] By December 1939, this figure had reached 5348.[139] Over the next six years, the original Marienfelde plant (Plant 40) produced all-terrain lorries and a range of tanks and armoured vehicles almost exclusively for the military. A second plant (Plant 90) was added, also exclusively for military production, which began contributing to turnover in 1935. The turnover of the plant rose from a negligible RM 1.3m in 1932 to RM 77.4m in 1937.[140] The importance of Marienfelde to Daimler-Benz in the 1930s is underlined when this is expressed as a percentage of total turnover – in 1932, Marienfelde accounted for two per cent of the total turnover of Daimler-Benz, whereas in 1937 it accounted for 21 per cent.

Initially, contracts for the military were relatively small and irregular, so that the company had difficulty maintaining a continuous and steady production in the first two years of the rearmament programme. However, it was possible to offset the worst effects of this by taking in contracts from other authorities, and Hentig was always able to force contracts out of the HWA by threatening to lay off workers at the Marienfelde plant.[141] The company also opposed suggestions from the military in 1935 that it transfer some civilian production to Marienfelde, complaining that it had agreed to reopen Marienfelde on the basis of a promise that the plant would be guaranteed continuous employment through military contracts.[142]

The favoured strategy of keeping Marienfelde for purely military production created a dilemma in itself, however, which became the cause of occasional internal friction throughout the 1930s. The HWA only gave oral guarantees of future contracts, and, furthermore, the allocation of specific contracts for production was carried out informally (for reasons of secrecy) and only on the basis of a yearly budget. This meant that the company was guaranteed full employment and lucrative profits in the short term, but was unable to plan with any degree of certainty more than one or two years ahead. On the one hand, it wished to exploit the hugely profitable rearmament boom,

137   MBAG Kissel l/7, Report of the Board of Directors for the Quarter-year from 1.7.1933 to 36.9.1933.
138   MBAG Kissel l/7, Minutes of the Supervisory Board Meeting of DBAG on 16.5.1934.
139   MBAG DBAG 31, Special Report of Daimler-Benz AG, 22.11.1945.
140   Pohl et al., *Die Daimler-Benz AG*, p. 126.
141   MBAG Kissel/Marienfelde 1926–1937, Kissel to Deutsche Reichsbahn, 23.11.1934.
142   MBAG Kissel/Marienfelde 1926–1937, HWA to DBAG Stuttgart, 18.7.1935; Kissel to HWA, 11.6.1935; Kissel to DBAG Berlin-Charlottenburg, 21.6.1935.

participation in which offered some advantages compared to producing for the free market, and feared being 'elbowed out' of the lucrative military sector by other companies if it did not expand to cater for the increased demands of the military.[143] On the other hand, it was wary of over-expanding capacity to profit from a rearmament boom that could end at any time and that would leave Marienfelde in particular saddled with huge excess capacity and no civilian production to fall back on.

By the mid-1930s, once the effects of the Depression had been overcome and profitability restored, the attitude of the board oscillated between the idea of expansion to meet increased demand from the military agencies and caution at over-expanding in the expectation that the rearmament programme would, at some point, be scaled down. In February 1936, for example, the Charlottenburg office informed Kissel that Marienfelde had sufficient contracts to guarantee production at full capacity until March 1937, but recommended that instead of immediately expanding the workshops it be considered whether 'if, in view of the expected coming reduction in military contracts, the current capacity of the plant be retained and a corresponding number of contracts left to our competitors.'[144] The expectation that rearmament expenditure would soon be reduced was reinforced by the widely held view – which extended to the functionaries of the Reich Air Ministry (*Reichsluftfahrtministerium* – RLM) too – that 'rearmament can not be continued at the same pace as hitherto as otherwise the whole economy could be damaged.'[145]

The question of whether to increase capacity at Marienfelde for military production or whether to follow a more cautious approach became the subject of an intermittent dispute within the board in the later 1930s. Hentig, as the member of the board responsible for military production and contracts, was clearly keen to expand capacity and shift the basis of Daimler-Benz's production further towards armaments. This would naturally also increase his own importance within the company. Kissel, on the other hand, was more hesitant, and, in May 1936, opposed Hentig's attempts to procure contracts for armoured vehicles that would necessitate an expansion at Marienfelde.[146] This was not a question of opposition to rearmament, still less of opposition to the regime – Kissel closely identified both himself and Daimler-Benz publicly with the regime and its policies. It was rather an expression of a cautious approach to expanding capacity in a situation where industry could not foresee how far rearmament would go and what the consequences of National Socialist policy would eventually be. The raw materials situation reinforced

143 See Hayes, *Industry and Ideology*, p. 136.
144 MBAG Kissel/Correspondence with WiGruLFZ (Economics Group Aircraft Industry) 1933–1940, DBAG Berlin- Charlottenburg to Kissel, 3.2.1936.
145 MBAG Kissel I/10, Minutes of the Board Meeting of DBAG on 26 and 27.5.1937.
146 MBAG Kissel/Marienfelde 1926–1937, Kissel to Stauss, 9.5.1936.

this caution: although military production was affected much less than automobile production, Marienfelde came to feel the shortages of materials too, and the company was wary of creating capacity for which there would be insufficient materials. The experience of the First World War and its aftermath also undoubtedly influenced the attitude of the company towards expanding for military purposes.[147]

Hentig was, however, as a result of his contacts with the HWA and of the centrality of Daimler-Benz to the rearmament programme, able to procure a more or less constant stream of contracts and materials for Marienfelde.[148] Despite the continual friction between Kissel and Hentig, the fact that the company was losing contracts to competitors because of lack of capacity led it to consider a further expansion at Marienfelde in July 1936.[149] In 1936, RM 2.7 million were indeed invested in expanding tank production at the plant.[150] Partly as a result of this, overall turnover at Marienfelde rose from RM 45.7m in 1936 to RM 77.4m in 1937.[151] The turnover of Plant 40 itself doubled between 1936 and 1937, so that the materials situation obviously had little effect in the end.[152] As a result of Hentig's recommendations and his assurances that sufficient contracts would be forthcoming, a further RM 4.1 million were invested in Plant 40 in 1938.[153]

147 The friction between Hentig and Kissel over the extent to which Daimler-Benz should convert capacity to military production or create additional capacity for military purposes replicated itself in differing attitudes regarding how the company should respond to the army's wish that it should establish a production facility at Königsberg, East Prussia. In 1936, the military approached Daimler-Benz with the proposal that a repair and production plant be built in Königsberg, which Hentig was in favour of establishing. Kissel was far more cautious, mindful of the costs and of the issue of who should finance the project, and unwilling to construct the plant without guarantees of long-term employment. He did eventually agree to the establishment of the plant, but this was clearly to maintain good relations with the military and is not to be seen as part of an expansionistic strategy towards the east. The turnover of the plant in fact peaked at only RM 2.8m in 1944, accounting for approximately 0.5 per cent of Daimler-Benz's total turnover in that year, so that its significance can be assessed as marginal. (MBAG Kissel I/9, Minutes of the Board Meeting of DBAG on 24.11.1936; MBAG Kissel I/10, Minutes of the Board Meeting of DBAG on 5.1.1937; MBAG Kissel I/10, Minutes of the Board Meeting of DBAG on 26/27.5.1937; MBAG Kissel I/10, Minutes of the Board Meeting of DBAG on 12.11.1937).
148 The methods he used were unscrupulous in the extreme. A letter of Hentig to Stauss of June 1937 outlining the methods he used to gain extra materials gives some idea of his tactics: 'When the materials shortage became obvious, I visited General Liese with a graph showing the possible capacity of the Marienfelde plant on the basis of the materials allocations and showed it to him in front of the chief of staff, Oberst von Hanneken. I intentionally depicted an alarming decrease in the employment curve for the next months, in order to achieve a corresponding effect in the HWA. I was treated with the greatest understanding by the chief of the HWA and he has taken measures that will undoubtedly ensure an improvement in the near future . . . in the meantime, I have drawn up a curve that shows the actual employment on the basis of the available material, which is far more positive.' (BA (P) 80 Ba2 P3192, Hentig to Stauss, 26.6.1937.).
149 MBAG Kissel/Marienfelde 1926–1937, Memorandum of the Discussion on 2.7.1936.
150 Roth, 'Der Weg zum Guten Stern', p. 335.
151 Pohl et al., _Die Daimler-Benz AG_, p. 126.
152 BA (P) 80 Ba2 P3269, Hentig to Stauss, 18.1.1938.
153 BA (P) 80 Ba2 P3269, Hentig to Stauss, 11.8.1937; Pohl et al., _Die Daimler-Benz AG_, p. 130.

Despite this, however, the turnover of Marienfelde failed to increase substantially between 1937 and 1939. From 1938 to 1939 turnover at Plant 40 actually fell significantly, against a background of renewed belief that rearmament expenditure would soon have to be scaled down.[154] This led Kissel to renew his criticism of Hentig, whom he again accused of having painted an over-optimistic picture of military orders and the materials situation.[155] Immediately prior to the outbreak of war, he described the latter expansion of Marienfelde as a 'miscalculation' (*Fehldisposition*).[156] Far from perpetually expanding capacity in the expectation of permanently increasing military contracts, the example of Plant 40 shows how even a firm such as Daimler-Benz, which identified itself strongly with the regime and opted from the outset for large-scale participation in the rearmament programme, had considerable misgivings about the state of armaments production and the economy generally by 1939, and was uncertain how to frame its future strategy.

c) Production for the Luftwaffe 1933–39

The Marienfelde plant was also the focus of Daimler-Benz's initial involvement in the aero-engine sector, which was the other main area of rearmament in which Daimler-Benz's activities expanded rapidly after the National Socialist seizure of power. Compared with Heinkel and Junkers, who in 1933 were already capable of serial production of aircraft frames, Daimler-Benz was somewhat behind in this sector.[157] The company was intent, however, from the beginning, on carving out a position in the serial production of aero-engines, in anticipation of future military contracts.[158] By January 1934 at the very latest it was negotiating with the newly formed Reich Air Ministry over the issue of establishing serial production at one of its plants.[159] In view of its geographical position, the company was unable to get the RLM's agreement to the establishment of serial production at Untertürkheim, where BMW parts were then being produced, and which the RLM insisted could only be used for development purposes. Despite the fact that it was not ideally big enough, the ministry was, on the other hand, willing to entertain the prospect of serial production at Marienfelde.

In April 1934, however, in view of the potential threat of air-raid damage in the event of war, the RLM decided that it was not going to give further

154   Pohl et al., *Die Daimler-Benz AG*, p. 126.
155   BA (P) 80 Ba2 P3269, Kissel to Stauss, 7.7.1939; Kissel/Hoppe to Hentig, 5.7.1939; Kissel/Hoppe to Hentig, 20.7.1939.
156   BA (P) 80 Ba2 P3269, Memorandum of the Discussion with Stauss in the Deutsche Bank, 24.7.1939.
157   Hansen, *Reichswehr und Industrie*, p. 142.
158   MBAG Forstmeier 14, Report to the Board on the RLM's Guidelines to DBAG, 2.8.1934.
159   MBAG Kissel/Correspondence with RLM 1933–1938, Memorandum of the Visit to Mr Bullinger at the RLM, 15.1.1934.

contracts to factories in Berlin.[160] Instead of giving Marienfelde a contract for production of its own engines, it was henceforth only willing to sanction the use of Marienfelde as a repair plant at which a core of experienced workers in the aero-engine sector could be created.[161] The RLM insisted that Unter-türkheim transfer its BMW engine-parts production to Marienfelde in order to provide this initial experience.[162] Kissel attempted to dissuade the RLM from this approach, proposing instead that a contract for the production of complete BMW engines be given to Marienfelde. While he argued that this would be of equal use in developing experience and that it would be less disruptive, it is clear that the main motivation of the company was to establish Marienfelde as a location for the serial production of engines as soon as possible, producing under licence until the company's own prototype, the DB4, was ready for production.

Despite the refusal of the RLM to permit more than parts production and repairs at Marienfelde at this point, Daimler-Benz continued to prepare for an expansion of Marienfelde to allow for the eventual assumption of full serial production, confident that the RLM would soon be forced to integrate the plant into its plans. In August 1934, it began to plan the extension of the plant through the erection of a new building (which became Marienfelde Plant 90). Kissel insisted internally that, despite the RLM's position, 'we must under all circumstances stick to our plans and goals and ensure that Marienfelde is utilized not only for carrying out repairs but is as quickly as possible used for the production of new engines.'[163] His insistence on this course of action was confirmed as correct when, soon after, the RLM did indeed request that Marienfelde tool for the production of 30 aero-engines per month, beginning full delivery in April 1935.[164]

The initial misgivings expressed about the size of Marienfelde had, however, already by this point led to the development of a far more substantial project in the aero-engine sector. Kissel had first considered overcoming the RLM's refusal to allow serial production at Daimler-Benz's existing factories, by constructing a completely new plant for the production of locomotive engines, marine engines and aero-engines in April 1934.[165] In view of the envisaged large-scale public orders in these areas, the board felt that there was more than enough potential for a new factory. The idea was obviously floated with the RLM soon after, as in July 1934 the company was requested by the

160 MBAG Kissel/Correspondence with RLM 1933–1938, Memorandum of the Discussion with RLM, 9.4.1934.
161 MBAG Forstmeier 14, Report to the Board on the RLM's Guidelines to DBAG, 2.8.1934.
162 MBAG Kissel/Correspondence with RLM 1933–1938, Kissel to Milch, 4.9.1934.
163 MBAG Forstmeier 14, Kissel to K.C. Müller, 26.9.1934.
164 MBAG Forstmeier 14, Memorandum regarding Financial Requirements for the Completion of the Tasts set by the RLM, 15.10.1934.
165 MBAG Kissel/Correspondence with RLM 1933–1938, Memorandum of the Discussion with RLM, 9.4.1934.

RLM to produce plans for a completely new factory which in peacetime would produce a variety of large engines.[166] The details of this plan were discussed during extensive negotiations between the RLM and the various manufacturers in July and August 1934. The initial intention was to build a factory capable of producing 25 aero-engines and 25 other engines per month, which could, in a situation of military need, be coverted to a pure aero-engine plant capable of producing 300 engines per month in three shifts.[167]

The company itself was under no illusions as to the significance of the project, noting that it would not only be a lucrative source of government contracts in peacetime, but that it would also be the 'most important engine plant in Germany in the event of war'. With the formulation of this project, the plans for which were developed over the following period, Daimler-Benz had in effect achieved its goal of establishing a position alongside Junkers and BMW as the main aero-engine producers for the military. In the early stages of the development of the Luftwaffe, these established manufacturers consistently attempted to dissuade the RLM from broadening the number of firms involved, arguing that the planned increases in production were best achieved by concentrating production at a few companies, rather than drawing new ones into the circle of competing contractors. Clearly the companies were keen to protect their monopoly position in an area that they recognized as highly profitable from the outset.[168]

By the time the RLM gave the official contract in October 1935, the location had been fixed, in line with Daimler-Benz's intentions, as Genshagen, near Ludwigsfelde on the south side of Berlin.[169] The initial plan for a mobilization capacity of 300 engines had in the meantime been scaled down to 220 per month, while the idea of manufacturing a wide range of engines in peacetime had been shelved in favour of a factory solely for the production of aero-engines, with a peacetime capacity of 85 engines per month.[170] The RLM had intended the formation of a separate company with RM 5m or RM 10m capital and the rest being financed with an RLM loan of RM 40m or RM 45m to Daimler-Benz. The latter refused, however, to incur such a large debt at this stage and undoubtedly also suspected that the RLM would finance the project

166 MBAG Kissel/Correspondence with RLM 1933–1938, Kissel to Milch 4.9.1934.
167 MBAG Kissel/Correspondence RLM 1933–1938, Report to the Board on the RLM's Guidelines to DBAG (I) on the Development of Aero-Engine Production (II) Projected Special Motor Factory, 10.9.1934; Forstmeier 14, Report to the Board on the RLM's Guidelines to DBAG, 2.8.1934.
168 MBAG Forstmeier 22, Confidential RLM-Discussion with the Heads of the Large Aero-Engine Producing Companies, 20.9.1934.
169 Geschäftsbericht der Daimler-Benz Motoren GmbH Genshagen 1936. The Annual Reports of the Daimler-Benz Motoren GmbH Genshagen from 1936 to 1942 are located in BA (P) 80 Ba2 P3320. A copy of the Annual Report for 1943 is held at the Mercedes-Benz-Archive, Stuttgart. Copies of the Reports for 1944 and 1945 could not be found.
170 MBAG Kissel/Correspondence with WiGruLFZ 1933–1940, Kissel to K.C. Müller/Gaggenau, 12.9.1935.

itself if forced to – which did in fact happen. In this way, the risk was immediately minimized and a profitable business was guaranteed from the outset, while Daimler-Benz retained the right to repurchase the plant at a later stage.[171] The company, a subsidiary of Daimler-Benz AG, was eventually formed in January 1936 as the Daimler-Benz Motor Company Genshagen (GmbH), with RM 14m capital (soon thereafter raised to RM 20m), of which the RLM provided RM 13.25m and Daimler-Benz a nominal RM 0.75m.[172]

Despite the immensity of the project and the shortage of building workers, the factory was constructed with breath-taking speed. Within eight months, virtually all the buildings had been completed and the installation of machinery in the first workshops had begun.[173] Machining in the workshops started in August 1936, under the management of K.C. Müller, the Daimler-Benz manager who henceforth took main responsibility for aero-engine production and who remained at Genshagen until the end of the war. The first engine, a DB 600 (developed from the DB4 prototype), made with parts delivered from Marienfelde Plant 90, was completed in February 1937.[174] The workforce was assembled and expanded with equal rapidity, despite the considerable labour shortages then existing, with the initial core of skilled workers coming from Daimler-Benz's south German plants and from BMW.[175] By June 1937 the plant already had 5813 workers.

Unlike the broad range of products aimed at a variety of markets made at the south German plants of Daimler-Benz, Genshagen was intended from the outset for the serial production of a small range of related engines for a single client. As such, the preconditions for the implementation of 'American' production methods were, in some respects, more easily satisfied. The specific circumstances in which the plant was built and the nature of the contracts it was completing, however, militated against the introduction of such production processes.

First, the layout of the plant was designed primarily for reasons of air-raid protection and only secondarily according to criteria of rational production methods. As well as spacing all workshops at a substantial distance from one another – negating the principle of reducing production costs by reducing transportation distances within the plant – the plant was built to comprise not one, but two identical production lines. These were built parallel to one another, two kilometres apart, and each produced half the volume that one

171   MBAG Kissel/Correspondence with WiGruLFZ 1933–1940, letter to Kissel, 12.11.1935.
172   MBAG Kissel/Genshagen 1936–1939, Contract between the German Reich and DBAG, November 1935 (Draft). The board of the company comprised Stauss (Daimler-Benz/Deutsche Bank), Rummel (Daimler-Benz/Deutsche Bank), Kissel (Daimler-Benz), Höfeld (RLM), Hellingrath (RLM), Maier (RFM). (BA [P] 80 Ba2 P3319, Minutes of the Board Meeting of Daimler-Benz Motoren GmbH Genshagen, 21.7.1936.)
173   MBAG Kissel/Genshagen 1933–1939, K.C. Müller to Kissel, 20.8.1936.
174   *Geschäftsbericht der Daimler-Benz Motoren GmbH Genshagen 1936.*
175   BA (P) 80 Ba2 P3319, Minutes of the Board Meeting of Daimler-Benz Motoren GmbH Genshagen, 14.4.1937.

unified production line would have achieved.[176] Second, the nature of military production was such that the turnover of models through obsolescence was greater than that in civilian production. Thus, the plant was forced partially or completely to re-tool far more regularly than Daimler-Benz's other factories. Moreover, the frequent changes in the design of each aero-engine meant that machinery was constantly being reset or altered to accommodate these changes. Even while tooling for the DB 600, the first Daimler-Benz aero-engine to be produced in series in the 1930s, the company was planning to switch to production of the more advanced DB 601, with even more advanced models already on the drawing board. The RLM in fact wanted Genshagen to switch to production of the DB 601 in 1938, while Daimler-Benz itself was keen to switch even earlier in order to maintain its advantage over competitor companies and ensure that it was not forced to produce another company's model under licence.[177]

Finally, the huge wave of investments in machine-tools by German industry in the 1930s had created a huge backlog of orders, particularly for special-purpose machinery, so the company would have to wait two or three years for such machines. Not only would the purchase of these machines greatly delay the assumption of production at Genshagen, but they would also only be available at a time when they might no longer be suitable for the type of engine (aero-engine or other) that the factory was producing at that point.[178] Already by the late 1930s German industry was faced with a situation where the backlog was such that some machine-tools would only be delivered at a point where the company might no longer have a need for them, a factor which became of even greater significance in the uncertain context created by the war.

These factors all combined to cause the management of Genshagen initially to invest exclusively in universal machine-tools. The relatively short delivery times for these machines meant that by March 1937 97 per cent of machine-tools for one production line and 60 per cent for the other had already been procured.[179] This meant that a volume of production approximating the initial planned monthly output had been reached by November 1937, in which month 65 DB 600 and 19 DB 601 engines were made. In July 1938, when production of the DB 600 ceased, 94 DB 601 engines were produced, and by August 1939 the plant was producing, on average, 200 DB 601 engines per month.[180]

176 *Leistungsbericht der Daimler-Benz Motoren GmbH Genshagen 1940*, p. 48.
177 MBAG Forstmeier 14, Daimler-Benz Motoren GmbH Genshagen to Kissel, 29.12.1936; Kissel/Correspondence with RLM 1933–1938, Kissel to DBAG Marienfelde, 29.12.1936; Forstmeier 14, Confidential Minute of Discussion concerning RLM Program Requirements in Relation to Commencement of Production of Model DB 601, 5.1.1937. Daimler-Benz intentionally slowed down development of the DB 600 in order to increase the chance of the RLM bringing forward its order for the DB 601.
178 *Geschäftsbericht der Daimler-Benz Motoren GmbH Genshagen 1936*.
179 BA (P) 80 Ba2, P3315, Daimler-Benz Motoren GmbH Genshagen/Technical Report, 31.3.1937.
180 BA (P) 80 Ba2 P3322, Monthly Reports/Production Reports of Daimler-Benz Motoren GmbH Genshagen 1937–1942.

Although the company was very successful in assembling its initial labour force, the fact that it had elected to install flexible multi-purpose machinery, and its consequent reliance on a high proportion of skilled workers, meant that the shortage of skilled labour very soon started to make itself felt at Genshagen. The plant was faced with the problem of increasing its workforce at a time when the shortages of skilled labour in particular were becoming acute. In part this was offset by extensive retraining and the ongoing training of semi-skilled workers or workers from other branches.[181] In view of the substantial branch-by-branch shift of workers into the armaments industry, which was one of the main developments in the labour market in the 1930s, the retraining of workers from other branches (from textile workers to hairdressers and bakers) was a key feature in the period. Up until 1939 1200 workers were retrained at Genshagen, of whom only 15 per cent had come from metal-working industries.[182]

The company was also able to attract some skilled labour by planning the construction of a substantial number of company houses adjacent to the plant, where 76 workers were initially housed in 1936.[183] However, the shortage of building workers and materials meant that the pace of construction never kept pace with the demand for labour. Although by 1940 925 houses had been built, the incompatibility of an armaments-orientated economy with large-scale social projects ensured that the settlement never achieved anything like its intended size or quality.[184]

In addition, the company reacted to the shortages by attempting to recruit skilled workers from the newly annexed Austria, and soon after from the Sudetenland.[185] It also attempted to increase the number of women workers at the plant – in 1937 it had already engaged 800 women to replace skilled workers, which it assessed as a success.[186] Between 1937 and 1939 the proportion of women in the Genshagen workforce rose from 5.1 per cent to 18.6 per cent. Finally, the management followed the common strategy of engaging more workers than it needed, in the knowledge that some of these workers would soon leave again.[187]

181 *Geschäftsbericht der Daimler-Benz Motoren GmbH Genshagen 1936.*
182 *Leistungsbericht der Daimler-Benz Motoren GmbH Genshagen 1940,* p. 46. Initially much of the retraining was directed at the remaining reserve of unemployed workers recruited from the Berlin labour market who had become unused to industrial labour through years of unemployment or who were, as a result of unemployment, no longer acquainted with contemporary production methods.
183 BA (P) 80 Ba2 P3319, General Report of Daimler-Benz Motoren GmbH Genshagen, 14.4.1937. On the Ludwigsfelde housing project see Birk, G., *Ein Düsteres Kapitel Ludwigsfelder Geschichte 1936–1945. Entstehung und Untergang der Daimler-Benz Flugzeugmotorenwerke Genshagen-Ludwigsfelde,* Ludwigsfelde, 1986, pp. 9–13.
184 *Geschäftsbericht der Daimler-Benz Motoren GmbH Genshagen 1940.*
185 *Geschäftsbericht der Daimler-Benz Motoren GmbH Genshagen 1938;* BA (P) 80 Ba2 P3322, Report of the 7 and 8 Monthly Report 1938.
186 *Geschäftsbericht der Daimler-Benz Motoren GmbH Genshagen 1937.*
187 MBAG Kissel/Genshagen 1936–1939, Kissel to K.C. Müller, 25.8.1938.

These solutions proved inadequate in themselves, however. The women workers on the shop floor were exclusively unskilled or semi-skilled, so that the problem of skilled labour was only alleviated insofar as they released male workers to be trained for more highly skilled work. This in itself often brought problems of falling quality, and the management often found that production problems were caused by workers not being up to the tasks set for them.[188] Some of this was owing to poor materials or poor subcontractors' work, rather than problems at Genshagen itself, but it still reflected the basic difficulties the acute labour shortages in the German economy were causing.[189] In addition, many of the workers recruited from Austria or the Sudetenland left very quickly or were dissatisfied at having to live so far away from their families. The problem of having to transport workers out of Berlin created by the decision to site the plant away from the industrial centres and thus from the necessary infrastructure also led many skilled workers to leave. The higher wages in the Berlin area also contributed to the difficulty of retaining labour and, as the company noted laconically, 'the protection of the labour offices has not been particularly effective.'[190]

The shortage was made particularly acute by the introduction of a new RLM programme on 1 July 1938, following the regime's radical acceleration of the pace of rearmament that summer.[191] The new programme envisaged an increase in production at Genshagen of 50 per cent, to 180 engines per month.[192] In addition to the shortage of labour, which demanded the adoption of production processes that would facilitate the greater use of semi-skilled labour, the company was now faced with the need to abandon its current production methods and install semi-automatic and automatic machine-tools in order to cope with the increased volume of production.[193] This would also allow a reduction in the cost of each engine, which, in view of the company's constant attempts to keep production costs below those of Henschel or Büssing-NAG (both of whom produced Daimler-Benz engines under licence), was a further impetus towards installing labour-saving machinery.[194] In view

188 MBAG Kissel/Genshagen 1936–1939, List of occasionally occurring Production Difficulties during Start-Up of Production of the DB 601 in our Genshagen Factory (undated 1938); BA (P) 80 Ba2 P3319, Minutes of the Board Meeting of Daimler-Benz Motoren GmbH Genshagen, 15.12.1938.

189 MBAG Kissel/Genshagen 1936–1939, Kissel to Daimler-Benz Motoren GmbH Genshagen, 9.5.1938.

190 BA (P) 80 Ba2 General Report of Daimler-Benz Motoren GmbH Genshagen for the 3 monthly Reporting Period, 21.4.1939; Geschäftsbericht der Daimler-Benz Motoren GmbH Genshagen 1938; see also Hachtmann, 'Arbeitsmarkt und Arbeitszeit', p. 206.

191 BA (P) 80 Ba2 P3319, Minutes of the Board Meeting of Daimler-Benz Motoren GmbH Genshagen, 28.6.1938.

192 MBAG Kissel/Genshagen 1936–1939, K.C. Müller to Kissel, 31.5.1938.

193 BA (P) 80 Ba2 P3316, Daimler-Benz Motoren GmbH Genshagen to Stauss, 8.11.1938.

194 MBAG Kissel/Genshagen 1936–1939, Kissel to K.C. Müller, 3.6.1939. Daimler-Benz used its rights as the licence-giver to visit Henschel and Büssing factories to observe the production methods there and copy ways of reducing production costs (MBAG Kissel/Genshagen 1940, Kissel to Wolf/Genshagen, 12.7.1939).

of this, and knowing that German machine-tool manufacturers had delivery backlogs of two to three years, the company sent one of its managers, Wilhelm Künkele, to the USA to study production methods there and to procure machinery from American manufacturers.[195] However, the foreign currency situation was such that the RWM was turning down all applications for currency allocations, which forced the management to scale down greatly the number of machines it could import.[196] As a result, the bulk of Genshagen's productive capacity remained based around universal machinery, and single-purpose machines were only introduced for a minority of operations.[197]

Despite this, the plant was able to produce 2249 engines in 1939, compared with 1427 in 1938, an increase of 58 per cent, while the blue-collar workforce rose only from 5453 in August 1938 to 5777 in August 1939, or by 6.5 per cent.[198] Some of this increase in productivity is undoubtedly accounted for by the introduction of labour-saving production processes; a substantial element is also, however, accounted for by the increases in workhours in the pre-war period and by the ongoing process of reducing piece-rates.[199]

Both Marienfelde and Genshagen were producing at less than full capacity in the immediate pre-war period, owing to shortages of raw materials and labour, which intensified greatly from 1938 to 1939 as a direct result of the forced pace of rearmament. However, the significance of these two Berlin armaments plants to Daimler-Benz in the later 1930s, and the shift of gravity from the south German to the Berlin plants that had occurred as a direct result of the expansion of armaments production, can be seen by their growing proportion of total turnover. In 1936, the two Marienfelde plants together accounted for 15 per cent of Daimler-Benz's total turnover. In 1939, the Marienfelde and Genshagen plants together accounted for 32 per cent of turnover.[200] Despite the levelling of automobile production in the later 1930s, the expansion of armaments production meant that gross profits continued to increase.

d) The South German Plants

Up until 1937–8, only a relatively small proportion of the capacity of the south German plants had been used for military production.[201] Most of the company's car and lorry models were produced in military versions prior to this point, and it had been keen for all plants to participate from an early stage

195 BA (P) 80 Ba2 P3316, Daimler-Benz Motoren GmbH Genshagen to Stauss, 8.11.1938.
196 BA (P) 80 Ba2 P3316, Daimler-Benz Motoren GmbH Genshagen to Stauss, 3.1.1939.
197 *Leistungsbericht der Daimler-Benz Motoren GmbH Genshagen 1940.*
198 BA (P) 80 Ba2 P3322, Monthly Reports/Production Reports of Daimler-Benz Motoren GmbH Genshagen 1937–1942.
199 BA (P) 80 Ba2 P3322, Report of the 12th and 13th Accounting Month 1937.
200 Calculated according to Roth, 'Der Weg zum Guten Stern', p. 334.
201 MBAG Kissel I/10, Minutes of the Board Meeting of DBAG on 26 and 27.5.1937; Minutes of the Supervisory Board Meeting of DBAG on 27.5.1937.

in order to overcome the impact of the Depression. However, the geographical position of the plants – specifically, their proximity to the French border – made them problematic from a military point of view, and the great expansion of civilian production up until 1937 guaranteed Daimler-Benz full utilization of capacity without large military contracts anyway. Essentially, Daimler-Benz was happy to follow what, until 1937, amounted to a strategy of dividing civilian and military production between the south German and Berlin plants. This allowed the company to profit from the rearmament boom and at the same time preserve its core of civilian production lines, which could supply the military but whose continuation would be guaranteed after the rearmament boom had ended.

The restriction of materials allocations to the consumer sector from 1936–7 onwards was instrumental, however, in effecting a gradual conversion of the capacity of the south German plants to military purposes. In order to maintain existing production levels of the 1.7l car at Untertürkheim in the face of allocations reductions, the board moved to procure contracts for an extra 1000 models of the armoured military version of the car, for which extra materials allocations were made. Similarly, it moved to make up the difference between civilian and export production at Gaggenau and the total capacity of the plant by gaining extra contracts from the HWA. Over the course of 1938–9 the centre of gravity of production at the south German plants was in this way successively shifted towards military contracts. This growing importance of military orders was also a key factor in the reorientation of the Mannheim factory towards lorry production in the period after 1936. Especially after 1938, lorry production was conditioned more and more by criteria of military demand. The decision to increase the capacity of Mannheim's 3-ton lorry production from 300 to 700 lorries per month, for example, was caused by the awareness of a pending RLM contract for 40,000 3-ton lorries, divided between Daimler-Benz and Opel, that would guarantee production for three or four years.[202]

Although in the short term the substitution of military for civilian production guaranteed fixed profits from public orders and full employment of the plants affected, the Daimler-Benz board did not view the accelerated production of armaments and its impact upon the company with complete equanimity. In May 1937, K. C. Müller reported to the board of Daimler-Benz that his impression, gained at a discussion with RLM officials, was that the current pace of rearmament could not be forced. From this point onwards, the company was caught in the dilemma of observing a growing tension in the diplomatic arena that might eventually lead to war, while wishing to avoid a further conversion of capacity to armaments production in case the regime's armaments expenditure were to recede.

---

202 MBAG Kissel I/11, Minutes of the Board Meeting of DBAG on 13.7.1938.

As late as January 1939 the board was still acting very cautiously over the issue of expanding in the aero-engine sector. This was partly because of fears that adequate materials would not be forthcoming to allow full utilization of additional capacity, but primarily because, as Müller formulated it, 'in the long run it cannot be expected that the public contracts will continue at their current high level.'[203] As a result of this, the board decided to invest in machine-tools that would allow a reduction in production costs, but refrained from investment in machinery that was intended to increase capacity. Far from increasing aero-engine capacity at Genshagen in 1939, the company was trying to procure contracts for locomotive and marine engine production – clearly with the aim of diversifying production at the plant in order to offset the impact of a potential reduction in RLM orders for aero-engines. In the event, the strategy failed due to the opposition of the majority share-holder – the RLM.

The company's strategy with regards to lorry production at Mannheim and Gaggenau was similarly characterized by considerable uncertainty in the period 1938–9 as to where the bulk of the plants' business would come from in the mid-term. The components for the military and civilian versions of the LGF 3000 (the all-terrain 3-ton lorry) were deliberately standardized as far as possible, partly of course in order to achieve a higher volume of production of fewer parts, but also with the intention of 'hedging' between military and civilian production, depending on which way things developed.[204] The insecurity created by the diplomatic situation also led to an unwillingness to invest in some areas – the Mannheim management recommended in April 1939, for example, that 'the procurement of additional machinery could have no impact within two years, due to long delivery backlogs, so that investments in machinery for stationary motors are not to be continued until future turnover can be clearly foreseen.'[205]

The changing response of Daimler-Benz to the rearmament boom of the 1930s and to its impact on the German economy shows how even a company that had opted for immediate large-scale participation in 1933, and had derived substantial profits from it from a very early stage, nursed considerable misgivings by the years immediately prior to the war. Having welcomed rearmament in the early years, and having been able as a result to overcome the effects of the Depression with remarkable rapidity, the company was now fearful of over-expansion and wary of becoming too dependent on state contracts, at a time when demand for Daimler-Benz's consumer- and commercial-orientated production was great but could not be satisfied as a

203 MBAG Kissel I/12, Minutes of the Board Meeting of DBAG on 12.1.1939.
204 MBAG Kissel I/25, Minutes of the Meeting in Untertürkheim on 10.1.1939 concerning the Production Program for the Gaggenau and Mannheim Factories as a result of the Type Reduction Program.
205 MBAG Kissel VI/19, Paulus to Kissel, 11.4.1939.

result of the regime's channelling of economic capacity towards military production. Far from merrily converting more and more capacity to military production to profit from what was seen as guaranteed demand, the company in the immediate pre-war period acted with caution and uncertainty.

IV. Profit and Plunder: Daimler-Benz in the Second World War – An Overview

1. Mobilization and 'Blitzkrieg' Economy 1939–41

Both the real level of the regime's expenditure on military output and the proportion of total economic activity for which military expenditure and production accounted increased greatly from the beginning of the war onwards. Real expenditure on military production rose from RM 17.2 billion in 1938–9 to RM 73.3 billion in 1941–42, and by 1943–4 had reached RM 99.4 billion.[1] Expressed as a proportion of GNP, military expenditure accounted for 38 per cent in 1940, 55 per cent in 1942 and 61 per cent in 1943.[2] Despite this further intensive channelling of economic capacity towards military production in the first half of the war – which also manifested itself in substantial shifts in labour deployment from the non-essential to essential industries – armaments output remained doggedly stagnant from 1939 to 1941. Both raw materials and finished goods production failed to increase substantially (except in one or two areas). Overall production of military goods was the same in 1941 as in 1940.[3]

Much of this is explicable by the inadequacy of the regime's management of the war economy and the inefficiency of the war economic apparatus as it had evolved by 1939. Upon the outbreak of war, there had existed neither a clear organizational structure with clearly defined areas of jurisdiction on the one hand, nor a comprehensive and unified mobilization plan on the other, both of which were necessary to enable such a complex process as the simultaneous mobilization of the military and the economy to take place. First, a fundamental dualism existed between the supervision of essential civilian production under the Reich Economics Minister, Walther Funk (in his capacity as General Plenipotentiary for the War Economy), and the supervision of official armaments factories by the Economic Armaments Office (*Wirtschaft- und Rüstungsamt*) of the Army High Command (OKW),

---

1 Overy, 'Blitzkriegswirtschaft?', p. 389.
2 Noakes and Pridham (eds.), *Nazism 1919–1945. Volume 2*, p. 298.
3 Müller, 'Mobilisierung', p. 523.

under General Thomas. The institutional rivalry between the two was the source of both major bureaucratic friction between the offices themselves and irritation on the part of industry, which demanded clear leadership from one or the other.[4] Meanwhile, raw materials production and much of the task of overall allocation was under the control of Göring's Four Year Plan office – itself hardly a model of efficiency. Within the armed forces themselves, materials and contracts allocation was carried out via complex procedures involving the Economic Armaments Office on the one hand and the individual ordnance offices of each branch on the other, who for their part acted with little consideration for each other or for the needs of industry. Finally, allocation of labour remained under the control of another institution, the Reich Labour Ministry, with its regional and local labour offices. Coordination between the various organs was virtually non-existent.[5]

The creation of the Reich Ministry for Weapons and Munitions (*Reichsministerium für Bewaffnung und Munition* – RMfBuM) in March 1940, under Fritz Todt, marked the first step towards transfer of overall control into civilian hands. The founding of the RMfBuM was typical, however, of Hitler's habit of responding to a problem by creating a new institution rather than addressing the problem itself. Todt's role was limited to production for the army, and, as the pre-existing institutions remained, with their spheres of jurisdiction largely unaltered, the basic problem was unresolved. Above all, General Thomas continued to oppose Todt's attempts to unify power over the economy in his own hands, and as Todt lacked control of the various mid-level and regional offices in the economic apparatus, including the Armaments Inspectorates and Armaments Commandos of the OKW, the RMfBuM was unable to solve the underlying problems. Meanwhile, successive military victories and the expectation of a quick end to the war relieved the pressure that occasionally built up on Hitler to resolve the conflicts.

As an examination of lorry production at Daimler-Benz's Mannheim plant shows, the frictions and inefficiency caused by the failure of the military to establish an effective apparatus and a positive relationship with industry in the first half of the war was responsible for considerable losses in output.[6] The argument that the chaotic inefficiency of the war economy apparatus until early 1942 was itself the sole cause of the failure to raise armaments output rests, however, upon the assumption that industry itself had a clear interest in an immediate and ongoing expansion of military production, an assumption that needs further examination. This is even more the case when one recognizes that the outbreak of war in September 1939 did little to alleviate

---

4 On the relationship between the RWM and the WiRüAmt/OKW see Müller, R.-D., 'Die Mobilisierung der Wirtschaft für den Krieg – eine Aufgabe der Armee?' in: Michalka (ed.), *Der Zweite Weltkrieg*, pp. 353–4.
5 See also the summary in Müller, 'Mobilisierung', p. 685.
6 See below, Chapter V.2.a.

the uncertainty that characterized the board of Daimler-Benz's strategy in the immediate pre-war period. Indeed, if anything, it exacerbated the innate uncertainty of the war situation, which was compounded by the proximity of its south-west German plants to the French border, which tended further to encourage a cautious attitude in the first months of the war.

This initial caution only faded with the German military successes in the west in 1940, culminating in the defeat of France in June 1940. While this both reduced the immediate threat to Daimler-Benz's capacity and ushered in the prospect of a pan-European trading zone within the German-dominated 'New Order', the bombing of Britain over the summer and autumn of 1940 and the high priority accorded to aircraft production by the regime for 1941 offered the company potentially lucrative opportunities in the aero-engine sector. In any case, the demands of the RLM for expanded output placed strong limits on Daimler-Benz's options for doing otherwise.[7] This formed the context for the adoption of an overtly expansionist policy by the company from the summer of 1940 onwards, centred around a programme of massive investment in the aero-engine and (less so) the tank sector, and the takeover of numerous plants in both occupied west and east in the following four years. In addition, under the direction of the RLM, more and more plants were converted to produce Daimler-Benz engines and parts under licence. Hence, by 1944 Daimler-Benz had built up varying amounts of influence over a very major portion of the Reich's aero-engine production plants and were suppliers of a significant amount of the military's demands in many other key sectors as well.

However, despite the adoption of an expansionist policy – which in the context of the war economy was the result of unavoidable political pressure as much as long-term strategic planning – the company's successive responses to the changing military and economic situation were still characterized by a high degree of caution and uncertainty, and by a reluctance to commit itself to long-term decisions in a war in which short-term events could very rapidly change the position of the Reich and with it the company. This was reinforced by the fact that within industry there was a widespread expectation that the war would be a short one and that a return to peacetime conditions and competition in a primarily consumer economy was therefore imminent. Even after the adoption of an expansionist policy in the summer of 1940, the company continued to operate on this assumption for some time. In effect, the conflict between the short-term potential of armaments production and the need to retain a core of consumer-orientated peacetime production lines which had characterized the pre-war period remained, from the point of view of private company strategy, the dominant issue until the autumn of 1941. Only with the failure of the 'Barbarossa' campaign and the start of a long war

---

7   See below, Chapter V.1.a.

of attrition on the eastern front did immediate considerations of post-war issues recede from the foreground – only gradually to re-emerge eighteen months later with the reverses of 1943 at Stalingrad and Kursk.

Throughout the period up until the autumn of 1941, the company therefore continued – despite greatly expanding investment at Genshagen, and despite the partial conversion of further capacity in its south German plants to armaments production, which was seen as an interim measure of short duration – to plan on the basis of an imminent return to peacetime conditions. In December 1939, for example, Kissel was participating in the WiGruFa's formulation of plans for the reconversion of the automobile industry from a war to a peacetime economy.[8] In July 1940, after the defeat of France, plans were being formulated internally for an expansion of capacity at Sindelfingen to enable Daimler-Benz to exploit the German-dominated post-war pan-European trading zone, based around a greatly expanded civilian and military vehicle production capacity.[9]

As part of these plans, which envisaged a virtual doubling of the company's pre-war automobile production, the Sindelfingen management undertook a detailed examination of the required investments, additional machine-tool capacity and extra presses, planning a doubling of the number of presses in the press shop.[10] At the same time it assessed the capacity of the regional machine-tool industry and its potential available capacity after the war, attempting to persuade local manufacturers to earmark a part of their capacity for Daimler-Benz to ensure favourable conditions for a rapid conversion to peacetime production.[11] This was carried out so that 'if needed, the necessary orders can be authorized by the board now, in order not to lose out in the transition to peacetime.'[12] The machine-tool manufacturers were obviously more than willing to oblige with offers and thus secure their own prospects for the post-war period.[13] Similarly, at the Gaggenau lorry plant, plans were made for the restructuring of the machine-shops on the basis of a peacetime programme, and while it was realized that these plans could only be implemented after the war, the board nonetheless made sure that 'the most important preliminary work be carried out now.'[14]

During the period up until late 1941, the company also worked intensively on reducing production costs of its main car and lorry models, with a view to

8   MBAG Kissel/Correspondence with WiGruFa 1935–1939, Egger to Kissel, 21.12.1939.
9   MBAG Huppenbauer 533, Report on the Possibilities for Procuring Tools for Peacetime Production, 5.7.1940. See also Seebold, G.-H., *Ein Stahlkonzern im Dritten Reich. Der Bochumer Verein 1927–1945*, Wuppertal, 1981, p. 111.
10 MBAG Huppenbauer 531, Memorandum concerning Need for Presses, 30.10.1940.
11 MBAG Huppenbauer 533, Report on the Possibilities for Procuring Tools for Peacetime Production, 5.7.1940; MBAG Huppenbauer 531, Memorandum concerning Expansion of Press Shop to the level of the Peacetime Production Program, 23.10.1940.
12 MBAG Huppenbauer 533, Communiqué of Sindelfingen Factory, 8.8.1940.
13 MBAG Huppenbauer 532, Maschinenfabrik Weingarten to DBAG, 8.8.1941.
14 MBAG Kissel VI/8, Dir. Hoppe to DBAG Gaggenau, 24.3.1941.

improving competitiveness after the war, and continued development of existing and new models.[15] Throughout the winter of 1939–40, regular and extensive discussions of the company's plans for the car sector took place, the assumption being that the war would be of short duration and that the imminent post-war period would witness an increased demand for which it was important to be prepared in advance.[16] Throughout 1941, the company continued to devote much energy to reducing production costs and improving the design of the 1.7l car, again in order to create good foundations for its post-war production.[17] Even after the invasion of the Soviet Union in June 1941, the company was examining the possibilities of converting its existing military models to peacetime uses, and testing new versions of its 1.5- and 3-ton lorries for the civilian market. In August 1941, a total of six models were being tested in complete secrecy, with the six models being listed internally as one single project to disguise the extent and nature of the plans.[18] Only in the autumn of 1941 did these plans recede into the background.

The expectation that the war would soon be over and the belief that the long-term core of the company's business would remain in car and lorry production also conditioned the board's attitude to the further conversion of capacity at its south German plants to armaments production upon the outbreak of war. In order to prevent another company (Auto-Union) gaining a foothold in naval engine production, the board immediately moved to fulfil the navy's demands for a second production line of Daimler-Benz marine engines by setting up a second line at Marienfelde – allowing the retention of Daimler-Benz's monopoly in an area that it saw as remaining highly profitable even after the war.[19] At Gaggenau, where lorry production had been accorded a low level of priority by the military and was correspondingly unprotected against call-ups and jeopardized by lack of materials, extensive efforts were made to gain munitions contracts with a high level of priority, thereby guaranteeing the utilization of its capacity, the retention of its labour, and the supply of material. Similarly, part of Sindelfingen's capacity was reorganized for the production of aeroplane frame components in order to guarantee the utilization of the press shop despite declining car production.[20] In general, however, it attempted to maintain its car and lorry production lines as far as possible and, when reorganizing capacity to cope with the new demands of the war situation, attempted to ensure that at least a part of each of its south

15 MBAG Kissel VI/6, Hoppe to Jungenfeld, 31.10.1939.
16 MBAG Kissel I/27, Memorandum concerning Car Types, 5.1.1940; Minutes of the Discussion of our future Car Type Program, 13.1.1940.
17 MBAG Kissel I/29, Memorandum of the Technical Discussion on 11.2.1941; Memorandum of the Technical Meeting on 13.2.1941; Memorandum of the Technical Discussion on 19.5.1941.
18 MBAG Kissel I/30, Report concerning the Technical Meeting No. 83 on 21.8.1941.
19 MBAG Kissel I/12, Minutes of the Board Meeting of DBAG on 18.9.1939; Minutes of the Board Meeting of DBAG on 12.10.1939.
20 MBAG Kissel I/13, Minutes of the Board Meeting of DBAG on 2.4.1940.

German plants remained engaged in vehicle production, even at a reduced level, in order to avoid having to dismantle the production lines.

In fact, for the first half of the war, most of the capacity of the south German plants remained devoted to vehicle production. At Untertürkheim, substantial capacity was given over to naval engine production, and car production capacity was gradually converted to the production of aero-engine parts and to research and development work in this sector. However, the inclusion of the 1.7l car in Schell's 'War Programme' (which superseded the Schell Programme on the outbreak of war) meant that the main car production line was kept intact and producing for military and civilian demand at a continually high level long after most other companies had been forced or had chosen to abandon car production.[21] In February 1940, Oberbaurat Schmidt was actually pressing the GBK to sanction an increase in production of the 1.7l car at Untertürkheim.[22] Kissel himself was in favour of trying to expand this production line, in order to ensure that all demand for cars was catered for solely by Daimler-Benz, preventing other manufacturers from being allowed to resume car production and thereby retaining Daimler-Benz's competitive advantage in the event of a rapid return to peace.[23] On the basis of the War Programme, Untertürkheim was still allowed to produce 1400 1.7l cars per month (excluding military and export quotas), a programme that was later reduced to 2500 per quarter, and finally to 800 per quarter in July 1941.[24] The company continued to take in contracts for private cars after the outbreak of war and refused to release customers from their contracts, in order further to justify claims that it needed to continue production of cars into the war. Not wanting contacts with private buyers to be broken during the war, Kissel ordered Schmidt to ensure that no more than one-third of its production of cars was allocated to public contracts and the authorities (as demanded by the GBK), and explicitly ordered these deliveries to be rationed to ensure that sufficient stock was left to sell to private buyers.[25]

Despite its opposition, and despite the interventions of Jacob Werlin, Daimler-Benz was finally forced to give up production of its 1.7l car, most of which was by now supplied to the military, in the third quarter of 1942.[26] Production fell from 18,042 in 1939 to 11,210 in 1940, 8298 in 1941 and 3951 in 1942.[27] Production of the 2.3l and 3.2l cars also continued into the war as 'redundant types' (*Auslauftypen*) under the War Programme, similarly coming to a virtual stop in 1942. The gradually released capacity was mostly converted to aero-engine parts production.

21   Kirchberg, 'Typisierung', p. 139.
22   MBAG Kissel/War Program, O.B. Schmidt to Kissel, 2.2.1940.
23   MBAG Kissel/War Program, Kissel to O.B. Schmidt, 5.2.1940.
24   MBAG Kissel I/13, Minutes of the Board Meeting of DBAG on 2.4.1940; Kissel I/14, Minutes of the Board Meeting of DBAG on 28 and 29.7.1940.
25   MBAG Kissel/War Program, Kissel to O.B. Schmidt, 5.2.1940.
26   MBAG Kissel I/15, Minutes of the Board Meeting of DBAG on 23 and 24.3.1942.
27   MBAG DBAG Statistics, Annual Production of Cars at DBAG 1927–1944.

Similarly, the reorganization of capacity that took place in the initial mobilization phase was also carried out with a view to avoiding, where possible, any measures that would disadvantage a rapid reconversion to peacetime production. Rather than produce all 500 LGF 3000 lorries per month that the military demanded at Mannheim, which would have been possible from February 1940 (once Mannheim had completed the tooling process begun prior to the war), the board elected to produce 150 of them at Untertürkheim, 'so that the lorry production line at Untertürkheim is safeguarded.'[28] It also attempted to diversify production at Genshagen by renewing its attempt to gain permission for the production of naval engines at the plant – partly to prevent Auto-Union participating in their manufacture, but primarily 'with a view to the future, to the period after the war'.[29] (Again, this failed owing to the opposition of the RLM.[30]) Likewise, it considered relocating its aero-engine development facilities from Untertürkheim to Marienfelde, and Marienfelde's actual aero-engine production to Genshagen, thereby ensuring that Genshagen would have sufficient contracts to ensure its profitability after the war.

The uncertainty created by the outbreak of war, combined with the expectation that it would be of limited duration, also conditioned the board's attitude to new investment and expansion in the first twelve months of the war. Kissel's immediate demand following the outbreak of war was that 'Investments should be reduced as far as possible. In particular, the current large volume of machine-tool orders should be examined and cut back as far as possible.'[31] The awareness that turnover at the south German plants would inevitably drop as a result of reductions in car production and whilst the plants re-tooled for armaments production, combined with the unwillingness to purchase machine-tools for car and lorry production when existing capacity was not being utilized, led indeed to the implementation of a wide review of running investments with a view to cancelling as many contracts as possible. At Gaggenau, all running orders except for 35 machine-tools were annulled, and of these 35, only ten were installed at Gaggenau, while the rest were transported to Untertürkheim to be mothballed for the duration of the war.[32] The suspended orders were eventually renewed in the spring of 1940.[33]

From the beginning of the war onwards, the company was naturally keen to profit from increases in armaments output – the attempt to procure munitions contracts undoubtedly stemmed partly from awareness of the huge shortages of munitions from which the military suffered following the defeat of Poland – and, while attempting to keep its civilian production intact, tried to increase

---

28 MBAG Kissel I/12, Minutes of the Board Meeting of DBAG on 12.10.1939.
29 MBAG Kissel I/13, Minutes of the Board Meeting of DBAG on 2.4.1940.
30 MBAG Kissel I/13, Minutes of the Board Meeting of DBAG on 22.4.1940.
31 MBAG Kissel I/12, Minutes of the Board Meeting of DBAG on 12.10.1939.
32 MBAG Kissel VI/7, Director Wrba/Gaggenau to the Board of DBAG, 29.3.1940.
33 MBAG Kissel VI/7, DBAG to Factory Management Gaggenau, 1.4.1940.

its armaments production. The possibility that the war might develop into a long one demanded that the plants ensure adequate participation in immediate war production programmes as much as the expectation that it would be short conditioned the fear of becoming over-reliant on them. However, the board avoided initiating an immediate expansion of capacity and, up until the summer of 1940, attempted where possible to facilitate this increase without any further investment in new machinery. The large backlog in the machine-tool industry discouraged the company from investing in machinery that would only be delivered a year or two later.[34] Instead, it transferred existing idle machinery between its plants, to alleviate bottlenecks and raise output in the short term without embarking on an investment programme that would only come to fruition months after the demand for armaments might have receded. Above all, machine-tools were transferred from the car and lorry plants to Genshagen and Marienfelde, where the outbreak of war brought far less disruption – and, of course, much more business – than to the south German plants.[35]

The impact of the outbreak of war and the subsequent mobilization process varied greatly according to what was being produced and where. An assessment of the relative effect of call-ups to the Wehrmacht, of labour shortages and fluctuations in materials supply, and of the inefficiencies caused by the complexities and inadequacies of the various administrative structures demands an examination on a plant-by-plant basis. The shifts in production priorities and the relevance of each production line to the war effort at different times meant that labour, materials and components bottlenecks tended to hit each plant at different times, and thus within a different overall economic, military and organizational-institutional context. As such, generalizations concerning the efficiency of different elements of the regime's mobilization and administration of the war economy are problematic.

Generalizations on the basis of one company's experience or strategy in the period prior to the winter of 1941–2 about the war economy are equally problematic insofar as different firms, producing in different fields, will undoubtedly have developed a range of responses to the war situation and may have viewed their prospects differently. If the example of Daimler-Benz is at all representative, however, the failure substantially to increase overall output of armaments prior to 1942 is explicable not only in terms of the inability, for whatever reason, of the regime to mobilize the economy effectively, but also of the reluctant attitude of industry to a short-term mobilization of capacity to cope with an atypical situation that might disadvantage its ability to exploit its mid- and long-term markets.[36] The failure to rationalize production in the

34 MBAG Kissel VI/6, DBAG Untertürkheim to DBAG Gaggenau, 5.10.1939.
35 MBAG Kissel VI/7, DBAG to Factory Management Gaggenau, 1.4.1940.
36 See Freyberg and Siegel, *Industrielle Rationalisierung*, p. 286, which suggests a similar strategic choice by Siemens, and similar passive resistance from the machine-tool industry (p. 172).

interests of an expansion of military output was thus not only a product of the chaotic inefficiency of the regime during this period, but also of the fact that (at least some sectors of) industry did not perceive it as being in their private interests to do so.

2. Expansion and Expansionism: Daimler-Benz and the New Order 1940–4

The cautious response to the outbreak of war gave way to a policy of massive expansion in the summer of 1940, an expansion that took two forms. First, from September 1940, in response to RLM demands, a huge investment programme at Genshagen was introduced, based initially on a RM 50m plan to raise the capacity of Genshagen to 800 engines per month (later increased to 1200 in the summer of 1941). This expansion, which was carried out over the following three years, and which provided the preconditions for the great increase in output in the second half of the war, brought with it a rise in the turnover of Genshagen from RM 116m in 1940 to RM 351m in 1944, in which year the plant accounted for well over one-third of the company's turnover.[37] Turnover at the Marienfelde plants rose from RM 94m in 1940 to RM 218m in 1944, as a result of expanded tank, armoured vehicle, and aero-engine production; expressed as a proportion of the company's total turnover, the Berlin plants' contribution rose from 39 per cent in 1940 to 58 per cent in 1944. This in itself is a reflection of the huge expansion of Daimler-Benz's aero-engine and tank sector in the war.

Company investment overall also rose substantially during the war:

Annual Investments at Daimler-Benz AG 1939–44 (Million RM):

| 1939 | 44.0 | 1941 | 127.0 | 1943 | 120.0 |
| 1940 | 62.0 | 1942 | 112.7 | 1944 | 133.0 |

The extent to which these investments – though substantial in themselves and an indicator of the extent of the increase of Daimler-Benz's activities in the war – represent a long-term expansion of capacity must be qualified by the comment that in the second half of the war substantial proportions of the company's investment were directed towards areas that were specific to developments in the war, such as barracks for foreign workers or air raid shelters. A cautious estimate, which it is impossible to substantiate fully owing to the lack of detailed evidence, would suggest that ten per cent of company investment went on such areas in 1942, rising to up to 35 to 40 per cent in 1944, primarily as a result of the huge dispersal programme.[38] While the

---

37 Pohl, et al., *Die Daimler-Benz AG*, p. 126.
38 Evidence concerning the cost of the dispersal programme is extremely sporadic. It would appear from the underground dispersal sites for which figures are available that each such project cost

overall level of investment remained relatively high during the war, strategic investment thus probably started falling much earlier. In fact, genuine investment in productive capacity probably peaked in 1941, which suggests – taking investment levels to be a broad indicator of confidence – that the board was sceptical about the prospects for the war from an early stage. In particular, sharply falling investment from 1943 onwards points to the fact that the Allies' bombing of Germany had a much greater impact upon German companies than the continued short-term high levels of output in 1943 and 1944 might otherwise imply.

The expansion of Daimler-Benz's activities is reflected in the development of turnover and profits in the war:

Turnover of Daimler-Benz AG 1939–44 (Million RM):

1939 527.6	1941 645.9	1943 942.0
1940 540.0	1942 839.2	1944 953.9

Gross Profits at Daimler-Benz AG 1939–44 (Million RM):

1939 + 101.19	1941 + 111.20	1943 + 185.90
1940 + 112.06	1942 + 149.00	1944 + 175.10

Net Profits at Daimler-Benz AG 1939–44 (Million RM):

1939 + 3.25	1941 + 3.61	1943 + 7.21
1940 + 3.76	1942 + 5.41	1944 − 3.53

In addition, the company built up substantial reserves during the war, in obvious anticipation of eventual demobilization.[39] Moreover, the workforce, which had already grown from 14,000 in 1933 to 42,776 in 1939, also further expanded greatly. In September 1944, the number of employees at Daimler-Benz AG, including the direct subsidiaries founded before and during the war, stood at 68,961.[40]

From the summer and autumn of 1940 onwards, the company also took over the management of plants in the occupied areas, greatly expanded its sales and repair network throughout Europe, and oversaw the introduction of production of Daimler-Benz aero-engines under licence in many other factories in both

between RM 3m and RM 8m. A conservative estimate, allowing RM 4m for the cost of each of the ten underground dispersal projects listed by the official company history, would put the overall cost at RM 40m; assuming a similarly conservative RM 10m for the plethora of surface dispersals, for air raid protection measures and the construction of blast walls, etc, at the main plants, the cost of protecting the company's capacity in 1944 can be estimated at approximately RM 50m, or 38 per cent of the company's investments in that year. For figures see MBAG Huppenbauer 476, DBAG Sindelfingen to Haspel, 14.7.44; Pohl et al., *Die Daimler-Benz AG*, pp. 91–2.
39 On the build up of reserves see Roth, 'Der Weg zum Guten Stern', p. 334.
40 MBAG Haspel 19, Statistical Monthly Reports 1942–1944.

east and west. By the end of the war, Daimler-Benz directly controlled plants in France (Colmar), Poland (Rzeszow), Czechoslovakia (Neupaka) and the Soviet Union (a huge repair facility at Minsk). It also oversaw licensed production at numerous German and Austrian plants (Henschel at Kassel, Nimo at Braunschweig, Pomo at Stettin, Steyr-Daimler-Puch at Graz and the huge Flugmotorenwerk Ostmark at Vienna, which it managed from 1941 to 1943), as well as abroad (Manfred Weiss, Budapest, and Avia, Prague). Finally, in western Europe, either Daimler-Benz engines or parts were produced at a Hispano-Suiza plant in France, and by Fiat and Alfa-Romeo in Italy.

Following the defeat of France, the company moved immediately to secure control of a factory in Colmar, which was tooled for the production of Daimler-Benz aero-engine parts. RM 14.9 million was invested in this plant, which was also equipped with large amounts of plundered machinery, in whose procurement Daimler-Benz managers actively participated.[41] It also expanded its sales and repair network in Alsace-Lorraine, setting up branches in Metz and Strasbourg.[42] Werlin tried, unsuccessfully, to gain control of the Bugatti plant in Alsace. The board member responsible for Gaggenau, Arnold von Jungenfeld, also tried, without success, to gain control of additional capacity for the production of lorry parts, complaining that 'useful sites have gone without our having been asked'. Kissel described the failure of the company to gain in this respect as 'very regrettable'.[43] The rapidity with which the new plant and workshops were established, the substantial investments made, and the aggressive policy pursued with regard to gaining additional sites suggest a long-term strategy of expansion in Alsace-Lorraine aimed at exploiting a secure post-war market in an area that the company could be reasonably certain would remain in German hands on a permanent basis.

Compared to its aggressive policy in Alsace-Lorraine, the attitude of the company towards expansion in the rest of occupied France was slightly less clear-cut. The desire to make sure it secured its 'share' of the new opportunities that might or might not present themselves, and the fear of being disadvantaged in the distribution of the spoils, had to be balanced against an assessment of the advisability of expanding under atypical conditions and of the long-term development of the political, legal, economic and, above all, military situation in Europe.[44]

Daimler-Benz managers were initially keen to visit the plants of French competitors in the automobile industry and to ensure that their interests were represented in any allocation of French factories to German companies.[45] The company was especially interested in Peugeot, seeing in a possible takeover

41   MBAG Kissel IX/War Plants Colmar, Kissel to K. C. Müller, 15.11.1940; Kissel to DBAG Gaggenau, 25.11.1940; DBAG Untertürkheim to DBAG Colmar, 14.2.1941.
42   MBAG Kissel I/13, Minutes of the Board Meeting of DBAG on 13 and 14.10.1940.
43   MBAG Forstmeier 14, Minutes of the Board Meeting of DBAG on 4.11.1940.
44   On the attitude of German industry to expansion in France see Müller, 'Mobilisierung', p. 496.
45   BA (P) 80 Ba2 P3195, Kissel to State Minister Pflaumer, 18.9.1940.

the establishment of a position in France and the elimination of a rival in the French market, and, upon hearing that Auto-Union was also trying to take it over, intervened with the military administration to delay this until its own managers could visit the plant. The attractiveness of French plants was greatly reduced, however, by the fact that French industry had been the object of a massive wave of plundering in the aftermath of the military campaign, so that many of potentially the most valuable machine-tools had been taken.[46] Upon visiting the plant, supervisory board member Carl Schippert, who played a leading role in the administration of the regime's policy towards the French automobile industry during the war, reported that the workshops were 'completely worn out and full of old machines', leading Daimler-Benz to lose interest – as, evidently, did Auto-Union.[47]

Schippert was also able to use his position as Commissar for the Renault and Unic factories to try to gain a controlling influence for Daimler-Benz over the capital of French firms, especially lorry firms, in line with the regime's policy of encouraging capital penetration and thus cementing German dominance of the 'New Order'.[48] Of particular interest, given that the company already produced Daimler-Benz lorries under licence, was Unic itself. The opportunity to gain control of these shares was presented by the fact that the assets of Rothschild, who owned 40 per cent of Unic, had been sequestrated.[49] Throughout the first half of 1941, Daimler-Benz attempted to gain control of Rothschild's Unic shares, believing that, although a minority shareholding would not give overall control, it would still bring substantial influence over a company well-placed to exploit what it saw as a profitable French lorry market. Above all, it saw the shares as ensuring a good source of 'all information concerning the French automobile industry, its interests and its relationship to the Reich'.[50] Negotiations were eventually broken off in July 1941, however, Daimler-Benz having either failed or changed its mind.[51] In addition, the board attempted to gain control of the capital of two further companies, Latil and Saurer, believing, as Kissel argued, that in the envisaged reorganization of the French lorry industry, 'we would have such influence that no decisions could be taken without our agreement.'[52] It is unclear, however, if Daimler-Benz was successful here either.

46 Umbreit, H., 'Auf dem Weg zur Kontinentalherrschaft' in: Kroener et al., *Organisation und Mobilisierung des Deutschen Machtbereichs*, p. 223.
47 MBAG Kissel I/13, Minutes of the Board Meeting of DBAG on 13 and 14.10.1940.
48 MBAG Kissel I/13, Minutes of the Board Meeting of DBAG on 21 and 22.1.1941. On the regime's policies towards the French economy in the initial phase of the occupation see Milward, A., *The New Order and the French Economy*, Oxford, 1970, pp. 23–110; on the issue of capital penetration, pp. 47, 50. For the appointment of Schippert as Commissar for the Renault and Unic plants see Roth and Schmid, *Die Daimler-Benz AG 1916–1948*, p. 240.
49 MBAG Forstmeier 14, Minutes of the Board Meeting of DBAG on 4.11.1940.
50 MBAG Kissel I/14, Minutes of the Board Meeting of DBAG on 25 and 26.3.1941.
51 MBAG Kissel I/14, Minutes of the Board Meeting of DBAG on 28 and 29.7.1941.
52 MBAG Forstmeier 14, Minutes of the Board Meeting of DBAG on 4.11.1940.

Daimler-Benz managers also played a leading role in the RLM commissions to France for the purposes of assessing the potential of the French aircraft industry in 1940–1. K. C. Müller was in France with the RLM twice in July 1940, on the first occasion just four days after the occupation was completed, for the purposes of 'plundering the factories' (*die Ausschlachtung von Fabriken*).[53] The company itself was also offered control of plants confiscated by the RLM for the production of aero-engines and components. In response to an offer of Hispano-Suiza's main plant, however, the board found that it 'has been largely cleared out, and only a few old machines remain, so that it can only function as a supplier to us with great difficulty.'[54] Another Hispano-Suiza plant was nevertheless visited soon after by Müller, and although the equipment was equally poor, he intervened to have the plant confiscated for Daimler-Benz because of the skilled workforce there.[55] It was then tooled for parts production and integrated into the network of Daimler-Benz engine-producing companies.

Overall, however, the initial expansionist aims in France yielded little, and it is probably true that the company benefited from the occupation of France less in terms of control of French companies (despite its efforts to undermine development and production of cars in the French companies its managers administrated), than as a source of plundered machine-tools, materials and, above all, French labour.[56] Given that National Socialist policy in the occupied territories tended, as a result of both ideological factors and immediate pressures, to give priority to short-term economic exploitation, it was difficult for industry to implement long-term plans predicated on a stable future and geared to long-term needs. In view of the chaotic and inefficient administration of the French economy, and the incompatibility of policies that plundered machinery and deported labour in one direction whilst trying to disperse contracts in the other without any effective coordination, Daimler-Benz soon adopted a policy based more around optimizing its share of machinery and labour for deployment in Germany rather than expanding production in France itself.

The idea that Daimler-Benz consciously prepared a policy of expansion in eastern Europe in anticipation of the regime's invasion of the Soviet Union is without foundation.[57] In contrast to the west, it is also doubtful whether

53   BA (P) 80 Ba2 P3316, Memorandum/Stauss, 24.7.1940.
54   MBAG Kissel I/13, Minutes of the Board Meeting of DBAG on 13 and 14.10.1940.
55   MBAG Kissel I/14, Minutes of the Board Meeting of DBAG on 21 and 22.1.1941.
56   Roth, 'Der Weg zum Guten Stern', pp. 221–2. French manufacturers had, in fact, often been able to obtain high-quality American machine-tools before the war that German companies had not been able to buy owing to currency shortages (Milward, *The New Order and the French Economy*, p. 37).
57   Roth argues that the formation and expansion of workshops in eastern Europe from 1937–8 onwards were in direct anticipation of the regime's later military campaigns (Roth, 'Der Weg zum Guten Stern', p. 217). This argument seems to rest too much on hindsight, however.

Daimler-Benz had any long-term expansionist aims in the east, which it aimed to pursue in the context of the war itself, once the war had been extended in June 1941. The takeover or establishment of production or repair plants naturally provided a basis for possible expansion in the event of a victorious conclusion to the war, but it is improbable that this was the main motive behind the company's collaboration in the exploitation of the eastern occupied territories. It did expand its sales and repair network in eastern Europe, again with a view to exploiting the export opportunities of the 'New Order'; but given the permanent fear of post-war over-capacity at Daimler-Benz's existing plants, it is unlikely that the company planned to use the plants it took over in the east (with the possible exception of the Flug-motorenwerk Ostmark, Vienna) as the basis for an expansion of actual production there after the war – certainly there is no concrete evidence to suggest this.

In the case of the Flugmotorenwerk Rzeszow, in Poland, for example – a plant that Daimler-Benz took over as trustee from Henschel in November 1941 – the company categorically refused to invest more than the minimum necessary to keep production going. This cautious policy was shown in April 1942 in its rejection of the Bank der Deutschen Luftfahrt's demand that the financing of the plant through its initial stage of unprofitability take the form of a credit loan, repayable by Daimler-Benz. The company resisted all such pressure strongly, arguing that it was doing its best to bring production into order, but that 'beyond that, and specifically in view of the conditions of production and the location of the plant in Poland, our company can under no circumstances assume liability for credits etc.'[58] Despite pressuring the RLM, the Bank der Deutschen Luftfahrt was unable to force Daimler-Benz to accept its terms, and, following a further refusal by Kissel to undertake a financial risk on the part of Daimler-Benz, the RLM was forced to continue financing the plant itself.[59]

In fact, upon taking over the trusteeship of the plant, Daimler-Benz set up a separate company, with a very low capital sufficient only to cover basic running production costs, to administer the plant and lease the buildings and machinery from the RLM.[60] In this way, the financial liability was reduced to a minimum, and the plant was kept completely separate from the core of the Daimler-Benz concern. Clearly, the uncertain legal and political situation in Poland compounded the general military unpredictability of the war situation and reinforced Daimler-Benz's unwillingness to take over either property or large-scale financial obligations in the east. Similarly, the board saw the plant it took over in Neupaka as purely 'an alternative war plant', one 'whose task

58 BA (P) 80 Ba6/7126, DBAG to Bank der Deutschen Luftfahrt, 21.4.1942.
59 BA (P) 80 Ba6/7126, Memorandum, 26.5.1942.
60 MBAG Kissel IX/Reichshof, Haspel to Cejka, 22.10.1941.

will be completed with the end of the war'.[61] It was also sometimes reluctant to comply with the regime's demands to establish licensed production at plants outside Germany, for fear of technology transfer and the danger of establishing competitors for itself in the post-war period.[62]

Finally, the issue of expansion eastwards caused the re-emergence of the underlying division within the board between those who favoured using the situation created by the Nazi occupation of Europe to expand capacity and orientate further the company's production towards armaments on the one hand, and those who were naturally more cautious and who already recognized the seriousness of Germany's military position on the other. When the issue of participating in a possible Armaments Ministry venture to establish tank production in Romania was discussed at the board meeting of 4–5. November 1942, it was again the Marienfelde manager Wolfgang von Hentig who argued that the company should participate in the project. He claimed that it would need a foothold in south-east Europe in order to compete in the post-war Greater German Reich, and that 'it would be wrong not to take advantage of this opportunity, as one day it will be very lucrative for us.' Despite making encouraging noises, however, Wilhelm Haspel, who took over the chairmanship of the board following the death of Kissel in July 1942, was very noncommital, saying that he was getting 'gradually more nervous' about such projects. In the event, it appears that little came of Daimler-Benz's participation in the project.[63] Whereas in 1937 the conflict between Kissel and Hentig over the expansion of Marienfelde had been resolved in the latter's favour, significantly, in 1942, the views of the more cautious Haspel won through. From this point onwards, those of Hentig's persuasion carried less and less weight within the board.

Nevertheless, the fact remains that Daimler-Benz massively expanded its operations in all areas of occupied Europe during the war, which, in the suggested absence of a long-term expansionist agenda, needs explanation. The motives of the company for participating in the takeover of plants in the occupied east are never explicitly revealed in the surviving written evidence, inasmuch as the minutes of board meetings, for example, do not contain lengthy discussions of the advantages and disadvantages of expansion; the essential fact that individual plants were taken over tells us nothing in itself about the motives of the company for doing so. Insofar as expansion was discussed, decisions were always informed by the assumption that the company's engagement would be limited to the period of the war. Moreover, they were influenced by the recognition that a failure to take over plants would mean accepting that other companies would acquire them instead. The

61 BA (P) Ba6 7446/3, Credit Record of the Bank der Deutschen Luftfahrt, 8.7.1944; Memorandum Regarding the visit to Daimler-Benz, Stuttgart, 5.5.1944.
62 MBAG Kissel I/14, Minutes of the Board Meeting of DBAG on 25 and 26.3.1941.
63 MBAG Kissel I/15, Minutes of the Board Meeting of DBAG on 4 and 5.11.1942.

unwillingness to see this happen, however, was not a product of the desire to acquire as many plants as possible to form the basis for an expanded post-war production, but derived from a fear of being marginalized as a producer for the war economy itself. The evidence is inconclusive, but the answer probably lies as much in the nature of competition between private manufacturers within the context of the war itself, as in plans that actually went beyond the war.[64] As often as not, the decision to accept the takeover of a new plant into the Daimler-Benz production circle was taken primarily to prevent Junkers or BMW doing so, and thus to avoid the possibility of being 'elbowed out' of particular production spheres – or, conversely, to try to gain a monopoly of particular production areas for the duration of the war. In the case of the Neupaka plant, for example, Haspel was highly sceptical about the proposal, describing it as 'very risky'. He argued, however, that the company would have to take it over 'in view of the overall situation, and especially in view of the tactics of Junkers.'[65] Similarly, the decision to comply with RLM demands that the Pomo plant in Stettin be tooled for Daimler-Benz aero-engine production was based largely on the fear that the plant might otherwise have been used to produce Junkers engines.[66]

The production of spare parts in Poland was in itself financially insignificant to Daimler-Benz, but, insofar as it improved the overall effectiveness of the Daimler-Benz production circle, it was vital in safeguarding the company's prospects for producing its own models at its own plants, rather than being forced to produce the models of another company under licence. Similarly, while taking over management of the huge Flugmotorenwerk Ostmark from Junkers and re-tooling it for the production of Daimler-Benz engines created the potential for huge licence-fee income for Daimler-Benz, it was equally important for the fact that Junkers's own efforts to dominate the aero-engine sector had been thwarted. That, within the context of the war economy, individual companies were competing for control of each area of production and seeking to frustrate the interests of their competitors does not, however, necessarily mean they were using the war to pursue an expansionist agenda going beyond the war itself. Of course, none of this reduced the impact of the exploitation of the occupied territories on the populations of those territories – in fact, the assumption that the company's engagement in the plants would be of limited duration tended to intensify it – and none of it reduces the responsibility of industry for the collaboration in that process, a process that in one form or another was still a source of substantial profit.

64 Cf. Hayes, *Industry and Ideology*, p. 264.
65 MBAG Kissel I/15, Minutes of the Board Meeting of DBAG on 4 and 5.11.1942.
66 MBAG Kissel I/14, Minutes of the Board Meeting of DBAG on 25 and 26.3.1941.

3. The Speer Period and the 'Production Miracle' 1942–4

Although, as recent research has demonstrated, the regime was trying to
mobilize the economy for a lengthy war to a far greater extent than has generally
been accepted, it remains the case that the crucial military reverses of the winter
of 1941–2, and with them the radically altered situation that faced the regime
from this point onwards, necessarily mark a significant break in the history of the
war economy too. While, as has been argued, this was not the only 'turning
point' in a war of two simple halves – the defeat of France in June 1940 marked
the first clear strategic readjustment on the part of Daimler-Benz, and at least
one more was to follow – the defeats on the eastern front and with them the
failure of the 'Barbarossa' campaign were the occasion for a radical shift in
perspectives, not only of the military and the regime itself, but also of the
industry upon which both depended to provide the means to prosecute the war
at all. Having been characterized up to 1941–2 by successive victories in a series
of limited campaigns against militarily inferior opponents, the war evolved in
the space of literally one or two months into a lengthy, increasingly defensive
war of attrition against an enemy far stronger in economic capacity and, above
all, human reserves than those previously faced. The entry of the USA into the
war in December 1941 further strengthened the forces facing the Axis powers.

While the unprecedented material losses of the 'Barbarossa' campaign and
the opening up of the huge eastern front created much greater demand for
replacement armaments than had been the case before, the enormous human
losses experienced by the army from the autumn of 1941 onwards resulted in
a qualitative change in the manpower requirements of the military.[67] The
mass call-ups of workers, and their replacement by mainly unskilled,
inexperienced and physically mistreated foreign workers, greatly changed the
conditions under which industry had to cope with the new situation, so that
in this respect too, the winter of 1941–2 represents a radical break from the
previous period. Both the prospect of a lengthy war and the massive increase
in military demand on the one hand, and the rapid dissolution of the core
workforce and its replacement by primarily unskilled foreign workers on the
other, created pressure to reorganize production in a way that had hitherto not
been the case. As Hitler's decree of 3 December 1941, which called for
concentration of production on the most productive (i.e. largest) plants and
the implementation of mass-production methods, shows, this pressure for
intensified rationalization was now coming from the highest levels.[68]

---

67 On the mass losses on the eastern front and their effects see Kroener, B., 'Die Personelle
    Ressourcen des Dritten Reiches im Spannungsfeld zwischen Wehrmacht, Bürokratie und
    Kriegswirtschaft 1939–1942' in: Kroener et al. (eds.), *Organisation und Mobilisierung des Deutschen
    Machtbereichs*, pp. 877–984.
68 BA (K) R41/289, Excerpt from the Führer Decree of 13.12.1941. On the impact of the military
    events of the winter of 1941–2 and the 'search for new perspectives' see Müller, 'Mobilisierung',
    pp. 630–89.

Above all, the events of the winter of 1941–2 also finally created the sense of urgency in the regime – not least in Hitler himself – to resolve the conflicts within the administration of the war economy that had themselves been at the root of the failure to expand armaments production quickly and efficiently, and provided the context in which overall power could be transferred to Todt's successor as RMfBuM, Albert Speer, who was appointed on 8 February 1942, following the former's death. Speer's appointment as General Plenipotentiary for Armaments Tasks in the Four Year Plan (*General-bevollmächtigter für Rüstungsaufgaben im Vierjahresplan*) on 1 March 1942 effectively subordinated the Four Year Plan structures to his control, insofar as they affected armaments and production. Most significantly, Speer's formation of the Central Planning Board (comprising himself, Milch and State Secretary Körner from the Four Year Plan office) on 22 April 1942 gave him unified control of raw materials allocation to the armaments industry.[69] When the incorporation of the Reich Associations (*Reichsvereinigungen*) gave Speer control of actual production of the main raw materials as well as their allocation, the marginalization of the Four Year Plan office and the transfer of its functions to the RMfBuM were complete.[70]

In May 1942, the Economic Armaments Office was also effectively sidelined and its most important powers given to the RMfBuM.[71] The office was split into two, with its main part, the Armaments Office (*Rüstungsamt*), transferred to the RMfBuM. A rump counterpart, the Defence Economy Office (*Wehrwirtschaftsamt*), remained under the control of Thomas until November 1942, when he resigned from this too. By May 1942, the military was already more or less completely marginalized in the economic apparatus, as with the transfer of the Armaments Office to the RMfBuM Speer had gained control of the crucial Armaments Inspectorates and Commandos.

Speer did not assume total control of the economy in 1942. Civilian production remained under the RWM until September 1943, when it was handed over to Speer under the renamed Reich Ministry for Armaments and War Production (*Reichsministerium für Rüstung und Kriegsproduktion* – RMfRuK). Above all, labour mobilization, procurement and deployment fell under the jurisdiction of Gauleiter Sauckel in his capacity as General Plenipotentiary for Labour Deployment, which superseded the Labour

69 Naasner, W., *Neue Machtzentren in der Deutschen Kriegswirtschaft 1942–1945. Die Wirtschafts-organisation der SS, das Amt des Generalbevollmächtigten für den Arbeitseinsatz und das Reichs-ministerium für Bewaffnung und Munition/Reichsministerium für Rüstung und Kriegsproduktion im Nationalsozialistischen Herrschaftssystem*, Boppard am Rhein, 1994, p. 165. The text of the decree establishing the Central Planning board is printed in Noakes, J., and Pridham, G. (eds.), *Documents on Nazism 1919–1945*, London, 1974, p. 645.

70 On the Reich Associations for Coal and Iron see Kehrl, H., *Krisenmanager im Dritten Reich*, Düsseldorf, 1970, pp. 260–5.

71 Janssen, G., *Das Ministerium Speer. Deutschlands Rüstung im Zweiten Weltkrieg*, Frankfurt/M., 1968, p. 50; Naasner, *Neue Machtzentren*, p. 166.

Ministry in this area on 21 March 1942.[72] However, the concentration of power in Speer's hands that occurred in early 1942 was nonetheless substantial, and the overall level of coordination this allowed provided one of the main pre-conditions for the expansion of output in the second half of the war.

Speer's reorganization of the overall management of the economy was combined with measures to rationalize production in each sector of the armaments industries. The main vehicle for this was the expansion of the reforms initiated under Todt in 1940, by which the industrialists responsible for each area of production were organized into committees to coordinate rationalization measures in the area concerned. Whereas Todt had only co-opted some army producers into the committees, Speer gathered all sectors of the armaments industries into this system and greatly expanded the committees' role. End-producers were organized into Main Committees (such as Main Committee for Engineering, Main Committee for Fine Mechanics, Tanks, for Munitions, for Vehicle Production and so on), with each one having a system of Special Committees responsible for the details of rationalization in each area (in the case of Vehicle Production, the Special Committee for 3-ton Lorries, the Special Committee for 4½- and 6½-ton Lorries, etc). Subcontracting industries or components producers were organized into Main Rings (Main Ring Forgings, Main Ring Machine Elements, etc), with each one similarly having subsidiary Special Rings for each component.

By transferring responsibility for production to the industrialists themselves, under the system of 'industrial self-responsibility', Speer hoped to exploit the technical and organizational expertise of industry in coordinating contracts allocation and the utilization of capacity, the best possible division of labour between plants, the simplification of the production programmes of each plant, the rationalization of production through further standardization and the usage of labour- and materials-saving production processes on the shop floor.[73] In addition to coopting their expertise, Speer also appealed to their profit-making instincts by replacing the existing 'cost-plus' pricing system – which had encouraged industry to produce expensively, as prices were calculated on the basis of production costs plus a percentage profit (thus the more expensive the production, the higher the profit) – with a 'fixed-price'

---

72   On Sauckel see Naasner, *Neue Machtzentren*, pp. 25–162.
73   BA (K) R3/288, Decree of the Reich Minister for Weapons and Munitions (RMfBuM) and General Plenipotentiary for Armaments Tasks within the Four Year Plan concerning the Division of Responsibility and Operating Procedures for the Organs of Self-Administration (Committees and Rings) in the War Economy of 20.4.1942; BA (K) R3/288, Implementation Decree of the RMfBuM of 20.4.1942. The role of the Committees and Rings was redefined and extended during the reorganization of the RMfBuM in the autumn of 1943, but remained the same in all its essential features as in April 1942 (BA [K] R3/288, Decree on the Distribution of Tasks in the War Economy of 29.10.1943; copy also in MBAG Haspel 5,49).

system. This allowed the producers to keep the difference between the fixed price and their own production costs (thus the cheaper the production, the higher the profit), encouraging the manufacturers to rationalize production and undoubtedly also stimulating a further intensification of labour on the shop floor.[74] Again, the establishment of this pricing system represented the completion of a process set in motion by Todt, but once more it took the crisis of 1941–2 for it to be finally achieved.

Daimler-Benz managers and engineers participated in the system of Committees and Rings on the same basis as those of other companies. Oberbaurat Schmidt, for example, was head of the Special Committee for 3-ton Lorries in 1942 and then the Special Committee for 4½- and 6½-ton Lorries from 1943 onwards. In the aero-engine sphere, first K.C. Müller and then Haspel chaired the Special Committee 'T2' (Daimler-Benz aero-engines) within the Main Committee for Engine Production (*Hauptausschuss Triebwerke*), which had initially been formed as the 'Daimler-Benz Ring' following the reorganization of the Aircraft Industry in August 1941 and which was integrated into the RMfBuM in April 1942.[75] In addition to this, and as part of the transfer of jurisdiction from military to civilian control, Werlin, the member of the board with the closest contacts to Hitler, was appointed as the Führer's General Inspector for the Vehicle Industry on 16 January 1942, signalling the final marginalization of Schell.[76] This provided an invaluable further source of information for the company.

While the extent of the freedom accorded to industry under this system can be overestimated – overall direction of the war effort remained with the political and military leadership and overall direction of the armaments economy remained with Speer, while the expertise of industry was only used in each particular sphere – industry nonetheless welcomed the end of the military's attempts to establish a 'command economy' under its control, and was able within the 'self-responsibility' system to utilize the limited autonomy it had to defend its own interests both collectively and individually against some of the pressures coming from above. In its public pronouncements, the Daimler-Benz board identified itself strongly with the aims and policies of further concentration and macro-rationalization, proclaiming that everything that was incompatible with this, 'including considerations of and planning for the coming peacetime', must be stopped.[77] In practice, criteria based on post-war considerations and private company interest continued to condition the response of the board to government pressures. Internally, the management

74 Werner, *Bleib Übrig*, p. 114.
75 On the reorganization of the aircraft industry and the Daimler-Benz Ring see below, Chapter V.1.b. For the full range of functions fulfilled by Daimler-Benz managers within the war economy apparatus see Roth, 'Der Weg zum Guten Stern', pp. 326, 330.
76 Pohl et al., *Die Daimler-Benz AG*, p. 40.
77 MBAG Kissel VI/8, Communiqué of the Directorate of DBAG, 2.7.1942.

was also highly sceptical of the immediate benefits to the military of Speer's type-reduction programme, as it was recognized that existing models would be in use for years to come and would thus continue to need spare parts, and companies forced to re-tool for production of new standard types would thus have to produce parts for their old models in addition to producing the new ones. At Daimler-Benz it was argued that if the military had wanted to enjoy the fruits of mass type-reductions it would have had to introduce the measures five years before the outbreak of war, not during it.[78] This scepticism was proven to be correct by the experience of having to re-tool for production of the Opel 3-ton lorry at Mannheim, which turned out to be a costly mistake.[79]

Within the company, a substantial process of internal concentration was instituted following the overall reorganization and successive exhortations of 1942, which yielded considerable results. In response to the new pressures from above to rationalize production, the board itself elected to transfer the newly established tank parts production line from Mannheim back to Marienfelde (Plant 40), allowing an increase in the space devoted to large-scale lorry production there. Meanwhile, the second naval engine production line, which had been established at Marienfelde in 1940, was to be transferred back to Untertürkheim, allowing a concentration of large-scale naval engine production there and an expansion of tank production at Marienfelde. According to the board, this internal rationalization would permit substantial increases in output without the need for large amounts of new capital, equipment or extra labour.[80]

This process of internal concentration did, when it was eventually instituted in January 1943, produce very considerable increases. Monthly output of naval engines at Untertürkheim, which had stood at ten in January 1942 and 15 in July 1942, rose to 21 in March 1943 and reached 27 in December of the same year. During the same period, the workforce on this production line had risen from 1340 to 1620, while the proportion of German workers had fallen from 90 per cent to 53 per cent, and the number of machine-tools in the production line had risen only from 403 to 599.[81] Thus, with 21 per cent more workers and 49 per cent more machine-tools, a 170-percent increase in output was achieved at Untertürkheim. Similarly, at Marienfelde, where tank and armoured vehicle production had slumped to around 30 to 40 per month over the winter of 1942–3, the company was able, partly as a result of this reorganization, to increase production to over 100

---

78   MBAG Haspel 7,60, Memorandum (The Orientation of the Car Industry to the Needs of War), 18.12.1942.
79   On the history of the Opel 3-ton Licence Production at Mannheim see below , Chapter V.2.b.
80   MBAG Kissel VI/8, Communiqué of the Directorate of DBAG, 2.7.1942.
81   BA (K) R3/1576, Development of Production, Work-Force and Machine Inventory in the Years 1942–4, DBAG Plant 60 Naval Engine Production (Enclosure with Letter of 2.2.1944). Both documents are reproduced in Roth und Schmid (eds.), Die Daimler-Benz AG 1918–1948, pp. 280–1.

tanks per month throughout 1944, peaking at 134 in September of that year.[82]

While this internal process yielded tangible and quantifiable results, a broader assessment of the overall impact of Speer's reforms is far more difficult. Obviously, hard conclusions about the administration of the war economy as a whole cannot be extrapolated from the experience of one single company, as different branches of the economy were affected in different ways and to different degrees. As the overall indices of armaments output show, production rose dramatically in some branches – the index of tank production peaked at 598 in December 1944 and the index of overall aircraft production peaked at 367 in July 1944 – but stagnated in others, as in the case of vehicle production, which reached 120 in 1942, 138 in 1943 and fell to 109 in 1944 (January–February 1942 = 100 in all cases).[83] Each sector also experienced periods of increasing or stable production at different points, depending on given strategic priorities at any time.[84]

It is also hard to assess how much the massive expansion of output in the armaments industry from 1942 onwards was the direct product of organizational changes made by Speer in his capacity as RMfBuM, and how far one should seek to relativize his importance by stressing the extent to which improvements in productivity and aggregate output were a result of decisions taken prior to Speer's appointment. At least the first rise in overall output, from February to July 1942, occurred before Speer's measures can have had any time to take effect. It is also clear both from general macro-indices and the experience of Daimler-Benz itself that the increases in output that were achieved from 1942 onwards took place primarily in sectors where there had been substantial reorganization at administrative or shop-floor level prior to Speer's appointment. This is the case, for example, in tank production, which had been the object of reorganization under Todt, and in aero-engine production, where the key investment decisions at Daimler-Benz had been taken in 1940 and 1941, and where the main reorganization process was set in motion under the RLM in the summer and autumn of 1941.

Part of the increase is also explicable by the further conversion of capacity. Such a conversion took place at Untertürkheim and Sindelfingen in 1942 which was the result of the cessation of production of the 1.7l, 2.3l and 3.4l cars, and contributed to increases in output in other sectors over the following two years. In 1941, the Sindelfingen plant had still been mainly engaged in vehicle production, which took up 64 per cent of its capacity in that year, but from then onwards it was converted more to production of aero-engine and fuselage parts mainly for Daimler-Benz and Messerschmidt models, so that by

---

82 MBAG Haspel 19, Statistical Monthly Reports 1942–1944. On tank production at Marienfelde (Plant 40) during the war see the overview provided by Roth, 'Der Weg zum Guten Stern', pp. 273–83.
83 BA (K) R3/1732, Comparison Chart of Group Production Indices 1941–1944.
84 Milward, *The German Economy at War*, p. 100.

1944 only 21 per cent of its capacity was still devoted to vehicle production.[85] Overall, 93 per cent of Daimler-Benz's total turnover in 1944 was derived from armaments production, compared to 79 per cent in 1941 (and 65 per cent in 1939), so that, despite the conclusions of recent research, it must still be recognized that further conversion of capacity from 1942 onwards played at least some role.[86]

Finally, for the period after Speer's appointment, it is impossible to assess with any certainty the relative importance of each aspect of his reforms. Above all, assessing the relative importance of his reforms to the overall management of the economy on the one hand, and the adoption of new labour- and materials-saving production processes, simplification of construction, etc, at shop-floor level on the other, is difficult. An examination of developments at shop-floor level suggests, however, that scepticism is required with regard to the extent to which reorganization of the production process was the product of optimal rational calculation rather than improvised crisis management. Similarly, the contribution of genuine materials- and labour-saving devices in most sectors should not be over-stressed.[87]

In the case of aero-engine production, significant savings in the use of some materials in short supply were indeed achieved. From October 1943 to October 1944 the amount of chrome used in each DB 605 aero-engine, for example, was reduced from 27.41 kg to 19.01 kg (a saving of 31 per cent), while the amount used in the DB 603 was reduced in the same period from 37.03 kg to 21.95 kg (a saving of 41 per cent). Similarly, from October 1943 to May 1944 the amount of nickel used in the DB 603 was reduced from 9.82 kg to 2.16 kg (a saving of 78 per cent).[88] This was achieved through extensive development work and undoubtedly also to some extent by more efficient machining methods which reduced wastage.

In other sectors, however, it is clear that labour- or materials-saving design and production changes and the concomitant savings in working hours were not always the product of 'simplification of construction' in the sense of extensive design alterations to individual components to allow more effective machining methods or easier assembly, although these continued to play a role. Increasingly, 'simplification of construction' meant not extensively researched engineering solutions of long-term technical significance, but simply the stripping away of fixtures and fittings and the elimination of non-

85 Daimler-Benz AG Factory Sindelfingen, *Unser Werk in den Kriegsjahren 1939–1944*, Sindelfingen, 1944, p. 6. In addition, the Sindelfingen plant produced parts for the Peenemünde project.
86 Roth, 'Der Weg zum Guten Stern', p. 333.
87 On the pressures involved in the reorganization of the production process from the middle of the war onwards see below, Chapters V.1.c) and V.2.a).
88 MBAG Haspel 1/11, DBAG Marienfelde (Conversion Supervisor of DBAG Plant 90) to the Working Group for Metal Conversion in the Reich Office for Iron and Metal, 6.5.1944; DBAG Untertürkheim to the Scarce Materials Commissions of the Defence District Deputy V (Stuttgart), 1.10.1944.

essential components from the standard model. Even in 1940 Daimler-Benz managers were noting that production costs of the 1.7l car body were falling, owing to the fact that, in place of the expensive laquering and polishing processes carried out for consumer production, it now simply had to be painted field grey for the army.[89] In April 1942 Schell demanded that 'all cosmetic refinements which only improve external appearances cease.'[90] In the case of Daimler-Benz's cars and lorries, this meant the removal of door-handles, lamps, ventilators, clocks and number-plates – henceforth the registration number was to be painted onto the bumper of the vehicle. From the middle of the war onwards, even the famous 'Mercedes Star' was to be left off the vehicle.[91] The significance of this can been seen in the example of lorry production at Gaggenau. Here, for example, the production time of Daimler-Benz's 4½-ton lorry was reduced by 26 per cent from 1940 to 1944.[92] Of the 149 working hours saved, 57.5 hours (39 per cent) came from the reduction of unnecessary 'trimmings'.[93] Simultaneously, a reduction in the quality of the parts caused by using less suitable materials was accepted, in view of the fact that long life of components was less necessary in the war owing to the short 'life expectancy' of a vehicle on the front.[94]

The extent to which long-term rationalization measures at shop-floor level were responsible for increases in output must also be questioned when one considers that exhortations to rationalize production were in response to successive military reversals and to the permanent decline in the German military position. Each attempt tended to coincide with a further growth in awareness on the part of industry of the way the wind was blowing and thus encountered the increasing reluctance of industry to expend energy on long-term measures to raise productivity in areas that would not represent the main area of company activity in the long term. Especially from early 1944 onwards, the reallocation of production lines was a part not of wide-ranging rationalization programmes but of crisis-management responses to bombing and bottlenecks, which were beginning to cripple the economy. Where production increases were nonetheless achieved, they were increasingly less the result of fundamental reorganization than of lengthening working hours and the intensification of labour at shop-floor level.

Overall, the extent to which the 'production miracle' was based on widespread shop-floor rationalization under Speer's control and represented a genuine qualitative change in the nature of industrial production compared to

89   MBAG Kissel VI/17, DBAG Sales Management to Haspel, 2.10.1940.
90   MBAG Kissel VI/8, Circular Concerning Concentration of Production/Simplification of Finishing and Saving of Material on the Vehicles of the War Programme of the GBK, 8.4.1942.
91   BA (K) R13 IV/12, Decree of the GBK, 25.6.1942.
92   BA (K) R3/517, Statistics on Material Usage, Work Time and Labour Costs, 11.8.1944.
93   BA (K) R3/517, Manager of the Special Committee 4 1/2 and 6-ton Lorries (at DBAG Gaggenau) to Main Committee for Vehicles Production, 12.7.1944.
94   MBAG Kissel VI/8, Circular of the GBK regarding Concentration of Production, 8.4.1942.

the first half of the war must be regarded as limited. In some branches, such as aero-engine production, fundamental reorganization did indeed occur – as the example of Genshagen, discussed below, shows – but here, too, the restructuring of production was as much a response to the peculiar situation of the war economy, and to the need to exploit the available labour, as it was indicative of long-term developments in the organization of production. At least the first sudden increase in aggregate output was owing to measures implemented prior to Speer's appointment, and much of the third short period of rapid growth, from December 1943 to July 1944, was more the result of desperate crisis management and intensification of labour than rational reorganization.[95] Speer's reforms at administrative level – in particular the establishment of the Central Planning board – were probably more important, in that they allowed the more efficient utilization of existing capacity through better allocation of contracts and materials. While internal concentration yielded very substantial results in some instances, reorganization at shop-floor level under Speer was probably modest rather than overwhelming in its significance.

4. 'Total War' and Post-War Planning 1943–5

Developments from the winter of 1943–4 onwards were characterized increasingly by two apparently conflicting tendencies, tendencies that, furthermore, seemingly became more pronounced in direct proportion to one another as the war moved into its final phase. In each case, rational and irrational factors intertwined in managerial responses to a situation over which both industry and the regime had less and less control. On the one hand, industry collaborated in the implementation of successive measures to mobilize the economy for 'total war', participating in (and indeed competing over) the concentration of scarce labour, material and resources in an increasingly desperate final defence of German territory. Under the coordination of the Fighter Staff (Jägerstab) and then the Armaments Staff (Rüstungsstab) of the RMfRuK, this final mobilization saw the output of the German armaments industry peak in July 1944, before it collapsed in the autumn of 1944 as transportation and supply problems, fuel and power shortages, and bottlenecks in actual production caused a rapid decline in German armaments production.[96] The participation of industry was motivated partly by rational profit-seeking in a market that, in the short term, remained highly lucrative, and in a situation in which industry was still dependent on the regime for contracts and materials in order to be able to carry on producing. It was also, however, characterized by a clear element of irrational 'flight forwards' in a paradoxical situation where, from mid-1944

95   Milward, The German Economy at War, p. 100.
96   Ibid., pp. 162–89; Wagenführ, Die Deutsche Industrie im Kriege, pp. 178–81.

onwards, the objective effect of a continuation of production was to maintain the survival of a regime whose policies had long since ceased to be in the interests of industry.

Parallel to this, the period from mid- to late 1943 onwards witnessed a clear tendency towards disengagement from the regime and reorientation towards a peacetime scenario, into which, it later became increasingly clear, the regime itself would be unlikely to survive. Partly in collaboration with elements within the RWM, partly on its own, industry began to prepare for the post-war period.[97] This manifested itself in the attempts of some companies to return to their core areas of peacetime activity, or at least to prepare these for the resumption of peacetime production. It also manifested itself in the willing participation in the regime's attempts to decentralize and disperse industrial capacity, which from industry's point of view ensured the rescue of its capital goods for the post-war period. Like other companies, Daimler-Benz took part in the dispersal programme from 1943 onwards and almost simultaneously began planning for the post-war period, underlining the fact that, for industry, the former was an integral part of the latter.[98] Long after production at its main plants had ceased as a result of bombing, industry continued to produce at the numerous dispersal sites, and went to desperate lengths to continue some form of production after both the military position and war production itself had all but collapsed. This preparation for the post-war period was not a product of ideological rejection, nor did it manifest itself in political opposi-tion of any sort – representatives of industry were conspicuous by their absence from conservative opposition circles throughout the war. It can be characterized better as opportunistic abandonment of a regime in a situation in which the regime was not only no longer acting even partially in the interests of industry, but was instead, by its continued prosecution of the war, destroying the basis for industry's continued existence. Here again, rational self-preservation – in a situation where the self-destructive dynamism of National Socialism had become incompatible with the self-reproductive func-tion of capital – combined with responses to a crisis situation that were totally devoid of any long-term aim or strategy. Paradoxically, again, the rationality of long-term disengagement and reorientation seemed to recede in impor-

---

97 On the preparations of the RWM see Herbst, L., *Der Totale Krieg und die Ordnung der Wirtschaft. Die Kriegswirtschaft im Spannungsfeld von Politik, Ideologie und Propaganda 1939–1945*, Stuttgart, 1982, pp. 348–453; Herbst, L., 'Kontinuität und Diskontinuität in den Deutschen Nachkriegsplanungen 1943–1947' in: *Bulletin des Arbeitskreises 2. Weltkrieg* (1985), pp. 49–69; on the preparations of industry see Herbst, *Der Totale Krieg*, pp. 383–7, pp. 402–9; Schumann, W., 'Nachkriegsplanung der Reichsgruppe Industrie im Herbst 1944' in: *Jahrbuch für Wirtschaftsgeschichte* 3 (1972), pp. 259–95; Schumann, W., 'Die Wirtschaftspolitische Überlebensstrategie des Deutschen Imperialismus in der Endphase des zweiten Weltkrieges' in: *Zeitschrift für Geschichtswissenschaft* 27 (1979), pp. 499–513; Piskol, J., 'Zur Entwicklung der aussenpolitischen Nachkriegskonzeptionen der Deutschen Monopolbourgeoisie 1943 bis 1945' in: *Jahrbuch für Wirtschaftsgeschichte* 2 (1969), pp. 329–45.
98 On the dispersal process see below, Chapter VII.

tance in favour of apparently irrational short-term responses as the end of the
war drew tangibly nearer.

The desperate attempts of industry to maintain production through the
winter of 1944–5 are undoubtedly partially explicable by the fear of reprisals,
by the sense that its fate was tied up in a very concrete way with that of the
soldiers at the front, and by the lack of any sense of an alternative in the given
situation. When one examines the way in which individual companies strug-
gled with each other for control of labour, machinery, materials and dispersal
sites in the final few months of the war, however, one is struck by the extent
to which the attempts to continue production (and to elbow other companies
out) were also motivated by the clear desire to gain a competitive advantage
over other firms for the transitional phase into the post-war period.
Continuing production (or maintaining the illusion of doing so) was also
essential in order to keep capacity intact in the short term, to avoid the conscription of labour and the confiscation of machine-tools for other purposes,
and thus to provide the basis for the transition into the post-war period.
Without wishing to over-state the rationality of managerial responses to the
collapsing war economy, the continued participation in armaments production in the short term and the process of reorientation towards consumer production in the long term were two sides of the same coin and equally
motivated by the fundamental aim of self-preservation. Until such time as a
new market presented itself – and there was no knowing when this would happen – industry was reliant upon the old, and the ability of each individual
company to make the eventual transition to the new was thus at least partly
dependent upon its ability to keep producing for the war as long as it lasted.

The process of conscious disengagement and reorientation was preceded by
a phase in which cautious optimism over the prospects for a successful
conclusion of the war gradually gave way to a more sceptical attitude about
Germany's military position. Ascertaining exactly when this change of
attitude set in is difficult, not least because the nature of the regime and the
supply of information inevitably meant that the position was not discussed
openly and awareness of the position did not spread uniformly. However, the
close contacts which big business had with the various ministries and party
organs, and the obvious conclusions it was able to draw from the development
of the war economy, meant that pessimism undoubtedly spread through
industry much sooner than through most sectors of the population in general.
The indications are that the board of Daimler-Benz was sceptical about the
prospects for a German victory from the winter of 1942–3, i.e. after the battle
of Stalingrad. This scepticism first manifested itself in January 1943 in a
reluctance to over-invest in the aero-engine sector, for fear of exhausting the
company's ability to borrow in the long term purely in order to finance an
expansion that would be of value only in the short term. In response to a
suggestion that the company finance its expanded production programme at
Genshagen through a loan to the parent company, Haspel pointed out that

Daimler-Benz itself had already made substantial investments in the aero-engine sector, whereas the vehicle sector had been treated 'very modestly'. In order to ensure that Daimler-Benz was in a position to borrow to finance the post-war reconversion to vehicle production on a large-scale and profitable basis, he insisted that further loans for the financing of aero-engine production be raised directly by the Genshagen subsidiary.[99]

The fear of over-investing in the military sector for short-term gain at the expense of longer-term interests gradually developed into a more cautious attitude concerning any form of investment. This was undoubtedly partly a product of the gradual increase in Allied bombing, which was, even if it initially caused no real disruption to production, still a clear indicator of the way things were developing. It was reinforced by emergent downward tendencies in the company's turnover from late 1943, which led Haspel to demand general caution with regard to expenditure from this point onwards.[100] In the case of investments in machine-tools, reluctance to invest was reinforced by the fact that the backlog of the machine-tool industry was such that it was unclear whether the war would still be being fought at the point where machinery ordered for military production would be ready for delivery.[101] Ordering machine-tools for armaments production thus had little point, while the company had more than enough capacity to cope with the inevitably much smaller volume of post-war production.

The clearest indication of the way the war was developing was, of course, the growing intensity of Allied bombing. Sporadic damage in 1943 was followed by recurring raids in the first half of 1944, which both severely disrupted production and caused substantial damage to factory buildings. Finally, in September and October 1944, a huge wave of bombing brought production at nearly all Daimler-Benz's plants to a virtual standstill and all but destroyed many factory buildings. Haspel was already aware of the hopelessness of Germany's military situation and the implications for Daimler-Benz.[102] In the summer of 1944, however, the collapse of the eastern front, the intensification of Allied bombing, and the launching of the second front caused a further shift in his expectations of the length of the war and a further reorientation in his thinking towards the post-war period. In August 1944, by which point air-raid damage to Daimler-Benz's plants was already considerable, Haspel ordered a virtual stop to all investment.[103]

99   BA (P) 80 Ba2 P3244, Haspel to Rummel, 29.1.1943.
100 MBAG Minutes of the Board Meetings of DBAG 1943–1945, Minutes of the Board Meeting of DBAG on 14 and 15.9.1943.
101 MBAG Haspel/'Arbeitskreis Lastwagen', Meeting on Lorry Production, 31.5.1944.
102 Thus, in the discussion on lorry production in May 1944, he stated that the situation was 'much worse than many in the company seem to grasp' and that he did not intend 'to sit and calmly watch as the situation drifts towards catastrophe' (MBAG Haspel/'Arbeitskreis Lastwagen', Meeting on Lorry Production on 31.5.1944).
103 MBAG Minutes of the Board Meetings of DBAG 1943–1945, Minutes of the Board Meeting of DBAG on 18.8.1944.

From this point onwards, Daimler-Benz followed a strategy of keeping substantial amounts of its capital liquid, avoiding expenditure other than on the removal of air-raid damage, limited rebuilding, and that incurred as a result of the dispersal of its factories. This reflected a trend visible in German industry in general in the summer of 1944.[104] In view of the clear inflationary pressures in the German economy in the final phase of the war, it is in some respects surprising that a flight into capital goods or similar policy aimed at hedging against inflation did not manifest itself in the company's attempts to manoeuvre into the post-war period. For the period up to the autumn of 1944 this is perhaps explicable by the expectation that a functioning economy and perhaps the regime itself would survive the war intact and on the basis of a negotiated peace, so that inflationary pressure might be brought under control. However, even in March 1945, when it was clear that defeat would be total and surrender unconditional, and by which point the economy had practically collapsed, Haspel still refused to countenance 'blind purchases' (*Luftkäufe*) of machine-tools, and insisted that machinery should be purchased only if it were directly usable for future production.[105] Even at Gaggenau, where preparations were under-way for a resumption of peacetime production, the management was busy annulling orders for machine-tools immediately prior to the end of the war.

This was probably motivated by the awareness that the company's existing machine-tool inventory would be adequate for the needs of the immediate post-war period, so that purchasing additional machine-tools was of secondary importance compared to the need to rebuild bombed-out factory buildings. While the relative stability of machine-tool technology meant that any excess capacity could still be utilized productively in the mid-term, when Germany's foreign currency position would still be such that additional imports of equipment would be impossible and new machine-tools correspondingly scarce, it seems that the company saw the retention of liquid reserves for the immediate task of rebuilding as more important than avoiding the risk of inflation.

The formulation of a strategy for guiding the company through the final phase of the war was combined with the development of plans for the post-war period itself. This itself was naturally based on expectations of what Germany's political and economic position would be at the end of the war, what forms of regulation would be retained in the transitional phase, and on prognoses for the development of the economy in the post-war period. In order to evaluate the significance of developments in the war, their impact on the German economy and the likely growth of the post-war economy, Haspel received regular confidential reports from Felix Lauscher, a figure associated

104   Herbst, *Der Totale Krieg*, p. 406.
105   MBAG Minutes of the Board Meetings of DBAG 1943–1945, Minutes of the Board Meeting of
       DBAG on 20.3.1945.

with the WiGruFa who throughout the war furnished the company with assessments of the diplomatic, military and economic situation.[106] These were based on extensive contacts with high-ranking military figures, figures in the RWM and Foreign Office and with private banking and industrial circles; taken together, they form a clear picture of 'Berlin' opinion in the last third of the war.

Lauscher had initially been employed by the Reich Association of Automobile Producers (*Reichsverband der Deutschen Automobilindustrie* – RDA) and the WiGruFa as a press and news agent, but his contract was terminated in 1941 after complaints from the RWM that the information he was circulating was confidential.[107] The company continued to procure his reports on a private basis, however, and they became one of Haspel's main sources for evaluating developments in the closing stages of the war. Although Lauscher was not a Daimler-Benz employee and his views were not necessarily synonymous with those of the board, the fact that Haspel went on receiving the reports in secret suggests that he placed considerable weight on Lauscher's views, and as such they provide an interesting insight into industry's changing expectations from 1943 onwards.

In their analysis of both military and diplomatic affairs, Lauscher's reports are characterized by a substantial amount of uncertainty. With regard to military events in particular, they fluctuate greatly between periods of optimism and pessimism, although the underlying trend is one of an increasingly dominant pessimism. From the summer of 1944 onwards, the reports reflect a growing expectation of an imminent end to the war, but the view that growing divisions among the Allies would allow a negotiated peace permitting the retention of German sovereignty and the survival of the regime persists into the late autumn of 1944, and it is not until December 1944 that hopes of a negotiated peace with the Soviet Union are abandoned.

Of greatest interest for the post-war planning of Daimler-Benz is Lauscher's prognosis for the development of the vehicle market and the prospects for the German automobile industry after the war. This is even more so the case in view of the fact that Daimler-Benz clearly pursued a strategy closely based on the assumptions and opinions contained in the reports. Lauscher argued that the limited consumer demand of the immediate post-war period would be directed towards satisfying everyday needs and the replacement of essential items lost, destroyed, or simply unreplaced during the war. The car industry would experience only limited demand for at least five years, and in a highly regulated economy Lauscher argued that priority would be given to the Volkswagen plant by the post-war government, and that any demand for cars

---

106 See the extensive collection of Lauscher's reports in MBAG Haspel 7,74.
107 MBAG Kissel/Economic Group Vehicles Production, Circulars and Communiqués 1936–1942, Minutes of the Advisory Board of the Economic Group Vehicles Production, 8.7.1941.

would be met therefore by Volkswagen.[108] By contrast, he provided a far more positive prognosis for lorry production in the immediate post-war period. The need to rebuild German cities meant that it could be predicted with virtual certainty, even in 1943, that 'the building industry will be the key industry in the post-war economy.'[109] For this reason, Lauscher predicted that the production of lorries would be directly relevant to any reconstruction programme and would thus be assured an important role.[110]

That Daimler-Benz would be reliant upon lorry production in the immediate post-war phase was confirmed by the very fact that its lorry production lines were the only peacetime lines that were still largely intact in 1944. The importance of this area was underlined by Haspel in the board meeting of 15–16 April 1944, in which he argued that 'if the conclusion of the war follows the usual pattern, the company will be dependent upon income from lorry production for at least half a year, as car production will probably not get going for half or three-quarters of a year.'[111] From the spring of 1944, lorry production assumed the key role in Daimler-Benz's post-war planning, and all decisions taken in the sphere of lorry production were based upon considerations of the post-war period. The internal forum for this was the company's 'working group on lorry production' (*Arbeitskreis Lastwagen* – AKL), which had been set up in February 1943 to coordinate research, development and production in the lorry plants, and to resolve problems related to the re-tooling of the Mannheim plant for the production of the Opel 3-ton lorry.[112]

At a meeting in March 1944, when the AKL became the forum for the post-war planning of the company, Haspel surveyed the state of Daimler-Benz's vehicle production with a view to assessing the company's position in this sector for the post-war period. Untertürkheim and Sindelfingen, the main car-producing plants, had completely ceased car production. Untertürkheim's production lines had not only been dismantled completely, but as yet it was also 'completely unclear what and how we will produce there', while at Sindelfingen 'virtually nothing' remained of its former production lines. The Berlin plants were even less in a position to make the transition into the post-war period. Gaggenau and Mannheim, on the other hand, were in a position to continue straight into the post-war period with the production lines they already had. Haspel therefore demanded that 'both works must prepare themselves to produce a cheap, competitive vehicle in peacetime.' This aim

108   MBAG Haspel 7,74, Lauscher to Haspel, 14.3.1944/Lauscher to Doerschlag (Off-Print), 14.4.1944; Lauscher to Haspel, 9.5.1944.
109   MBAG Haspel 7,74, Lauscher to Haspel, 17.11.1943.
110   MBAG Haspel 7,74, Lauscher to Haspel, 14.3.1944/Lauscher to Doerschlag (Off-Print), 13.3.1944.
111   MBAG Minutes of the Board Meetings of DBAG 1943–1945, Minutes of the Board Meetings of DBAG on 15 and 16.4.1944.
112   MBAG Minutes of the Board Meetings of DBAG 1943–1945, Minutes of the Board Meetings of DBAG on 16 and 17.2.1943.

had to be reached 'at all costs', because 'lorry production is the activity with which Daimler-Benz will be left after the war.'[113]

The preparation of the lorry production lines manifested itself in various ways. As the end of the war drew perceptibly closer, Haspel intensified his efforts to get the 3-ton Opel line functioning at Mannheim in order to have it ready for the transitional phase.[114] To secure this objective, machine-tools were transferred from Untertürkheim to Mannheim, and, after the collapse of tank production at Marienfelde, machinery was also transferred to Mannheim from Marienfelde.[115] As well as pushing through the immediate re-tooling of Mannheim for the Opel model, Haspel initiated plans for the eventual re-tooling of the plant for Daimler-Benz's own model.[116] In addition, he instituted an extensive rationalization programme at Gaggenau and Mannheim, based on a comparison of their respective production methods, the most efficient of which in each area then being adopted at the other plant.[117]

While Mannheim had relatively efficient production methods as a result of the investments of the late 1930s and of the re-tooling for the Opel model, the Gaggenau plant was in a far less positive position. In comparison to Mannheim, however, which in early 1944 was still re-tooling, Gaggenau had a fully operational production line which, furthermore, was engaged in manufacturing one of Daimler-Benz's own models. As such, it was the key plant, of the two, for the transitional phase.[118] However, Haspel concluded as a result of the study that 'incredibly little' had been done during the war to rationalize production at Gaggenau.[119] In the summer of 1944, extensive plans for a modernization of its capacity were therefore formulated and the post-war conversion prepared. Although it was impossible to procure the necessary 550 machine-tools during the war itself, Haspel demanded of the Gaggenau management that lorry production costs be reduced by 20–25 per cent and plans for an expansion of capacity to 1000 lorries per month be made.[120] The intensified rationalization measures of 1944, in this sector at least, were thus the result less of the regime's mobilization of the resources of the Reich in the pur-

---

113   MBAG Haspel/'Arbeitskreis Lastwagen', Minutes of the Discussion on Lorry Production, 9.3.1944.
114   See below Chapter V.2.b.
115   MBAG Haspel/'Arbeitskreis Lastwagen', Minutes of the Meeting on Lorry Production on 31.5.1944; Memorandum of the Discussion on Lorry Production on 2.10.1944. The latter case is interesting in that it reflects at once the attempt to activate consumer-orientated production lines rather than reactivate bomb-damaged military production, the insistence upon retaining control of machinery rather than see it transferred to another company (in this case Krupp) and the clear tendency to transfer machine-tools from east to west as the Soviet troops advanced.
116   MBAG Haspel/'Arbeitskreis Lastwagen', Meeting on Lorry Production, 10.7.1944.
117   MBAG DBAG 21, Comparison of Materials and Wages Costs: Mannheim and Gaggenau Production, 5.2.1944.
118   MBAG Minutes of the Board Meetings of DBAG 1943–1945, Minutes of the Board Meetings of DBAG on 15 and 16.4.1944.
119   MBAG Minutes of the Board Meetings of DBAG 1943–1945, Minutes of the Board Meetings of DBAG on 18.8.1944.
120   MBAG Minutes of the Board Meetings of DBAG 1943–1945, Minutes of the Board Meetings of DBAG on 15 and 16.4.1944; MBAG DBAG 22, Memorandum Gaggenau, 12.4.1944.

suit of 'total war' than of private company preparation for a highly competitive peacetime market whose return was imminent.

Throughout the war, the strategy of the company was conditioned, first, by a
recognition that the changing pressures of the war would of necessity cause
substantial and regular changes in the demands made of the company by the
regime, and, second by a defensive caution born of the fear of embarking upon
short-term projects that might jeopardize the long-term prospects of the company. Defence of these long-term interests had to be balanced against the need
to profit from a war that provided the company with its only market – a market that, exploited skilfully, was a highly profitable one. Throughout the war,
attitudes to investment, the takeover of additional plants and the reorganization of capacity internally were conditioned both by the demands of wartime
competition between manufacturers and pressure from the regime on the one
hand, and criteria of post-war considerations on the other. Initial caution following the outbreak of war gave way to a renewed wave of expansion in the
summer of 1940, as pressure from above combined with recognition of the
potentially lucrative rewards of expansion, led the board to increase investment radically after the fall of France. In the case of aero-engine production,
this investment, along with the implementation of industry-wide measures
from 1941 onwards, formed the basis for the huge expansion of output from
1942. In the short term, the inefficiency of the regime's apparatus compounded the effects of the company's unwillingness to let go of its strategically
vital consumer-orientated production lines, and led to consistently poor levels
of output in the first half of the war, notably in lorry production.

In addition to facilitating further the increases in output in the company's
aero-engine sector, Speer's reforms brought about positive results in other
areas of the company's activity in the second half of the war, during which
period an increasing element of 'flight forwards' characterized the company's
participation in measures to increase armaments output. Nonetheless, as the
case of the 3-ton licence project at Mannheim shows, the Speer period also
had its share of costly failures. Attempts to raise output in the final third of the
war were made increasingly difficult by the impact of Allied bombing, which
not only had a disruptive impact in terms of immediate production, but also
caused a marked shift in the attitude of the company towards the war. This
manifested itself in a gradual reorientation of the company towards a strategy
focused on peacetime, as evidenced by the extensive post-war planning
activities of the company. It also appeared in a growing reluctance to commit
capital to armaments production. Specific areas of production (above all aero-
engine production) notwithstanding, investment in plant probably peaked in
1941. In the final third of the war in particular, the company opted
increasingly for a substitution of labour for capital, which enabled it to
maintain high levels of armaments output while gradually manoeuvring itself
into position for the resumption of peacetime production.

V. Chaos and Improvization: Armaments Production during the War

1. Arming the Luftwaffe: Daimler-Benz Motoren GmbH Genshagen 1939–45

a) Mobilization and Stagnation 1939–41

The board of Daimler-Benz was aware from the beginning that for the duration of the war – whether it was long or short – increased demand for military goods on the one hand, and restrictions on non-military production on the other, would see a further growth in the importance of the Berlin plants. It was keen to raise production at Genshagen from the outset, aware that the increased demand for aeroplanes would necessarily translate into increased demand for aero-engines, and that it must therefore augment output or accept that engines from other manufacturers would be built into planes that had previously relied solely on Daimler-Benz engines. This the company wished to avoid at all cost.[1] On the other hand, it was wary of the risks of expanding capacity and undertaking new investment – for the reasons already stated – as it feared that Genshagen would not be fully utilized after the war even at its existing size.[2]

In order to augment output without expanding capacity, the management of Genshagen immediately opted for an increase in working hours. In October 1939, the ten-hour day was introduced for all workers.[3] In addition, and in order to compensate for falls in productivity owing to the influx of inexperienced new conscripted labour, night shifts and Sunday shifts were brought in.[4] A substantial number of skilled workers had been called up, to work at RLM repair facilities at the front, while their replacements were, in the majority of cases, semi- or unskilled workers who needed training and time

---

1 MBAG Forstmeier 14, Minutes of the Meeting in Untertürkheim concerning the Production of Aero-Engines, 28.12.1939.
2 MBAG Kissel I/12, Minutes of the Board Meeting of DBAG on 12.10.1939.
3 BA (P) 80 Ba2 P3322, Management of Daimler-Benz Motoren GmbH Genshagen to the Board, 18.10.1939.
4 BA (P) 80 Ba2 P3322, Management of Daimler-Benz Motoren GmbH Genshagen to the Board, 14.9.1939.

to familiarize themselves with their new tasks. All the same, this extension of working hours enabled the management not only to avoid a fall in output, but to increase monthly production from 202 single engines in September 1939 to 220 in December 1939.[5]

By December 1939, however, the company board believed that the lack of labour in Berlin was such that the limits of such a strategy had already been reached and that production could not be increased further in this way.[6] In order to overcome this, and in order to retain within the firm labour that was otherwise liable to be called up to the Wehrmacht, it initiated a substantial transfer of skilled workers from its south German plants to the Berlin plants, which took place on a more or less continuous basis in the first half of 1940.[7] In addition, as car production at Untertürkheim was gradually cut back to the levels decreed by the 'War Programme', some of Untertürkheim's capacity was converted to the production of aero-engine parts for Genshagen. By this process of transfer and conversion, the Daimler-Benz board expected to be able to raise output at Genshagen to 375 engines per month without any new investment beyond that already under-way, so that it could be seen to be responding to the demands of war without undermining its central aim of avoiding any expansion that was inappropriate from the company's private viewpoint.[8]

In fact, despite the inevitable disruptions caused by the outbreak of war, the Genshagen plant was able in this way to increase its production of aero-engines month on month for the first eight months of the conflict, reaching 290 in May 1940.[9] With the exception of July 1940, however, when an exceptional short-term intensification of production was achieved in order to supply Luftwaffe demand during the Battle of Britain, this level was not reached again until May 1941. From mid-1940 to mid-1941, monthly production at Genshagen fluctuated greatly, but overall levels of output remained static.

Following the defeat of France, the plant's position was changed in two ways. First, it was repurchased by the company from the RLM, which until this point had remained the majority shareholder. The Daimler-Benz board had originally planned to try to delay the repurchase (which had always been the eventual goal) until after the war, believing that the lower level of production

5   BA (P) 80 Ba2 P3322, General Reports (September, December 1939)
6   MBAG Kissel I/12, Minutes of the Board Meeting of DBAG on 13.12.1939.
7   An initial 250 skilled workers were transferred from Gaggenau to Genshagen in December 1939. By July 1940, 324 skilled workers from Gaggenau and 230 from Untertürkheim had been transferred to Genshagen and to Marienfelde. MBAG Kissel/War Plants Genshagen, Kissel to K. C. Müller, 27.6.1940; Kissel to Daimler-Benz Motoren GmbH Genshagen, 18.7.1940. In addition, workers were transferred from Sindelfingen (MBAG Kissel XIII/4, Hoppe to DBAG Sindelfingen, 4.4.1940).
8   MBAG Forstmeier 14, Minutes of the Meeting in Untertürkheim concerning the Production of Aero-Engines, 28.12.1939.
9   BA (P) 80 Ba2 P3322, General Report (May 1940).

at that time would ensure a lower price.[10] However, the RLM wished to sell the plant sooner, and in order to make sure that it was not sold to a competitor, the board elected to agree to the repurchase in September 1940 – paying RM 23 million, for a plant whose actual value K. C. Müller estimated at RM 80 million.[11]

Second, as part of the planned diversion of resources to production for the Luftwaffe in 1941, the RLM demanded a huge increase in output from Genshagen which could only be achieved by the substantial expansion of capacity that the Daimler-Benz board had hitherto avoided. In July 1940, the Quartermaster General for the Luftwaffe, Ernst Udet, demanded that Daimler-Benz formulate two projects for the expansion of Genshagen from its current capacity (275–300 engines per month) to a capacity of 750 and 1000 engines per month respectively.[12] By August, this had evolved into an initial project for a capacity of 800 engines, together with a project for a possible further expansion to allow the production of up to 1800 Daimler-Benz engines per month.[13]

Given that at this point – immediately following the defeat of France – the board was framing its strategy on the assumption that a return to peacetime conditions was likely, the demands of the RLM created a dilemma. While an expansion of capacity to 800 engines per month might represent a lucrative opportunity in the event of a longer war and might not necessarily prove excessive in the event of a return to peacetime conditions in the context of the envisaged 'New Order', the prospect of expansion to 1800 engines per month presented the obvious threat of chronic over-capacity. This was especially so since such an expansion would, under current conditions, take three or four years, and would be completed under conditions possibly completely different from those of the moment. Kissel was aware, however, of the dangers of non-compliance, especially as the company was in the process of negotiating the repurchase of Genshagen at this point. If it refused to expand, it was conceivable that the plant would be sold to a competitor, and, as Kissel recognized, if the company did not ensure that it repurchased Genshagen itself its position in the lucrative aero-engine sector would be very difficult to sustain.

Kissel argued that 'from the national standpoint' Genshagen must therefore be expanded, but insisted that in order to avoid creating excess capacity for the long term the expansion should be carried out in such a way as to ensure

10   MBAG Kissel I/12, Minutes of the Board Meeting of DBAG on 12.10.1939.
11   MBAG Kissel I/13, Minutes of the Board Meeting of DBAG on 13 and 14.10.1940. The RLM members thereupon left the board of the Genshagen company, and were replaced by Daimler-Benz/Deutsche Bank personnel. In December 1940 the board contained Stauss (Deutsche Bank), Rummel (Deutsche Bank), Kissel, Haspel, Hentig and Nallinger (all Daimler-Benz board members). (BA [P] 80 Ba2 P3317, Wörner to Rauchfuss, 30.12.1940.)
12   BA (P) 80 Ba2 P3316, Memorandum/Stauss, 24.7.1940.
13   MBAG Kissel I/13, Minutes of the Board Meeting of DBAG on 16.8.1940.

that the plant could revert to producing 300 engines per month while remaining profitable. The initial programme, labelled '15940', envisaged an expansion of capacity to 800 engines per month in accordance with the RLM's wishes – i.e. practically a trebling of capacity.[14] When completed the plant would require an additional 9000 workers (compared to a current workforce of approximately 8500 workers), and almost 1000 additional machine-tools, with the total cost of the project planned as RM 50 million.[15]

While the initial work for this expansion was being carried out, however, the '15940' project was superseded by another, even larger project. In June 1941, immediately prior to the invasion of the Soviet Union, Göring demanded that production for all sectors of the Luftwaffe be increased four-fold.[16] The 'Elch' programme and the subsequent 'Hermann Göring' programme, formulated in accordance with this decree by the RLM in the summer of 1941, envisaged an expansion of output at Genshagen from its current level of 300–50 to a massive 1200 engines per month.[17] In response to this, and undoubtedly on the basis of considerations similar to those that gave rise to the '15940' project, a new investment programme was formulated, proposing in addition to the RM 50m of the initial project a further huge investment of RM 120m. Over the following two to three years, the massive expansion envisaged in these successive projects was carried out, forming the basis for the substantial increases in output that occurred in the second half of the war.[18]

The long-term process of expansion of the plant took place against the immediate background of stagnating military production, which was, given the impending launch of Operation 'Barbarossa', reaching crisis proportions by the spring of 1941. Since the summer of 1940, successive efforts to mobilize additional capacity and use existing capacity more effectively had failed. Attempts to set clear priorities and switch resources between different branches of military production had foundered on bureaucratic inefficiency, conflicts between state, party and military authorities, and the tendency of each branch of the armed forces to pursue its interests in competition with, rather than in cooperation with, the other two.[19] The effect of this lack of coordination was that overall military output was the same in 1941 as in 1940.[20] This stagnation was particularly noticeable in production figures for the Luftwaffe – aircraft output

14 MBAG Forstmeier 14, Daimler-Benz Motoren GmbH Genshagen to RLM, 15.9.1940.
15 MBAG Kissel I/13, Minutes of the Board Meetings of DBAG on 13 and 14.10.1940.
16 MBAG Forstmeier 14, Announcement of the Reichsmarshall of the Greater German Reich (June 1941).
17 BA (P) 80 Ba2 P3319, Minutes of the Board Meeting of Daimler-Benz Motoren GmbH Genshagen on 20.11.1941.
18 Eventually, a somewhat smaller total of RM 98m was invested from 1940–4, on top of the RM 48m invested in the plant up until 1939 (MBAG Forstmeier 14, Daimler-Benz Motoren GmbH Genshagen, Overview of Investments, 27.6.1945).
19 Müller, 'Mobilisierung', pp. 532–40, p. 557.
20 Ibid., p. 523.

rose by 30 per cent from 1939 to 1941, but the resources allocated to the sector rose by 100 per cent in the same period, a broad reflection of the inefficiency
and wastefulness that characterized both the overall administration of production and organization at shop-floor level.[21]

This global stagnation was apparent, although not as starkly as in the sector
as a whole, in the experience of the Genshagen plant during the first two years
of the war. After the summer of 1940, all attempts to expand production
beyond the 290 engines achieved in May of that year failed owing to the
inability of subcontractors to keep pace with the increased demands for many
major components. First, whenever the management tried to do so, shortages
of casings, cylinders or other large items immediately emerged.[22] Second, as a
result of the offensives in the west in the first half of 1940, greatly increased
demand for spare parts meant that components intended for the regular serial
production engines had to be taken from those supplied for serial output,
reducing the number of engines that could be completed.[23] Effectively,
bottlenecks in the production of components meant that production at
Genshagen could not rise above a ceiling of 300 engines for any length of
time. In fact, in the second half of 1940, production levels actually dropped
virtually month after month for six months, falling back to 219 engines in
December 1940. Continued shortages of material, late deliveries of
components and increased demands for spare parts combined to ensure that
output at the end of 1940 was thus the same as at the end of 1939, despite the
fact that over 1000 more workers were employed at the plant.[24]

In 1941, in addition to these shortages, the worsening supply of labour itself
increasingly became a barrier to the further expansion of production. The
Genshagen management permanently pressured the RLM for extra labour as a
prerequisite for increased output, demanding in February 1941 an extra 1000
workers – the majority of whom would have to be skilled – and stating that it
would be impossible to increase production above 300 engines per month without them. With the extra 1000 workers, the company promised it could produce
up to 350 or, with an extra 750 workers on top of that, 400 engines per month.[25]

---

21 Overy, R. J., *Goering. The Iron Man*, London, 1984, p. 148.
22 MBAG Kissel/Correspondence with RLM 1939–, Memorandum of the Discussion in
    Wernigrode, 17 and 18.5.1940.
23 BA (P) 80 Ba2 P3322, Management of Daimler-Benz Motoren GmbH Genshagen to the Board,
    23.5.1940.
24 The inadequate and irregular supply of components continued through 1941 and is reflected in
    the huge fluctuations in monthly output in the first half of the year (January 251 engines, February
    287, March 257, April 224, May 307, June 287). This was caused by the fact that large numbers
    of basically complete engines had to sit at Genshagen often for weeks on end, waiting for the
    delivery of one or two parts. (BA [P] 80 Ba2 P3322, Management of Daimler-Benz Motoren
    GmbH Genshagen to the Board, 20.12.1940; Management of Daimler-Benz Motoren GmbH
    Genshagen to the Board, 22.2.1941; *Geschäftsbericht der Daimler-Benz Motoren GmbH Genshagen*
    1940.)
25 MBAG Kissel/War Plants Genshagen 1941, Memorandum regarding Discussion with Chief
    Engineer Tserschisch, 25.2.1941.

The continuing need for a high level of skilled labour was partly a product of the fact that Genshagen underwent a complete re-tooling in the first half of 1941, which was also a contributory factor in ensuring that output remained roughly at the same level as in the previous year. From January to March 1941, the plant re-tooled for production of a substantially modified DB 601 model, which was produced for the next twelve months. It then immediately began re-tooling for production of a completely new model, the DB 605, which began production in May 1941. This was produced alongside the DB 601 until March 1942, when it became the main serial engine to be manufactured at Genshagen. Despite repeated moves to introduce its successor model, the DB 603, the DB 605 remained the main serial engine produced at Genshagen until the end of the war. While full-scale production levels were being reached for the new models, the plant was reliant upon a high level of skilled labour; at the point where a relatively stable volume of production was established, a greater deployment of semi-skilled labour became possible.

The continuous demands for skilled labour are also, however, a reflection of the limited extent to which the plant made any attempt to raise output by utilizing flow production methods, favouring instead the retention of production processes demanding a high proportion of skilled labour. The tendency to rely upon increased labour supply rather than rationalize production methods is shown in the development of the structure of the workforce from 1939 to 1941 and is seen most clearly when these increases are compared to production level increases in the same period. Output at Genshagen rose from approximately 200 engines per month at the outbreak of war to an average 300 per month during 1941 i.e. by approximately 50 per cent. However, the blue-collar workforce rose from 5681 in December 1939 to 8180 in December 1941, an increase of 44 per cent.[26] Thus, although compared with the sector as a whole labour productivity remained relatively constant, increases in output were only keeping broad pace with those in the workforce. Moreover, the skills structure of the workforce was practically constant from 1939 to 1941. It is impossible to give an exact breakdown of the workforce in terms of skilled, semi-skilled and unskilled status, as statistics on skills differentation are only available for the male workforce. However, given that no women were deployed as skilled workers, it is still possible to give precise figures for the overall proportion of skilled workers in the workforce during the period. Since the great majority of the workforce in the period 1939–41 were men (89 per cent of the blue-collar workforce in December 1941), the broad skills structure of the workforce as a whole can be therefore also be established from the statistics on the male workforce. It should be borne in mind, however, that women tended to be proportionately more represented in the unskilled than

---

26 These and the following figures are from MBAG Forstmeier 16, Workforce, Wages, Turnover, Production 1937–1942.

in the semi-skilled bracket compared to men, and that figures on the semi- and unskilled male workforce therefore tend to overstate the proportion of semi-skilled to unskilled workers in the workforce as a whole.

In December 1939, of a total male workforce of 4744 workers, 2630 (55.5 per cent) were skilled workers, 1332 (28 per cent) were semi-skilled and 782 (16.5 per cent) were unskilled. The production of aero-engines was the preserve of skilled workers, with the minority of unskilled workers being used primarily in storage, loading or transportation work. By December 1940, out of a total of 5790 male workers, 3082 (53 per cent) were skilled, 1735 (30 per cent) were semi-skilled and 973 (17 per cent) were unskilled. Despite a slight increase in the proportion of semi-skilled workers, there was therefore effectively no change in the first year of the war. By the end of 1941, the total male workforce had increased to 7197. Despite the shortage of skilled workers in the economy, the number of skilled workers at Genshagen had increased to 3563 (49.5 per cent), the number of semi-skilled workers to 2118 (29.5 per cent) and the number of unskilled to 1516 (21 per cent). This increase in unskilled workers in both real and percentage terms was undoubtedly owing to the prisoners of war and foreigners who began to account for a substantial proportion of the Genshagen workforce in 1941. However, the key feature of the statistics is that they show a constantly high level of skilled workers at the plant from 1939 to 1941. If women are included in the calculations, the proportion of skilled workers among the Genshagen employees was 46 per cent in 1939, still 46 per cent in 1940 and 44 per cent in December 1941.

b) The Industrial Council and the Ring System

Underlying all this was the company's desire not to undertake any large-scale reorganization that would jeopardize the transition to peacetime conditions, reflecting the reluctance within the industry as a whole to effect a rationalization that would reduce individual companies' capacity to manufacture whole engines independently after the war. By 1941, however, the policy of expanding the workforce instead was reaching its limits. In February 1941, K. C. Müller grumbled that in place of the skilled workers demanded by the company it was receiving workers who were 'anything but fully usable.'[27] In June 1941, the company complained of the complete impossibility of getting the necessary labour and lamented the failure of all its attempts to get either additional German or foreign skilled workers.[28] By the summer of 1941, the difficulty of further increasing output was, according to Kissel, primarily a question of labour, with shortages of components responsible only for bottlenecks of limited duration.[29]

27 MBAG Kissel/War Plants Genshagen 1941, Memorandum regarding Discussion with Chief Engineer Tserschisch, 25.2.1941.
28 MBAG Kissel/Correspondence with WiGruLFZ, Daimler-Benz Motoren GmbH Genshagen to WiGruLFZ, 16.6.1941.
29 MBAG Kissel/War Plants Genshagen 1941, Kissel to Daimler-Benz Motoren GmbH Genshagen, 19.6.1941.

By mid-1941, the RLM and the German aircraft industry as a whole were in a position where it was impossible to rely on ever-increasing supplies of high-quality labour by continuously conscripting skilled workers from the wider economy as the manufacturers demanded. The system of production which pandered to company egoism by allowing the production of complete engines or fuselages in several places in moderate volume – as the manufacturers themselves preferred to do – using production processes that relied on a high proportion of skilled workers could no longer be continued. Shortages of labour had to be overcome by an industry-wide rationalization of production which would allow greater output by more effective utilization of the available workforce and greater deployment of unskilled and semi-skilled workers.[30]

The crisis of production in the aircraft industry led Göring to appoint an Industrial Council (*Industrierat*) in May 1941 to tackle the problem. Under the overall chairmanship of Udet (until his suicide in November 1941), the Auto-Union and Junkers director Werner chaired a committee of leading industrialists, each of whom was responsible for coordinating one area of production. In addition to Werner himself, who was responsible for overall production, the council comprised the head of the Economic Group for Engineering, Lange (responsible for machine-tools), Koppenberg of Junkers (raw materials and semi-finished goods), Frydag of Henschel (aircraft frames), Egger of Büssing-NAG (coordination with other Economic Groups) and another figure from the automobile industry, Bruhn, who was responsible for questions of organization.[31] The strong representation of the automobile industry on the council was itself a reflection not only of the fact that many automobile manufacturers were by now involved in aircraft production, but also of the desire to utilize the experience of the automobile industry in the introduction of flow production methods. The imperative to follow this policy was reinforced by the proclamation at this time of the 'Hermann Göring' programme, with its demands for a quadrupling of production.

This initial step towards transferring responsibility for production to the industrialists was soon followed by the introduction of a new organizational system which was of far greater significance than the Industrial Council itself and which the latter formulated in cooperation with the State Secretary at the RLM, Milch. Three months after the formation of the Industrial Council, Udet ordered the formation of production 'Rings' for each main item of production.[32] This system, which was essentially the same as Todt's reorganization of Munitions and Tank production under civilian control within the RMfBuM, demanded the coordination of firms with the same or

---

30   On the position of the aircraft industry in general in 1941 see Overy, *Goering*, pp. 183–9.
31   MBAG Kissel/Correspondence with WiGruLFZ, WiGruLFZ to Member Firms, 31.5.1941. On the formation of the Industrial Council see Overy, *Goering*, p. 149; Müller, 'Mobilisierung', p. 561.
32   BA (P) 80 Ba2 P3315, Udet to Daimler-Benz Motoren GmbH Genshagen, 15.8.1941.

Bodywork production at Sindelfingen, 1928 (*top*) and 1938

Motor assembly
line at Mannheim,
c. 1940

Aero-engine production at Genshagen, c. 1940

Finished tanks, Marienfelde, *c.* 1940

Day of national labour, Mannheim, May 1940

Morning roll call of apprentices, Mannheim, *c.* 1940

Training of female workers, *c.* 1940

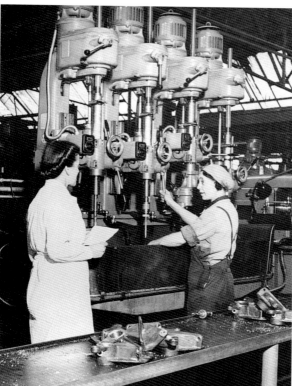

Factory social worker and female machine operator, Mannheim, *c.* 1940

Propaganda image of Polish forced workers under the supervision of a German foreman, Rzeszow, 1943–44

Barracks for Polish forced workers, Rzeszow, 1943–44

Factory security,
Rzeszow, 1943–44

Destroyed
administration
buildings at
Untertürkheim
following the air raid
of 5 September 1944

Untertürkheim following the air raid of 5 September 1944 (*top*) and after rebuilding, 1949

related production into Rings under the leadership of the main firm in that
field, which was to supply two managers as head and deputy head of the Ring.
These figures were responsible for coordinating production at all the plants
within the Ring and for ensuring that each plant produced according to an
overall plan. This was to overcome the inefficiency and lack of coordination
caused by the previous system, whereby firms produced under their own
management and according to their own plans. By coordinating the greatest
possible rationalization within and between firms, by reallocating components
production for the whole Ring to fewer firms, rather than each producing its
own parts or subcontracting on an individual basis, by coordinating the
distribution of materials and components in response to specific bottlenecks,
and by fully utilizing the potential of a second shift, substantial increases in
output were to be achieved using just the existing labour.

As part of this system, all firms producing Daimler-Benz aero-engines were
coordinated into the Daimler-Benz Ring, which was set up under the control
of Daimler-Benz itself and managed by K.C. Müller and Wilhelm Künkele,
the technical director of Genshagen. The Ring, which was to rationalize
production of the DB 601, the DB 605 and the DB 603 aero-engines, initially
included, in addition to the Genshagen, Untertürkheim and Marienfelde
(Plant 90) plants, Büssing-NAG, Henschel, Pomo (Stettin), Steyr-Daimler-
Puch, Manfred Weiss (Budapest) and Fiat (Turin), all of whom produced
these engines under licence.[33] The implications of the formation of the Ring
system and the new line to be pursued were discussed by the Daimler-Benz
board on 23 October 1941.[34] While recognizing the necessity of rationalization and its potential benefits, the board rejected the idea of reallocating
production on the scale demanded by Werner, who the previous day had told
Milch and General Thomas that 75 per cent of the aircraft industry was using
'pre-Flood' production methods, and who was clearly the most vociferous
advocate of a huge reorganization of the industry.[35] K.C. Müller argued that
Werner's proposed reallocation of contracts and redistribution of productive
capacity would cause disruptions for half a year in the case of the major
components and therefore considered it 'out of the question' that such a policy
be pursued.[36] Kissel was also opposed to such a large-scale restructuring, on the
basis that it would make an eventual reversion to the existing set-up
impossible, apparently subscribing to the same view as other industrialists who
saw the issue as one of ensuring that a short-term measure aimed at raising

33 Despite the transfer of the Daimler-Benz Ring to the control of the RMfBuM in early 1942, where
it became the Special Committee T2 within the Main Committee for Engine Production, as part
of the overall centralization of control of armaments production under civilian administration
that was occuring at the time, and despite the addition of further plants over the next three years,
this system of organization remained effectively unchanged until the end of the war.
34 MBAG Kissel I/14, Minutes of the Board Meeting of DBAG on 23.10.1941.
35 Müller, 'Mobilisierung', p. 602.
36 MBAG Kissel I/14, Minutes of the Board Meeting of DBAG on 23.10.1941.

production within the war context did not jeopardize the company's prospects for the post-war period.

Werner was apparently insistent, however, that at least small-parts production be centralized in one place and that minor components be produced in volume. Even this raised objections from the board, which realized that the smaller manufacturers would be opposed to this measure and would accuse Daimler-Benz of using their dominant position within the Ring to put them in a position where they would be incapable of producing complete engines after the war. Udet's directive on the establishment of the Ring system had explicitly stated, in fact, that 'the reallocation of contracts may not be hindered by private company interests.'[37] This in itself was a recognition that the failure to rationalize production in the sector over the previous two years was in part owing to the unwillingness of private industrial companies to give up the production of complete aero-engines.

Werner renewed his demands for the introduction of 'American' production methods in the wake of Hitler's decree of 3 December 1941, with the express support of Hitler.[38] Even in the face of this, and despite the obvious failure of the 'Barbarossa' campaign – certainly obvious to all in business circles – the board reiterated the opposition it had expressed in October in the next board meeting, on 11 December. Kissel was increasingly mindful of the possibility of air-raid damage and saw this as a further argument against over-concentration, while K. C. Müller continued to push the line of raising production by increasing labour supply. Initially Müller therefore instituted only a limited concentration of production, confined to the reorganization of production of smaller parts within the Ring, thereby underlining the extent to which peacetime considerations continued to influence company attitudes even at this very late stage in the 'Barbarossa' campaign, and the extent to which business reticence militated against some attempts to effect reorganization of industry in the interests of war production.

c) The 'Production Miracle' 1942–4

In the second half of the war, the production increases achieved by the rationalization programme under the Ring system were remarkable compared to the modest ones of the period 1939–41. Output of single engines at Genshagen reached 400 for the first time in May 1942, 500 in October 1942, averaged 563 per month in 1943, and in January 1944 reached 800. Finally, following the formation of the Fighter Staff within the RMfRuK, from April to July 1944 the plant produced 1200 or more engines every month. In December 1944, production was still higher than in the second half of 1943, although it collapsed soon after.[39]

37   BA (P) 80 Ba2 P3315, Enclosure with Letter of GLM of 15.8.1941 (Tasks of the Ring Managers).
38   MBAG Kissel I/14, Minutes of the Board Meeting of DBAG on 11.12.1941.
39   MBAG Haspel 19, Statistical Monthly Reports 1942–1944.

Assessing the relative importance of the various measures taken from the summer of 1940 onwards in achieving the increases in output is incredibly difficult. Clearly, both the main pre-conditions for the growth in production were established prior to the military reverses of 1941–2 and Speer's appointment as Armaments Minister in February 1942. First, the introduction of the successive investment programmes '15940' and 'Hermann Göring' programme in 1940 and 1941 came to fruition in 1942 and 1943. Second, the key point in the transfer of jurisdiction and responsibility to civilian control came with the formation of the Industrial Council and the Ring system in mid-1941, and the rationalization programme which was implemented in the second half of the war was already under-way – albeit initially in limited form – in late 1941.

How far the new context created by the military reverses of the winter of 1941–2 affected the plant in detail is also difficult to assess. The relative importance of general exhortations to increase production, specific decrees from Hitler, the RLM or the RMfBuM, and the changing perceptions of industry itself during the period cannot be established, as there was often little direct link between specific decrees and movements in production levels. Production of aero-engines at Genshagen actually took off substantially in the second half of 1941, before the rationalization programme carried out under the Ring system could have any effect and before the impact of the '15940' project could be felt. The fact that average monthly output in the second six months of 1941 was 340 engines, compared to 268 engines in the first, is probably a reflection of the earlier attempts of the regime to switch resources to the aircraft sector in 1940 and 1941. At what point this ceased to be the main factor in the increases and at what point other factors took over is, however, impossible to say with certainty.

Finally, assessing the impact of specific measures either during the winter of 1941–2 or in the following period is also made difficult by the fact that, while the overall level of production increased year on year (3659 in 1941, 4920 in 1942, 7702 in 1943, 10,535 in 1944), monthly output fluctuated even more greatly than in the first half of the war.[40] Decisions taken within the overall administrative apparatus of the war economy did not affect monthly output at factory level until months later (if they affected it at all), making it difficult to trace movements in output back to specific measures. Moreover, increases in output over any three- or four-month period were as often as not the result of the alleviation of one or two specific bottlenecks rather than a product of overall planning, strategic decision-making or administrative reorganizations several stages removed from the shop-floor in the apparatus of the war economy. The relationship between overall planning and rationalization on the one hand and short-term crisis management on the other is impossible to

40   MBAG Forstmeier 18, Total Production of Daimler-Benz Aero-Engines (Statistics), 28.8.1945.

quantify, but it is plainly the case that as the war moved into its final two years, improvization and crisis management became more and more the dominant factors.

Despite these qualifications, it is clear that the winter of 1941–2 marked an important break in at least two ways. First, as already argued, the failure of the 'Barbarossa' campaign brought about a marked change in the subjective attitude of the company which should not be ignored. The new situation created by the failure of Barbarossa in the late autumn of 1941 radically altered the perspectives and expectations of industry, and with them their priorities with regard to utilizing capacity. The prospect of a lengthy war of attrition presented for the first time a situation in which it would be necessary and beneficial (if only in the negative sense that the fate of industry was tied up with the fate of the armed forces) to expand military output greatly. As the expectations of a rapid end to the war receded, measures to increase output over two or three years could be introduced without fear that an imminent return to peacetime conditions would leave industry in a disadvantaged position for the future. This was reinforced by the sense of crisis that the failure of Barbarossa had stirred up within the regime itself, creating intensified pressure from above to increase output. As Kissel warned in February 1942, immediately after the appointment of Speer as Armaments Minister, 'we are operating under consistently critical eyes, so that, the way things stand, if we do not soon achieve a smooth and adequate flow of production, we can expect unpleasant interventions from outside.'[41]

Second, in 1942, the workforce at Genshagen underwent a radical restructuring which greatly changed the situation within which the management of the plant had to achieve the demanded increases in production. On the one hand, in the first six months of 1942, 539 German workers, representing approximately 7-8 per cent of the male German workforce, were called up to the armed forces in preparation for the summer offensives of 1942.[42] More importantly, the first half of 1942 saw a huge influx of (mainly Russian) foreign forced labour into the plant.[43] This presented the management not only with the difficulty of integrating the mostly unskilled workers into a production process hitherto dominated by skilled labour, but also with radical problems caused by the need to achieve this in conformity with the ideological policies of the regime. When these workers arrived at Genshagen they had been brutalized and starved to the point where they were scarcely capable of any work at all. Both their physical state and the regulations governing their deployment stood in stark contradiction to the regime's demands to raise output and rationalize production.

---

41 MBAG Kissel/War Plants Genshagen 1941, Kissel to Ring Management T2, Genshagen, 13.2.1942.
42 MBAG Haspel 19, Statistical Monthly Reports 1942–1944.
43 The issue of foreign forced labour is treated in detail below, Chapter VI.3.

The changed context created by the military events and administrative reorganization of the previous months, combined with the need to restructure the production processes to accommodate the loss of German workers, led K. C. Müller to abandon the company position of December 1941 and institute a wide-ranging reorganization of production utilizing flow production methods in March 1942.[44] The RLM's demands for 600 aero-engines per month in 1942 meant that the volume of production was sufficient to allow the utilization of these methods even before the main influx of foreign forced workers made it imperative to reorganise the production process to allow the deployment of a far greater proportion of lesser skilled labour.

In June 1942, the structure of the labour force was radically altered by the arrival of roughly 2500 Russian male and female forced workers.[45] In December 1941 there had already been 1899 foreign workers at Genshagen, corresponding to 23 per cent of the workforce, and, in addition to this, 428 prisoners of war.[46] However, all but 24 of these had been west European workers, among whom were sufficient numbers of skilled and semi-skilled workers for there to have been no need to restructure the production process dramatically in order to integrate them into the plant. Nor did political factors dictate a restructuring of production to allow their deployment in line with the racist ideology and police and security policy of the regime.

With the arrival of the 2500 Russian, the proportion of foreign workers rose from 23 per cent in the winter of 1941 to 53 per cent in the winter of 1942. In addition, the number of prisoners of war rose to 793. The effect of the call-ups to the armed forces on the one hand and the influx of Russian workers on the other is reflected in the changed skills structure of the workforce in December 1942 compared to the previous year. Having increased in real terms in 1940 and 1941, the number of skilled workers in the male workforce fell in 1942 from 3563 to 3236; at the same time the total male workforce increased from 7197 to 9490 and the blue-collar workforce rose from 8180 to 11,303. In percentage terms, the proportion of skilled workers in the male workforce fell from 49.5 per cent in December 1941 to 34 per cent in December 1942. As a proportion of the total workforce, including women, it fell from 44 per cent to 28 per cent over the same period. Figures for the following two years are, unfortunately, unavailable, but it can be safely assumed that the proportion of skilled workers fell even further in 1943 and 1944.[47]

The arrival of the Russian workers coincided with demands from the RLM for even greater quantities of the DB 605 engine as a result of changing overall strategic policies. However, as the board complained in August 1942, 'the

44   MBAG Kissel I/15, Minutes of the Board Meeting of DBAG on 23 and 24.3.1942.
45   BA (P) 80 Ba2 P3322, Daimler-Benz Motoren GmbH Genshagen to the Board, 11.7.1942.
46   MBAG Forstmeier 16, Work-Force, Wages, Turnover, Production 1937–1942.
47   On the collapsing skills structure of the German workforce in the second half of the war see Salter, 'Mobilization', p.p 67, 99–103.

Russians who have recently been allocated to us are not suitable for this production.'[48] In fact, soon after the proportion of foreign workers in the workforce began rising at an accelerated rate, problems with the DB 605 started to occur at the front which could at least partly be traced back to the fact that they were increasingly being produced by ill-trained, inexperienced and half-starved workers living in appalling conditions.[49] Nonetheless, the proportion of foreign workers and prisoners of war in the workforce rose continuously through 1943 and 1944, reaching 58 per cent in August 1943 and 67 per cent in October 1944, when in addition over 1000 women from Ravensbrück concentration camp were deployed in the assembly hall.[50] In the face of this, the management was forced continuously to adapt the production processes to accommodate these changes in the composition of the workforce. Over the following two years, successive production lines or workshops were converted to flow production methods, as the expansion of the plant was simultaneously brought to a conclusion. The increased proportion of foreign workers in the workforce and the terror apparatus that stood behind the management undoubtedly made it much easier to introduce new production methods that reduced the dependence of the plant upon skilled labour, in a way that might not have been possible in the first half of the war owing to the opposition of the skilled German workforce. The conversion to flow production methods not only allowed the deployment of large numbers of east European workers at the bottom of the skills hierarchy, but also facilitated greater control over the workers by virtue of the 'disciplining' function of the flow process. That this was a key factor in the restructuring of production in the aero-engine industry in general is shown by the suggestion at an RLM meeting in March 1943 of Dr Frydag of Henschel that, in place of supervisory personnel who had been called up to the armed forces, factories could use 'the production methods themselves – if one uses flow production, the people have to go with it.'[51] The presence of a large proportion of completely powerless foreign workers with no effective means of asserting or defending their interests undoubtedly also made it easier for management to implement a 'speed-up' of the production process – the significance of which must be taken into account when assessing how far reductions in production time were the result of a 'production miracle', and how far the result of an increasing intensification of labour in the latter part of the war.

48 MBAG Kissel I/15, Minutes of the Board Meeting of DBAG on 14.8.1942.
49 MBAG Kissel I/15, Minutes of the Board Meeting of DBAG on 30.6 and 1.7.1942; MBAG Minutes of the Board Meeting of DBAG 1943–1945, Minutes of the Board Meeting of DBAG on 12 and 13.4.1943; BA (P) 80 Ba2 P3315, Minutes of the Board Meeting of Daimler-Benz Motoren GmbH Genshagen, 29.10.1943.
50 BA (P) 80 Ba2 P3323, Management of Daimler-Benz Motoren GmbH Genshagen to the Council, 25.11.1944. On the deployment of concentration camp inmates at Daimler-Benz see below, Chapter VI.3.c.
51 BA-MA (Freiburg) RL 3/19, GL-Discussion, 2.3.1943.

In November 1942, having largely completed the initial reorganization envisaged following the formation of the Ring, the management began converting some of the large component lines to flow production.[52] This was intended to raise the level of production to 1000 engines per month. In December 1942, it was decided to follow this by a conversion of the whole of the plant to serial flow production, a process that was intended to be completed by the early autumn of 1943.[53] The production time for a single engine had already been lowered from 1379 hours in May 1941 to 1200 in December 1942, and the board intended another reduction in production time and costs and an increase in output by this further rationalization.[54]

The imperative to accelerate and expand the introduction of these methods was reinforced by the call-up of a further 497 German male workers from January to July 1943, in response to the second disastrous defeat on the eastern front at Stalingrad in February 1943.[55] By October 1943, the proportion of German workers at Genshagen had become so small that production was near to breaking point – with K.C. Müller voicing his desperation over the difficulties of producing aero-engines when 65 per cent of the workforce were foreign workers 'with no inner interest' in their work. He complained of the 'great and difficult, if not impossible task' of producing such a complex item as an aero-engine under these conditions, but could only attempt to overcome this 'dreadful situation' (*Übelstand*) by 'the furthest possible division of labour.'[56] As a result of this continuous process of conversion to flow methods of production, however, average monthly output rose to 469 per month in the second half of 1943, 658 per month in the first half of 1943 and, after falling to an average of 626 engines per month in the second half of 1943, reached 806 engines in January 1944, its highest point yet.[57]

Statistics on aggregate production times for Daimler-Benz engines are unfortunately unavailable for the second half of the war. The huge increases in output during this period, when the workforce only increased very moderately, were, however, comparable to those achieved by other companies. At BMW, production times were reduced from 3260 hours in the summer of 1940 to 1250 in 1944 (a saving of 62 per cent in time), while at Henschel production times were reduced by 64 per cent from 1939 to 1943.[58] The figures for Daimler-Benz aero-engines were undoubtedly comparable. The

---

52   MBAG Kissel I/15, Minutes of the Board Meeting of DBAG on 4 and 5.11.1942.
53   BA (P) 80 Ba2 P3319, Minutes of the Board Meeting of Daimler-Benz Motoren GmbH Genshagen, 4.12.1942.
54   MBAG Kissel V/21, Müller to WiGruLFZ, 16.6.1941; BA (P) 80 Ba2 P3244, Memorandum (Rummel), 13.1.1943; *Geschäftsbericht der Daimler-Benz Motoren GmbH Genshagen 1942.*
55   MBAG Haspel 19, Statistical Monthly Reports 1942–1944.
56   BA (P) 80 Ba2 P3315, Minutes of the Board Meeting of Daimler-Benz Motoren GmbH Genshagen, 29.10.1943.
57   MBAG Haspel 19, Statistical Monthly Report 1942–1944.
58   Overy, 'Rationalization and the Production Miracle', pp. 370–1.

development of individual machining processes at Daimler-Benz during the
second half of the war gives a good idea, however, of how production methods
were adapted to changes in the nature and skills structure of the labour force
on the one hand, and in response to the need to raise output on the other, and
what productivity increases were simultaneously achieved. As an example of
this one can look at the development of precision grinding machines at the
company during the war.[59]

Briefly, the precision grinding process came at the end of the various
machining operations, after the workpiece had been through the basic
operations such as drilling, cutting, milling and turning. It involved passing a
fine-grained grinding stone over the surface of the workpiece, to smooth its
surface and remove blemishes or imperfections remaining from the previous
operations. This was necessary, first to improve the surface of the piece, and
thus facilitate smoother functioning within the overall finished engine, and,
second to ensure uniform heat transfer during operation, thus reducing the
likelihood of engine failure through over-heating. Machine-tools for this had
been developed in the USA, but not only was it no longer possible to procure
these, they were also inadequate in that they only polished the surface of the
workpiece and did not remove the imperfections remaining from the other
operations. In the second half of the war, however, these foregoing machining
operations were being carried out by less skilled and less experienced workers,
which led to deteriorating quality of workmanship and made the polishing
process more important.

In the face of this, Daimler-Benz developed at its own workshops machines
for use 'even under difficult circumstances', such as the declining quality of
raw materials and the growing shortage of 'responsible and trustable' workers
– a clear reference to the poor motivation of the foreign workforce. Despite
the increased precision demanded from these machines, they were designed
with the 'greatest emphasis on simplicity of use' as only 'overwhelmingly
unskilled workers' were available for their operation, again a reference to the
impact of the influx of foreign workers on the skills structure of the workforce.
As more operations were converted to flow production methods, the number
of operations on which they could be employed increased, so that in 1942
special-purpose machine-tools were being developed for the grinding of
bearings, camshafts, crankshafts and other major components. By the
introduction of such machinery, the worktime for the polishing of a cylinder
liner was reduced from 20 to 6 minutes, while the grinding of other parts of
the same cylinder was reduced from 30 to 4 minutes, a reduction of 87 per cent
worktime per piece.

The significance of this special-purpose machinery in the second half of the

---

59   The following is based on Daimler-Benz AG (ed.), *Die Entwicklung des Feinziehschleifens bei der
     Daimler-Benz Aktiengesellschaft. Ein Beitrag zur Leistungssteigerung* (undated, 1942).

war is highlighted by the figures for investment in new machinery at Genshagen from 1938 to 1943. They show a substantial increase from 1940 onwards, but above all huge investments in 1942 and 1943:

Annual Investments in Machinery and Machine-Tools 1938–43 (RM)

1938	2.4M	1940	4.1M	1942	13.5M
1939	1.1M	1941	7.5M	1943	12.7M

In 1943, of the total RM 12.7m spent, RM 10.7m were invested in special-purpose machinery.[60]

The success of the rationalization programme instituted under the Ring system from late 1941 onwards is underlined when one compares the growth of output with the development of the workforce in the second half of the war. While average output rose from 340 engines per month in the second half of 1941 to over 1200 aero-engines per month from April to July 1944 (an increase of 253 per cent), the workforce increased in size from 8180 in December 1941 to only 10,909 in July 1944 (an increase of 46 per cent) while the proportion of skilled and German workers steadily deteriorated.[61]

The extent to which the increases in output from 1941 to 1944 represented genuine shop-floor productivity gains has to be seen in perspective, however. When compared against 1939, the figures for the second half of the war appear slightly more modest. Taking the war as a whole, average monthly output rose from 264 in 1940 to 1079 in the first six months of 1944 (an increase of 309 per cent), while the blue-collar workforce rose from 5681 in December 1939 to 10,909 in July 1944 (an increase of 92 per cent). Although these increases are still significant and substantial, it is clear that the great growth in output per worker from 1942 to 1944 is as much a reflection of the inefficiency and poor productivity of 1940 and 1941 as of the rationalization of the administrative system and production process from mid-1941 onwards.

The extent to which genuine rationalization was responsible for the increases up to 1944 is also questionable when one considers that nearly half of the growth in monthly output at Genshagen in the second half of the war was achieved in 1944 itself, after the investment programmes had been completed, and well beyond the point when the board of Daimler-Benz was secretly devoting its main energies towards the rationalization of lorry production for the post-war period. The increase achieved from January to July 1944 (806 to 1200 aero-engines) was almost as great as that from late 1941 to January 1944 (an average of 340 per month to 806). While some of the increases in 1944 were the result of the ongoing effects of K. C. Müller's

---

60   BA (P) 80 Ba2 P3319, Minutes of the Board Meeting of Daimler-Benz Motoren GmbH Genshagen, 4.12.1942.
61   MBAG Haspel 19, Statistical Monthly Reports 1942–1944; MBAG Forstmeier 16, Work-Force, Wages, Turnover, Production 1937–1942; BA (P) 80 Ba2 P3322, General Report 1937–1944.

rationalization programme, a growing proportion was undoubtedly owing to the lengthening of working hours under the Fighter Staff, the intensification of labour through piece-rate reductions, and the 'speed-up' of the production process by accelerating the pace of transportation and assembly lines. That the company resorted to these measures is shown by Haspel's comments at this time in another context (lorry production), when he demanded that targets be achieved 'with brutal force, if necessary', and that 'the last ounce be squeezed out of people'[62] This policy was, however, pursuable only in the context peculiar to the latter phases of the war and only with the specific labour force of the time, at whose expense at least some of the increases in output were achieved.

d) Production under Licence 1941–44

In addition to managing the introduction of flow production methods at Genshagen, the Daimler-Benz aero-engine experts also had the task of organizing the rationalization programme within the Ring and overseeing the tooling-up process at the numerous additional licence production plants that were added to the Daimler-Benz Ring in 1941–2. Given the chronic shortage of technicians, engineers and skilled workers, the simultaneous task of setting up production and training a workforce – often from scratch – placed incredible burdens on the Daimler-Benz management and gave rise to considerable delays beyond those caused by bottlenecks in supplies, machinery and so on. It took from January 1941 to mid-1942 for the Colmar plant to tool for aero-engine parts and achieve a steady volume of production, and even with plundered and requisitioned machinery the full number of machine-tools had not been procured by this point.[63] As such, this relatively small plant provides a further example of how increases in output were as often as not the result of cumulative efforts going back into the early phase of the war, which by their very nature took many months to come to fruition.

At those licensed plants that already had fully established production lines by the outbreak of the war (Büssing-NAG and Henschel), similar increases in output were achieved under the Ring system to those at Genshagen. Output of Daimler-Benz aero-engines rose from 1709 in 1941 to 6037 in 1944 at Büssing, and from 1283 in 1941 to 5313 in 1944 at Henschel.[64] These plants had their own technical personnel and engineers and could thus implement rationalization measures themselves, under the overall direction of Daimler-Benz, which simply had to reallocate contracts and liaise over issues such as changes in design. Furthermore, as privately owned companies, the same

62 MBAG Haspel/'Arbeitskreis Lastwagen', Minutes of the Meeting on Lorry Production on 31.5.1944.
63 MBAG Kissel IX/Colmar, Kissel to K. C. Müller, 15.11.1940; Kissel to Daimler-Benz GmbH Kolmar, 6.2.1941; Report of the Management, 12.5.1942.
64 MBAG Forstmeier 18, Total Production of Daimler-Benz Aero-engines 1936–1945, 28.8.1945.

issues of self-interest ensured full cooperation in measures to increase output in the second half of the war as at Daimler-Benz itself.

This was in marked contrast to some of the other plants (especially those in occupied territories) that were integrated into the Daimler-Benz Ring and tooled for Daimler-Benz production during the war itself. At these plants the same shortages or backlogs of machine-tools that slowed the pace of tooling at Daimler-Benz's own plants were exacerbated by the tendency of the Ring management to satisfy the immediate demands of running production lines at the main plants. The lack of trained personnel at the plants themselves, and the multitude of burdens placed on Daimler-Benz's own engineers, meant that it took roughly two years for even a small plant to be tooled. In addition to shortages of components, materials and machinery, these plants had to contend with untrained, poor-quality labour drawn mainly from the locality, and thus depended upon a workforce whose poor food supply and brutal treatment intensified problems of low productivity, absenteeism, non-compliance and resistance.

The Avia factory in Prague, for example, was allocated to the Daimler-Benz Ring and ordered to tool for production of the DB 605 in August 1942.[65] Initially, it was to produce 500 aero-engines per month in 1944.[66] However, the plant only actually began production in July 1944, and in total only 311 aero-engines were ever built at the plant.[67] Similarly, the Pomo plant in Stettin, which was taken over in March 1941, was designated to produce 400 aero-engines per month in 1943, but only managed a total of 1724 in the year, corresponding to an average monthly production of only 144. This only increased marginally to 1877 aero-engines in the whole of 1944.

The problems of tooling plants from scratch were further exacerbated by the RLM's regular orders to re-tool for the production of a different model, often halfway through the tooling process for the last model. Avia, for example, had been initially meant for production of the DB 605, but before a single engine had been produced it was ordered to re-tool for the DB 603. Similarly, the Steyr-Daimler-Puch plant at Graz was first earmarked for production of the DB 603, of which it was supposed to deliver 700 per month by 1943.[68] It eventually began production in October 1942 – but of the DB 605, to which it had obviously been switched as part of the RLM's efforts to increase output of the DB 605 in 1942.[69] By October 1943, however, it was re-tooling for the DB 603, a task that proved so difficult under the conditions prevailing by then that it only produced 688 engines in 1944 compared to 1177 in 1943.[70] Even

65   MBAG Kissel I/15, Minutes of the Board Meeting of DBAG on 14.8.1942.
66   MBAG Kissel I/15, Minutes of the Board Meeting of DBAG on 4 and 5.11.1942.
67   B.I.O.S. (ed.), *Report on Visit to Daimler-Benz AG at Stuttgart-Untertürkheim*, London, n.d. p. 5;
      MBAG Forstmeier 18, Total Production of Daimler-Benz Aero-engines 1936–1945, 28.8.1945.
68   MBAG Kissel I/14, Minutes of the Board Meeting of DBAG on 23.10.1941.
69   B.I.O.S. (ed.), *Report on Visit to Daimler-Benz*, p. 5.
70   BA (P) 80 Ba2 P3315, Minutes of the Meeting of Daimler-Benz Motoren GmbH Genshagen,
      29.10.1943; MBAG Forstmeier 18, Total Production of Daimler-Benz Aero-engines 1936–1945,
      28.8.1945.

in 1943, the average monthly production of 98 aero-engines compared appallingly with the initial projection of 700 per month. The net result of this was that, with the exception of the fully established Henschel and Büssing-NAG plants, the additional capacity integrated into the Daimler-Benz Ring consumed a huge amount of resources (human, physical and financial) in return for minimal output, which bore no relationship whatsoever to the enormous investment in time, material and money made in them.

This is seen above all in the development of the Flugmotorenwerk Ostmark (FMO) in Vienna, the huge Reich investment project in which Daimler-Benz was directly involved from 1941 to 1943. The FMO was a massive RM 450m factory in Vienna, with subsidiary plants in Brünn and Marburg, financed by the Reich itself and conceived in the early stages of the war. Initially, it had been intended to manufacture the Junkers Jumo 222 aero-engine, and the project had been developed in cooperation with the Junkers management.[71] However, in 1941, as part of its moves to increase output of its currently favoured Daimler-Benz engines, the RLM began considering the possibility of converting capacity devoted to Junkers production to Daimler-Benz engines – a process in which Daimler-Benz managers were undoubtedly less than completely passive. Rather than convert plants already engaged in full serial production, which would result in a fall in output during the changeover, the RLM decided in September 1941 to transfer responsibility for the fledgling FMO from Junkers to Daimler-Benz and to produce DB 603 engines there instead.[72] In addition to the fact that the transfer of this embryonic project would not cause the same fall in output, the RLM was probably persuaded by Daimler-Benz's promise that it could produce 1200 DB 603 engines per month with a total of just over 3000 machine-tools at Vienna, which compared favourably to the Junkers project of 1000 Jumo 222 engines per month with an inventory of nearly 4500 machine-tools.[73] The project thus envisaged 20 per cent higher output with 30 per cent less machinery. Precisely how far Daimler-Benz was motivated in submitting these plans by its eagerness to take over the plant is unclear, but it clearly played some role. Kissel's view of the takeover was in any case unambiguous, describing it as 'the greatest success our company has ever had.'[74]

According to the initial plans, production was to begin in March 1943 and was to have reached a level of 800 per month by December 1944 and 1200 per month during 1945.[75] The shortages of building workers and materials, however, and the complications caused by the conversion from Junkers to

71   MBAG Kissel IX/FMO, Kissel to Jahr, 24.9.1941. On the background to the FMO project see Perz, B., *Projekt Quarz. Steyr-Daimler-Puch und das Konzentrationslager Melk*, Vienna, 1991, pp. 105–7.
72   MBAG Kissel IX/FMO, Milch to Kissel, 19.9.1941.
73   MBAG Kissel IX/FMO, Minutes of the third Board Meeting of FMO GmbH, 16.12.1941.
74   BA (P) 80 Ba2 P3322, Kissel to Stauss, 24.9.1941.
75   MBAG Kissel IX/FMO, Kissel to the Management of FMO GmbH, 15.11.1941.

Daimler-Benz, meant that the building and tooling process experienced successive delays. The pace of building was slowed by the poor quality of the building workforce (nearly 11,000 in total), the great majority of whom were forced foreign workers and prisoners of war, whose work-rate was, unsurprisingly in view of their dreadful treatment, particularly poor. The priority accorded to DB 605 production in 1942 meant that the Ring management consistently filtered off machine-tools delivered to the FMO for deployment in other production lines. This compounded the general delays caused by lack of capacity in the machine-tool industry, which experienced reductions in its raw materials allocations year on year after 1941.[76] By October 1942, fewer than half of the 2500 machine-tools needed to start production had been delivered. Meanwhile, changes in programmes and planning created further difficulties in meeting deadlines, as each involved changing orders to materials and components suppliers as well as to machine-tool manufacturers, causing not only delays but considerable friction with suppliers as well.[77]

By February 1943, the building of the factory was finally complete. However, Haspel informed the RLM that with regard to the accumulated machinery there were still 'gaping holes' (*gähnende Leere*) in the inventory, describing the delivery rate as very unsatisfactory and stating his view that the machine-tool situation would cause even greater problems as things progressed.[78] In fact, of the 2280 universal machine-tools ordered by the main Vienna plant, only 46 per cent had arrived by March 1943, the original planned start-up date. Of the relatively large numbers of single-purpose machines ordered – a reflection of the poor quality of the workforce and the need to simplify production processes as far as possible to allow the effective exploitation of the foreign workers – only 17 per cent had arrived at Vienna and four per cent at Brünn.[79]

As a result of this, the production programme was inevitably postponed, with the new date for the start-up set as December 1943. Even with this delay, however, the management of the FMO concluded that the output figures envisaged would not be achieved, at least for the first few months.[80] Meanwhile, with the failure of Daimler-Benz to deliver on its promises now obvious, Göring became increasingly irritated with the state of affairs at the plant, which was rapidly turning into an expensive disaster.[81] After repeatedly criticizing the Daimler-Benz management – at a time when Daimler-Benz was

76   Freyberg and Siegel, *Industrielle Rationalisierung*, p. 157.
77   MBAG DBAG War Plants 26, Minutes of the fourth Board Meeting of FMO GmbH, 16.10.1942.
78   MBAG DBAG War Plants 26, Haspel to Cejka/RLM, 9.2.1943.
79   *Geschäftsbericht der Flugmotorenwerke Ostmark GmbH für 1942–1943*
80   MBAG DBAG War Plants 26, Minutes of the Fifth Board Meeting of FMO GmbH, 9.4.1943.
81   MBAG DBAG War Plants 26, Göring to the Management of FMO, 14.5.1943; Perz, *Projekt Quarz*, pp. 117–18.

out of favour with the RLM for other reasons too – Göring eventually ordered in June 1943 that management of the plant be taken over by the Steyr-Daimler-Puch director Georg Meindl.[82] Following friction with Meindl, who was following his own expansionist agenda, Haspel, K.C. Müller and Fritz Nallinger (head of development and board member at Daimler-Benz) resigned their positions at the FMO.[83] Henceforth, their relationship with the FMO was confined to overseeing production within the Daimler-Benz Ring, on the same basis as the other licensed production sites. Production in Vienna finally began in August 1943, with 515 aero-engines being delivered by the end of the year and a disastrously low 2375 being completed in the whole of 1944.[84] The RM 450m, 1200-engines-per-month project thus ended up achieving an average output in 1944 of only 198 aero-engines per month.

Despite its protestations of injured innocence, the Daimler-Benz board was clearly glad, by this point, to be relieved of responsibility for the plant. Far from being designed to regain control over the FMO, the resignations of Haspel, Müller and Nallinger from the board suggest that the company was keen to make as complete a break as possible.[85] In fact, the removal of the factory from Daimler-Benz control came at a particularly fortunate moment for the company, as the FMO was in the process of raising its basic capital to finance the start of production, which would have necessitated a substantial financial commitment on the part of Daimler-Benz at a time when it was already trying to refrain from further investment in the aero-engine sector.[86] The supervisory and managerial board agreed, in fact, that 'the disengagement from the Ostmark plant represents a release from future financial engagements and from the responsibility for production in Vienna' – a statement that, when compared with Kissel's joy over the initial takeover in September 1941, shows how far the perceptions of the company had changed in the intervening two years.[87]

The experience of trying to tool a major factory for production of the DB 603 under the conditions prevailing in the latter third of the war was also of great significance for Haspel's attitude towards the idea of a further re-tooling of Genshagen in 1944. The difficulties in setting up the production lines in Vienna – against a general background that, as Haspel was aware, was going to get worse rather than better and that would make re-tooling harder still (if not impossible) as time went on – suggested that any attempts to do the same at Genshagen would be doomed to failure. As 1944 progressed, the growing

82 MBAG DBAG War Plants 26, Haspel to Cejka/Roehnert/K. C. Müller, 5.6.1943; on the detailed events Perz, *Projekt Quarz*, pp. 118–121.
83 MBAG DBAG War Plants 26, Haspel to Roehnert, 17.8.1943.
84 MBAG Forstmeier 18, Total Production of Daimler-Benz Aero-engines 1936–1945, 28.8.1945.
85 For a contrary view see Perz, *Projekt Quarz*, p. 117; in a far more extreme form Roth, 'Der Weg zum Guten Stern', pp. 259–64.
86 MBAG DBAG War Plants 26, Memorandum, 17.8.1943.
87 MBAG Minutes of the Presidium Meeting of DBAG, 12.8.1943 (no cat. no.).

problems in the German war economy were such that if production at Genshagen collapsed, which it might well do were it to attempt a major re-tooling, resources, labour and machinery would inevitably end up being transferred to new priority production lines, leaving Genshagen in an irretrievable position.

By early 1944, however, after three years of serial production of the DB 605, the RLM was apparently intent upon finally pushing through the conversion of Genshagen to production of the DB 603. Seeing that the materials supply was getting more and more catastrophic (in his words, 'downright gruesome'), Haspel was opposed to the changeover, which he saw as an impossibility from the technical viewpoint and a disaster from the private company viewpoint.[88] The RLM apparently wished the Genshagen plant to be re-tooled for production of the DB 603 from March 1945. Even given the most optimistic scenario for future developments, the planning engineers of Genshagen calculated that it would be impossible to achieve this before June 1945.[89] According to them, the RLM's demands 'have the marks of a theoretical prognosis which bears no relation to reality' and had 'impossible' stamped all over them. The management of the plant opposed the decision to re-tool on the grounds that such impossible targets depressed the workforce and caused declining morale and productivity.

Haspel himself was aware from his previous experience with the FMO that even a timetable orientated to June 1945 would inevitably end up being delayed, given the deteriorating situation, and would probably not be complete by the end of the war. In order to avoid having to produce the DB 603, the company therefore offered the RLM a new, improved version of the existing DB 605, the DB 605 D. With this, the company was able to regain the RLM's enthusiasm for the DB 605, which had become 'completely uninteresting', in one go.[90] Even re-tooling for this adapted model in 1944 caused Genshagen huge problems – owing above all to the poor quality of the available labour – and was not carried out at the rate required by the RLM programme; but compared to the problems that the DB 603 would have created, these difficulties were minimal.[91]

Aware nonetheless that the RLM demanded some progress towards production of the DB 603, but unwilling to put the interests of Daimler-Benz in jeopardy, Haspel used his position as chairman of the dominant company in the Ring to force the risks of re-tooling onto one of Daimler-Benz's main competitors, Büssing-NAG. Having gained permission to produce the DB 605

---

88   MBAG Forstmeier 16, Haspel to K. C. Müller, 3.6.1944; Haspel to Büssing-NAG, 19.6.1944. On the declining raw materials situation of the Reich in 1943–4 see Janssen, *Das Ministerium Speer*, pp. 208–16.
89   MBAG Haspel 3/26–27, Daimler-Benz Motoren GmbH Genshagen to Haspel, 10.3.1944.
90   MBAG Forstmeier 16, Haspel to Büssing-NAG, 19.6.1944.
91   MBAG Haspel 3/26–27, Daimler-Benz Motoren GmbH Genshagen to Haspel, 10.3.1944.

D at Genshagen on the grounds that it would be impossible to re-tool the plant for the DB 603, Haspel wrote to persuade Büssing-NAG, saying: 'It would undoubtedly be good if you committed your energies fully to the DB 603.' Pointing out that the RLM programme only demanded a low level of initial output and that many of the parts for the DB 603 were similar to those for the DB 605, he argued that 'the changeover will not cause too many difficulties.'[92] What then happened at Büssing-NAG is unclear – what is certain, however, is that, in the desperate conditions of mid-1944 onwards, the Daimler-Benz Ring operated less and less for the interests of the Reich, and more and more as a source of influence and power for Daimler-Benz.

The Ring management was, of course, powerless to prevent the intensifying air raids on the Reich. Production at Genshagen was severely disrupted for the first time in August 1944 after a major raid. Whereas in July 1944 1200 single engines were built, in August production fell to 472.[93] Despite the fact that the machine-shops had been transferred in their entirety to an underground dispersal site by this point, production never fully recovered, collapsing completely in the winter of 1944–5 under the combined impact of disrupted supplies, worsening communications, growing transportation problems and perpetual air raids.

The case of Genshagen shows how difficult it is to divide the development of production into phases that coincide neatly with military developments in the war. Nonetheless, four main phases are discernible. First, the period up to the summer of 1940 was characterized by caution concerning expansion and attempts to increase output without investment that would condemn the plant to over-capacity after the war. Second, the period from the summer of 1940 until the winter of 1941–2 witnessed the formulation of expansion plans under pressure from the RLM and the introduction of organizational changes designed to effect industry-wide rationalization to overcome the stagnation of the first two years of the war. During this period, the attitude of the company towards rationalization had been determined by the same views regarding prospects for the post-war period that had informed its feelings about expansion. The third period, that of early 1942 to the winter of 1943–4, witnessed a mass rationalization programme designed, first, to raise output in response to the radically altered military situation and, second, to allow the continuation of production in the face of a changing labour force. Even here, what was termed rationalization often meant crisis management and improvization, and, as the study of the Daimler-Benz Ring shows, often yielded poor results. Finally, the period 1944–5 witnessed a last mobilization of resources and radical intensification of labour in pursuit of further increases in output under the Fighter Staff, at a time when bombing not only caused the eventual collapse in production but also led the company to devote its energies to rationalizing production in areas of longer-term interest to the company.

92   MBAG Forstmeier 16, Haspel to Büssing-NAG, 19.6.1944.
93   BA (P) 80 Ba2 P3322, General Reports (July, August 1944).

2. Strategies for Survival: Lorry Production at Mannheim 1939–45

a) Lorry Production and the 'Blitzkrieg' Economy

The development of the Mannheim plant during the war stands in stark contrast to that of Genshagen. Compared to the latter, which developed into one of the biggest aero-engine factories in Germany and expanded to form the core of a huge production network covering the whole of Europe, Mannheim was much more modest in size and significance to the war effort. Not only was it smaller than most of Daimler-Benz's other plants, but within the lorry sector in general it played a smaller role than the Ford plant in Cologne, or the massive Opel lorry plant in Brandenburg, which was the largest and most efficient truck factory in Europe. The experience of Mannheim during the war is of interest precisely because, as a smaller plant, it ended up producing the lorries of another company – Opel – under a state-sanctioned licence agreement forced on both parties in the context of Speer's rationalization drive. It thus allows the examination of rationalization policy from the other end, from the perspective of the smaller, licensed plant. Despite its relatively modest size – its workforce rose from 3231 in December 1939 to 4601 in December 1944, and the proportion of Daimler-Benz's total turnover for which it accounted fell from 6.7 per cent in 1939 to 4.1 per cent in 1944 – the plant also merits detailed examination because, as one of the key vehicle-producing plants within the Daimler-Benz concern during the war, it attained a significance within the company's overall strategy that was far greater than its size would suggest.[94]

At the outbreak of war, the Mannheim plant was in the latter stages of the restructuring process that had followed the decision to convert it to lorry production. This restructuring had itself been the occasion of a substantial transformation of the production process and of the widespread introduction of more rational working methods. The company's own literature stressed the contrast in extensive 'before' and 'after' pictures of the shop floor, which detailed the replacement of old and noisy belt-driven machinery with quieter and faster electrically driven machine-tools and the introduction of new labour-saving equipment. Pictures of earlier assembly lines 'without lifting gear or transportation equipment' were contrasted with engine assembly 'on the moving conveyor and with modern equipment to ease the workload', and with pictures of electric trolleys, carriages on runners to transport the semi-finished frames and similar labour-saving improvements to reduce the work burden.[95] According to this public voice, 'all possibilities that contribute to raising productivity in any way are worked on collectively and systematically', including both the extensive training of workers and 'technical improvements

---

94 MBAG DBAG 31, Special Report of Daimler-Benz AG, 22.11.1945; Pohl et al., *Die Daimler-Benz AG*, p. 126.

95 *Leistungsbericht der Daimler-Benz AG 1940. Werk Mannheim.*

to work methods, improvements to machinery and appliances and improve-ments to the transportation system.'[96]

The real development of the plant during the first two to three years of the war is, however, hard to reconcile with the image of high productivity, rationality and organizational efficiency presented in public by the firm. In fact, as a plant situated reasonably close to the French border, it experienced substantial disruption during the mobilization phase immediately preceding and in the months following the outbreak of war. The general disruption to Mannheim's production caused by call-ups to the Wehrmacht of both the plant's own workers and those of its subcontractors and materials suppliers was compounded by the fact that it had previously drawn upon the industry of the Saar for many of its supplies. The military and geographical vulnerability of this region had led to the closure of many of its factories by the military authorities, necessitating the search for new suppliers and causing delays while new subcontracting relationships were established.[97]

As a result, the Mannheim plant experienced substantial shortages and irregular deliveries of many major components in the first six months of the war.[98] Production was characterized by hold-ups which forced the plant to store many incomplete lorries whilst additional parts were procured.[99] Despite the board's demands for an immediate intensification of labour at Mannheim following the outbreak of war, the initial volume of production of 500 lorries per month which the plant was supposed to achieve by January 1940, was not reached until March 1940, by which point the restructuring process had still not been completed.[100] The exact extent of the problems caused is difficult to assess due to the self-contradictory statistics available for this period, but clearly the low volume of production achieved in the first half of 1940 was not a result of low levels of demand, themselves derived from a strategy of limited economic mobilization, but rather a reflection of the disruption caused by the outbreak of the war to a plant that itself was already in a transitional phase as it converted to lorry production.[101]

96 *Leistungsbericht der Daimler-Benz AG Werk Mannheim (Vol. 7)*, p. 58.
97 MBAG Kissel VI/19, Hoppe to Werner/DBAG Mannheim, 15.11.1939; Memorandum of the Discussion at Mannheim, 22.12.1939; Salter, 'Mobilization', pp. 14–15.
98 MBAG Kissel VI/19, DBAG Mannheim to Hoppe/Untertürkheim, 3.11.1939; Hoppe to Werner/DBAG Mannheim, 15.11.1939.
99 MBAG Kissel VI/20, Hoppe/Untertürkheim to Decker/DBAG Mannheim, 11.3.1940.
100 MBAG Kissel VI/19, Kissel to Werner/DBAG Mannheim, 28.10.1939; MBAG Kissel I/12, Minutes of the Board Meeting of DBAG on 12.10.1939; MBAG Kissel I/13, Minutes of the Board Meeting of DBAG on 2.4.1940.
101 MBAG Kissel VI/20, Overview of Deliveries of the LGF 3000 Lorry in the First Half of 1940 (2.7.1940); MBAG Kissel I/28, Minutes of the Discussion at the Mannheim Plant 8.7.1940. Both sets of statistics agree that the plant was meant to produce 3240 lorries in the first six months of 1940 (540 per calender month). However, one suggests that a total of 2736 was produced (a shortfall of 506, or 16 per cent), while the other suggests that only 1985 were produced (a shortfall of 1255, or 39 per cent).

The company management was in no doubt as to where the blame for the poor performance of the lorry sector lay. The general uncertainty that characterized the company's response to the outbreak of war was reinforced in the case of lorry production by the lack of clear orders from the military procurement agencies. In December 1939, at a meeting between the Economic Armaments Office and leading industrialists, Kissel complained to General Thomas that industrialists 'could manage much more if clear tasks were given to them.'[102] One year later, the continued duplication of jurisdiction between the various authorities, the lack of coordination between ministries, offices and agencies, and the conflicting signals emanating from all quarters led Kissel to repeat his complaint internally, stating that it was impossible to plan lorry production in advance 'as we do not know what we are supposed to be producing.'[103]

In place of regular orders and a guaranteed stable volume of production, which Kissel demanded as the precondition for the fulfilment of military demands, the company was forced to chop and change at short notice and as a consequence was never sure what it was going to be expected to produce from one month to the next. The constantly changing demands and the failure of the military agencies to set clear priorities or fixed programmes were a source of permanent friction between the company (and industry in general) and the military. Kissel, for whom the priority was large-scale peacetime production of a 3-ton lorry in as few variations as possible, demanded the guarantee of a long production run of a fixed model, 'as we cannot accept the adoption of yet another model after two years and with it a new reorganization of production.'[104] For the vehicle sector, where the regular renewal of models for reasons of military superiority was not as crucial as in the aero-engine sector, Kissel argued that it must be possible to fix production requirements in advance and for the long term.[105]

Not only did the military's constant changing of programmes and specifications cause problems, but considerable friction was generated by what the company management perceived to be the unrealistic demands that the military made with regard to orders that, by their nature, would take industry months to complete. Programmes were formulated, orders were given too late for industry to be able to adapt, but materials allocations were also released too late for companies to plan production runs and coordinate deliveries with suppliers, or, in the case of new models, to find and liaise with new sub-contractors. Not so much shortages of material *per se*, but late allocation and

---

102 Overy, 'Mobilization for Total War', p. 623; the document is reprinted in Eichholtz, D. and Schumann, W. (eds.), *Anatomie des Krieges. Neue Dokumente über die Rolle des Deutschen Monopolkapitals bei der Vorbereitung und Durchführung des Zweiten Weltkrieges*, (East) Berlin, 1969, pp. 235–40.

103 MBAG Kissel XIV/31, Kissel to Oberbaurat Schmidt, 23.9.1940.

104 MBAG Kissel I/13, Minutes of the Board Meeting of DBAG on 20.9.1940.

105 MBAG Kissel VI/7, Kissel to DBAG Gaggenau, 21.9.1940.

irregular deliveries were responsible for the failure to utilize capacity effectively. As Kissel emphasised, the failure to meet demand did not mean that the capacity was not available, 'but has its cause above all in the difficult and irregular material supply.'[106]

Again, the protests of industry seem to have had little effect, and little seems to have changed in the first year of the war. In September 1940 Kissel was still complaining of the unrealistic and unreasonable attitude of the military authorities and of their complete lack of understanding of the nature of industrial production. Referring to army orders for the first three months of 1941, he remarked scornfully that 'even a child knows that if material is allocated now . . . it is complete nonsense to expect deliveries to begin in the first quarter, let alone function remotely smoothly.' From the industrialist's point of view, the military's attitude was 'inexplicable', given that the armed forces would obviously need lorries permanently and were thus in a position to order a year in advance .[107]

Unsurprisingly, the first two years of the war witnessed little that can be genuinely termed rationalization in the sense of long-term reorganization of production on the basis of a clearly defined strategy. In view of the poor materials and components supply situation on the one hand, and the lack of clear overall coordination from the military authorities on the other, the company board and the management of the plant were forced to improvise much of their production on a monthly basis and come up with ad hoc responses to situations as they developed. The failure of the authorities to coordinate materials, labour and contracts allocation, and the resultant inability of the company to establish an effective functioning relationship with its subcontractors, forced the plant to resort regularly to production of its own components in response to each successive bottleneck as it arose. Especially from 1941 onwards, as labour shortages in the components industries began to delay supplies even more than in 1940, the plant reverted to the improvised production of small volumes of components in its own workshops to alleviate the shortages. This policy allowed production to continue but was highly disruptive, inefficient and time-consuming, and meant that the plant's machinery was being utilized to a far lower extent than would have been the case had it been able to maintain a fixed, constant production of one or two parts on each machine-tool or machine group.

How extensive this crisis management approach was and how much capacity was tied up in alleviating bottlenecks is hard to assess, but regular references can be found to such measures being used at both Mannheim and Gaggenau in all phases of the war. In mid-1941 both plants were complaining of what the Mannheim management referred to as the 'permanently recurring

106   MBAG Kissel/Correspondence with WiGruFa 1940–1942, Kissel to WiGruFa, 20.1.1940.
107   MBAG Kissel VI/7, Kissel to DBAG Gaggenau, 21.9.1940.

demands for back-up.'[108] In July 1942, at the point when Speer's rationalization programme was supposedly alleviating precisely this kind of problem, the Mannheim management said that it could not fulfil production requirements because it was having to waste time producing several components alternately on the same machines, which involved the regular and time-consuming resetting of machinery. This meant that nominal times set for the production of each piece could not in practice be achieved, and that actual utilization of each machine-tool remained effectively much lower than the paper calculations of the plant's production managers suggested.[109] In March 1943, the plant was still having to resort to self-production of additional parts at short notice in order to prevent production from coming to a complete standstill. On this particular occasion, the plant had been forced to produce washers which it had hitherto procured externally. Although the Mannheim management viewed this inefficient form of production as 'no longer acceptable' given the desperate shortages of labour in the war economy as a whole by this point, it was informed by the authorities that it was not allowed to procure the washers from outside any more but had to continue manufacturing them itself. The frustration of the management is clearly expressed in its response: 'No comment necessary.'[110] If anything, the deteriorating quality of components – a reflection of the shortages of quality labour in the components industries and of restrictions concerning raw materials utilization – led to these problems intensifying as the war went on, as further amounts of subsequent machining became necessary to improve the supplied components to allow their final assembly at Mannheim. This inevitably compounded the problems caused by the improvised reversion to self-production.[111]

The high degree of flexibility that this demanded conditioned a continued preference for universal machine-tools that could be adapted to successive short-term needs. The purchase of special-purpose machinery, which had already become difficult in the pre-war phase because of foreign currency exchange problems, became virtually impossible during the war anyway, so that the extent to which the company could make free choices on the issue should not be overestimated.[112] Even in the case of general-purpose machinery, the management sometimes preferred to avoid ordering machine-tools that had long delivery backlogs in favour of using machines that were not necessarily the most suitable for the job in hand, but that were immediately

108 MBAG DBAG Mannheim 23, DBAG Mannheim to DBAG Untertürkheim/ Purchasing Department, 28.7.1941; MBAG Kissel VI/8, Kissel to DBAG Gaggenau, 17.5.1941.
109 MBAG Kissel/3-ton Opel, Minutes of the Meeting of 15.7.1942 at Mannheim.
110 MBAG DBAG Mannheim 25, Dexheimer/Mannheim to Utech/Mannheim, 25.3.1943.
111 MBAG DBAG Mannheim 25, Appointments Office/Mannheim to Decker/Mannheim, 15.1.1943.
112 MBAG Kissel I/13, Excerpt from the Meeting in Untertürkheim on 18.6.1940 regarding Standardization in the Vehicles Industry.

available or could be more easily procured.[113] The overall uncertainty caused
by the failure of the military to set clear priorities or guarantee long production
runs – which resulted in a fear of ordering machinery that might be redundant
when it was eventually delivered – was compounded in the vehicle sector by
continued doubts as to whether and when the pre-war Schell Programme
would be implemented, which might necessitate further reorganization of
Gaggenau and Mannheim and even the introduction of different types. This
too led the board to insist that the company's lorry-producing plants should
continue to invest in machinery that was of general application and capable
of transfer between production lines or plants.[114]

The reliance upon highly flexible production methods caused by perpetual
improvization, crisis management and short-term responses to bottlenecks
also ensured a continued need for a high level of skilled labour at Mannheim.
Up until the winter of 1940–1 there were no serious threats to production
methods, however ad hoc, from shortages of skilled labour. From 1940 to 1941
the male workforce of Mannheim rose from 3119 to 3348, and in 1940 the
proportion of skilled workers in the workforce (52.7 per cent) still compared
relatively well with that of 1937 (56.7 per cent).[115] However, even by late
1940 production was beginning to suffer from a lack of properly trained or
experienced workers at individual machines, leading to problems of quality
deterioration.[116] During 1941, the plant began to experience severe shortages
of labour, in particular of skilled workers, which it clearly found harder to
retain (from call-up) than Genshagen because of the lower level of priority
that army production was accorded. From December 1940 to December 1941
it lost 11.3 per cent of its German male workforce, a reflection of the qualitative change in the armed forces' manpower demands following the invasion of
the Soviet Union, while their replacements were mainly women or foreign
workers who were usually less skilled and experienced and who could not be
deployed in the same way as their skilled German counterparts.[117]

From late 1941 onwards, the Mannheim management was forced to resort
increasingly to a widespread division of labour on the individual production
lines to allow the integration of these new workers into the production
process. In the case of gears production, for example, it complained of the
difficulties caused by the lack of skilled workers, as 'this affects the setting up
of the machinery to a very great extent, and we are forced as a result to
implement an extremely extensive subdivision of the work tasks to allow the

113 MBAG Kissel VI/22, Memorandum, 6.11.1941.
114 MBAG Kissel VI/7, Hoppe/Untertürkheim to DBAG Gaggenau, 2.10.1940; MBAG Kissel
     VI/21, Hoppe/Untertürkheim to DBAG Mannheim, 15.10.1940.
115 MBAG DBAG 10, Work Force Statistics for the Mannheim Plant, July 1937; *Leistungsbericht
     der DBAG Werk Mannheim (Vol. 7)*, p. 14; MBAG DBAG 31, Special Report of DBAG,
     22.11.1945.
116 MBAG Kissel VI/21, Hoppe/Untertürkheim to DBAG Mannheim, 23.9.1940.
117 MBAG DBAG 31, Special Report, 22.11.1945.

production of gears with these semi-trained people at all.'[118] As with the case of Genshagen, the accelerated dissolution of the core workforce from 1941 onwards undoubtedly facilitated the restructuring of production processes in a way that might previously have encountered the opposition of skilled workers. However, it is clear from the Mannheim management's description of its adoption of these solutions that it did not regard these changed methods as the optimal rational solution to a particular problem, but rather as a short-term improvised response to allow production to continue at all. The division of labour forced on the management by the peculiar labour supply situation was not necessarily indicative of long-term developments in the production process that would continue beyond the war itself. What in the context of the war may have been a rational response to an immediate problem was not necessarily the optimal solution under 'normal' conditions, and the adjustment of production techniques to the lower skills level of the wartime labour force was not synonymous with long-term skills dilution in the automobile industry, which remained in essence a high-skills industry. The Mannheim management itself stressed with regard to the utilization of flow methods for gears production that 'it is much less an issue of production in volume than one of production at all.'

In any case, the ability of management to raise production by the division of labour and the utilization of flow methods was limited by the shortages of machine-tools that the plant experienced at this time. In order to subdivide a set of tasks performed by one worker on one machine so that two workers could each perform a reduced set of (simpler) tasks, a second machine-tool was obviously needed. The conversion to flow production methods thus caused, of necessity, a greater shortage of machine-tools and forced even more extensive multiple utilization of individual machines, as production lines had to be converted or reset to produce several parts in alternate shifts or rotation. In some cases, tank and lorry parts were produced alternately on the same production line. Combined with the necessity of self-manufacturing individual components that were in short supply, this led to some machine-tools being used to produce up to ten or twelve different parts simultaneously, which had significant repercussions on productivity and effective utilization of capacity.[119]

Overall, an examination of the Mannheim plant in the years 1939 to 1941 gives an impression of chaotic inefficiency, short-term improvization and poor productivity, the inevitable results of flaws in the management of the war economy and the poor coordination of materials, parts and labour supply. In total, the plant produced 6049 lorries in 1940, a monthly average of 504, and

---

118   MBAG Kissel VI/22, Memorandum regarding Start-up of Production of the Faks-40 Gears at the Mannheim Plant, 13.12.1941.
119   MBAG Kissel VI/23, Decker/Mannheim to Hoppe/Untertürkheim, 9.1.1942.

6431 in 1941, a monthly average of 556.[120] This compared to a nominal capacity of 1000 lorries per month, which the plant was supposed to have achieved following the reorganization of the late 1930s, and is a reflection not of a limited 'Blitzkrieg' strategy but of the poor management of the economy in the first half of the war, itself a product of deeper flaws in the National Socialist system.

b) The Opel licence 1942–5

The Daimler-Benz board was aware from the outset what the possible consequences of failure to overcome the problems in the lorry sector might be. Sooner or later, the combination of military losses on the one hand and stagnant production figures on the other would create pressure for state-sanctioned rationalization, type-reduction and standardization beyond that achieved under the direction of Schell in the immediate pre-war phase. In September 1940, in anticipation of imminent demands for a further programme of type-reduction, the company was already developing a new 3-ton lorry, which it hoped would be light enough and cheap enough to produce that, in the event of such a forced industry-wide rationalization, other companies would be ordered to produce Daimler-Benz's model, rather than the other way round.[121]

The expectation that the regime would sooner or later respond to the stagnation of output in the sector by adopting this policy was confirmed in January 1941 by Schell's decision to organize the lorry manufacturers into 'production groups' (Baugemeinschaften), each of which was to produce a fixed type decreed by Schell himself. This policy went beyond the previous type-reductions ordered under the pre-war Schell Programme, as not only was the number of types a plant was allowed to produce to be further limited, but more than one company was now to produce the same model. This was intended to simplify spare parts procurement for the military and allow the block allocation of components contracts to subcontractors, reducing production costs and administrative effort.[122]

Over the course of 1941, however, the issue of type-reduction in the lorry sector receded in importance somewhat. For the Daimler-Benz board a more immediate problem for Mannheim and Gaggenau emerged in the form of the regime's diversion of capacity away from army production in the summer of 1941, in the wake of the initial successes of the Barbarossa campaign. Despite its desire to retain its lorry capacity intact and thus ensure the continued

120   MBAG Statistics 2, Annual Production of Lorries and Omnibusses at DBAG 1927–1944.
121   MBAG Kissel I/28, Memorandum concerning Construction and Production of Lorries, 23.9.1940.
122   MBAG Kissel XIV/31, Additional Clarification of the Agenda of the Meeting of the Technical Committee of the GBK, 30.1.1941; Oberbaurat Schmidt to Kissel, 29.4.1941. On the GBK during the war in general see Müller, 'Mobilisierung', pp. 643–51.

existence of a core of peacetime-orientated production lines, the board was forced in the summer and autumn of 1941 to consider aero-engine or tank parts production for Mannheim and Gaggenau, since this would guarantee a regular supply of contracts and with it the retention of labour that might otherwise be conscripted elsewhere.[123] In the case of the Mannheim plant in particular, the company fought constantly to keep the lorry production lines intact. However, the conflict between Daimler-Benz's long-term strategic intentions on the one hand and the immediate imperative to keep the core of the plant's capacity intact on the other, eventually forced the company to accept contracts for the production of tank parts in October 1941.[124]

The military reversals of the winter of 1941–2, and the catastrophic material losses suffered by the German forces on the eastern front, altered this position within the space of a few weeks. From December 1941 to March 1942, the army lost a total of 31,100 lorries.[125] To put this in perspective, the German vehicle industry produced fewer than 85,000 lorries for the domestic market in the whole of 1941.[126] The demand for replacements and for sufficient supplies for the summer offensive of 1942 ensured Mannheim's continued utilization as a lorry plant, overturning the board's fears of the previous six months that the capacity of the plant would eventually be diverted to other uses. However, the material losses of 1941–2 also created renewed pressure for rationalization in the sector, emanating now from the highest levels of the regime, and fresh threats of type-reductions. These now came primarily from Speer at the RMfBuM, with the backing of Hitler. Speer had effectively marginalized Schell in the first half of 1942 as overall control of armaments production finally passed from military into civilian hands.

The RMfBuM initially planned to overcome the huge losses incurred in the east and raise production in line with the demands of the changed military situation by pushing through an expansion of Opel's Brandenburg plant, where the main German 3-ton lorry was produced, from an existing capacity of 2000 lorries per month to a new production level of 6000 per month. Hitler himself, placing the pragmatic need to exploit Opel's experience of mass-production methods above political and ideological objections related to the American ownership of the company's capital, agreed to this proposal on 10 May 1942. However, the majority of Opel's board was opposed to such an expansion, on the grounds that the labour supply situation would prevent full

---

123 MBAG Kissel I/14, Minutes of the Board Meeting of DBAG on 28 and 29.7.1941.
124 MBAG Kissel VI/8, Kissel to DBAG Gaggenau, 17.9.1941; MBAG Kissel I/14, Minutes of the Board Meeting of DBAG on 23.10.1941.
125 Kugler, A., 'Die Behandlung des Feindlichen Vermögens in Deutschland und die Selbstverantwortung der Rüstungsindustrie. Dargestellt am Beispiel der Adam Opel AG von 1941 bis Anfang 1943' in: *1999. Zeitschrift für Sozialgeschichte des 20. und 21. Jahrhunderts* Heft 2, 1988, p. 62.
126 Müller, 'Mobilisierung', p. 644.

utilization of the extra capacity in the war itself, while for the period beyond
the war such an expansion would condemn the plant to over-capacity. Opel
was also able to wriggle out of a proposed new production facility for its 3-ton
lorries in Riga.[127]

Pressure was also coming from the army for increased production of the
Opel 3-ton lorry, which it preferred to other models. Compared to the
Daimler-Benz model, the Opel lorry was 1000 kg lighter and more suited to
conditions in the east.[128] From the military viewpoint, raising output by
converting other plants to Opel production offered the benefits of simplified
spare parts and fuel supply (Daimler-Benz's lorry was a diesel lorry), while
licensing production at other plants offered Opel a way out of expanding its
own capacity. This led Speer, in covert cooperation with Opel's board
member Heinrich Wagner and a Daimler-Benz manager Gottlieb Paulus (a
former Opel employee), to examine the possibility of setting up licensed
production of the Opel model at Mannheim. This occurred during mid- to late
May, not only behind the back of the Daimler-Benz board, but initially
without the knowledge of the Opel board either.[129]

At Daimler-Benz, Kissel was aware that the issue of type-reduction and
concentration was at the forefront of debate again, as it was due to be discussed
at the forthcoming meeting of the Main Committee for Vehicle Production
within the RMfBuM; but he was completely unaware that the issue of licensed
production of Opel's 3-ton model at Daimler-Benz was already being
considered and that a decision had all but been reached. At the Daimler-Benz
board meeting of 3 June 1942, discussion of the imminent type-reduction
measures proceeded on the assumption that in future only one 3-ton model
would be produced in unison by Opel, Daimler-Benz, Ford and Magirus, but
Kissel was still optimistic that the new version of Daimler-Benz's 3-ton lorry,
which he described as 'path-breaking', would be chosen. Only at this point did
Werlin, who had become aware of the plans in the previous week, inform
Kissel of what amounted to a *fait accompli* in favour of the Opel model.[130]

The issue of building the Opel 3-ton model under licence, and the
consequences of accepting or opposing Speer's (and Hitler's) demands, were
the subject of lengthy discussion at the meeting of 3 June. Kissel himself was
angered by and bitter at a decision that he saw as undermining the board's
right to make its own choices and as an illegitimate intervention in the private
affairs of the company. On a purely practical level, he was aware of the
immense difficulties of undertaking a complete re-tooling of a factory in the

---

127 On the complexities of the pre-history of the 3-ton licence agreement and the relationship
     between economic calculation and power-political issues at Opel see Kugler, 'Die Behandlung
     des Feindlichen Vermögens', especially pp. 64–7.
128 MBAG Haspel/Volkswagen, Haspel to Nordhoff (draft), 5.2.1947.
129 Kugler, 'Die Behandlung des Feindlichen Vermögens', p. 68.
130 MBAG Kissel I/15, Minutes of the Board Meeting of DBAG on 3.6.1942.

middle of the war, especially for production of a model developed by another factory and thus not necessarily tailored to suit production methods at Mannheim. It would, according to Kissel, represent 'the largest and most difficult reorganization that the company has ever had to carry out.'

Haspel also saw huge difficulties in undertaking such a re-tooling, and was equally aware of the attendant dangers, but argued that it was preferable to accept the order to build Opel lorries under licence than to risk being elbowed out of the strategically vital mid-sized lorry sector. Accepting production of the Opel lorry would guarantee the continued participation not only of Mannheim but also of Sindelfingen and Untertürkheim in lorry production, which was of vital significance for the post-war period, for, as he observed, 'Were we to lose our position in this sector, we would find it very difficult to resume vehicle production again.' Likewise, K.C. Müller argued that producing the main army lorry type would ensure long-term participation in large-scale production and prevent the loss of Daimler-Benz's position to other companies. The board as a whole, concurring with Haspel's assessment that under the circumstances there was no alternative but to accept the decision, and recognizing the possibility of making a virtue out of a necessity in using the situation further to expand Mannheim's capacity and gain knowledge of Opel's mass-production techniques, opted to agree to the proposal at the forthcoming meeting of the Main Committee. The licence project was eventually finalized by a decree of Schell (who remained nominally in charge of the whole issue) on 23 June, which also decreed that Borgward produce the Opel 3-ton on the same basis and formed similar production groups for lorries in other classes.[131]

Kissel, however, a tradition-minded patrician obsessed with company tradition, found it impossible to come to terms with the idea of Daimler-Benz, the inventors of the automobile, having to build the superior model of another company. As a national-conservative orientated man and NSDAP member with at least some sympathy for the regime and its ideology, he found it particularly hard to accept the notion of having to produce the model of an American-owned company – the very same firm that he himself had abused in the past on account of its alleged 'Jewishness'. This affair, together with the personal grief caused by the loss of his son in the war, led Kissel to commit suicide shortly afterwards.[132]

His replacement, Haspel, was a skilled technocrat whose interventions at board meetings had always been determined by commercial considerations of the long-term impact of war-time decisions on the development of the company. His appointment reflected not only the new pragmatism of the RMfBuM in encouraging and promoting engineers and technocrats to

131 MBAG Kissel/3-ton Opel, GBK to Main Committee for Vehicles Production, 25.6.1942.
132 MBAG Haspel/Volkswagen, Haspel to Nordhoff (draft), 5.2.1947. My thanks to Dr. Heidrun Edelmann (Tübingen) for drawing my attention to this material.

positions of prominence in the economy – at the expense where necessary of ideological considerations (in Haspel's case, the fact that his wife was Jewish) – but is also indicative of the concerns of the company itself in the changed circumstances of the second half of the war. Haspel was not only younger than his board colleagues Hentig, Jungenfeld, Werlin and K.C. Müller, and a more recent arrival on the board than all but the last of these, he was the only one of these not to identify personally and publicly with the regime or to hold a party membership card. While the issue of complicity in the regime cannot be reduced to a simple matter of party membership, Haspel's appointment over the head of his more senior colleagues can be taken as an early manifestation of the gradual process of the company's distancing itself from the regime.[133]

Despite leading the wing of the Daimler-Benz board that was in favour of accepting the Opel licence contract, if only as the lesser evil, Haspel recognized that the whole project presented major difficulties for the company, not only in terms of the re-tooling process, but owing to the fact that soon after the war, precisely at the point where lorry production would be vital to the company, the plant would have to be converted to production of Daimler-Benz's own model again. The fear of being caught halfway through the re-tooling process at the point when the war ended, and thus being forced to break it off and revert to production of the existing 3-ton model, led Haspel to refuse the initial one-year notice period built into the draft contract for the Opel licence and demand instead that two years' notice of withdrawal from the contract (starting from the end of the war) be incorporated into the agreement. This agreement, which was included in the final contract signed on 12 August 1942, provided at least some safeguard that Opel would not be able to give notice of withdrawal of the licence immediately the war was over in such a way as would severely disrupt Daimler-Benz's production and gain a crucial competitive advantage for Opel.[134]

As far as the immediate conversion to production of the Opel model was concerned, Haspel was aware from the outset that the planned start-up date for the new model of March 1943 was far too optimistic. The planning of production, the procurement of machinery, the allocation of individual production lines between Opel, components suppliers and Daimler-Benz itself (and here between Mannheim, Sindelfingen and Untertürkheim), and the arrangement of materials supply and so on represented a huge organizational challenge at the best of times, and would take many months. He recognized above all that if the plant ceased manufacturing Daimler-Benz's own model before the Opel model went into production, then the daily pressures caused by the shortages of labour and materials in the German war economy as a

133 On the background to Haspel's succession to the chairmanship see below, *Chapter VI.2.*
134 MBAG Kissel I/15, Minutes of the Board Meeting of DBAG on 14.8.1942; Kissel XI/12, Contract between Opel AG und Daimler-Benz AG (Opel 3-ton Licenced Production), 12.8.1942.

whole would lead inevitably to Mannheim's workforce being gradually conscripted elsewhere, and that the plant would find it incredibly difficult to reverse this process once it had set in.

The management thus planned instead for a start-up of production in July 1943, basing its preparations on a production of 250 in the first month, rising to 1000 per month in October 1943, 2000 per month in April 1944 and reaching the required 2600 per month by June of the same year.[135] Haspel, a realist, recognized that even this goal was unattainable. In order to avoid the gap between the two production runs which he feared most, he intervened with Schell to gain extra contracts for production of a further 1500 Daimler-Benz 3- and 1½-ton lorries at Mannheim and Untertürkheim, allowing the continuation of their production for an extra three months or so. His scepticism regarding the achievability of the deadline was proven correct when the high priority category promised by Speer for the project, which Haspel knew was essential for the procurement of machine-tools and materials and without which this already difficult undertaking would be rendered virtually impossible, was not forthcoming. Although the board was aware that the other company that was supposed to build the Opel lorry under licence, Borgward, had manufactured a reason to reverse the licence order, it is unlikely that it was pursuing a conscious delaying tactic at this point in gaining these extra contracts, given Haspel's own strong advocacy of the Opel option. The latter remained keen to keep delays to a minimum and the deadline was thus initially revised only slightly, envisaging a start-up of production in August or September 1943.[136]

At the same time, planning of the Opel 3-ton project was conditioned by the recognition that sooner or later the plant would be reverting to Daimler-Benz's own model. Although Haspel was enthusiastic to ascertain which of Opel's production methods were patented and which could be adopted at Daimler-Benz, plans for the new model were still formulated using as much as possible of Mannheim's existing machinery, and in the majority of cases where purchase of a new machine-tool was necessary, the management was sure to order machinery that could be used for other purposes. Its initial survey of machinery required for the start-up of production found that nearly half could be converted or modified from pre-existing equipment, thus avoiding new purchases, while of the 120 new machine-tools needed, 88 were to be universal machines that could be guaranteed an alternative function after the war.[137] Despite the immediate demands of the Opel project, the company continued to develop its own engines, partly for the post-war period, and

135 MBAG Kissel/3-ton Opel, Memorandum regarding Discussion on 28.7.1942 of the preliminary Planning of the 3-ton Standard Lorry, 28.7.1942.
136 MBAG Kissel I/15, Minutes of the Board Meeting of DBAG on 14.8.1942.
137 MBAG Kissel/3-ton Opel, List of Expenditure on Machinery and Items for Production, 28.7.1942.

partly in the hope that it would be able to produce an engine that it could build into the Opel lorry, avoiding the need to convert the existing production line and allowing the retention of one single mass-production line for both Mannheim and Gaggenau, with the cost benefits this entailed.[138]

Haspel's sense that the initial deadline for the conversion was wildly optimistic given the general situation of the war economy by this point was proven correct by the subsequent planning and re-tooling process. Speer's failure to give the project priority treatment compounded the general backlog of machine-tool orders and shortage of engineers and skilled workers and caused inevitable delays in the procurement and installation of the necessary new equipment. By March 1943, hardly any progress had been made, and the July 1943 deadline was put back by six months. At this point, Haspel was still committed to pushing through the conversion to the Opel model, although his awareness that the war situation could change at any point led him to ensure that the whole process was carried out in such a way as to allow the option of a quick reversion to full production of the Daimler-Benz model, which at this point was still continuing.[139]

However, in the summer of 1943, the slow rate of progress at Mannheim, combined with the general reorientation of perspectives engendered by the development of the war in the previous six months, caused Haspel to question the advisability of the whole project and to reconsider the possibility of attempting to reverse the decision. On the one hand, the failure of Daimler-Benz's technical staff to find a way of converting the company's own engine to allow its installation in the Opel frame meant that the conversion of Mannheim's engine line would now be a necessity. Not only would this complicate and delay production of the Opel lorry, with all the disadvantages this would bring from the military point of view, but from Daimler-Benz's own viewpoint the expectation that diesel engines would soon increase in attractiveness as fuel shortages intensified presented the likelihood of having to reconvert to production of the company's own model almost immediately after completion of the initial switch-over to the Opel engine. This the company naturally wished to avoid. From both a military and private company perspective – the latter increasingly conditioned by thoughts of the post-war period – the conversion appeared to make much less sense than it had done a year before. In addition, the board had begun to realize that production of the Opel model had the added disadvantage that it entailed breaking long-standing links with Mannheim's own subcontractors, who for their part were only too pleased to have an excuse to convert to production of tank

138   MBAG Minutes of the Board Meetings of DBAG 1943–1945, Minutes of the Board Meeting of
       DBAG on 16/17.2.1943; MBAG Haspel/'Arbeitskreis Lastwagen', Minutes of the Meeting on
       Lorry Manufacture on 3.3.1943.
139   MBAG Haspel/'Arbeitskreis Lastwagen', Minutes of the Meeting on Lorry Manufacture on
       3.3.1943.

components, guaranteeing their own materials and labour supply much better than if they stayed with lorry production.

Having initially pursued the conversion project as the best possible option, Haspel was led by the experiences of the previous twelve months to see the project as 'no longer purposeful'. He now argued that both military and private company interests demanded that the project be ditched before it was too late and the plant be allowed to revert to its former production. Continuing production of an item of which the plant had plenty of experience was more advisable, in the given context, than launching further into something completely unknown, of which, he said, 'we don't even know whether it is realizable or not.'[140] Having come to the conclusion that the point of no return had now been reached, Haspel intervened at least once with Schaaf, the head of the Main Committee for Vehicle Production, around June 1943 in an attempt to reverse the decision, but obviously without success. Despite gradually intensifying air raids, which also made going on with existing production appear more advisable than pushing forward with the re-tooling, the company was forced to continue converting the plant for the Opel model.

In the autumn of 1943 it was clear that even the latest deadline, which had now been set back to February 1944, was not going to be achieved. Continued shortages of machinery, increasing air raids and lack of priority treatment were exacerbated by the fact that Opel, which had initially been supposed to assist in the start-up of production by supplying some of the necessary components, was falling behind with its own production figures and was thus not in a position to help.[141] Heinrich Nordhoff, the Opel manager in charge of the Special Committee for 3-Ton Lorries at this point, obviously had the private interests of his own company to consider. In allocating supplies to his own factory first he was in any case acting in line with his duties as head of the Special Committee as Opel was, after all, the main producer of the lorry and was producing in sufficient volume to cater for immediate demand. Meanwhile, at Mannheim, as a result of air raids, 41 per cent of working hours were lost in September 1943, 59 per cent in October, 49 per cent in November, and 44 per cent in December, further delaying the conversion process.[142] Of the initial 100 extra machine-tools that were vital for the start-up, only 21 had been delivered by the end of October 1943.[143]

Haspel, for whom lorry production was becoming the key aspect of Daimler-Benz's activity, was now faced with the scenario that he had dreaded all along.

---

140 MBAG Minutes of the Board Meetings of DBAG 1943–1945, Minutes of the Board Meeting of DBAG on 9.6.1943.

141 MBAG Minutes of the Board Meetings of DBAG 1943–1945, Minutes of the Board Meeting of DBAG on 14 and 15.9.1943.

142 MBAG Haspel 2,15, Impact in Hours of Air Raids and Alarms from September 1943 to February 1944, (undated, 1944).

143 MBAG Haspel/'Arbeitskreis Lastwagen', Minutes of the Meeting on Lorry Manufacture on 29.10.1943.

Production of the old 3-ton model was gradually being wound down and was obviously going to cease before the Opel model had started to take its place. This created the prospect of a gap in production, possibly of several months, with the result that the plant would inevitably experience the 'dissolution' that Haspel had wanted to avoid at all costs. However, though he had reached the conclusion that the conversion was virtually impossible to carry through, especially given that overall conditions were more likely to deteriorate than improve, his only alternative was to refuse outright, which meant risking that Speer might order the transfer of Mannheim's machinery and labour to Opel itself, effectively closing the plant down. While open admission of failure could lead to the complete dissolution of the Mannheim plant, maintaining the illusion of attainability offered the chance to continue working towards achievement of a rationally functioning large-scale lorry plant which, if it was not completed in time to contribute towards the war effort, would nonetheless be of crucial importance to Daimler-Benz in the post-war period. The strong interdependence of the Mannheim and Gaggenau plants also meant that ongoing participation in the Opel project offered the chance to improve production methods and expand capacity not only at Mannheim itself, but also at Gaggenau. The recognition that Daimler-Benz's private interests were still best served by pushing on thus reinforced the company's continued participation, though, as Haspel realized, there was no real alternative anyway.

In June 1944 the old Daimler-Benz 3-ton lorry finally ceased production, so that, although the new type was not ready, the paper option of reverting to the old model would now give no more rapid results than continuing with the new project. Meanwhile, the deteriorating supply situation was such that, according to Haspel, 'the Mannheim plant can go neither forwards nor backwards', but had now gone so far down the original road that 'there is no alternative but to keep going down it.'[144] In mid-July, two years after the original decision had been taken, after the collapse of the German army on the eastern front and after the launch of the second front, and in an overall economic situation that had in the meantime radically changed, production of the Opel model finally began.[145] In August, at a time when the plant was already supposed to have reached a production level of 2600 lorries per month, the first 20 lorries were delivered.[146] This rose to 297 in September and 637 in October, as the collapse of production at Brandenburg following a huge air raid in August raised Mannheim to the status of the main 3-ton lorry producer and ensured the supply of materials to keep production going.[147] By gaining an

144   MBAG Minutes of the Board Meetings of DBAG 1943–1945, Minutes of the Board Meeting of DBAG on 15 and 16.4.1944.
145   MBAG Haspel/'Arbeitskreis Lastwagen', Minutes of the Meeting on Lorry Manufacture, 10.7.1944.
146   MBAG Haspel 19, Statistical Monthly Reports 1942–4.
147   See below, Chapter VII.3.

allocation of concentration camp inmates to work on the assembly lines, the management was also able to ensure that production continued and thus to keep the plant intact in the chaotic circumstances of the closing stages of the war. Between August 1944 and the end of the war, a total of 3500 Opel lorries were produced, a significant achievement in the context, but, measured against the original aims of the Opel project, a total failure.

From the viewpoint of the RMfRuK and the army, the decision to force the licensed production of the Opel lorry at Mannheim proved to be a disastrous miscalculation, the project only coming to fruition at a time when the military reverses Germany had suffered were such that production could no longer bring any of the advantages envisaged in June 1942. The performance of the plant was no better in the second half of the war than in the first half. From the viewpoint of the company, however, the Opel licence project was of crucial importance, as it ensured that Daimler-Benz retained a firm foothold in the vital lorry sector for the post-war period – and as such fulfilled one of the key preconditions for the company's ability to emerge from the wreckage of 1945.

VI. Big Business and Racial Barbarism: Labour at Daimler-Benz 1939–45

1. Company Social Policy 1939-1945

The National Socialist seizure of power and the rearmament-led economic boom of the 1930s not only created the conditions in which an accelerated transition to more capital-intensive production methods could occur, but also, through the destruction of the organized labour movement and the erosion of Weimar social legislation, a context which the company social policy initiatives developed in the 1920s could expand. The Law for the Ordering of National Labour of 20.1.1934 (AOG), which relied heavily on the input of industry for its conception, combined the exclusion of all 'external elements' (*werksfremde Elemente*) from the formulation of company social policy and the restoration of industry's status as 'master in its own house' with a decentralization of responsibility for the formation of pay, conditions and welfare provision from state to factory level.[1] This devolution of welfare provision to the individual factory was intended to break down collective class-based activism and mentalities among the workers in favour of a company-orientated identity embodied in the notion of the 'factory community.'[2] Despite the establishment of the external regulatory office of Trustee (later Reich Trustee) of Labour under the Reich Labour Ministry (*Reichsarbeitsministerium* –RAM), however, the language of 'trust' and 'duty' which supposedly defined the relationship between workers and management could not conceal that the law represented a codification of the huge shift in the balance of power between capital and labour that had occurred as a result of the Depression and the National Socialist seizure of power.

Like all other companies, Daimler-Benz greatly expanded its voluntary social policy provision in the 1930s.[3] Initially, expenditure rose modestly,

---

1 Siegel, T., 'Lohnpolitik im Nationalsozialistischen Deutschland' in: Sachse et al., *Angst, Belohnung, Zucht und Ordnung*, p. 68.
2 Frese, *Betriebspolitik*, pp. 100, 112.
3 For a detailed examination of Daimler-Benz's social policy in the 1930s see Stahlmann, *Die Erste Revolution*, pp. 213–18.

with the relatively easy labour supply situation making it possible to recruit additional labour and exact disciplined work from them without the need for extensive social policy offerings. The increase in Daimler-Benz's expenditure from RM 459,000 in 1933 to RM 2.7m in 1937 was substantial, but, given the increase in Daimler-Benz's labour force over the same period, not excessive compared with what came after.[4] As the acute labour shortages of the pre-war years began to give rise to an increase in labour fluctuation and to intense competition for workers between companies, and as the regime responded by continually increasing its regulation of the labour market and wage levels, so business in turn attempted to reduce labour fluctuation and circumvent controls by using social policy as a form of indirect wage increase. At Daimler-Benz, this manifested itself in an increase of social policy expenditure from RM 2.7m in 1937 to RM 9.14m in 1938 and RM 12.1m in 1939. This was accompanied by a marked growth in the proportion of social policy expenditure made in the form of direct money payments (Christmas bonuses, etc).[5]

The outbreak of war did not represent a complete break in the development of either state or company labour policy, as both growing state dirigism in the labour market and the criminalization of labour law had begun prior to 1939.[6] Nonetheless, both the context within which company social policy was formulated and the aims which it pursued were necessarily altered by the substantial increase in state control over the allocation of labour and by the even more marked expansion of the terroristic state apparatus that stood behind the employers during the war. State direction of labour deployment reduced the significance of social policy as a means of recruitment on the free market, while the expansion of state terror in the war underpinned internal company measures to discipline and control the workforce. The extent to which the latter formed the context for the development of internal company policy is underlined by the fact that whereas in 1938 86 workers were executed by the regime, in 1943 and 1944 this figure was over 5000 per year. In the same way, Gestapo arrests rose from 7311 in June 1942 to 43,505 in June 1944.[7] While a major proportion of this is accounted for by the extension of terror towards foreign workers, the war nonetheless witnessed a major escalation of overt coercion of German workers too. This was most visible in the emergence of the Labour Education Camps during the period 1940–1.[8] With their brutal regime of hard forced labour, undernourishment and lack of sleep, these were again primarily used to 'educate' foreign workers, and the shortage of German workers was such that employers were often reluctant to resort to such

4   Pohl et al., *Die Daimler-Benz AG*, p. 173.
5   Ibid., p. 173; Stahlmann, *Die Erste Revolution*, p. 218.
6   Salter, 'Mobilization', p. 209.
7   Werner, *Bleib Übrig*, pp. 318–19.
8   Ibid., pp. 175–82.

external bodies, but the existence of these camps, combined with the threat of being sent to the Russian front, undoubtedly had a major disciplining effect on native workers too. Thus, although the war witnessed an extension of the internal disciplinary function of company social policy, through withdrawal of holiday pay, fines, loss of 'reserved status' and so on, it tended to be concerned with measures to integrate new workers into the factory environment, with training them quickly and with raising and maintaining their productivity in the changing situation provided by the war.

The immediate context in which company policy towards the workforce had to be formulated upon the outbreak of war was provided by the War Economy Decree (*Kriegswirtschaftsverordnung*) of 4 September 1939.[9] As part of the regime's measures to mobilize the economy for war, this stipulated the cessation of bonuses for overtime, Sunday work, nightshifts or working on public holidays, and allowed the extension of working hours beyond those usually permitted. The company, recognizing the need to expand armaments production, but reluctant to undertake an immediate expansion of capacity to cope with what was widely seen as an anomalous situation of short-term duration, took immediate advantage of these stipulations to try to raise output without large-scale reorganization or investment. Taking advantage of the fact that no overtime or other bonuses had to be paid, the company introduced a ten-hour day (at Genshagen at least), and combined this with demands for an 'immediate intensification of labour', which manifested itself in a cross-the-board piece-rate reductions of up to 12 per cent.[10] Even when the stipulations of the War Economy Decree concerning bonuses and overtime were gradually withdrawn over the winter of 1939–40, following a wave of labour unrest, the company continued to exact longer hours than the norm from its workers, as the 'cost-plus' pricing system in operation at this point meant that the producer could pass on the costs of overtime and bonus pay to the purchaser in the form of increased prices. In September 1940, the 60-hour week was introduced at Untertürkheim.[11] Thus, while many companies regarded 54 to 56 hours per week as the optimal balance between longer hours and the maintenance of long-term labour productivity, workers at Daimler-Benz had to suffer very long hours from an early stage.[12]

Given the hours that Daimler-Benz workers were forced to work, the issue of maintaining and raising productivity assumed great significance at an early point in the war. This was particularly the case when it came to the thousands of new workers who came to the company as substitute labour for called-up male workers and who had to be integrated into the production lines as

---

9 MBAG Huppenbauer 226, War Economy Decree, 4.9.1939.
10 MBAG Kissel VI/9, Kissel to Werner/DBAG Mannheim, 28.10.1939; Kissel XIII/10, Kissel to Kemmler/Gau Office for the Iron and Metal Industries, 20.9.1939.
11 MBAG DBAG Untertürkheim 19/2, Administration Decree No. 1271, 25.9.1940.
12 Werner, *Bleib Übrig*, p. 149.

quickly and efficiently as possible. One of the major sources of additional labour at Daimler-Benz from 1939 to 1941 was female labour, which increased substantially in the period. Whether or not the regime was successful in mobilizing female labour reserves in the macro-economy as a whole, either through transfer from non-essential to essential industries or through mobilization of previously economically inactive women, the number of women specifically in the metal-working sector rose markedly in the first two years of the war, and Daimler-Benz was no exception, as the statistical evidence clearly shows.[13]

At Mannheim, the number of German women rose from 112 out of a total of 3119 workers in December 1939 (3.4 per cent) to 505 out of 3572 workers in December 1941 (14 per cent), an increase of 350 per cent.[14] Thereafter, it rose only moderately from 505 in December 1941 to 633 in December 1944, at which point German female labour still only accounted for 14 per cent of the total workforce. Similarly, at Gaggenau, the number of German women rose from 320 in December 1939, out of a total of 5083 workers (6.3 per cent), to 608 in December 1941, out of a total workforce of 4877 (12.4 per cent). Thereafter, it similarly rose only marginally further in the second half of the war. Thus, at both Mannheim and Gaggenau, the main phase in the expansion of the German female labour force was clearly 1939 to 1941. A similar trend is discernible for Sindelfingen, where the number of German women rose moderately from 1939 to 1941, before actually falling away. The modesty of the increase in the first half of the war at Sindelfingen, compared to Gaggenau and Mannheim, is probably explained by the relatively high proportion of women workers in the Sindelfingen workforce prior to the war, a product of the fact that as a body-work plant it had a higher number of 'feminized' operations (upholstery, polishing, etc.).

The overall figures for Daimler-Benz (excluding Genshagen) replicate the pattern of a rising proportion of female labour in the first half of the war followed by relative stagnation in the second half, albeit in far less marked form than at Mannheim or Gaggenau. At Untertürkheim, the number of German women in the workforce increased at a more or less constant rate throughout the war. At Marienfelde, the main increases occurred in the second half of the war, probably a product of the fact that female labour reserves in the Berlin area had been mobilized more fully in the pre-war years and that they were also the object of competition from more feminized industries such as the electrical engineering industry, which was centred on Berlin.[15] Overall, however, the greatest expansion of the German female labour force at Daimler-Benz's core plants occurred from 1939 to 1941, during

13 Ibid., p. 82.
14 These and the following statistics are from MBAG DBAG 31, Special Report of Daimler-Benz AG, 22.11.1945.
15 Freyberg and Siegel, *Industrielle Rationalisierung*, p. 280.

which period the number of German women workers rose from 4038 to 5533, an increase of 37 per cent in real terms, and in proportional terms from 11.3 per cent of the workforce in December 1939 to 13.6 per cent of the workforce in December 1941. Thereafter, again, it rose more moderately, from 5533 in December 1941 to 6151 in December 1943. The proportion of German women in the workforce as a whole in the second half of the war fluctuated between about 12 and 13.5 per cent.

As with the development of shop-floor organization and production itself under war conditions, it is difficult to penetrate beneath the company's public projection of an image of efficiency, rationality and ideological conformity to the daily realities of the situation and the experience of women workers on the shop floor. The company stressed to the DAF, for example, that it recognized that the deployment of female labour brought 'especially important responsibilities' regarding their care, as 'the woman is undoubtedly more damage-prone than the man'. Hence it would 'do everything to keep her from even the smallest of dangers.' For this reason, the company claimed that working women, and especially mothers, were comprehensively looked after and always deployed in such a way that 'their health can in no way be endangered.'[16] In reality, however, insufficient stocks of protective clothing, shortages of engineers and daily pressures to fill immediate gaps on the production line meant that women were put to work with little regard for their health, and in one case at least – at more or less the same time as the above claims were being made by the Mannheim management – new workers, and especially women, were being made to operate machines without any protective clothing at all, so that it was reported internally that 'the danger of an accident is exceptionally great.'[17]

The integration of large numbers of additional women workers into a factory environment traditionally dominated by males and structured accordingly, and into a production process characterized by a high level of skilled and semi-skilled labour, was less problematic than it had been in the First World War. Although the automobile and aero-engine industries remained high-skills sectors, the ability to retrain workers for specific and limited functions had nonetheless been made easier by the evolution of serial production, of mechanization and semi-automation, and the routinization of work functions these engendered. This was especially the case on large-scale production lines where the division of labour was sufficient to allow tasks previously carried out by skilled workers to be performed by semi-skilled workers, as long as the specifications of the given product remained constant – thus releasing skilled male workers for more complex tasks or for work on small-volume production lines such as naval engine production or

16 *Leistungsbericht der Daimler-Benz AG Werk Mannheim/Ergänzungsbericht 1940–1941*, p. 39.
17 MBAG DBAG Mannheim 23, Circular of Mannheim Management regarding Supply of Women's Workclothes, 11.11.1941.

aero-engine development, where genuinely skilled labour was needed.[18]

Initially, women workers tended thus to be deployed on car production lines, where the high volume of production, relatively routinized labour functions and the relative lack of changes to design specification during the war meant that they could be integrated into the production process as semi-skilled labour with relative ease. Thus, at Untertürkheim, skilled workers in car production were transferred to naval and aero-engine production and development and replaced by semi-skilled women, so that by December 1939 some car production workshops had as little as 7 per cent skilled workers.[19] However, even in the first half of the war, the extent of the call-ups of German male workers to the Wehrmacht was such that the company soon had to broaden the deployment of female labour to other areas, and by mid-1940 women were also being drafted into aero-engine production in increasing numbers.[20] Consequently it was forced to engage in extensive training of female labour from a very early stage – the alternative was to effect a widespread subdivision of labour to reduce the dependence of the plants on semi-skilled and skilled workers, but this would have undermined the long-term flexibility of the factories at a time when this was precisely what the company, operating on the assumption that a return to peacetime was imminent, wished to protect. As argued in the case of Mannheim, it was only when the labour shortages began to intensify really seriously, in 1941, that the company reluctantly started to do this.

In fact, despite the changes in the organization of production in the preceding twenty years, the capital-intensive and high-skills nature of the automobile and aero-engine industries meant that, as with all substitute labour in the war, extensive training was still essential for the integration of female labour into the production process in even the most rationalized sectors. While a substantial proportion of German women were utilized as white-collar workers, their blue-collar counterparts were for the most part trained for semi-skilled activities. For example, whereas in July 1940 59 per cent of women on the shop floor at Mannheim were deployed as semi-skilled workers and 41 per cent were unskilled, by June 1941 75 per cent were semi-skilled and only 25 per cent unskilled.[21] However, no women were ever deployed as skilled labour, and the pattern of under-representation of women in high-skilled small-volume production lines continued well into the second half of the war at least.[22]

As far as social policy initiatives and the structuring of working hours

---

18 DBAG Sindelfingen (ed.), *Report on our Measures and Results in the Area of Professional Training 1940–1* (undated, 1941).
19 MBAG Kissel VI/1, Kissel to Gauleiter Mürr, 2.12.1939.
20 MBAG Kissel XIII/3, DBAG/Hoppe to Armaments Commando Stuttgart, 18.5.1940.
21 *Leistungsbericht der Daimler-Benz AG Werk Mannheim/Ergänzungsbericht 1940–1.*
22 MBAG Haspel 1,2, Work-force Statistics for Naval Engine Production at Marienfelde (1.10.1942), 31.3.1943.

designed specifically to recruit and retain female labour are concerned, at Daimler-Benz they were developed on a similar basis to those of other large industrial companies.[23] The company employed numerous social workers who visited women in the factories to ensure that they were not deployed in unsuitable work and to monitor their experience and performance, and attempted to attract female labour by measures such as the establishment of more kindergartens and crèches to look after their children.[24] Some workers were also deployed on a half-shift basis, to give them time to carry out their extensive domestic chores, although, like many other companies in the sector, Daimler-Benz found that this caused a variety of problems, not least of which was friction between half-shift women and those women who had to work a full shift, the latter resenting the privileged position of their comrades.[25] As a result, Daimler-Benz, again like other companies, preferred to give women workers one or two (unpaid) days off a month to perform household chores.[26] Nonetheless, at Untertürkheim 363 out of 2038 German women (18 per cent) were employed on half-shifts by April 1944.[27]

Despite the efforts of the company to structure the work and environment of the female labour force in such a way as to optimize their productivity, women workers were a regular source of complaint in the early part of the war. In May 1940 the women's social worker at Sindelfingen observed that the low productivity of women workers was often a product of lack of will and a 'poor attitude to work'.[28] At around the same time, the manager of Marienfelde complained of a lack of sense of responsibility among workers who stayed at home for 'any triviality' such as headaches or 'a little cough', directing his comments specifically at women workers.[29] While this is as much a reflection of the hardline attitude of the management as it is of the alleged idleness of women workers – anyone who had to perform long hours of industrial labour and simultaneously manage a household in the war hardly had it easy – it nonetheless underlines the fact that women workers were perceived to be a particular problem when it came to discipline and absenteeism.[30]

Not only for the female labour force, but for all the new workers drafted into the production lines at Daimler-Benz in the war, the second means of

23   See Sachse, C., 'Hausarbeit im Betrieb. Betriebliche Sozialarbeit unter dem Nationalsozialismus' in: Sachse et al., *Angst, Belohnung, Zucht und Ordnung*, pp. 209–74.
24   MBAG Kissel XIII/4, Half-Yearly Report of the Factory Social Worker at DBAG Sindelfingen, 10.5.1940; *Geschäftsbericht der Daimler-Benz Motoren GmbH Genshagen 1940.*
25   MBAG Haspel 4,36, Minutes of the Meeting of the Main Committee for Vehicles Production, 11.11.1943.
26   *Leistungsbericht der Daimler-Benz AG Mannheim/Ergänzungsbericht 1940–1.*
27   National Archives Washington D.C., RG 243 USSBS Docs 79a1, Work-force Statistics Daimler-Benz Untertürkheim Plant, 30.4.1944.
28   MBAG Kissel XIII/4, Half-Yearly Report of the Factory Social Worker at Daimler-Benz AG Sindelfingen Plant, 10.5.1940.
29   MBAG Kissel XIII/8, Factory Roll Call at Marienfelde, 11.4.1940.
30   Werner, *Bleib Übrig*, p. 80; Salter, 'Mobilization', p. 197.

integrating them into the production process and bringing their productivity up to standard quickly was the wage system in the factories. This itself had undergone an extensive transformation, beginning in the immediate pre-war years, and had evolved by 1941 into a key aspect of the company's system of discipline and incentive for the workers. It was based upon Taylorist methods of factory management which involved the breaking-down of work processes into their individual component movements not only as the basis for the optimization of efficiency in each process as an end in itself, but also as the foundation for a 'scientific' calculation of wages based on the nature of the labour being performed.[31]

The previous system of individual timed piece-rates at Daimler-Benz had meant that, although the productivity of each worker increased, differences in the work-rate of each worker, problems with materials supply or inadequacies in the time-and-motion studies on which basis wages were calculated, meant that in practice some components continued to reach the assembly lines at a different rate to others. The uniformity and regularity of production speed of each machine or machine group, which were the preconditions for a genuine flow production process, were thus still not assured. Furthermore, with the semi- rather than fully integrated production processes of the type that existed at Daimler-Benz, which were characterized by intermediate materials or semi-finished goods storage at the end of each machine group, there remained a limited potential for informal control of production speed on the part of the workers. The management was aware that, despite the pressure caused by the overall tempo of production it was still possible for workers to conceal bottlenecks, as 'when workers see a bottleneck, those who stand at the immediately preceding work stations instinctively slow down, so that the bottleneck is not visible by the pile-up of material.'[32]

In part, such problems could be overcome by the removal of workers suspected of slowing down the pace of production and their replacement by 'uninfluenced' workers, i.e. those less given to passive resistance or informal shop-floor control of output. More fundamentally, however, the management pursued a strategy of countering the scope for resistance at a sub-strike level by undermining the solidarity between workers by a dual strategy revolving around the use of group piece-rates on the one hand, and the simultaneous stimulation of worker individualism on the other.

Beginning with the Mannheim plant, where the fundamental reorganization that followed its conversion to a lorry plant formed the basis for a complete overhaul of its wage structures from 1938 onwards, the company gradually moved to introduce group piece-rates on the shop floor at all its plants. This involved the organization of the workers on each individual

31 For a more detailed analysis of wages structures at Daimler-Benz see Stahlmann, *Die Erste Revolution*, pp. 199–213.
32 MBAG Kissel XIII/11, Job Evaluation and Wages Systems in Flow Production, 6.12.1941.

production line into work-gangs (*Kameradschaften*) consisting of ten to 80
workers, depending on the size of machine group, and paying the workers on
the basis of the output of the work-gang as a whole. Thus, instead of being
dependent upon his or her own output, a worker's wage was now based upon
the output of the whole production line. All at once, the management noted,
'each member of the work gang is equally interested in high output and in high
productivity.'

The consequences of this were obvious – whereas previously, slower
workers would be 'absorbed' and concealed, now the group as a whole was
forced to ensure as regular and uniform a production flow as possible, and
indeed did so without pressure from the foreman. In place of the previous
tendency to collective support, the management observed that 'the workgangs
now recognize the unsuitable workers themselves . . . the group effort is never,
however, directed towards absorbing weaker members.' This was reinforced by
an intentional interspersal of highly productive and politically reliable
workers among the others, both to keep work rates up and to undermine
further the ability of less compliant workers to organize slow-downs, which, in
a group of up to 80 workers, would be next to impossible to arrange without
discovery.

This method of discipline and control proved itself to be particularly
suitable to the conditions of the war economy. First, pressure from German
male workers to keep work-rates up meant that the large numbers of new
workers drafted into the factories were quickly forced to achieve a high level
of productivity too.[33] This was brought to bear on both German women and
foreign workers with great effect. Second, it was used by the management to
help overcome the problems that shortages of materials and irregular supplies
caused to attempts to optimize the through-flow of production. As the new
group piece-rates were calculated on the basis of aggregate output over a
period of weeks, any delay or disruption that caused the group to fall behind
with its targets forced the workers to make up lost production over the
following days if they wanted to achieve their full wage. The pressure placed
on them by this system was such that the management found it much easier to
get the workers to work overtime than before. With the group piece-rate
system, the company was thus able to ensure that when the supply of materials
was inadequate, which was often the case, the burden was passed on to the
workforce, who were forced to catch up or bear the financial cost of not doing
so, even when the backlog was not their fault.[34]

Bonus pay for output beyond the production target was also calculated on a
group basis, with each worker receiving a uniform bonus in proportion to the
complexity of the task he or she was performing within the group (i.e. skilled

33 *Leistungsbericht der Daimler-Benz AG Werk Mannheim/Ergänzungsbericht 1940–1*.
34 MBAG Kissel XIII/11, Job Evaluation and Wages Systems in Flow Production, 6.12.1941.

workers received a higher bonus than semi-skilled workers). The bonuses were such that a good worker could, in principle, achieve a maximum of 15 per cent above the wage paid to a worker of average ability.[35] The bonuses themselves were calculated according to the second element in the new pay system, a new, more differentiated eight-scale wages structure that replaced the old distinctions between skilled, semi- and unskilled, and that was intended not only to reinforce the atomizing impact of the group piece-rate, but to stimulate the emergence of a new, more individualistic worker type.

Again, the roots of this development are to be found in the immediate pre-war years, with the process of implementation extending into the middle years of the war. The new, eight-scale wage structure was, essentially, born of the need to update the traditional three-tiered gradation of workers based on skills level to reflect the more differentiated range of skilled and semi-skilled vocations, that had developed as a result of changing methods of production and that could not be adequately incorporated into the traditional categories. The introduction of more gradations of skills levels, and the increase of pay differentials between each, was intended to encourage individual upward mobility and, at the same time, make such mobility easier, because the skills gap between each gradation was smaller. The upward-mobility ethos functioned in line with the atomization strategy aimed at promoting a more self-orientated worker improving his or her position through individual self-advance, not collective action. In the context of the war, this was in some ways difficult to introduce, as increasing pay differentials without flouting the regime's policy of an overall wage freeze naturally meant reducing some workers' pay and increasing others, potentially causing extreme unrest. This demanded, as Kissel regularly pointed out, an 'intense psychological education of the workforce'.[36] However, in other ways the war created a context in which this could be all the more easily implemented. Not only did the company have a huge terror apparatus behind it that could be brought to bear on recalcitrant workers, but also, as a result of changes in the structure of the workforce during the war, those lower-skilled functions that would experience a pay reduction were increasingly being performed by prisoners of war and foreign workers. These groups were marginal to the core German male workforce and were faced with far greater and more consistent state terror, so their scope for resistance to managerial measures was far less.[37]

The second significant aspect of this eight-scale wage system was that, in

---

35 MBAG Kissel XIII/11, Clarification of the Guidelines for the Implementation of Wages Policy Measures in Relation to the Raising of Productivity in the War Economy, (undated, 1941). In practice, competition for labour and the stipulations of the cost-plus pricing system encouraged piece-rate bonuses to gravitate upwards – at Genshagen, for example, workers were achieving, on average, bonuses of 40 per cent above supposed average productivity by 1942.
36 MBAG Kissel XIII/10, Kissel to Jäzosch/Office for Iron and Metal of the DAF, 5.4.1940.
37 MBAG Kissel XIII/11, Clarification of the Guidelines for the Implementation of Wages Policy Measures in Relation to the Raising of Productivity in the War Economy, (undated, 1941).

place of paying the individual worker according to his or her skills level, the wage was calculated according to the specific activity being carried out.[38] This was based on job evaluation methods developed in the 1920s and 1930s that aimed to pay not the worker, but the work being performed, and were intended to re-establish a 'fair' relationship between the pay of skilled and semi-skilled workers. Whereas with the previous system the inflation of piece-rates for semi-skilled workers in times of labour shortage (such as in the late 1930s) often meant that they could be paid more than skilled workers on an hourly rate, henceforth wage increases for semi-skilled workers could only be achieved by their rising to perform a more complex work operation. Inevitably, this encouraged workers to seek higher wages by promotion to higher-paid activities, so that the system gave rise to an 'automatic and natural process of selection' within the workforce by which the most capable rose to the top. Once the workers grasped this, the management maintained, the age of collective wage disputes would be succeeded by one in which wages would be a depoliticized issue, in which the notion of a 'just wage' would be divorced from distributional conflict and relegated to the status of a technical issue, disputable only insofar as the individual work activity was not placed in the correct category.[39]

While in the long run this system, which formed the basis for wage structures in the 1950s and 1960s, undoubtedly played a major role in stimulating individual upward mobility, in the short term its ability to function as a stimulus to increased productivity was dependent upon money wages retaining their status as an incentive to work. However, from 1943 onwards the scarcity of consumer goods was such that there was little in the way of rationed goods to buy, while black-market prices for unrationed goods remained beyond the reach of ordinary workers.[40] The declining value of money wages thus forced the company, and the regime, to find other ways of maintaining labour productivity, containing absenteeism and enforcing labour discipline generally.

A key role here was played by food allocations, which emerged as central to a broader system of non-financial incentives and rewards in the second half of the war. The allocation of food rations to workers had, from the outset, been closely linked by the regime to the nature of the work they performed, with basic rations being supplemented by extra rations for those who performed hard or long hours of work.[41] The company had also, like other companies, been keen to ensure that these extra rations actually went to the workers for whom they were intended, as opposed to being shared amongst their family

38 MBAG Kissel XIII/11, Short Memorandum on the Introduction of Pay according to Job Specification in the Aero-Engine Industry, 1.2.1941.
39 MBAG Kissel XIII/10, Kissel to Jäzosch/Office for Iron and Metal of the DAF, 5.4.1940.
40 Werner, Bleib Übrig, p. 323.
41 Ibid., p. 44.

members. In order to force workers who qualified for extra rations to eat them themselves, the management of Marienfelde, for example, began directing a proportion of their extra ration cards direct to the factory canteens in April 1940. As a result, the number of workers eating in the canteens more than doubled in a single week.[42] It was thus only a small step, especially in the given climate, to instrumentalizing food allocation as a disciplining measure, making the receipt of rations dependent upon the achievement of given levels of work and, above all, upon the maintenance of a given standard of discipline. This was particularly the case as, compared to the relatively satisfactory levels of nutrition in the first half of the war, the calorific intake of German workers fell substantially in the second, when longer hours and the stress caused by air raids both intensified the physical strains of the war and made the workforce increasingly reliant upon food and goods procured by the company.[43]

The period 1943–4 witnessed the implementation and extension of this practice, which culminated in the gradual replacement of money wages by food and goods as the prime lever by which to exact hard work and strict discipline. In November 1943, the value of money was still such that Fritz Sauckel ordered that ill-discipline be met with fines of up to one day's or week's wages, depending on the severity of the offence, with state organs to be involved if necessary.[44] In March 1944, by contrast, those who went absent from the factories or worked at an inadequate rate were to be disciplined by the withdrawal of their extra rations.[45] Workers who failed to turn up on Saturday afternoon or Sunday night, when absenteeism was particularly marked, or who clocked on late and clocked off early had their extra rations withheld for one week.[46] The occasional receipt of cigarettes or similar items was also dependent upon not having fallen foul of the regulations on absenteeism.[47] Finally, hours lost through absenteeism were to be taken off holiday entitlement, forcibly made up on other days or countered with withdrawal of Sunday, night-shift or overtime bonuses.[49] The radicalization of state terror that accompanied these measures saw at least one German worker – a female typist – sent to a Labour Education Camp in November 1944, for absenteeism.[49]

By this process of disciplining and terrorizing absentee workers, the company was able to ensure that most continued to turn up to work. Further, the

42 MBAG Kissel XIII/8, Factory Roll Call at Marienfelde, 11.4.1940.
43 Werner, *Bleib Übrig*, p. 51.
44 MBAG Haspel 3,32, First Decree for the Securing of Order in the Factories, 1.11.1943.
45 MBAG Haspel 3,32, Circular of the Manager of Untertürkheim regarding the Combating of Work-Shirking through withholding of Supplementary Rations 4.5.1944.
46 MBAG Haspel 3,32, Announcement regarding the Observation of Working Hours, 18.5.1944.
47 MBAG Haspel 3,32, Circular to all Departmental Heads regarding Special Allocations, 12.5.1944.
48 MBAG Haspel 3,32, Second Decree for the Securing of Order in the Factories, 23.9.1944.
49 MBAG Haspel 3,32, Announcement of Punishment due to Unwarranted Absence, 27.11.1944.

growing reliance of the workers on the plant for food and goods was such that the company could instrumentalize this in combination with piece-rate reductions to exact an ever-more intense rate of work, which was in turn related to the company's desire to keep raising output in the short term as far as possible, whilst not disadvantaging the company's interests for the (post-war) long term. However, the period from late 1943 onwards was also characterized by developments that apparently ran counter to the radicalization of discipline and terror, and which are probably as important in explaining why labour discipline held up to the extent that it did in the last phase of the war. As the intensification of bombing destroyed residential areas in the cities – Mannheim, Stuttgart and Berlin were all subjected to intense and highly destructive air raids – so the pre-existing social routines and daily normalities of the working people who lived there (shopping, going to the barber's, etc) necessarily underwent a process of dissolution, which was quickened by the dispersal of production to other sites outside the cities and by evacuations, which also accelerated the dissolution of family and social ties. Parallel to the process of radicalization experienced at the factory, the workplace also became under these circumstances an agent of stabilization, developing into the focal point of a surrogate normality.[50] In April 1944, for example, a shop was established at Untertürkheim to enable workers to carry out essential purchases in breaks or after work.[51] Soon after, a hairdresser's was set up to allow German male workers to have their hair washed and cut on the same basis.[52] A shoe-repair workshop was also created, as was an extra dental surgery.[53] While this was obviously primarily aimed at reducing absenteeism among workers, it is likely that such measures functioned not only in a strictly disciplining sense, in that they increased the workers' reliance upon the factory because of the lack of alternative sources of supply, but also played a crucial role in recreating a 'normal' context within which workers could continue to engage in their 'normal' occupations and routines under conditions that were otherwise anything but the norm. Radicalizing and stabilizing developments thus existed side by side in the final phase of the war, and the ability of the company and the regime to keep workers at work depended upon the interaction of both these processes simultaneously.

2. The German Labour Front and Company Social Policy 1939–45

The social policy programmes developed by the DAF in the 1930s went very much with the grain of the employers' practices that emerged in the 1920s and that were themselves greatly expanded in the 1930s as competition for labour,

50 Werner, *Bleib Übrig, passim.*
51 MBAG Haspel 3,32, Announcement of the Establishment of a Food Shop, 17.4.1944.
52 MBAG Haspel 3,32, Announcement of the Establishment of a Hairdresser's, 4.5.1944.
53 MBAG Haspel 3,32, Announcement of the Establishment of Dentist Appointments, 24.5.1944; Announcement of the Opening of a Shoe-Repair Shop, 12.6.1944.

the need to circumvent the regime's wage restrictions and the need to maintain labour productivity in the face of lengthening working hours forced employers to increase their provision in this area more and more. The DAF itself, recognizing the significance of these developments, underwent a process of perpetual expansion throughout the 1930s and into the war, developing its initial 'Beauty of Labour' (Schönheit der Arbeit – SdA) and 'Strength through Joy' (*Kraft durch Freude* – KdF) campaigns into a far broader range of programmes encompassing virtually every aspect of social policy within and outside the workplace, designed not only for the sake of the policies themselves but also to assert the DAF's right to function as the sole determinant of social policy within the regime. Its activities combined initiatives aimed at integrating the workers socially and politically into the regime and, increasingly, at raising labour productivity within the workplace, with efforts to influence company social policy in line with the ideological objectives of the regime. By the outbreak of war it had built up a multitude of offices with representatives in each large company or factory, including Daimler-Benz, ranging from youth officers, women's officers and sports officers to legal advisers and work safety advisers, and to KdF functionaries for each main area of KdF activities, all under the direction of the DAF plant foreman (*Betriebsobmann*) for each factory.[54] By sidelining or 'coordinating' rival party organs (the Hitler Youth, the National Socialist Factory Cell Organization, the National Socialist Women's Organization), the DAF was able to become the main party organ responsible for industrial social policy and could establish itself as the dominant National Socialist presence on the shop floor.[55]

According to its annual reports, the company enjoyed a highly harmonious relationship with the DAF, manifesting itself in 'close cooperation' on all issues relating to the establishment of the 'factory community'.[56] In comparison to many other companies, which often maintained an attitude of thinly veiled hostility and even refused to take part, Daimler-Benz does seem to have enjoyed a good relationship with the DAF in many areas, especially up to the war. It was an enthusiastic (and very successful) participant in the annual Model Plant competition, and placed great emphasis on the achievement of the various awards, even if only through recognition of the benefits of such gestures of outward conformity with the regime.[57] It also entered its

---

54 *Leistungsbericht der DBAG 1940 Zentralverwaltung und Werke Untertürkheim*, Band 1, p. 99ff, (Circular of the Gau Foreman for Württemberg of DAF concerning DAF Organization at Daimler-Benz AG), excerpts reprinted in Roth und Schmid (eds.), *Schlüsseldokumente*, p. 182 (Doc. 70).
55 On the development of the DAF up until 1939 see especially Frese, *Betriebspolitik*.
56 *Geschäftsbericht der Daimler-Benz AG 1938*; *Geschäftsbericht der Daimler-Benz AG 1939*.
57 On the differing attitudes of companies to the Model Plant Competition see Frese, M., 'Vom NS-Musterbetrieb zum Kriegsmusterbetrieb. Zum Verhältnis von Deutscher Arbeitsfront und Großindustrie 1936–1944' in: Michalka (ed.), *Der Zweite Weltkrieg*, pp. 382–401. For Daimler-Benz's attitude see for example MBAG Kissel I/14, Minutes of the Board Meeting of DBAG on 28.5.1941.

apprentices for the Reich Apprentice Competition (*Reichsberufswettkampf*), regularly sent managers and foremen on DAF 'human leadership' courses and donated large sums of money to local DAF organs or for DAF workers' holidays and holiday hostels.[58]

While the management was supportive of the DAF's efforts to indoctrinate workers through speeches, roll-calls and courses, and of its attempts to redefine shop-floor culture in line with National Socialist ideology, it was, like other companies, fiercely defensive of its managerial autonomy and resisted all attempts by the DAF to encroach upon what it regarded as private company matters or to establish a precedent for its right to co-determine managerial policy.[59] While it was keen to avoid unnecessary conflict – if only because 'we have enough battles to fight' – the board was also aware of the predatory nature of the DAF's activities with regard to expanding its jurisdiction in social and labour policy, and was very wary of entering into agreements or commitments with the DAF that would facilitate DAF intervention in managerial decisions. As Kissel formulated it in 1937, 'Once the Labour Front has established a position in public, it isn't so easy to keep it at bay.'[60] Conceptual questions over the specific content of policy were less significant than the principle of managerial autonomy itself. This was especially the case in view of the fact that, although the higher organs of the DAF had embraced modern factory management methods by the outbreak of war, residual tensions between management and the DAF remained very much in evidence at a lower level, suggesting that the tendency of the DAF to intervene far more directly in the interests of the workers in the early years of the regime had not disappeared at the local level to the extent that it had at the top.[61]

The company continued to cooperate with the DAF in some areas after the outbreak of war in September 1939. It sent both workers and managers on externally run training courses (but refused to allow the DAF to set up courses at Daimler-Benz itself, for fear of giving away business secrets).[62] It was also willing to invoke the support of the DAF against other institutions where the general line of the DAF was similar to that of the company and its interests, such as in the prevention of call-ups to the Wehrmacht. When Sindelfingen's training manager was threatened with call-up, for example, the firm enlisted the DAF's support to pressurize the recruitment agencies to reverse the

58 For example MBAG Kissel XIII/1, Memorandum on the visit of Labour Leader Tuchscheerer/Local Youth Officer of the DAF, 3.8.1937; *Geschäftsbericht der Daimler-Benz AG 1938*; *Geschäftsbericht der Daimler-Benz AG 1939*.
59 Werner, *Bleib Übrig*, p. 76.
60 MBAG Kissel XIII/7, Kissel to Wilhelm/DBAG Marienfelde, 6.8.1937.
61 MBAG Kissel XIII/7, Wendt/DBAG Marienfelde to Kissel, 26.7.1939; see also Werner, *Bleib Übrig*, p. 6.
62 MBAG Kissel/Correspondence with the German Automobile Trust 1939–1942, Report of the Meeting on Training of 25 and 26.10.1940 in the Office of Vocational Training and Management, 28.10.1940; MBAG Kissel I/13, Minutes of the Board Meeting of DBAG on 20.9.1940.

decision, in this case successfully.[63] When the KdF Office at Untertürkheim was found to be RM 6000 in debt, the board paid its arrears, although it was formally nothing to do with the company.[64] In addition, the DAF helped run barracks for German and for foreign workers and, in the closing phase of the war, assisted in setting up shops at Daimler-Benz's factories to enable the workers to purchase essential goods.[65] The DAF also tended to cooperate with employers on issues such as pressing for extra food allocations for armaments workers.[67]

Generally, however, the outbreak of the war marked a clear turning point in the relationship between the company and the DAF, which from this time became increasingly tense and combative, and occasionally developed into one of outright conflict. The war brought questions of both productivity and ideology to the fore – the latter above all owing to the issues of female labour and foreign labour – and it is tempting to see the intensifying conflict between the company and the DAF as a product of the ideological radicalization of the DAF and the regime generally during the war and, as a consequence, of the growing incompatibility of productivist and racist goals. However, while the increasing prominence of ideological issues undoubtedly exacerbated pre-existing conceptual differences, the extent to which these were responsible for the increasing animosity between the company and the DAF should not be overestimated.

In its published literature, especially that submitted to the DAF for the 'Model Plant' competitions, the company was keen to stress the extent to which its social policy was formulated in support of the ideological goals of the regime. Its presentation of developments in production technology stressed the improvements these made to the condition of the workforce and the reductions of the physical burdens placed on them. This was combined with details of the company's extensive 'Measures to Improve the Health of the Workforce', outlining the use of protective clothing, ergonomic seating, good lighting and ventilation, accident prevention measures, etc, and boasting of its canteens and kitchen and washing facilities – all these being presented in terms of company commitment to 'racial hygiene' (and all creating an image that conflicted strongly with the reality of the increasing hardships of life on the shop-floor during the war).

Worker groups who were the object of particular ideological interest, such as young people and women, were given especially extensive treatment. The role of the apprentices as the 'youth elite' was stressed, as was the strong

---

63   MBAG Kissel XIII/4, DBAG to Kissel, 9.10.1941.
64   MBAG Kissel I/14, Minutes of the Board Meeting of DBAG on 28.5.1941.
65   MBAG Haspel 3,32, Announcement of the Establishment of a Food Shop, 17.4.1944.
66   Werner, *Bleib Übrig*, p. 48.
67   On the role of company social workers see Sachse, C., 'Hausarbeit im Betrieb. Betriebliche Sozialarbeit unter dem Nationalsozialismus' in: Sachse et al., *Angst, Belohnung, Zucht und Ordnung*, pp. 209–74.

ideological element in their training, which was carried out in classrooms and workshops decked with National Socialist insignia and pictures of the 'Führer.' Similarly, the company stressed that 'Expectant mothers, new mothers and infants are cared for especially carefully', and provided the DAF with lengthy descriptions of company kindergartens, crèches and the activities of the company social workers, who visited women in the factories or, in the case of families with large numbers of children, at home.[67] Young women, in addition to their general training, were given ideological instruction in their duties as future German wives and mothers by the DAF Women's Officer, with the full support of the company.[68]

In many cases there was little conflict between the policies of the DAF and the company, despite the fact that the former was pursuing racist as well as productivist goals to a far greater extent than the latter. The need to mobilize labour led to the development of social policy initiatives aimed specifically at integrating women into an environment traditionally dominated by and structured towards the needs of a predominantly male workforce. The provision by the company of kindergartens, crèches and rest facilities, together with the expansion of maternity provision for (German) women and the adaptation of working hours, was designed to attract women by making it easier for them to carry out their dual tasks as industrial labourer and housewife and mother, which under the conditions of war was incredibly burdensome. Such measures, taken from a company point of view, to attract and retain female labour, coincided perfectly with the regime's racially motivated desire for the same facilities and provisions. Thus, while the racist vision of the DAF and the long-term aims of industry were far from synonymous, there were sufficient points of contact for conceptual issues to have played a minor role.

Not all the examples of friction with the DAF that occurred during the war can be easily bracketed together as having one underlying cause. Some disputes were clearly the product of localized tensions that were, as often as not, exacerbated by differences that were personal as much as political. In the case of Marienfelde, for example, a long-running dispute between the DAF foreman and the deputy manager, during which the 'interminable accusations' of the foreman apparently reduced the manager to a physical wreck, was solved by an agreement between Kissel and the DAF in Berlin to transfer both individuals to other posts.[69] Similarly, at Gaggenau, relations between the management and the local party and DAF appear to have been less than cordial at points.[70]

68 *Leistungsbericht der DBAG Untertürkheim 1940* (Vol. 2); *Leistungsbericht der DBAG Untertürkheim 1940* (Vol. 3); *Leistungsbericht der DBAG Mannheim 1940* (Vol. 7); *Geschäftsbericht der Daimler-Benz Motoren GmbH Genshagen 1940.*
69 MBAG Kissel XIII/8, Wendt/DBAG Marienfelde to Kissel, 12.1.1941; Kissel to DAF Foreman Genth. 9.9.1941; Kissel to Hentig, 23.9.1941.
70 MBAG Kissel XIII/3, Kissel to DBAG Gaggenau, 4.1.1941.

The war itself necessarily forced the DAF to cut back on its KdF and leisure activities, causing it to search for new areas of activity that would legitimize its role in central aspects of labour and social policy. In part, this was achieved by the development of housing and insurance plans for the post-war period.[71] However, it also manifested itself in growing efforts to influence wage structures, training and shop-floor labour deployment – policy areas that the Daimler-Benz management had hitherto defended as its own preserve. Insofar as both the permanent latent tensions and the increasing number of open conflicts between the company and the DAF during the war had one common characteristic, it was precisely that they arose primarily out of the ever-growing attempts of the DAF to encroach upon internal factory management and assert its right to co-determination of policy not only in issues of shop-floor culture, but also in issues of shop-floor organization and factory management.

This was not a clear-cut development – in some ways, the gradual evolution of the DAF's attitude towards productivity-orientated factory management methods actually resulted in a more cooperative relationship with the company. Whereas its attempts to integrate the workers socially and politically into the new regime, and its compensatory function as a replacement for the Free Trade Unions had previously led it to oppose piece-rate reductions, its adoption of scientific management and its self-appointed role in raising industrial efficiency caused it to endorse such measures increasingly. In a discussion of piece-rate reductions at Genshagen in early 1942, for example – doubtless brought on by the new incentive to reduce production costs represented by Speer's fixed-price system – the board noted with satisfaction that 'the DAF used to cause difficulties in these cases, now it supports us,' and that similarly, at Untertürkheim, this had formerly been the case but now 'the DAF is behind us all the way.'[72]

In general, however, the DAF's habit of inviting itself to Daimler-Benz's factories to assess the efficiency of production and oversee the introduction of productivity-improving measures necessarily led to growing tension. From the beginning of the war onwards, the DAF regularly wrote to Kissel offering its services to help achieve a purposeful allocation of labour and resources within the factory in order to mobilize labour and productivity reserves.[73] As Kissel recognized, the agenda behind these offers was to establish a precedent for intervention in internal managerial issues, and with it influence over industrial production. As a result, Kissel always replied expressing polite interest but equally firm refusal, stating typically in March 1940 that 'as you

71 See Recker, *Nationalsozialistische Sozialpolitik*, pp. 98–154.
72 MBAG Kissel I/15, Minutes of the Board Meeting of DBAG on 23 and 24.3.1942.
73 See for example MBAG Kissel XIII/10, Office of Vocational Training and Management of the DAF to DBAG Marienfelde, 15.12.1939; Office of Vocational Training and Management of the DAF to Kissel, 9.3.1940; Kissel to the Office of Vocational Training and Management of the DAF, 23.8.1940.

know, I have been working on improvements to labour deployment at Daimler-Benz for a long time' and that he had 'a committee of excellent company men' working on the issue, implying that the DAF was simply not needed. Behind his polite but vague offer to discuss the issue in the future lay the clear desire to keep the DAF at bay.[74]

Having put the DAF off for six months in this particular instance, Kissel was forced to reply again to a similar offer in August 1940. While he again paid lip-service to the DAF's suggestions, he emphasized that for such work the very best in engineers and time-and-motion specialists were necessary. This was a pointed allusion to the widely held view in industrial circles that the DAF's time-and-motion 'experts' were ill-qualified and incompetent.[75] That Kissel subscribed to this view himself is underlined by his demand to meet the DAF engineers personally in order to assess their competence before letting them loose on Daimler-Benz's production lines. Most of all, however, Kissel asserted that the huge additional workload created by the war was such that Daimler-Benz's own engineers were too busy and that the timing was therefore 'highly unsuitable', and, again, that 'these procedures are routine for us', so that he was certain that 'absolutely everything is being done to achieve the tasks with the available people that is remotely possible.'[76] As the DAF became ever-more persistent, Kissel became ever-more blunt, to the point where he stated simply in response to one suggestion: 'I am pleased to inform you that we have been operating for years in the manner that you describe as necessary.'[77]

The failure of the DAF's attempts to influence managerial practices or shop-floor policy at Daimler-Benz in any important way is best highlighted by the issue of wages policy. The recognition of the significance of the new wage structures being developed by German industry, not only at Daimler-Benz but also at firms such as BMW and Klöckner-Humboldt-Deutz, where from the late 1930s onwards various five-, six- or eight-category wage systems had been evolved, had led the DAF to appropriate this as a key area in which it could not only contribute to the efficiency of the war economy, but also assert its role in factory management in the future. As such, an examination of the role of the DAF in the formulation of new wage structures during the war underlines the limited extent to which it was an active agent in evolving and disseminating new managerial practices within German industry.

From September 1939, the Office for the Iron and Metal Industries (*Fachamt Eisen und Metall*) of the DAF, under its head Jäzosch, had been

74 MBAG Kissel XIII/10, Kissel to the Office of Vocational Training and Management of the DAF, 12.3.1940.
75 Werner, *Bleib Übrig*, p. 231.
76 MBAG Kissel XIII/10, Kissel to the Office of Vocational Training and Management of the DAF, 23.8.1940.
77 MBAG Kissel XIII/11, Kissel to Local Departmental Head Thierauf of the DAF Gau Management Württemberg-Hohenzollern, 26.5.1941.

cooperating with the RAM and the Reich Group Industry (the employers' organization within the RWM) in the development of a new model wage structure, first as a means of raising wartime productivity, and second as the basis for an eventual fundamental restructuring of wages policy after the war.[78] By fixing womens' and foreign workers' wages in proportion to those of German male workers, it also served as an instrument of gender and racial hierarchicalization within the workplace. Conceptually, there was little to distinguish the DAF's project from that developed at Daimler-Benz or by the RGI, based as they all were on job evaluation, time-and-motion study and the related pursuit of the so-called 'just wage' – that is, a wage derived not from collective bargaining or through market forces, but one that reflected the individual work performed by each worker and that was dependent upon his diligence.[79] In addition to the atomizing impact of the individualization of pay calculation and the stimulation of upward mobility by the subdivision of job categories and the expansion of pay differentials, the adoption of a system that paid for the activity, not the worker, was designed, from the point of view of the regime, to allow the control of wage levels and to reduce employer's capacity to circumvent its wage freeze.[80]

Kissel himself, as head of one of the pioneering companies in this aspect of factory management, was a member of the DAF's committee of industrial experts that advised on the formulation of the system and regularly corresponded with the DAF's Office for the Iron and Metal Industries on the subject. Whilst he was happy to advise the DAF on its plans and to report in general terms on the progress being made on Daimler-Benz's own system, he was just as obstinate about not allowing the DAF influence over the issue at Daimler-Benz itself as he was about all other aspects of factory management. Thus, in reply to what was obviously an attempt to assert its right to participate in the development of Daimler-Benz's own wages policy, Kissel assured the DAF that the company was operating in line with the regime's wishes and interests, but left it in no doubt as to who was in charge: 'I have the impression that it will be possible to introduce a new wage system in our factories according to the guidelines set by me.' This was accompanied by a particularly pointed snub in Kissel's expression of his belief that 'they will also be acceptable to the Reich Trustees of Labour,' a reference to the fact that such regulation as was necessary lay within the jurisdiction of the RAM's officials, the DAF having no codified role in this area.[81]

The limit of the extent to which the DAF was an active agent in the development of new productivity pay structures at Daimler-Benz is underlined

---

78 Siegel, *Leistung und Lohn*, pp. 162–4; Hachtmann, *Industriearbeit*, pp. 210–23.
79 Siegel, *Leistung und Lohn*, p. 14.
80 Ibid., p. 247; Hachtmann, *Industriearbeit*, p. 214.
81 MBAG Kissel XIII/10, Kissel to Kemmler/Gau Office for the Iron and Metal Industries of the DAF, 20.9.1939.

not only by the fact that the company refused it any participatory role, but by
the fact that, if anything, the flow of ideas was from Daimler-Benz to the DAF,
not the other way round. Whilst Daimler-Benz was developing its new system
and expanding its application workshop by workshop, Kissel regularly sent the
DAF not only details of the progress being made, but also advice on how to
implement the system and what experience the company had had, together
with clarification of aspects that the DAF 'experts' did not understand fully.[82]
Above all, Kissel kept reminding the DAF of the complexity of the issues
involved, both in technical and political terms, in introducing such new
policies, and stressing that they had to be developed and implemented far
more carefully – even on a plant-by-plant basis – than the DAF seemed to
understand.

The DAF's lack of influence in this area at Daimler-Benz is highlighted
finally by the company's statement in February 1941 which said that 'we have
been working on the restructuring of the previous system of wages at the plants
of this company for years, and have now managed to bring the work to a
certain stage of completion.'[83] This was over a year before the DAF's final
version was published, in March 1942, and 18 months before Sauckel ordered
the introduction of the industry-wide Wages Group Catalogue Iron and Steel
(*Lohngruppenkatalog Eisen und Metall* – LKEM) in the following October,
on the basis of a project conceived more by the RGI than the DAF but
claimed by the DAF as its own work.[84] The company was correspondingly
sceptical about the propaganda claims of the DAF regarding the productivity
increases of up to 30 per cent recorded at (the relatively small number of)
factories that introduced the LKEM on the DAF's model. When the DAF
informed the company that it was hoping to apply its new system to
Genshagen as a test case, the board noted with satisfaction that it had already
been working according to the principles of job evaluation at Genshagen for
a long time, rendering the DAF's offer superfluous. Haspel was particularly
scathing, saying that the DAF was 'hawking its system with the claim that
some managers had achieved productivity gains of 30 per cent', but that these
figures were based on the performance of 'just the ones who haven't done
anything before now.'[85]

The success of the DAF in expanding its jurisdiction against other National
Socialist organs, the size of its organizational apparatus, the volume of
publications produced by the Labour Science Institute and the range of
functionaries within the workplace should not, therefore, create an
exaggerated idea of its importance with regard to factory management. The

82   MBAG Kissel XIII/11, Kissel to Jäzosch/Office of Iron and Metal, 5.4.1940; Kissel to
     Lahs/WiGruLFZ, 1.10.1940.
83   MBAG Kissel XIII/11, Kissel to Lahs/WiGrLFZ, 1.2.1941.
84   Siegel, *Leistung und Lohn*, pp. 164, 191–2.
85   MBAG Kissel I/15, Minutes of the Board Meeting of DBAG on 23 and 24.3.1942.

programmes of the DAF built upon pre-existing trends in industry, but these continued to be implemented with a substantial degree of autonomy by industry itself. While the DAF may have played a role in disseminating ideas, its influence was probably greater on smaller and medium-sized firms than on companies such as Daimler-Benz or Siemens.

The increasing attempts by the DAF to gain influence over internal company decisions also formed the background for the long-running dispute between it and Daimler-Benz over the replacement of Kissel by Haspel in the summer of 1942, following the former's suicide.[86] The DAF had already tried to assert its right to co-determination of senior personnel policy in June 1941, when it had proposed that a director at Untertürkheim and convinced National Socialist, Werner Romstedt, be appointed to the post of DAF foreman, carrying out both tasks in 'personal union.' Kissel, recognizing the dangers of having a senior manager directly answerable to the DAF, refused, on the grounds that Romstedt was too busy.[87] With the death of Kissel in July 1942, the DAF renewed its attempts to influence personnel decisions, this time with the backing of the SS, whose own antagonism to the Daimler-Benz board was rooted in the fact that Haspel's wife was half-Jewish, as was the wife of another board member, Otto Hoppe, while the wife of a director at Mannheim, Carl Werner, who also figured in the dispute, was completely Jewish.

Haspel's appointment as Kissel's successor on 10 August 1942 was accepted not only by Göring, Speer and Milch, for whom the pragmatic needs of the moment demanded that Haspel's undisputed abilities be fully exploited in the interests of the war economy, but by Hitler himself.[88] When the DAF renewed its pressure soon after, this time demanding that Romstedt be taken on to the managerial board, Haspel's position was thus relatively secure. However, despite the fact that the board was keen to ensure that 'there must be no disputes with the DAF', its refusal to entertain the DAF's proposals meant that a lengthy conflict was almost inevitable.

Following the confirmation of Haspel's appointment, a DAF representative of the Office for the Iron and Metal Industries, Dickwach, intervened with Strauss, the head of Daimler-Benz's supervisory board, to put forward the DAF's alternative views on the necessary restructuring of the managerial board after Kissel's death. Dickwach contrasted the achievements of Kissel, who had been well on the way to making Daimler-Benz a National Socialist 'model plant' that was not only economically successful but had also succeeded in advancing 'the political interests of the racial community', with the new, unacceptable situation. Whereas politically and ideologically

86 For a different view of the conflict over Kissel's successor see Roth, 'Der Weg zum Guten Stern', pp. 302–6; see also Bellon, *Mercedes in Peace and War*, pp. 254–7.

87 MBAG Kissel XIII/11, Kissel to Dickwach/Main Division Leader of the DAF Office of Iron and Metal 11.6.1941.

88 MBAG Kissel I/15, Minutes of the Board Meeting of DBAG on 14.8.1942.

exemplary men had previously been at the forefront of all genuine 'leadership' questions and had ensured that Daimler-Benz remained committed to the 'German struggle for freedom', while 'Jew-tainted' and thus politically un- acceptable managers had been confined to carrying out low-profile technical and organizational functions, the recent changes at managerial level had led to this being reversed. According to Dickwach, 'it is impossible for the board with its current composition to fulfil the leadership function in the factory community' – the supposed Jewish connections of the board meant that 'all it can do is pursue business interests.' By misrepresenting the nature of the changes (he made out that both Hoppe and Werner had just joined the board, whereas Hoppe had been a member since 1930 and Werner never became a member at all), Dickwach suggested that Daimler-Benz had virtually been taken over by a Jewish coup. To safeguard the political and ideological reliability of the company, he demanded that Romstedt, whom he depicted as Kissel's virtual chosen successor, be taken onto the board.[89]

Stauss was as defensive of the autonomy of Daimler-Benz and the Deutsche Bank as Kissel had been. He pointed out that both Göring and Hitler had formally approved Haspel's appointment, and made only a vague offer to discuss the matter further with other Daimler-Benz board members. Dickwach, however, recognized that this was mere manoeuvring, and, the next day, rejected Stauss's supposedly conciliatory attitude on the grounds that 'it was obvious that you have no intention of following the suggestions of the Party and the German Labour Front.'

Dickwach was also able to mobilize the support of the SS, and Himmler in particular, by asserting that Stauss had claimed that Himmler had also person- ally approved Haspel's appointment, a suggestion that greatly angered Himmler. The head of the SS Main Office, Gottlob Berger, offered his help on the grounds that this was a vital struggle, because 'it demonstrates whether the DAF and the party have a say in such issues, or whether the appointment is made by the board according to the old principles, regardless of how the individual is disposed towards the Third Reich.' Berger likewise claimed that Kissel had envisaged Romstedt as filling his place on the board, but that the company had instead been taken over by men whom Kissel himself had rejected owing to their 'Jew- taintedness' (again, a falsehood, since it was Kissel himself who had sought Haspel's appointment to the board in 1936).[90] Finally, on 25 August, Himmler himself intervened with Daimler-Benz board member and contact man to the regime Werlin, clearly furious that he had been cited as having supported the appointment of three 'Jew-tainted' managers to the board, describing the mere suggestion as an 'affront to the National Socialist state' and threatening to go to Hitler and Göring if the decision was not reversed immediately.[91]

89   BA (K) NS 19/776, Dickwach to Stauss, 20.8.1942.
90   BA (K) NS 19/776, Berger/Head of the SS Main Office to Himmler, 20.8.1942.
91   BA (K) NS 19/776, Himmler to Werlin, 25.8.1942.

In addition to his party connections and his function as the Führer's 'General Inspector for the Vehicle Industry', which allowed him to mediate between the company and Hitler, Werlin, as a high-ranking SS officer, could also use his good connections with Himmler to smooth over friction with the SS where it arose. In this case too, he was able, with K.C. Müller and Hentig, the other solid Nazis on the board, to engineer a compromise that satisfied Himmler. By offering to remove Hoppe from the board and eventually to dismiss Werner from his directorship, Werlin was able to insist that Haspel stay in his position.[92] This proposal, together with Stauss's later assurances that he had never suggested that Himmler had agreed to Haspel's appointment, was enough to placate Himmler, who agreed to the compromise on 4 September 1942.[93] Berger complained bitterly that 'despite the fact that the Führer spoke of the Jews in the Speech to the German Nation, heavy industry has won. The German Labour Front . . . has capitulated.'[94] However, with Himmler's acceptance of the compromise, the company had successfully neutralized the issue as far as the SS was concerned.

Having failed in its initial intervention, the DAF nonetheless continued to agitate for a change in the company board that would involve the promotion of Romstedt to a position of power. Following Himmler's withdrawal from the fray, Dickwach renewed his attacks on Haspel and Werlin, complaining that events had shown that 'the supervisory and managerial board wish to return to the old system of management', that the board functioned not according to the 'leadership principle' but 'as a democratic forum', and that 'there is obviously no inclination to build up an organically ordered leadership structure in accordance with the nature of National Socialism.'[95] While he was now forced to admit that Haspel's undisputed abilities necessitated his retention in a managerial capacity, he demanded that he be removed from his post as 'factory leader', leaving all 'leadership' of the workforce to someone politically and ideologically suitable. This would only be achieved by appointing Romstedt to the board and entrusting him with all such functions.

Again, however, the company was able to resist this pressure, with the result that Haspel remained chairman. Hoppe, though formally removed from the board, continued in practice to fulfil the same functions as before, while the promise to dismiss Werner was never carried through. Although the SS and party continued to harass them on this issue, Hitler's renewed statement of support for the Daimler-Benz board ensured that all three were able to avoid

92 BA (K) NS 19/776, Werlin to Himmler, 27.8.1942; letter to 'Wölffchen' (= SS-Obergruppenführer Karl Wolff, SS Headquarters), 27.8.1942.
93 BA (K) NS 19/776, Himmler to Stauss, 27.8.1942; Stauss to Himmler, 18.9.1942; Personal Staff of the RFSS to Berger, 4.9.1942.
94 BA (K) NS 19/776, Berger to SS Obersturmbannführer Brandt/Personal Staff of the RFSS, 2.10.1944.
95 BA (K) NS 19/776, Dickwach to Haspel, 6.9.1942; Dickwach to Jäzosch, 18.9.1942.

further serious problems through to the end of the war.[96] Soon after, Romstedt was transferred by the company to fill a vacancy at the Rzeszow plant, safely out of the way in Poland; and though Haspel feared that the DAF would see this as an 'open declaration of war', Romstedt proved to have been effectively marginalized.[97]

While the conflict over Kissel's successor was ostensibly a product of Haspel and his colleagues' alleged 'Jewishness', it is clear that, seen in the broader context of the development of relations between the company and the DAF, the issue at stake was essentially that of managerial autonomy. That Haspel's personal circumstances were as much a convenient excuse as the reason itself (this is not to say that the DAF did not take the ideological aspect seriously) is underlined by the fact that the DAF tried to influence all appointments, not just those where supposed Jewish connections were at stake. Not only managerial board appointments, but also supervisory board appointments were contested. In November 1942, for example, the management complained that Speer, the party and the DAF were all trying to influence an appointment, although it could not tell whether the interventions were co-ordinated or individually conceived.[98] Such interference had become so bad by 1943 that, in one case, when a senior manager withdrew from a specific position he retained it formally 'for political reasons', that is, to avoid the need for an announcement of the change, which might arouse the interests of the DAF.[99]

As with its attempts to influence wage and social policy, however, the interventions of the DAF on matters of senior personnel were a failure. In none of the areas in which it sought to assert its jurisdiction vis-à-vis private company interests was it successful. While this is partly explained by the fact that Daimler-Benz was one of the first companies to implement some of the social policy initiatives that the DAF later appropriated and tried to implement elsewhere, the DAF had just as little success with other large companies.[100] As such, an analysis of the role of the DAF that stresses its 'modernizing' function with regard to factory and 'human' management methods probably overstates the significance of the Labour Science Institute within the overall structure of the DAF, whose active centre of gravity was far lower and whose real significance is probably to be found more in the functions it carried out at shop-floor and local level.

96   BA (K) R3/1578, Speer to SS-Gruppenführer Fegelein, 5.11.1944.
97   MBAG Kissel I/15, Minutes of the Board Meeting of DBAG on 4 and 5.11.1942. Bellon argues that the transfer of Romstedt to this plant is an indication of the importance of Rzeszow to Daimler-Benz (Bellon, *Mercedes in Peace and War*, p. 257). In fact, given that Romstedt's transfer was obviously intended to marginalize him, it is more the case that the transfer is an indicator of the lack of long-term interest in the plant.
98   MBAG Haspel/Correspondence regarding Board of Directors 1942–1943, Naumann to Haspel, 28.11.1942.
99   MBAG Haspel 3,31, Report on the Management of Genshagen, 5.4.1943.
100 Freyberg and Siegel, *Industrielle Rationalisierung*, p. 380; Salter, 'Mobilization,' pp. 280–3.

3. Prisoners of War, Forced Foreign Workers and Concentration Camp Labour at Daimler-Benz 1940–5

a) Prisoners of War and West European Workers

The territorial expansion of the Reich also offered the possibility of exploiting a second form of additional labour.[101] Very soon, the shortage of workers led to the mass deployment of prisoners of war and civilian labour from the occupied territories of Poland and France – by December 1940 there were nearly 1.2m prisoners of war deployed in the Reich.[102] Initially the majority were put to work in agriculture, while the rest who were put to work in industry were used as miners or building workers, where the labour-intensive nature of the work lent itself to short-term physical exploitation.

While this was primarily a product of decisions taken within the regime, most branches of German industry only hesitantly began to consider the option of utilizing prisoner of war labour. At a discussion at the WiGruFa in June 1940, at the time of the occupation of France, fears of sabotage were raised and complaints expressed about the regime's demand that all prisoners of war be deployed in a single workshop in large colonies for security reasons.[103] While this may, again, have been possible in the mining industry, it was not compatible with the highly integrated, mechanized production processes characteristic of the vehicle and engine sector. At Daimler-Benz, the cautious attitude to expansion in the first ten to twelve months of the war, combined with the protection of its skilled German workforce by their 'Reserved Status' (*UK-Stellung*) and the Wehrmacht's recruitment freeze after the initial wave of call-ups in September 1939, meant that the labour shortage did not represent a serious threat to production in the first half of 1940, certainly not to the point where the widespread deployment of prisoners of war was considered as a core strategy.[104] In the south German plants, the increase in the supply of female labour was substantial enough initially to prevent the necessity of procuring prisoners of war on a large scale.

During the second half of 1940, the attitude of the company began to change. As it began to expand its activities, the labour shortage gradually

---

101 On the history of the overall system of foreign labour see Herbert, U., *Fremdarbeiter. Politik und Praxis des 'Ausländer-Einsatzes in der Kriegswirtschaft des Dritten Reiches*, Bonn, 1985; Herbert, U., 'Arbeit und Vernichtung. Ökonomisches Interesse und Primat der Weltanschauung im Nationalsozialismus' in Diner, (ed.), *Ist der Nationalsozialismus Geschichte? Zu Historisierung und Historikerstreit*, Frankfurt/M., 1987, pp. 198–236; Homze, E., *Foreign Labor in Nazi Germany*, Princeton, 1967; Siegfried, K.-J., *Rüstungsproduktion und Zwangsarbeit 1939–1945*, Frankfurt/M., 1987; On Daimler-Benz in particular Schmid, M., 'Unsere Ausländische Arbeitskräfte. Zwangsarbeiter in den Werken und Barackenlagern des Daimler-Benz Konzerns. Ein Überblick' in: HSG (ed.), *Das Daimler-Benz Buch*, pp. 559–91; Hoppmann, B. et al., *Zwangsarbeit bei Daimler-Benz*, Stuttgart, 1994.
102 Herbert, *Fremdarbeiter*, p. 96.
103 MBAG Kissel/Correspondence of WiGruFa, Circulars and Communiqués 1936–1942, Minutes of the Advisory Meeting of WiGruFa, 6.6.1940.
104 On the recruitment freeze see Salter, 'Mobilisation', p. 40.

intensified. By the summer of 1940, the company was also sceptical about the prospects of procuring sufficient numbers of women workers to cover the shortfall.[105] At Marienfelde and Genshagen, where the first year of the war had failed to witness any real increase in the number of women employed, and where the expansion of production created greater labour shortages than in the south German plants, prisoners of war were in fact deployed immediately following the defeat of France. By the end of the year, there were 190 prisoners of war at Marienfelde and 267 at Genshagen.[106]

As argued above in the cases of Mannheim and Genshagen, it was during 1941 that the labour shortages at Daimler-Benz began to intensify seriously and it was during early 1941 that prisoners of war and foreign workers replaced women as the main focus of its attempts to procure additional labour. Their shift was both facilitated and reinforced by the regime's general policy of accelerating the deployment of prisoners of war and foreign workers in industry by this point. In January 1941, having been offered 50 to 60 prisoners of war by the local Labour Office, the management of the Gaggenau plant contacted the board to find out whether or not the deployment of prisoners of war was acceptable to the company, stating that 'in view of the ever-intensifying shortage of labour we are positively inclined towards this measure'. The reply came back 'there are no objections to the deployment of prisoners of war.'[107] By February 1941, this practice was obviously widespread and accepted by the company as a central element in its labour policy.[108] Where it was impossible to use prisoners of war on account of secrecy restrictions, such as in aero-engine or naval engine production, the company actively rearranged its labour force to allow German workers who had been engaged elsewhere to move to aero-engine production, replacing them with prisoners of war on less secret lines such as lorry production.[109]

By the end of 1941, all of Daimler-Benz's plants had large numbers of prisoners of war housed in barracks and working under extremely punishing conditions. The great majority were deployed in heavy physical labour, such as the loading and unloading of materials, suggesting that the peculiar labour supply situation of the war did not always result in the introduction of more capital-intensive processes. Indeed, even in industries such as the metal-working industry, it could lead to a reversion to more labour-intensive methods based on physical exploitation of 'expendable' labour.[110] At Genshagen, where by April 1941 over 400 French prisoners of war were being

105 MBAG Huppenbauer 226, Communiqué (DBAG Sindelfingen), 9.5.1940.
106 Hoppmann et al., *Zwangsarbeit bei Daimler-Benz*, p. 98.
107 MBAG Kissel XIII/3, DBAG Gaggenau to Hoppe, 17.1.1941; Hoppe to DBAG Gaggenau, 20.1.1941.
108 MBAG Kissel XIII/11, DBAG/von Viehbahn to RMfBuM, 6.2.1941.
109 MBAG Kissel XIII/3, Hoppe to DBAG Gaggenau, 5.2.1941.
110 MBAG DBAG Mannheim 23, Sales Management to Decker/Management of Mannheim, 22.1.1941; Arrangement for Layout of Halls 1 and 2 (Mannheim Plant), 9.9.1941.

deployed, a small minority were being employed as skilled labour, but the management placed most value on the mass of workers being used as unskilled labour, as 'every German unskilled worker has the desire and the opportunity to be trained as a machine operator and thus to earn far more than an unskilled worker, so that it is impossible to get German unskilled workers.'[111] According to the Genshagen management, the majority were hard-working and disciplined – the return of a few recalcitrant prisoners of war to the camps, where their fate is not hard to surmise, undoubtedly had a strong disciplining effect on those who remained.

Although the availability of prisoners of war allowed substantial numbers of German workers to retrain as machine operators, the immediate shortage of skilled labour in 1941 was such that there were limits to how far the deployment of prisoners of war alone could solve the underlying problems. From early 1941 onwards, the company began extensive recruitment of skilled foreign workers from the occupied and Allied west.[112] The initial experiences were not always overwhelmingly positive. Following the agreement of the regime with Italy of February 1941, by which large numbers of Italian civilian workers were to be sent to work in Germany, the Genshagen plant was supposed to receive a transport of over 500 skilled lathe workers and other machine operators. When they eventually arrived in May, they numbered only 219, the majority of whom were semi- or unskilled.[113] At Untertürkheim it had also been intended to deploy large numbers of Italian workers, but in view of the superior conditions that the Italian workers were supposed to enjoy while in Germany, the company withdrew its application at the Labour Office, for fear that their presence would create discipline problems among a resentful German workforce.[114] Even when it was able to recruit voluntary workers from the west, problems were caused by very high levels of fluctuation. Measured by the standards of treatment meted out to Soviet prisoners of war and civilian workers later in the war, the treatment of the west European workers was moderate, but the discrepancy between the promises of high wages, good conditions and generous holidays on the one hand and the realities of long hours, strict factory discipline, intensive labour and spartan housing on the other, ensured that many failed to return from holiday or refused to extend their contracts. Of the 200 Danish workers at

111   MBAG Kissel XIII/14, Daimler-Benz Motoren GmbH Genshagen to Kissel, 25.4.1941; Hoppmann et al., *Zwangsarbeit bei Daimler-Benz*, pp. 301–2.
112   Isolated cases of foreign workers engaged at Daimler-Benz's plants are mentioned for 1940, but early 1941 marks the point at which the recruitment of foreign workers became a core element of the company's labour procurement. Hoppmann et al., *Zwangsarbeit bei Daimler-Benz*, p. 85, mentions 400 Danish workers recruited to Untertürkheim and Sindelfingen in 1940, for example.
113   MBAG Kissel/Correspondence of WiGruLFZ, Daimler-Benz Motoren GmbH Genshagen to WiGruLFZ, 16.6.1941.
114   MBAG Kissel XIII/14, Kissel to Armaments Commando Stuttgart, 24.4.1941; Hoppe/Kissel to Labour Office, 24.4.1941.

Untertürkheim in the summer of 1941, for example, only 15 remained by early 1942.[115]

The main source of civilian foreign workers for Daimler-Benz prior to the influx of Soviet prisoners of war and civilians in early 1942 was France, from where 49,000 workers (compared to nearly one million prisoners of war) were transported before September 1941 with varying degrees of willingness to work in Germany.[116] Many German companies had begun recruiting on a voluntary basis in France prior to the occupation of June 1940 (Daimler-Benz apparently not among them, however), leading the regime to prohibit individual company action in July 1940 in favour of a centrally administered recruitment system organized by the military authorities and Labour Offices.[117] Henceforth, firms were required to register requests formally with the relevant authorities. However, even after the regulation and codification of the recruitment of French workers, companies such as Daimler-Benz were able to operate via both formal and informal channels simultaneously in order to procure labour. Daimler-Benz itself was able to exploit its extensive influence over the French automobile industry, and the leverage this gave it over the French firms it ran on a commissarial basis, to enlist 'voluntary' workers directly, thus circumventing Labour Office control. In fact, the processes by which French workers came to Daimler-Benz are illustrative of how, despite the existence of formal structures and procedures that ostensibly had to be utilized, in practice the formulation and implementation of policy evolved through a combination of personal and institutional contacts between business and the regime. Operating on various levels and with varying degrees of formality, the institutional relationship between industry and the authorities became blurred above all where industrial managers operated in an official or semi-official capacity within the structures created by the regime to manage the war economy.

From April 1941 at the latest, Daimler-Benz used the influence of Carl Schippert, the company representative responsible for managing Renault and Unic on a commissarial basis, to recruit directly for transfers specifically to Daimler-Benz's factories in Germany.[118] Initially, this occurred on a more or less voluntary basis, with the company suggesting to Schippert that French workers might actually want to work for Daimler-Benz in particular, in view of the famous name of the company, and that this, combined with the promise of good wages, conditions and holidays, would be attraction enough.[119] By making generous promises to the workers, the company was able to recruit 446 volunteers from Renault, although Kissel's request to Schippert that the latter 'ensure that

---

115 Hoppmann et al., *Zwangsarbeit bei Daimler-Benz*, pp. 113–14.
116 Herbert, *Fremdarbeiter*, p. 99.
117 Hoppmann et al., *Zwangsarbeit bei Daimler-Benz*, p. 40.
118 Ibid., p. 85.
119 MBAG Kissel XIII/14, DBAG/von Viehbahn to Schippert, 28.6.1941.

all the necessary steps are taken to give rise to voluntary recruits' suggests that the 'voluntary' nature of the process was dubious from the outset.[120] Quite what the kind of pressure Schippert applied is unclear, but, as Kissel stressed, the company's links with the French firms gave it a certain leverage over their managements, who for their part had an interest in collaborating with the Germans in order to ensure a supply of materials and contracts to allow them to continue production and guarantee their existence. None-too-subtle pressure on the French companies thus played an important role from the outset.

As is clear from the extensive correspondence between Kissel and Schippert in the summer and autumn of 1941, the board expended considerable effort and exerted consistent pressure through various channels to procure French automobile workers, while completion of Labour Office procedures was regarded as only a formality.[121] In June and July 1941, for example, the company tried to get 300 workers for Untertürkheim and 100 for Marienfelde from Renault and Unic directly via Schippert.[122] Simultaneously, it pressured via the military authorities in France for labour that had been procured by the officially organized procedures, expressing 'great interest ' in the allocation of workers who had been recruited directly by the authorities and requesting the OKW to make an allocation that reflected Daimler-Benz's status as 'a leading south German armaments manufacturer.'[123] By the autumn of 1941, the labour shortage was so severe that it was also attempting to take in as many prisoners of war as possible – when informed of the availability of 500 prisoners of war for Untertürkheim, it noted that the designated barracks had been planned for 200 workers 'but could possibly be increased to 250'.[124]

However, by September 1941 Kissel was forced to recognize that, measured against the shortfall of labour, the success in recruiting voluntary French workers had been minimal. By this point, the general failure of the regime's policy of voluntary recruitment had led to numerous discussions between the military authorities, the Labour Ministry and major industrialists contemplating an alternative approach, involving the direct transfer of whole sections of the workforces of French factories in closed groups to firms in Germany. Again, by promising adequate energy supplies and materials to continue production, this time officially, the cooperation of French firms would be guaranteed, and by a combination of direct contact with individual firms, pressure on French workers and pressure on the French government, a greater transfer of labour should occur.[125] In addition to Renault and Unic,

120   MBAG Kissel XIII/14, Kissel to Schippert, 11.6.1941.
121   MBAG Kissel XIII/14, Schippert to Kissel, 14.6.1941.
122   MBAG Kissel XIII/14, DBAG/von Viehbahn to Schippert, 28.6.1941; DBAG/von Viehbahn to Schippert, 9.7.1941.
123   MBAG Kissel XIII/14, Kissel to OKW/Defence Economy and Armaments Office, 15.8.1941; DBAG/von Viehbahn to OKW, 27.8.1941.
124   MBAG Kissel XIII/14, von Viehbahn to Kissel, 1.9.1941.
125   MBAG Kissel XIII/14, Kissel to Schippert, 11.9.1941.

whose workforces Daimler-Benz regarded as reserved by rights, Kissel attempted to intervene with the OKW to have other French companies (Simca, Latil, Laffly) earmarked for direct labour transfer to Daimler-Benz's plants, arguing that as automobile manufacturers the workers from these plants would be of great use to Daimler-Benz and requesting that other firms be prohibited from recruiting there.[126] This policy of direct group recruitment marked a further step towards coercive recruitment, which by 1942 had more or less become the norm and had escalated even further by 1943.[127] Only after the voluntary principle had been all but dispensed with did the flow of workers significantly increase – by 1943, for example, 4568 Renault workers had been transported to Daimler-Benz factories, compared to 446 initial volunteers in 1941.[128] Correspondingly, only after deportation had become standard procedure did Kissel rate the flow of workers from France as a success.[129]

By mid-1941, the recruitment of foreign workers had been established as the main method by which Daimler-Benz procured its additional workers.[130] By a similar process of more-or-less voluntary recruitment achieved by making false promises, followed by gradually escalating pressure and coercion, workers were procured from most countries in western Europe, especially Holland, Dennmark and Belgium. The methods by which they were brought to Daimler-Benz are often obscure, but by the end of 1941 and prior to the first deployment of Soviet prisoners of war, all of Daimler-Benz's plants were 'strongly dependent' upon foreign workers and French prisoners of war.[131] In December 1941, 6.3 per cent of the workforce at the company's core plants were foreign workers and 3.5 per cent prisoners of war, while at the Genshagen subsidiary the proportion of foreign workers had reached 18.6 per cent and that of prisoners of war 4.2 per cent. Including the FMO (Vienna), the plants in the occupied territories and the repair workshops at the various fronts, by the end of 1941 the total proportion of foreign workers and prisoners of war had reached 24.4 per cent, i.e. a quarter.[132]

While the west European workers were not always the skilled ones the company demanded, and while the high fluctuation levels were a source of complaint, the company was in general able to integrate them into the factory and its production processes with relative ease. All the time the influx of foreign workers was confined to those from west Europe, the skills structure of the workforce remained more or less constant at all plants. Certainly there was no change on a scale comparable with that of the period after the winter of 1941–2, and although the integration of foreign workers caused substantial

126   MBAG Kissel XIII/14, Kissel to OKW, 29.9.1941.
127   Hoppmann et al., *Zwangsarbeit bei Daimler-Benz*, p. 86; Herbert, *Fremdarbeiter*, pp. 180–4.
128   Hoppmann et al., *Zwangsarbeit bei Daimler-Benz*, p. 87.
129   MBAG Kissel/War Plant Genshagen 1941, Kissel to Ring Management T2, 13.2.1942.
130   MBAG Kissel XIII/3, Kissel to DBAG Gaggenau, 26.6.1941.
131   MBAG Kissel I/14, Minutes of the Board Meeting of DBAG on 11.12.1941.
132   Hoppmann et al., *Zwangsarbeit bei Daimler-Benz*, p. 100.

increases in wastage and broken tools, these remained at moderately tolerable levels.[133] Above all, as west European civilian workers could be deployed from the outset among German workers, their integration into the production lines was relatively unproblematic. In fact, the company did this to great effect, reporting that, by being placed in work gangs alongside Germans, they necessarily had to achieve the same work rate as that of their German colleagues, who for their part had an interest in encouraginging a high-work rate from the foreign labourers in order to maintain their own wage levels.[134]

The high degree of integration within the factory and the satisfactory wages and food provided for the west European foreign workers should not lead to an underestimation of the extent to which both strict factory discipline and, on occasion, physical violence or punishment were brought to bear upon recalcitrant or ill-disciplined workers, either at Daimler-Benz or elsewhere. The emergence of the brutal Labour Education Camps over 1940–2 as a central plank in the regime's system of terror was not only in response to declining work discipline among the German workforce in the first half of the war, but was also very closely linked to the gradual increase in foreign workers in Germany from 1940–2 onwards, and the camps were full of foreign workers even before the deployment of Russians was under way.[135] Daimler-Benz was no exception here, and many west European workers were transferred to the Labour Education Camps for poor work, suspected sabotage, alleged insubordination or, later, for colluding with the Soviet workers.[136] Of the 1169 west European workers at Sindelfingen in December 1943, for example, 22 were under some form of arrest, the majority undoubtedly in Labour Education Camps or concentration camps.[137] While the corresponding figures for Soviet workers were probably significantly higher, it remains the case that for the west European workers too the threat of state terror was a crucial factor in the equation.

b) Soviet Prisoners of War and Civilian Deportees

In the summer of 1941, the recruitment of foreign workers had become the central element of Daimler-Benz's attempts to procure additional labour, and the process of organizing their deployment and their integration into the factory had become correspondingly 'normalized'. By the autumn of 1941, therefore, as the invasion of the Soviet Union created the potential for the regime to exploit a vast new source of labour in the German war economy, it was in many ways only logical for the company to extend its efforts in

---

133   MBAG Kissel/Correspondence of WiGruLFZ, Daimler-Benz Motoren GmbH Genshagen to WiGruLFZ, 16.6.1941.
134   *Leistungsbericht der DBAG Werk Mannheim/Ergänzungsbericht 1940–1*, p. 28.
135   Werner, *Bleib Übrig*, pp. 176–8; Salter, 'Mobilisation', p. 229.
136   For examples see Hoppmann et al., *Zwangsarbeit bei Daimler-Benz*, pp. 122, 150.
137   MBAG Huppenbauer 406, Housing of West European Workers as of 13.12.1943.

procuring foreign workers to Soviet prisoners of war and civilian workers. Initially, however, ideological opposition of the regime to the deployment of 'racially inferior' and politically dangerous Soviet prisoners of war and civilians precluded this, especially in the wake of the initial victories in the east, which made this seem unnecessary and resulted in hundreds of thousands of Soviet prisoners of war being allowed to die in captivity each month (nearly two million had died by February 1942).[138] In any case, in the autumn of 1941, many German industrialists, those at Daimler-Benz included, shared the expectation of a quick end to the war and adopted a 'wait and see' attitude to the issue of Soviet labour.

However, the failure of the 'Barbarossa' campaign and the consequences for the German army and the economy led Hitler to overcome his ideological objections and order the deployment of Soviet prisoners of war in Germany on 31 October 1941.[139] As the realization spread through German industry that the campaign had been a failure and that a long war was in now prospect, so the desire to deploy Soviet workers increased, and it is no accident that the first attempts by Daimler-Benz to procure Soviet prisoners of war were made at this time.

Soon after the Führer Decree of 31 October, Daimler-Benz's Genshagen management, in contrast to many other firms, had declared its willingness to use 100 Soviet prisoners of war on an experimental basis.[140] However, the Soviets had suffered such brutal treatment at the hands of the Wehrmacht that thousands had died each day, and those that survived were in such a dreadful physical condition as a result that they had to be 'returned' to the Wehrmacht camp without being put to work. The first Daimler-Benz plant to deploy Soviet workers was Sindelfingen, whose management had by the end of 1941 requested 400-500 Soviet skilled workers to be put to work in Luftwaffe production.[141] How many workers came in the initial transports and exactly when is unclear, but by February 1942 at the latest a contingent had arrived, also evidently in an appalling physical state.[142]

With the renewal of mass call-ups to the Wehrmacht from early 1942 in anticipation of the Stalingrad campaign, and the simultaneous demand from the regime to increase armaments output radically, the board renewed its pressure for large numbers of Soviet prisoners of war to be allocated to Daimler-Benz in February 1942. In the same month Kissel asked the FMO management how far it had got, stating, 'We will undoubtedly be able to put the so-called 'helper races' [*Hilfsvölker*] to good use.' He continued that

---

138   On the fate of the Soviet prisoners of war see Streit, C., 'Sowjetische Kriegsgefangene-Massendeportation-Zwangsarbeiter' in: Michalka (ed.), *Der Zweite Weltkrieg*, pp. 747–60.
139   Herbert, *Fremdarbeiter*, pp. 139–43; Naasner, *Neue Machtzentren*, pp. 92–8.
140   Hoppmann et al., *Zwangsarbeit bei Daimler-Benz*, p. 303.
141   MBAG Huppenbauer 401, DBAG Sindelfingen to RLM 15.12.1941; DBAG to RLM, 16.12.1941.
142   MBAG Huppenbauer 401, DBAG Sindelfingen to RLM, 24.2.1942.

'although the workers deployed in Genshagen are causing all sorts of headaches', patience would bring rewards – 'I am sure that with correct treatment much can be got out of the workers from the east.' He concluded: 'I am therefore pleased that such workers are being put to work in Untertürkheim.'[143] In late March, by now aware of what the process entailed and conscious of exactly what it meant for the Soviet workers concerned, Kissel wrote to a contact in the RLM that he had heard of the availability of large numbers of 'refugees' in the Leningrad area, and requested to know 'how many men are involved, and what I have to do to procure as large an allocation as possible for my firm and above all Untertürkheim.'[144] This was followed up with a request for further allocations in April 1942.[145] Through the spring of 1942, Soviet prisoners of war and civilian deportees flooded into Daimler-Benz's factories, so that within the space of six months the workforce was radically transformed. At Untertürkheim there were 550 Russians by the end of June 1942, with a further 750 expected in the following two weeks.[4146] At Sindelfingen, 600 Russians arrived in early June, with a further allocation of 600 to arrive soon after.[147] At the same time, as noted already, a massive transportation of 2500 Soviet forced labourers arrived at Genshagen.[148]

It is difficult to ascertain the exact proportion of east and west European foreign workers at Daimler-Benz at any given point during the war, as aggregate figures for prisoners of war, forced foreign workers and (later) concentration camp inmates are often unreliable or self-contradictory.[149] However, under the impact of call-ups to the Wehrmacht on the one hand and the continuing influx of prisoners of war and foreign workers on the other,

143 MBAG Kissel IX/FMO, Kissel to General Management of FMO, 14.2.1942.
144 MBAG Kissel XIII/14, Kissel to Griep (RLM-Deputy), 19.3.1942.
145 MBAG Kissel XIII/14, Kissel to Griep, 14.4.1942. The volume of evidence documenting in unambiguous fashion the board's attempts to procure both west and east European foreign workers makes the assertion of Hoppmann et al., *Zwangsarbeit bei Daimler-Benz*, p. 79, that 'unfortunately there are no documents from either the supervisory or managerial boards to show whether a decision in principle was ever taken to deploy forced workers' untenable. While some ambiguity exists regarding the very early stages of the deployment of prisoners of war, in the crucial case of the Soviet workers in particular, it is clear that the board actively pressed for them from an early stage. Given the high degree of centralization of decision-making at Daimler-Benz scepticism is also necessary regarding the further claim of Hoppmann et al., p. 79, that the main decisions were taken at individual factory level and that 'as the deployment of foreign workers by the plants intensified, a decision from above was no longer necessary.' While the individual managements clearly pressed for their deployment, it is also evident that they referred back to the board for all major decisions, including that of the procurement of prisoners of war, and it is inconceivable that the recruitment of foreign workers would have occurred without the prior consent of the company board.
146 Hauptstaatsarchiv Stuttgart E397/65, DBAG Untertürkheim to Regional Food Office, 30.6.1942.
147 MBAG Huppenbauer 401, Memorandum regarding Expansion of Barracks at Böblinger-Allee Site, Sindelfingen, 23.4.1942.
148 BA (P) 80 Ba2 P3322, Daimler-Benz Motoren GmbH Genshagen to the Board, 11.7.1942.
149 For comprehensive statistics see Roth, 'Der Weg zum Guten Stern', pp. 343–4; Hoppmann et al., *Zwangsarbeit bei Daimler-Benz*, pp. 95–104; also MBAG Haspel 19, Statistical Monthly Report 1942–4.

the proportion of forced workers at the core plants rose from 9.8 per cent in December 1941 to 25.4 per cent in December 1942, 32 per cent in December 1943 and 35.2 per cent in December 1944. At Genshagen, the proportion was at all times much higher – the proportion had already reached nearly 50 per cent by the end of 1942 and 67.5 per cent by the end of 1944.[150] In December 1944, at all plants controlled by Daimler-Benz, a total of 26,958 forced foreign workers, 4887 prisoners of war and thousands of concentration camp inmates in both production and at dispersal sites were being put to work, for the most part under dreadful conditions.[151]

The percentage of foreign workers deployed at the company depends on whether one counts only the main factories of the pre-war concern or whether one also includes the workforces of the numerous subsidiary firms and firms managed under trusteeship in the occupied territories during the war. In the latter case, the proportion would be substantially higher. Aggregate percentages for the company as a whole tend to underplay the significance of the foreign workers in the blue-collar workforce and the extent to which production relied on the forced foreign workers from an early stage. For example, figures for Untertürkheim as a whole suggest only an average proportion of foreign workers at the plant, whereas in fact production was strongly dependent on this labour since a very high proportion of German employees were engaged in the research and development work that accounted for an increasingly large part of the plant's activity in the war.

In any case, focusing purely on statistical material – crucial as it is – does not in any adequate way reflect the degree of complicity of either industry as a whole or Daimler-Benz in particular in the overall process of foreign labour exploitation, or the function of industry within the system evolved to carry it out. More important than the precise statistical details is the recognition of the extent to which the deployment of foreign workers, in the case of Soviet workers and concentration camp inmates in particularly appalling conditions, involved – indeed, depended on – the collusion of industry, without which the use of forced labour in the German war economy would have been impossible. Above all, by putting the various categories of worker to work in the different conditions demanded by the ideologically defined criteria of the regime (it is possible to over-state the degree of divergence of priorities between industry and the regime on this issue), German industry not only collaborated in the exploitation of forced labour in the interests of the war economy (and of industry itself), but actively facilitated the establishment of the Nazi racial hierarchy within the workplace.

From the outset, the Soviet workers were deployed at Daimler-Benz under dreadful conditions, in line with the regulations laid out in February and

150 Hoppmann et al., *Zwangsarbeit bei Daimler-Benz*, pp. 101–2.
151 Ibid., pp. 98–9.

March 1942 in the so-called 'East Worker Decrees' (*Ostarbeitererlasse*).[152] They were to be kept strictly segregated from the German population, other civilian foreign workers and other prisoners of war, put to work under guard in large colonies, and housed in barracks surrounded by barbed wire, which they were only allowed to leave on the march to and from work.[153] There were no limits on their working hours – a situation brutally exploited by Daimler-Benz – and they were to receive no overtime, nightshift or Sunday pay.[154] Physical violence was expressly sanctioned as a means of keeping order within the workplace, while 'ill discipline', refusal to work or 'sloppy work' (*lässiges Arbeiten*) was punishable by the Gestapo and usually resulted in referral to a Labour Education Camp or concentration camp.[155] Finally, the racist paranoia of the regime demanded that the transgression of ideologically defined rules, above all sexual contact with Germans or other foreign workers, was to be met with summary execution or transfer to a concentration camp.

By April 1942, the experience of trying to exploit Soviet workers had led to widespread recognition within industry and the regime that an effective deployment was impossible under these conditions. Pressure from industry and the recognition of the regime of the need to modify some of the restrictions to make the use of Soviet workers more worthwhile and effective – essential given the military situation in 1942 – gave rise to a relaxation of some of the regulations regarding the segregation of Soviet workers from other workers.[156] The decision to remove barbed wire from the barracks and to permit Soviet workers to leave them under guard as a reward for good work was a further acknowledgment of the negative psychological impact the conditions were having on the Russians' willingness and ability to work.

However, while the removal of barbed wire may have had a positive psychological effect, and while the relaxation of the regulations regarding segregated deployment may have eased their integration into the production process – a factor of importance especially in the highly integrated production lines of the metal-working industry – changes in the regulations regarding their deployment in the plant did not mean an improvement in the physical treatment or physical conditions of the Soviet workers. In fact, at the same time, largely in response to public opinion in the wake of cuts for the German

152 On the 'Ostarbeitererlasse' see Herbert, *Fremdarbeiter*, pp. 154–7.

153 MBAG Huppenbauer 233, Excerpt from the General Stipulations of the RFSS and Head of the German Police regarding the Recruitment and Deployment of Workers from the East of 20.2.1942.

154 MBAG Huppenbauer 233, Decree on Labour Legislation in Relation to the Treatment of Workers from the Newly-Occupied Areas, 9.2.1942.

155 MBAG Huppenbauer 233, Circular of the Gestapo regarding Deployment and Guarding of Soviet Workers, 25.3.1942.

156 MBAG Forstmeier 22, Reich Group Industry to the General Plenipotentiary for Labour, 4.4.1942; MBAG Huppenbauer 233, Treatment of workers from the Former Soviet Areas/Addendum to Section A of the General Stipulations regarding the Recruitment and Deployment of Workers from the East of 20.2.1942 (9.4.1942).

population, the rations of the Soviet workers were cut from what was already an intolerably low level to one that condemned them to accelerated physical decline.[157] Despite the modifications, moreover, the basic conditions for Soviet workers remained those dictated by the initial decrees.

Initially, the Soviet workers at Daimler-Benz's plants were allocated food in uncritical compliance with the stipulations of the regime. On these starvation rations the men were put to work for up to 80 hours per week, including Sundays, and the women for 60 hours. However, by the end of June, the Russian workers, who had complained from the outset, were rejecting the food, and at Untertürkheim the Russian men were refusing to work. They were eventually forced to start again, with the 'ringleader' of the strike being sent to a concentration camp; but, as a result of their action, the Untertürkheim management pressed for extra food allocations, 'even if these larger amounts are achieved at the expense of quality.'[158] Other Daimler-Benz plants had similar experiences. At Mannheim, the bread given to the Soviet forced workers was of such poor quality that it caused widespread stomach complaints and digestion problems.[159] Likewise, at Genshagen, the management reported in June that their first experiences of the Soviet workers were generally positive, whereas two months later poor treatment was leading to problems in production that were causing the managers considerable worry.[160] The desperation of the Soviet workers in the summer of 1942 is reflected in the fact that, despite the heavy guarding of the barracks and the threat of the death penalty for attempted escapes, many tried to get away. The management's claim that the loss of 600 of the 2500 Soviet deportees by September 1942 was attributable primarily to escapes is still questionable, however: a substantial portion of these first deportees undoubtedly died through malnourishment or other mistreatment.

Similar experiences and complaints from other companies in the spring and summer of 1942, combined with the growing recognition within the regime of the extent to which the war economy was dependent on the Soviet forced workers, led to a gradual improvement in the rations and conditions of the Soviet workers, in an attempt to raise their productivity to the level the military situation required. In a succession of decrees in the summer of 1942, Sauckel ordered that the foreign workers, above all the Russians, be deployed in line with their pre-existing skills, be given adequate training and be treated in such a way as to maintain and increase their ability and willingness to work

157 MBAG Huppenbauer 233, Excerpt from the Decree of the RMfEuL, 17.4.1942; Herbert, *Fremdarbeiter*, pp. 162–3.
158 Hauptstaatsarchiv Stuttgart E397/65, DBAG Untertürkheim to Regional Food Office, 30.6.1942; Hoppmann et al., *Zwangsarbeit bei Daimler-Benz*, p. 134.
159 Stadtarchiv Mannheim, Food and Economy Office/1958 488, DBAG Mannheim to Reich Doctors' Chamber, 24.8.1942.
160 BA (P) 80 Ba2 P3322, Daimler-Benz Motoren GmbH Genshagen to the Board, 11.7.1942; Daimler-Benz Motoren GmbH Genshagen to the Board, 21.9.1942; see also BA-MA (F) RW 20–3/1, War Diary of Armaments Inspectorate (Berlin), 3.Q.1942, p. 35.

in the long run.[161] Similarly, in July 1942, Sauckel demanded that prisoners of war be used in such a way as to maximize their productivity, including the introduction of productivity-related pay, small bonuses for good work and withholding of rations for ill-discipine.[162] On the whole, the spring and summer of 1942 thus marked the transition from the short-term policy of 'Destruction through Work' (*Vernichtung durch Arbeit*) characteristic of the euphoric phase of the initial victories of the 'Barbarossa' campaign, to that of long-term exploitation of forced labour in the interests of the war economy. As such, the blanket brutality of the period up to mid-1942 gave way to a more differentiated system of incentive and discipline designed to maximize the output of the Soviet workers. However, this occurred within a broader policy framework which combined these concessions to the regime's economic pragmatists with continued racial discrimination and terror, ensuring that the experience of the Soviet workers remained dreadful.

Although the significance of these improvements to the rations and situation of the Soviet workers should not be underestimated, meaning as they did in many cases the difference between life and death, their working and living conditions were made only marginally better. Where the company did attempt to improve conditions, it was only so as to ensure the minimum standard of provision and hygiene to stop illness and disease from becoming rife. Such attempts on the part of the company were isolated rather than systematic, and, in any case, often met with little success. Even when it had notionally been allocated particular goods, such as extra blankets or extra clothes or shoes, suppliers were often unable to deliver.[163] At Sindelfingen, at least some of the barracks were made with rotten timber, the walls were mildewy and the buildings were not waterproof.[164] The minimum conditions decreed acceptable for housing in the barracks remained harsh – beds only had to be stool-width apart, while washing facilities were very basic and there only had to be provision for each worker to take a shower once a week.[165] Given the physical nature of the work and the general lack of clothing (many workers had only one set of clothes to live and work in), this was highly unsatisfactory from the point of view of hygiene, not to say unpleasant in the extreme for the foreign workers concerned, and, combined with a food supply that remained adequate at best, did nothing to help prevent the spread of illness and disease. For the Soviet women in particular, factory hardship was compounded by great suffering in the barracks. Many were forced to prostitute

161 MBAG Huppenbauer 233, Communiqué regarding Deployment of Foreign Labour, 25.8.1942.
162 MBAG Huppenbauer 226, Circular of DBAG Sindelfingen concerning the Raising of Productivity of Prisoners of War in the Economy, 6.8.1942.
163 MBAG Huppenbauer 233, DBAG Sindelfingen to Economy Office Böblingen, 21.7.1942; MBAG Huppenbauer 401, DBAG Sindelfingen to Economy Office Böblingen, 25.7.1942; DBAG Sindelfingen to Economy Office Böblingen, 10.8.1942.
164 MBAG Huppenbauer 405, DBAG to RMfBuM, 14.11.1942.
165 MBAG Haspel 3,32, Decree on the Housing of Workers in Barracks for the Duration of the War (RGBl.I 1943, s.388).

themselves to west European workers for bread. If they became pregnant, they were usually forced to have an abortion; those who did give birth mostly lost their infants through malnutrition or related illnesses. The experience of the Soviet women was thus in many fundamental ways much worse.[166]

The physical state of the workers, their lack of experience and their unfamiliarity with the factory environment, their depressing and frightening existence in the barracks and their obvious lack of interest in producing armaments for the German military combined to ensure that their productivity was poor, and the work they delivered was often of low quality. Following the arrival of the 2500 Soviet workers at Genshagen, the monthly wastage of material doubled, reflecting the poor work of these untrained and brutalized workers.[167] K.C. Müller summarized the situation in July 1942 in a comment that mixed racial contempt with recognition of the fact that the system of blanket exploitation was inappropriate to the needs of a high-skilled, capital-intensive production process such as that as Genshagen: 'You can't build engines with Russians.'[168]

In line with the general shift in policy of the regime in the summer of 1942, the company gradually moved towards better training and greater integration into the production process for the Soviet workers. The nature of production at Daimler-Benz was such that a minimal amount of training had to be given from the outset, and, at Sindelfingen at least, Russian workers were used according to pre-existing skills more or less from the beginning of their period of labour there. In July 1942, out of a detachment of 100 new labourers, 30 were selected and deployed as skilled workers immediately.[169] When the Sindelfingen management heard of a skilled Russian worker being used as an unskilled labourer, it immediately arranged for his redeployment as a lathe operator.[170] The positive results (clearly, the plants were as quick as anybody to realize that if the Soviet workers were given semi-decent treatment they were capable of working just as well as Germans) led Haspel to argue in November 1942 that the company should take the long-term view and accept the necessity of procuring as many Russian women as possible, train them for three months and accept the loss of output this involved, in order to have genuinely productive workers at the end whom the company could really use.[171] In its annual report for 1943, the Genshagen management noted that it had successfully given young male Soviet workers training not only for specific tasks but 'six months training on a broad basis.'[172]

Comprehensive statistics on the development of the skills structure of the

166   For examples see Hoppmann et al., *Zwangsarbeit bei Daimler-Benz*, pp. 135–6, 170–1.
167   BA (P) 80 Ba2 P3326, Accounting Report 1942.
168   MBAG Kissel I/15, Minutes of the Board Meeting of DBAG on 30.6 and 1.7.1942.
169   MBAG Huppenbauer 233, Deployment Plan for Russians on 8.7.1942.
170   MBAG Huppenbauer 233, DBAG Sindelfingen/Factory Management to Held, 24.8.1942.
171   MBAG Kissel I/15, Minutes of the Board Meeting of DBAG on 4 and 5.11.1942.
172   *Geschäftsbericht der Daimler-Benz Motoren GmbH Genshagen 1943.*

workforce at Daimler-Benz's plants for the second half of the war, and for the skills structure of the foreign workers within this, are unavailable. Detailed figures on the structure of the workforce for Unterturkheim in April 1944 give a clear idea, however, of the extent to which the reliance of the company on foreign workers forced it into extensive training of west and east Europeans alike. Of 15,589 workers at Unterturkheim in April 1944, 10,484 were German (67 per cent), 2883 were west European (18 per cent) and 1846 were Russian (12 per cent) – the remaining 376 workers were prisoners of war (3 per cent). While there is a clear hierarchy within the skilled workforce – 30 per cent of German workers, 10 per cent of west European workers, but only 0.1 per cent of Russian workers were skilled – overwhelmingly the most important fact is that for all the racially defined categories, the great majority were classified as skilled or semi-skilled workers by 1944. In April 1944, 55 per cent of German, 81 per cent of west European and 66 per cent of Soviet workers were performing skilled or semi-skilled functions, and even among the prisoners of war, 44 per cent were doing so.[173] As a key company in the high-skills metal-working sector, the proportion of west to east European workers was relatively high in most of Daimler-Benz's plants, and, if the figures for Unterturkheim are representative, which occasional evidence suggests them to be, then it seems that the training of both east and west European workers was sufficiently widespread for the deployment of foreign workers to have had little effect on the underlying development of the production processes at Daimler-Benz or on the skills structure of the workforce (specific areas such as aero-engine production at Genshagen notwithstanding).

Similarly, there is little documentary evidence concerning the productivity of the Soviet forced workers in comparison to that of the German or west European workers, but the occasional evidence suggests that it was similar to that of other plants in the engineering sector.[174] A broad picture of the development of the work-rates of Soviet workers in comparable plants, which undoubtedly reflect developments at Daimler-Benz, can be gained by examining the evidence collated by the Labour Science Institute of the DAF. In March 1943, the DAF estimated that the average productivity of a Soviet worker, measured against the average productivity of a German worker performing comparable tasks, was 70 to 75 per cent of the norm.[175] By 1944, the average productivity of Soviet workers had risen to around 80 per cent of that of a corresponding German worker, with 88 per cent of the Soviet

---

173   National Archives, Washington D.C., RG 243 USSBS Docs 79a1, Work-force Statistics Daimler-Benz Unterturkheim Plant, 30.4.1944.

174   BA-MA (F) RW 20–50/5, War Diary of the Armaments Commando Potsdam, 4.Q. 1942, Enclosure 16, Productivity of East Workers (December 1942), states the average productivity of the Soviet men to be 60–65 per cent of that of their German counterparts, and that of the women to be 65–70 per cent.

175   Arbeitswissenschaftliche Institut der DAF (ed.), *Der Arbeitseinsatz der Ostarbeiter in Deutschland*, Berlin 1943.

workers producing at 60 per cent productivity or higher, and 58 per cent at 80 per cent productivity or better. The productivity of Soviet women was notably higher than that of the men. Of the women, 92 per cent worked at 60 per cent of the work-rate of their German counterparts, and 74 per cent worked at 80 per cent productivity or better; while of the men, 85 per cent produced at 60 per cent productivity or better, and only 47 per cent produced at 80 per cent or more of the German work-rate.[176] Haspel's clear preference for Soviet women workers, expressed in November 1942, suggests that this pattern established itself at Daimler-Benz very early on. Clearly, however, the majority of both men and women examined registered stable or improving work-rates.

The reasons for the improving productivity of the Soviet workers are complex; the extent to which widespread improvements in the standard of provision for them was responsible should not be over-stated. Elementary, and later more extensive, training was a key factor; familiarization with both the factory environment and the specific tasks being performed within the production process was undoubtedly another. In a highly integrated production process in which each machine-tool and each production line was coordinated with the next (in principle at least, if often not, during the war, in practice), both the tempo of the overall flow of production and pressure from the German workers created a strong compulsion to achieve the work-rate demanded. In fact, the main area of production where the work processes had been so subdivided and mechanized that mainly semi- and unskilled workers could be deployed, that of assembly, was precisely the one in which the production process itself demanded the highest level of discipline. Beyond the pressures created by the general lack of workers, this undoubtedly explains why the restrictions regarding the deployment of foreign workers and prisoners of war in assembly work were gradually lifted.[177]

The second aspect of the integration of the Soviet workers into the production process and the raising of their productivity was the development of a differentiated system of incentive, reward, discipline and terror which encouraged conformity and forced hard work out of them. From mid-1942, productivity-related pay became the norm, while increasingly the allocation of food was instrumentalized as a means of incentive and discipline, with extra rations being given for good work and food withheld for failure to work hard or conform. Such measures were developed for the German workforce too, but affected the Soviet workers to a greater extent and were implemented according to far more brutal criteria. Given the abysmal level of nutrition the Soviet workers continued to receive, even the smallest premium would have

---

176   Arbeitswissenschaftliche Institut der DAF (ed.), *Arbeitseignung und Leistungsfähigkeit der Ostarbeiter in Deutschland*, Berlin, 1944.

177   On the integration of Soviet workers into the production process in the metalworking sector in general see Herbert, *Fremdarbeiter*, pp. 273–8.

Here the 2 references to journal articles I've come across
German History vol 19, n03, 2001
Discussing Slave Labourers p400-8
also several articles in German Studies Review, vol XXV No1, Feb 2002

had a substantial effect in raising work-rates, meaning as it often did the difference between adequate food and intolerable hunger. By 1944, food and items of consumption had more or less replaced increasingly worthless money as the main incentive, with cigarettes playing a key role. The assertion at the Fighter Staff meeting of 26 May 1944 that '5 or 10 cigarettes means more to a Soviet worker than RM 20' may have been an exaggeration, but not much of one.[178] The process of improving the position of the Soviet workers, on paper at least, and of refining the food allocation system to optimize the exploitation of their labour was completed in late 1944 when three categories of food ration were created – one for those who achieved over 100 per cent of the work-rate of the German workers, a second for those who achieved over 90 per cent, and a third for those who failed to reach 90 per cent.[79]

However, it is highly doubtful whether many consistently achieved a work-rate sufficient to allow the receipt of extra rations in this way, and in any case the collapsing supply situation of the Reich was such by this point that the rations increasingly existed on paper only. Soviet workers were more likely to be affected by the growing tendency to withdraw rations as a means of disciplining the workforce; conversely, they continued to be the objects of particular discrimination when it came to the allocation of extra items of consumption. When there was not enough to go round, they were always the first to be excluded from the list of recipients of extra cigarettes or vitamin pills.[180]

Furthermore, the evolution of the mechanisms of control and reward was one element in a renewed worsening of the Soviet workers' position, along with that of the west European workers in many respects, in 1944. During the period in which the growing dependence on Soviet labour manifested itself in successive moves to improve their productivity, strategic company planning for the post-war period began to assert itself and resulted in a reversion to more short-termist thinking regarding the maximization of armaments output and in a growing reluctance to achieve this through long-term capital investment. Along with the German workers, the forced workers, and later the concentration camp inmates, were caught between the successive demands of the regime to increase output and the growing reluctance to expand capacity or continue investment, which manifested itself above all in a radical intensification of labour in 1944 achieved through a reversion to short-term extensive exploitation of the foreign workers. As the post-war period came more and more into focus, these workers became once again increasingly 'expendable'; as a result, their suffering intensified once more. In May 1944, as noted, Haspel demanded that targets be achieved 'with brutal force if

178 BA-MA (F) RL 3/7, Minutes of the Fighter Staff Meeting of 26.5.1944.
179 Stadtarchiv Stuttgart Food and Economy Office 362, RMfEuL to Regional Economic Offices, 22.9.1944.
180 MBAG Haspel 3,32, Announcement regarding Distribution of Vitamin Supplements to Our Workers, 27.4.1944; Circular to all Heads of Department regarding special Allocation, 12.5.1944.

necessary' and that 'the last ounce be squeezed out of people.'[181] It was precisely the system of incentive and discipline evolved over the previous eighteen months, allowing the threat of withdrawal of rations for those who failed to keep up, combined with the increased integration of the Soviet workers into the flow process, permitting the 'speed-up' of production lines, that enabled this to take place. At Genshagen, for instance, the piece-rates in aero-engine production were cut successively in 1944.[182] Clearly, it did not demand identification with the imperialist or racist ideology of the regime to allow the company to participate in its barbarous criminality – the exploitation of some of the regime's most helpless victims was in many ways at its most intense when the company had already abandoned it and was looking only to save itself.

The other aspect in the renewed deterioration of the situation of the foreign workers in 1944 was a product of the intensifying bombing, diminishing supplies and later, from the winter of 1944–5 onwards, of the more fundamental disintegration of the regime. First, as successive air raids caused considerable damage to Daimler-Benz's plants and rendered many foreign workers superfluous as far as actual production was concerned, many of those who had hitherto been deployed as machine operators (which afforded them a degree of protection) were put to work in clearing up and rebuilding, occasioning a reversion to short-term physical exploitation in heavy labour. This was particularly the case for the Italian 'Military Internees' who were sent to work at Daimler-Benz's plants from late 1943 onwards and whose experience of brutality and deprivation matched that of the Soviet workers.[183] Even worse was the experience of the Soviet workers who were put to work as labourers at the underground dispersal sites. Detachment from the core plant meant the weakening of ties with the main supplier of food; deployment in heavy labour brought with it treatment not much better than that meted out to the concentration camp inmates there.[184]

For those at the main plants, the intensifying work-rate within the factory was paralleled by the escalating impact of Allied bombing raids. By 1943, shortages of building materials and sporadic air-raid damage were leading to increasing numbers of foreign workers being crammed into barracks that had been intended to take far fewer people. At Sindelfingen, for example, in June 1943, 800 Russians were being housed in a barracks complex originally

181 MBAG Haspel/'Arbeitskreis Lastwagen', Minutes of the Meeting on Lorry Production 31.5.1944.
182 Hoppmann et al., *Zwangsarbeit bei Daimler-Benz*, p. 220.
183 On the IMIs at Daimler-Benz see Schmid, 'Unsere Ausländische Arbeitskräfte', p. 70; in general see Herbert, *Fremdarbeiter*, pp. 259–63.
184 In April 1944, for example, 200 of Untertürkheim's Soviet workers had already been put to work at the dispersal sites, so that for some of the Soviet workers over a year of their time in Germany was spent in such circumstances (MBAG Haspel 1,2, Circular regarding Special Food Allocations for Russians, 22.4.1944).

designed for 660.[185] In an air raid on Sindelfingen in October 1943, 250 sleeping places in the barracks and all essential facilities were destroyed, causing even greater cramming together in barracks that were already heaving with workers.[186] The bombing damage to barracks led not only to a desperate shortage of replacement clothing, but to a situation where, already by March 1944, Russian workers were having to sleep in slit trenches.[87] Finally, in the attacks on Sindelfingen of 14 August, 10 and 13 September 1944, first a barracks for 170 Russian women and then the whole barracks complex for west European workers along with all kitchen and canteen facilities were destroyed; there were also numerous fatalities.[188] Similar events at Unter-türkheim in August 1944 led to a situation where not only all foreign workers, but all German workers too were eating together in the same makeshift facilities: where the situation of the Soviet workers approximated to that of west European workers, it was more a product of coping with the chaos on the ground, than a result of the relaxation of ideological restrictions by the regime.[189] The deteriorating supply situation and the impact of the bombing on conditions generally meant that, more often than not, the growing similarity between the experiences of west and east European workers was a product of levelling down, not levelling up.

Meanwhile, the effects of bombing and the fact that many prisoners of war and foreign workers were now deployed outside, in addition to the declining ratio of German personnel to the mass of forced labourers, led to an inevitable reduction in the effectiveness of the company's security provisions and to an increase in the opportunities for escape.[190] The rapid wane in the living standards of the prisoners of war and foreign workers from the summer of 1944 onwards simultaneously manifested itself in more regular attempts to escape. The firm obviously tried to counter the waning effectiveness of its internal surveillance and security system by increasingly resorting to external bodies, resulting in a clear radicalization of terror in the last phase of the war. As the plants started to experience over-employment, the need to retain scarce labour receded, reinforcing the willingness of the management to invoke external terror in its attempts to discipline recalcitrant workers and discourage escape attempts. Thus, for example, in response to continual absenteeism, lack of discipline and 'insubordinate behaviour' (*herausforderndes Verhalten*) on the part of Czech workers, and specifically for repeated refusals to get out

---

185 MBAG Huppenbauer 392, DBAG Sindelfingen/Heim to Haspel, 21.6.1943.
186 MBAG Huppenbauer 406, DBAG Sindelfingen to the General Plenipotentiary of the RMfRuK, 11.10.1943.
187 MBAG Haspel 2,16, Memorandum for Director Scheerer of RMfRuK, 3.3.1944.
188 MBAG Haspel 2,18, DBAG Sindelfingen to Haspel, 14.8.1944; DBAG Sindelfingen to Haspel, 10.9.1944; DBAG Sindelfingen to Haspel, 13.9.1944.
189 MBAG Haspel 3,32, Announcement concerning Working Hours, 30.8.1944.
190 Of the many escape attempts see for example MBAG Haspel 1,2, Confidential Communiqué regarding the Guarding of our French Prisoners of War and Italian Military Internees, 10.7.1944.

of bed in the mornings, four persistent offenders were sent to a concentration camp for six months. In a second case, when eleven French workers refused to do as they were told, and three continued to behave uncooperatively, all eleven were sent to a concentration camp for four months.[191] Here, again, the fact that the company had long since abandoned the regime and was desparately preparing for the post-war period did not prevent it invoking the state's terror apparatus; down to the end of the war, Daimler-Benz continued to send people to what amounted to almost certain death.

c) Concentration Camp Labour 1943-5

The growing shortage of labour also led to a shift in the function of the SS-run concentration camps in 1942. Whereas prior to 1942 they had been run primarily as institutions of 'destruction through work', with the work performed there having no real economic function, they were thereafter used as sources of additional labour for direct and indirect deployment in armaments production. In conjunction with industry, the SS transferred increasing numbers of inmates to 'outer camps' (*Aussenlager*) attached to industrial plants or to building sites, where they were put to work. As a result of this, up to half a million concentration camp inmates were working in the war economy at the end of 1944. Despite the partial shift in the role of the camps in 1942, however, the treatment of the internees remained barbaric and brutal, and countless tens of thousands died as a result of hunger, cold, illness and physical mistreatment or punishment.[192]

In the same way that the normalization of the use of foreign workers in 1941 paved the way for the mass exploitation of the Soviet workers from early 1942 onwards, so this in its turn paved the way for the final stage in Daimler-Benz's collusion in the regime's crimes, the widespread deployment of concentration camp inmates.[193] The vast majority were put to work as building labour on the dispersal sites; they were also used at numerous Daimler-Benz plants, however. Genshagen was the first, 180 inmates from Sachsenhausen being put to work there in January 1943. Of the south German plants, the first to utilize camp internees (although not, strictly speaking, concentration camp internees),

---

191 MBAG Haspel 1,2, Announcement of the Managers (Unterürkheim) concerning Foreign Workers, 10.11.1944 (reprinted in Pohl et al., *Die Daimler-Benz AG*, p. 319, Document 60).

192 On concentration camp labour in the German war economy see Pingel, F., *Häftlinge unter SS-Herrschaft. Widerstand, Selbstbehauptung und Vernichtung im Konzentrationslager*, Hamburg, 1978; Pingel, F., 'Die KZ-Häftlinge zwischen Vernichtung und Arbeitseinsatz' in: Michalka (ed.), *Der Zweite Weltkrieg*, pp. 784–97; Vorländer, H. (ed.), *Nationalsozialistische Konzentrationslager im Dienst der Totalen Kriegsführung. Sieben Württembergische Außenkommandos des KZ-Natzweiler/Elsaß*, Stuttgart, 1978; Benz, W. and Distel, B. (eds.), *Sklavenarbeit im KZ* (*Dachauer Hefte* 2), Dachau, 1986; Hamburger Stiftung zur Förderung von Wissenschaft und Kultur (ed.), *Deutsche Wirtschaft. Zwangsarbeit von KZ-Häftlingen für Industrie und Behörden*, Hamburg, 1991.

193 On the 'increasing moral indifference' of the conservative elites, of which this is a prime example, see Mommsen, H., 'Aufarbeitung und Verdrängung. Das Dritte Reich im Westdeutschen Geschichtsbewußtsein' in: Diner (ed.), *Ist der Nationalsozialismus Geschichte? Zu Historisierung und Historikerstreit*, Frankfurt/M., 1987, p. 85.

was Gaggenau, which transferred part of its production to the Security Camp (*Sicherungslager*) at Schirmeck, in Alsace, in late 1943, for the express purposes of exploiting the labour of the political prisoners kept there.[194] In January 1944, 250 Schirmeck inmates were working for Daimler-Benz, including skilled workers, while following the establishment of a second workshop there a further 250 inmates were forced to produce spare parts for Gaggenau's lorries.[195] Later, as the front moved towards Germany, this production was transferred back to Gaggenau, where an 'outer camp' was set up and inmates were deployed in both production and clearing up bomb damage.[196] Finally, in late September 1944, 1060 inmates from Dachau were transferred to an 'outer camp' in Mannheim for deployment in Daimler-Benz's factory there, while almost simultaneously around 1100 inmates from the women's concentration camp at Ravensbrück were put to work at Genshagen. In both cases, the great majority were used on the assembly lines.[197] The conditions under which the inmates lived and worked were indescribably bad, their existence consisting of both arbitrary brutality at shop-floor level and constant exposure to SS terror, of intense hunger, cold and illness, and of long hours of hard physical labour that were the cause of exhaustion and long-term damage to health.

While the shortage of labour in the macro-economy was clearly a key factor in the deployment of concentration camp inmates directly in armaments production from the regime's viewpoint (another was the attempts of the SS to gain influence in economic and labour issues), the motives of the individual companies concerned are less obvious, certainly at least at Daimler-Benz. While in the case of underground dispersal the issue is relatively clear-cut – the company board was willing, not to say eager, to sanction and participate in murderous exploitation in order to save its capital goods for the post-war period – more complex processes were at work in the decision to procure inmates for deployment in production itself.[198] Although there were some concentration camp inmates at Daimler-Benz plants before the autumn of 1944, the fact that by far the largest influx coincided with the accelerating

194 On Gaggenau in this context see Hoppmann et al., *Zwangsarbeit bei Daimler-Benz*, pp. 365–77.
195 MBAG DBAG 21, Report of the State of the Reorganization and Investment Costs at the Gaggenau Plant as of January 1944, 5.2.1944.
196 Hoppmann et al., *Zwangsarbeit bei Daimler-Benz*, p. 367; Schmid, 'Unsere Ausländische Arbeitskräfte', p. 376.
197 On the case of Mannheim see Schmitt, A., 'Die Geschichte des Konzentrationslagers Mannheim-Sandhofen. Ein Beitrag zur Zeitgeschichte im Regionalen Bereich', Zulassungs-arbeit, Ludwigsburg, 1976; Koppenhöfer, p. , 'Erster Wahl für Daimler-Benz: Erinnerungen von KZ-Häftlingen an die Arbeit im Daimler-Benz Werk Mannheim' in: *Mitteilungen der Dokumentationsstelle zur Nationalsozialistischen Sozialpolitik* 15–16 (1986) pp. 5–30; Koppenhöfer, P. , 'Im Buchenwald war die Verpflegung Besser. KZ-Häftlinge bei Daimler-Benz Mannheim' in: HSG (ed.), *Das Daimler-Benz Buch*, pp. 514–42; Hoppmann et al., *Zwangsarbeit bei Daimler-Benz*, pp. 424–36; On Genshagen Hoppmann et al., *Zwangsarbeit bei Daimler-Benz*, pp. 379–97; Schmid, 'Unsere Ausländische Arbeitskräften', pp. 580–1.
198 Herbert, 'Arbeit und Vernichtung', pp. 183–4.

collapse of production at the factories, and thus came at a point when the company's strategic intentions were focused on the post-war period, suggests that rational profit-seeking, still less the desire to utilize the presence of this unprotected labour to push through long-term changes in production technology, was not the primary motive.[199] The inmates were procured at a time when large-scale capital investment and reorganization of production had long ceased, and that most of these workers were deployed in assembly is again a reflection of the fact that this was already a highly rationalized sector of production, into which they could be integrated without expensive and time-consuming reorganization. Most of the inmates were at Mannheim, for example, for a matter of only one or two months before being transported to the underground dispersal sites instead, or being sent back to the concentration camp, so the idea that they marked a new stage in the organization of industrial production is to be treated with scepticism.

Clearly, as with all aspects of the company's behaviour during this period, an element of 'flight forwards' is involved. As production became more and more a question of crisis management on a daily basis, long-term strategic thinking, especially at shop-floor level, played a diminishing role. As far as rational motives were involved, these were undoubtedly short-term and, in the case of Mannheim especially, had to do with keeping production of the 3-ton lorry going in some form at all costs, for fear that if production should collapse, then the factories would – figuratively speaking – dissolve. As argued above, maintaining production, or at least the illusion of production, was essential to enable the company to keep its plant intact in the final chaotic months of the war. This imperative to keep producing, partly for reasons of short-term company interest, quite possibly partly out of identification with or sense of duty towards the soldiers at the front, and partly for lack of a conceivable alternative, undoubtedly played a greater role than rational profit-seeking or any new 'model' of industrial production or labour.

4. Business, Racial Barbarism and the New Order: The Flugmotorenwerk Rzeszow 1939–44

a) The Rzeszow plant under Henschel GmbH 1939–41

The extent to which industry's pursuit of its own interests in the second half of the war actively reinforced the tendency to intensify the labour process and thus the exploitation of the foreign forced workers at its mercy can be most clearly seen in an examination of Daimler-Benz's labour policy in the

---

199 For treatments of the issue that tend to this view see the collection of essays in Hamburger Stiftung für Förderung von Wissenschaft und Kultur (HSZFWK) (ed.), *Deutsche Wirtschaft*. An exception in the volume is that of Hans Mommsen, who persuasively argues that rationalization and profit-seeking were secondary factors (Mommsen, H., 'Zwangsarbeit und Konzentrationslager bei den Volkswagenwerken' in: HSZFWK (ed.), *Deutsche Wirtschaft*, pp. 221–225).

occupied areas. Here, the general uncertainty caused by the war situation and the growing reluctance to invest heavily in new processes specifically for war production in the latter third of the war was compounded by the more fundamental unwillingness of the company to make large-scale investments in the eastern occupied territories. The imperative to raise output on the one hand and the refusal to do this by investment and wideranging reorganization on the other resulted in an increasingly exploitative policy towards the labour force in the occupied territories. Its development can be traced clearly by an examination of the plant in Rzeszow, Poland, which Daimler-Benz took over in November 1941. This factory allows not only a detailed examination of the development of the system of incentive, discipline and terror applied to the foreign workforce, but also of how the suffering of the Polish population under National Socialist occupation was, although primarily a product of the regime's policy and ideology, also reinforced by the independent pursuit of private business interests by the companies that collaborated in the exploitation process.

Following the defeat of Poland in 1939, the Flugmotorenwerk Rzeszow was initially put under the management of Henschel GmbH, which produced Daimler-Benz aircraft engines under licence. Henschel was charged by the RLM with assembling and training a workforce out of the local Polish population and with reorganizing and re-tooling the plant for the production of parts for Daimler-Benz engines. Against the background of National Socialist policy in Poland and the impact of the occupation on the local economy, however, the process of setting up production proved difficult.[200] The disruption the military campaign caused to the Polish economy, ongoing Nazi terror in the initial phase of the occupation, combined with the practical difficulties of totally re-tooling a large industrial facility and working with a completely inexperienced workforce meant that the Henschel management made very slow progress.[201]

From the outset, Henschel attempted to make up for the slow pace of the reorganization process and the low work-rate of the Polish workforce by lengthening working hours. By 1941 the workshops were operating for 21 hours a day in two shifts.[202] The predominance of Polish workers, however – for most of the war 90 per cent or more of the workforce was Polish – meant

---

200   On the general background see Broszat, M., *Nationalsozialistische Polenpolitik 1939–1945*, Stuttgart, 1961; Gross, J.T., *Polish Society under German Occupation. The Generalgouvernement, 1939–1944*. New Jersey, 1979, especially pp. 92–117; Noakes, J. and Pridham, G. (eds.), *Nazism 1919–1945. A Documentary Reader. Volume Three: Foreign Policy, War and Racial Extermination*. Exeter, 1988, pp. 922–87.

201   See, for example, MBAG VO 175/25, Flugmotorenwerk Reichshof to Armaments Commando Krakow Region, 26.11.1940; Flugmotorenwerk Reichshof to Armaments Commando Krakow Region, 21.3.1941; Flugmotorenwerk Reichshof to Armaments Commando Krakow Region, 12.5.1941; Document/Development of the Flugmotorenwerk Reichshof (undated).

202   MBAG VO 175/25, Flugmotorenwerk Reichshof to Armaments Commando Krakow Region, 21.3.1941.

that from a relatively early stage the management was forced to develop more
extensive and long-term responses to their poor productivity. In March 1941
the management was already reporting, for example, on its efforts to increase
production by intensification of the work process. It reported that it had
introduced piece-rate pay in almost all of the machine workshops, which had
led to 'a considerable improvement in the material situation of the Polish
workers after the attainment of a noticeable improvement in productivity'.

However, although the regime's decision to halt all economic activity in
Poland in 1939 had been reversed by a policy of attempting to mobilize Polish
industry in the interests of the war economy soon after, the slow progress the
management was able to make in assembling a core of at least partially trained
workers was increasingly jeopardized by the harsh conditions suffered by the
Polish population.[203] The catastrophic food situation that had developed in
Poland since the occupation was, by 1941, starting to have a strong negative
impact on the ability of the company to maintain and increase production as
required.[204] Not only was it responsible for the deterioration of the health of
the workers to the degree that their capacity to work was severely affected, but
also for a continual increase in the rate of absenteeism.[205] The management
warned that, as a result of the latest reductions in rations for the Polish
workers, the latter were now being fed below subsistence levels, and that
consequently 'workers who have relatives in the countryside prefer to
disappear from the workplace, or at least to devote one or two days a week to
procuring food.'[206] The situation was becoming so desperate that the company
was increasingly powerless to keep at least enough workers attending the plant
with a sufficient degree of regularity to secure production. Punishing the
workers with fines was largely ineffective as the zloty was almost worthless, and
the workers in many cases actively wanted to be sacked.[207]

In the face of this the management began to put pressure on the regime for
a new policy towards the Polish population. It argued for a change in the
distribution of food to the various sectors of Polish society, suggesting that
only by improving the rations of the Polish armaments workers relative to the
rest of the population would it be possible to generate a corresponding desire
amongst the workforce to work in the industry. In July 1941, it wrote to the

203 Umbreit, 'Auf dem Weg zur Kontinentalherrschaft', p. 323.
204 The weekly food allocation in grams to German and Polish workers in the
      Generalgouvernement in 1941 is given in MBAG VO 175/25, Comparison of Reich Germans
      in the Old Reich and Reich Germans, Ethnic Germans and Poles in the Generalgouvernement,
      (undated, 1941). On the calorific intake of the Polish population during the war see Noakes and
      Pridham (eds.), *Nazism. Volume 3*, pp. 990–2.
205 MBAG VO 175/25, Flugmotorenwerk Reichshof to Armaments Commando Krakow Region,
      21.7.1941.
206 On the food situation in Poland see also Broszat, *Nationalsozialistische Polenpolitik*, p. 77.
207 MBAG VO 175/25, Situation Report of Flugmotorenwerk Reichshof on 1 to 30 Juny 1941,
      30.6.1941; on the decline of the real value of the zloty and of workers' wages see Noakes and
      Pridham (eds.), *Nazism. Volume 3*, p. 992.

Armaments Commando, using imagery that exemplifies the instrumentalist attitudes of German industry to the foreign workers at its mercy:

An objective and unemotive evaluation of the situation must inevitably lead to the conclusion that the needs of the Polish worker and his family have to be satisfied on the same basis as a German armaments worker ... in order to maintain and improve the willingness and capability of the Poles – who have no interest in the outcome of the war – to work, no other yardstick can be applied, just as one cannot according to whim reduce the amount of lubricant applied to a French machine-tool.'[208]

It argued that in order to strengthen the hand of the company:

It would be appropriate for an increase in the food supply to take place exclusively for those Poles working for the German interest in the General-gouvernement. Undoubtedly this would enable the definite securing of the food supply to the Poles in the armaments industry and to those employed by the authorities. The rest of the population would have to cover its needs, as previously, via the black market or by agricultural labour.

For an armaments worker, the loss of employment would therefore mean a significant reduction in living standards, which, in the context, could mean the difference between subsistence or starvation. The management argued that this would lead to a corresponding interest in gaining work in a public factory and that an increase in the productivity of the Polish workers would then be attainable.

Despite this pressure, however, the food situation deteriorated further over the autumn of 1941. The long-term impact of chronic undernourishment, lack of heating and inadequate clothing, combined with increasingly intensive industrial labour was a catastrophic deterioration in the health of the Polish workers. The number of illnesses at the plant steadily increased. The poor nutritional state of the Polish workers was leading to lung, stomach, and skin illnesses and disorders, and to dysentery – these, the plant doctor reported, were solely attributable to the fact that 'both the food consumed in our plant and that obtained from other sources is qualitatively and quantitatively exceptionally inadequate.' The doctor suggested further that a high proportion of all industrial accidents in the factory were a result of the poor physical state of the workforce, and as such could also be linked to the lack of adequate food.

Not only did the number of illnesses increase dramatically through 1941, but the absenteeism rate rose substantially too. This again was a direct product

208   MBAG VO 175/25, Flugmotorenwerk Reichshof to Armaments Commando Krakow Region, 21.7.1941.

of the food situation. The Polish workers were increasingly having to resort to purchasing food on the black market, as the allocated rations were too low to live on. Absenteeism over the summer months was exacerbated by the Polish workers helping with the harvest, for which they were paid in food by the farmers. The decline in the value of the zloty and the minimal rations that could be purchased officially meant that bartering or payment in kind in the black economy – alongside theft – was becoming the main means of procuring and paying for goods. The company reported that

> the small allocation of food and items of clothing . . . can be paid for with only a part of the weekly wage. The mentality of the Poles leads them to the conclusion that, given the impossibility of buying anything on the free market with their low wages, it is pointless to work more days per week than those necessary to pay for the rationed food and goods.[209]

The appalling physical condition and low level of skills of the Polish workers, the high rate of absenteeism and the lengthy process of tooling, which had to take place with the assistance of a minimal number of German engineers, meant that Henschel made very slow progress in bringing the plant to a level of production satisfactory to the RLM. The latter soon became frustrated with the management's failure effectively to reorganize the plant and bring it to the point where it could start making a positive contribution to the regime's armaments programme. In April 1940, therefore, General Udet sent K.C. Müller to Rzeszow in order to see how it could be brought to work productively.[210] Although the plant remained for the time being formally under Henschel control, Müller's visit marked the start of a process whereby Daimler-Benz gradually gained influence over Rzeszow.

By 1941, it had begun supplying tools and parts directly to the Daimler-Benz plants in Marienfelde and Genshagen.[211] In May 1941, it was also visited again by a representative of the RLM – in all likelihood a Daimler-Benz

---

209 The poor physical state of the Polish workers also, inevitably, had a negative impact on the quality of production at the plant. The management complained that 'the aircraft plant produces both in its spare parts production and in its tool- and appliance-making departments parts which in many cases demand precision down to a few thousandths of a millimetre. This labour demands a high-quality workforce which, especially with regards to its nervous constitution, must be totally healthy.' It argued further that 'the tiredness symptoms that unavoidably manifest themselves in, on average, 10½-hour shifts of highly concentrated metal-cutting work have to be kept to a minimum in order to avoid costly wastage. This is only possible if the worker in question is well fed and not burdened with additional worries about obtaining necessary clothing and a minimum amount of heating and cooking fuel for himself and his family.' MBAG VO 175/25, Flugmotorenwerk Reichshof to Armaments Commando Krakow Region [Special Report on the Food Situation], 23.9.1941.)
210 MBAG Kissel IX/Reichshof, Memorandum regarding Henschel Altenbau and Rzeszow, 27.4.1940.
211 MBAG VO 175/25, Flugmotorenwerk Reichshof to Armaments Commando Krakow Region, 1.5.1941.

engineer – to examine the situation with regard to improving the production process, productivity and profitability. This was followed in August 1941 by the transfer of responsibility for the actual production process to a Daimler-Benz engineer.[212] Despite the fact that Henschel had by the autumn of 1941 essentially completed the reorganization and was in a position to expand production substantially, it drew the logical conclusion from this gradual usurpation by Daimler-Benz and in September 1941 informed the RLM that it was unwilling to continue managing the plant.[213] Daimler-Benz took over completely as of the beginning of November 1941, just after production began to increase.[214]

b) Polish forced labour and the Daimler-Benz Management 1941–4

Under the management of Daimler-Benz both the size of the workforce and the volume of production increased greatly. In February 1942 the workforce consisted of 2549 workers, of whom 1812 were male and 299 were female blue-collar workers.[215] The vast majority of these were Polish, with the 438-strong white-collar workforce consisting overwhelmingly of Germans. Over the following two years the total number of workers increased almost continuously to reach 4251 by the end of April 1944.[216] Of these, 3757 (88 per cent) were Polish civilians.[217] Throughout the period, approximately 90 per cent of the civilian workforce were Polish.

Throughout the period of its responsibility for the plant, Daimler-Benz managers implemented limited measures to improve productivity through training and reorganization. The expansion of the workforce was paralleled, first, by an increase in the training of the Polish workers.[218] This process did not, however, extend to proper and thorough vocational training in the sense of an industrial apprenticeship. Rather, it consisted of short-term, improvised training with the aim of imparting a minimum of competence in a narrowly defined sphere of production, which would allow basic tasks only to be carried out. As far as skilled workers went, the Rzeszow management informed its Genshagen counterpart in September 1942 that 'we honestly have out of a total workforce of 2800 blue-collar workers only 122 skilled workers, i.e. not even five per cent. We can only alleviate the situation by getting the half-wild

212   MBAG VO 175/25, Flugmotorenwerk Reichshof to Armaments Commando Krakow Region, 1.8.1941.
213   MBAG Kissel IX/Reichshof, Kissel to Henschel GmbH., 22.9.1941.
214   MBAG Kissel IX/Reichshof, Haspel to Cejka (RLM), 22.10.1941.
215   MBAG VO 175/25, Flugmotorenwerk Reichshof to Armaments Commando Krakow Region, 1.2.1942.
216   These and the following figures are based, unless stated otherwise, on the comprehensive internal 'Statistical Monthly Reports' for 1942–4 contained in MBAG Haspel 19.
217   This figure does not take into account the Russian prisoners of war who came to Rzeszow in February 1944. They numbered 112 in February, 190 in March and 189 in April, the last month for which detailed statistics are available.
218   MBAG VO 175/24, Flugmotorenwerk Reichshof to Armaments Commando Krakow, 10.3.1943.

Poles accustomed to some sort of work, which they then usually deliver in good quality.'[219] The management constantly reported a shortage of skilled workers and a need for more trainees.[220]

Second, in addition to training workers, the company undertook a partial reorganization in early 1942 as part of the process of reallocating contracts among the various plants in the Daimler-Benz 'Ring' that took place at this time.[221] The attitude to the task of arranging a rational production process was also, however, characterized by a high degree of improvization and adaptation of available machinery, rather than by investment in new, more suitable machinery. This was the case even when it entailed substantially lower output. Thus, for example, the company reported that, of the machine-tools in the plant when Daimler-Benz took over, 'approximately 20 per cent . . . are unsuitable for current tasks, but can in time be adapted for these purposes, although they will then on average reach only 60 per cent of the productivity of a corresponding German machine.'[222]

The lack of willingness to invest in long-term measures to improve the productivity of the workforce was partly conditioned by the fact that the poor physical state of the workers, the possibility of their being deported to Germany or the real possibility of their falling victim to the brutality of the regime made it impossible to assume that they would stay at the plant for any length of time. On the other hand, it can be seen as part of Daimler-Benz's more general unwillingness, in the light of the innate uncertainty of the war situation, to make a long-term commitment to the plant. The reluctance to improve productivity by rationalization and investment was reinforced by the fact that, given the defenceless position of the Polish population, it was easier and less costly to raise production by a continual intensification of the labour process. Instead, over the two and a half years during which the plant was under Daimler-Benz control, the range of measures that Henschel had begun to introduce was continuously expanded and adapted to the context to optimize its effect at any given time. These measures mirrored in many respects the social policy introduced in Germany throughout the war.

First, the Daimler-Benz management continued the process of lengthening working hours begun by Henschel. In January 1943, the basic minimum working week was increased to 54 hours, although in practice the Polish workers were already working much longer hours. The management demanded that this manifest itself in either one-eighth more output or in a personnel reduction of one-eighth without loss of output. Implementation of

219   MBAG VO 175/23, Flugmotorenwerk Reichshof to Daimler-Benz-Motoren GmbH Genshagen, 17.9.1942.
220   See, for example, MBAG VO 175/24, Reichshof/Memorandum 30.3.1943, in which a shortage of 303 skilled workers is mentioned.
221   BA (P) 80 Ba6/7126, DBAG to Bank der Deutschen Luftfahrt, 28.3.1942.
222   MBAG War Plants 27, Memorandum regarding Flugmotorenwerk Reichshof GmbH, 19.11.1943.

the latter would have the advantage of making it possible to 'reduce the number of unsuitable workers without any problem'.[223] By May 1943, the Polish workforce was working a minimum 67¼-hour week.[224] As a plant producing under the Fighter Staff, the working week was finally increased to 72 hours in early 1944, although by this stage shortages of coal and disruptions to the energy supply meant that the number of productive hours fluctuated greatly.[225]

Second, the process of lengthening work hours was compounded by the introduction of measures to increase the amount of productive labour exacted from each worker. In cases where workers were being deployed to operate individual machines, for example, they would be forced henceforth to operate two simultaneously. This was the process that had been perfected by the management of Daimler-Benz during the Depression and represented a major way of saving labour for the management, achieved by greatly increasing the physical exploitation of each worker.[226]

The pressure to raise output was increased by the allocation of a new production programme to Rzeszow in March 1943, in order to fulfil which the plant was required to double its output over the course of 1943.[227] The management planned to achieve this partly through a further reorganization of the production process and a lengthening of working hours. It also immediately reduced the set times in which each unit of production had to be completed, effectively forcing the workers to work harder for the same amount of money – part of an ongoing process throughout the war, a process that became more and more marked as the company's awareness of the military situation led it to realize that its engagement in the east was, in all likelihood, going to be of limited duration.

The management aimed to achieve the necessary output primarily, however, through a further set of wide-ranging measures designed to intensify the labour process even more. An extensive report of March 1943 submitted to the Armaments Commando gives a detailed insight into precisely how the Polish workforce was treated and to what ends.[228] In addition to lengthening the work hours of the Polish workforce and further reducing piece-rates, the management reported that it had undertaken 'intensive instruction of all our shop-floor functionaries, to make each one aware of his responsibility as demanded by the current war situation.' Each week the manager assembled the representatives of the Polish workforce 'with whose help I can influence the workforce and receive valuable pieces of advice.' For the Polish shop-floor workers this 'intensive instruction' of the supervisory personnel meant, in

223 MBAG VO 175/39, Minutes of the Discussion on 29.1.1943.
224 MBAG VO 175/24, Flugmotorenwerk Reichshof to Armaments Commando Krakow, 31.5.1943.
225 MBAG VO 175/24, Flugmotorenwerk Reichshof to Armaments Commando Krakow, 4.5.1944.
226 MBAG VO 175/39, Minutes of the Discussion on 11.5.1943.
227 MBAG VO 175/39, Program Discussion, 9.3.1943.
228 MBAG VO 175/24, Flugmotorenwerk Reichshof to Armaments Commando Krakow, 9.3.1943.

practice, a further intensification of control, punishment and brutality within the workplace.

This was accompanied by the increasingly cynical use of items of everyday consumption as incentives to the workforce to work harder. Given the extreme scarcity of these items and the prohibitive prices charged on the black market, this became an increasingly effective measure for the factory, as the workers were dependent on the plant for their supply. The manager thus stated that 'in the last five weeks I have had the productivity rates of the whole Polish workforce measured and now distribute food allocations which we receive purely according to these productivity rates.' The cigarette and vodka rations of workers whose work-rate was deemed unsatisfactory were reduced in order to increase those of the more productive workers; those workers whose effort was not deemed adequate were given notes explaining why they had not been included in the extra food allocations.

The company also planned to introduce this system of allocation for all supplementary rations – again mirroring policy towards both German and foreign workers in Germany. It argued that this would enable the exclusion of those Polish workers 'who just happen to be present' and allow allocation solely to those who put in what the management deemed to be a full day's work. The workers who had clocked on for 54 hours per week but who, according to the set work-rate, only delivered 20 hours' worth of productive labour, 'have no right to such additional food allocations.' Not only were these workers to be excluded from food supplements, but, in view of the fact that 'they just hang around for the other 34 hours and prevent others from working', they were also to be registered with a 'combing-out' commission and placed at the disposal of the labour authorities for transfer to Germany. These measures were designed also to have an effect on those workers who were not yet producing enough to satisfy the demands of the management, as opposition to being transferred to Germany was extensive among the Poles.

These incentive measures were accompanied by limited provision to improve the material position of the workers. In addition to a general increase – in principle at least – in the rations of Polish armaments workers and their families implemented by the regime, the management attempted to improve the standard of food with the available means, by sending the factory cooks on courses run by the Armaments Commando.[229] The standard of food remained, however, appallingly low. Even those rations to which the Poles were officially entitled were not always delivered. The rations of particularly hard-working Poles were supplemented with extra food parcels, but these could only alleviate hardship in a minority of cases.[230] Similarly, the establishment of a kindergarten for the children of the increasing numbers of Polish women employed at the factory had the aim of improving productivity by reducing

229 MBAG VO 175/24, Armaments Commando Krakow to all Armaments Plants, 18.3.1943.
230 MBAG VO 175/24, Flugmotorenwerk Reichshof to Armaments Commando Krakow, 8.3.1943.

labour fluctuation. By providing for the children of Polish workers, who otherwise were especially malnourished and disadvantaged by the regime's rationing policy, the management hoped to force the Polish women to stay at the factory. Measures aimed at supporting the workers' families were felt to be particularly effective – as the manager reported: 'if it is possible to tie the Polish family to the company in this way, the Pole will be forced to deliver punctual and clean labour, as if we sack him he displaces his whole family. What he loses can hardly be bought on the black market.' The 'support' of the Polish families also manifested itself in other, more macabre ways. Reporting that it supported diligent workers in situations of difficulty, the company stated that these usually occurred when a family member died. In such cases, the company would pay for and procure the coffin, recognizing that 'these are opportunities to create the strongest ties to the plant, as worries about the family are very prevalent among the Poles.' That the catastrophic situation of the Poles was a direct product of the brutal German occupation seems not to have registered.

The company was able to report on the increased output achieved by the allocation of food on a productivity basis five months later. The new distribution system had, it stated, contributed to a further rise in the living standards of the willing members of the Polish workforce. The tailoring of the incentive system to allow improvement of the situation of the worker's family had had a particularly good effect – a mark of how appalling the supply of food to the Polish population was. The management found that 'precisely those with large families received the largest allocations, i.e. were among the hardest working.'[231] Only ten per cent of Poles with families fell into the category of workers who merely received the basic rations, the rest received some form of productivity-related supplement. The management clearly prided itself on the extent to which it had managed to instil in the workers an awareness of the direct causal relationship between specific patterns of behaviour and reward or punishment. The productivity of the workers was assessed on a weekly basis: 'an improvement, or conversely a drop, in the productivity of the worker is responded to immediately each time, so that the different levels of food distribution have become a very significant incentive for the willingness to work here.' The management declared itself satisfied with the current system of food distribution, provided that 'sufficient difference be maintained between the distribution to armaments workers and the rest of the population and that we can continue to distribute according to the principle of productivity.'

How far this system actually led to an improvement in the material situation of the Polish workforce, as the management claimed, must, in view of the continued decline in the health of the workers, be questioned. Any

231   MBAG VO 175/24, Flugmotorenwerk Reichshof to Armaments Commando Krakow, 5.8.1943.

increases in food supply were paid for by a greatly intensified labour process and clearly had to go at least partially to the workers' families.[232] The rate of absenteeism in general under the Daimler-Benz management also remained constantly high. In February 1942 an average 7.9 per cent of workers were absent.[233] In September 1942, ten to 15 per cent of the company's 552 machine operators were consistently absent through a combination of illness, holiday and simple absenteeism.[234] The food situation continued to be desperate, despite nominal increases in rations. As even the small amount of food to which the Polish workers were entitled was not always delivered, they were continually forced to go absent in search of food.[235] In addition, the huge shortage of coal in Poland in the winter of 1942–3 meant that the authorities – despite some pressure from management – refused to deliver more than 30 per cent of the official (in itself very low) quota for the workers.[236] This also contributed to absenteeism over the winter, as the Polish workers were faced with the choice of working and risking freezing to death, or going in search of coal for their families.[237]

The management responded to the continuously high rates of absenteeism not only by the range of social policies described, but also by an expansion of disciplinary and punishment measures, paralleled by the increased resort to terror on the part of the state.[238] First, in response to the shortage of German supervisory personnel, the management moved increasingly towards an internal system whereby the Poles would 'discipline themselves'. This was best achieved, according to the management, 'by punishing not individuals but the whole group or department for particular transgressions, so that a department in future ensures order of its own accord.'[239] In one case, for example, two departments working nightshifts had their rations stopped collectively, because they had allowed a colleague to sleep during the shift. This was combined with an intensification of control within the plant, with rigorous checks instituted on wash rooms, toilets, etc, to prevent the workers from

---

232 In early 1943, out of a workforce of approximately 3000, there were 372 cases of respiratory illnesses, 73 illnesses related to digestive problems, 22 cases of rheumatism and a total of 555 other illnesses. In addition, there were 75 industrial accidents and 59 cases of infection, attributable directly to working in the factory under these conditions. MBAG VO 175/24, Flugmotoren Reichshof to Armaments Commando Krakow 9.4.1943.

233 MBAG VO 175/25, Flugmotorenwerk Reichshof to Armaments Commando Krakow, 1.3.42.

234 MBAG VO 175/24, Report on the Usage of Floor Space and Machinery, 28.9.1942.

235 MBAG VO 175/24, Flugmotorenwerk Reichshof to Armaments Commando Krakow, 22.9.42.

236 MBAG VO 175/24, Flugmotorenwerk Reichshof to Armaments Commando Krakow, 18.9.1942.

237 The company exerted pressure for more coal to be delivered, arguing (and clearly exaggerating somewhat for effect) that otherwise up to 40 per cent of the workforce could be expected to go absent over the winter. The allocating official replied that 'the loss of 40 per cent of the workers would have to be tolerated, and in any case, that would still leave 60 per cent, enough if necessary to maintain production' (MBAG VO 175/24, Flugmotorenwerk Reichshof to Armaments Commando Krakow, 18.9.1942).

238 MBAG VO 175/24, Flugmotorenwerk Reichshof to Armaments Commando Krakow, 8.3.1943.

239 MBAG VO 175/24, Flugmotorenwerk Reichshof to Armaments Commando Krakow, 18.3.1943.

avoiding work.[240] Second, the intensification of internal control was complemented by an expansion of state-sanctioned terror in the General-gouvernement, led by the SS. As early as November 1942 the management attended a meeting of companies with the Armaments Commando in Warsaw, at which the issue of establishing Labour Education Camps directly attached to the larger firms was discussed.[241] During the following period, special factory Labour Education Camps were set up under the SS for the specific purpose of combatting 'idleness' (*Bummelantentum*). Workers were to be transferred to these camps if other disciplinary measures, such as forced overtime, punishment labour, withdrawal of food, etc, failed to achieve the desired effect. The workers continued to work in the factory, but spent all other time in the camp, where, under SS supervision, they could be forced at any time of day or night to perform hard physical labour.[242]

The management at Rzeszow seems to have been initially unwilling, or at least reluctant, to establish a camp attached to the plant. It was clearly aware that conditions in these camps were so brutal that in many cases the workers would not survive. In view of the shortage of labour, the management preferred to discipline workers within the firm and reduce 'idleness' through internal measures, rather than allow the SS to gain too much influence over company policy. Thus, in February 1943, it informed the Armaments Commando that it had not yet built a camp, but was attempting instead to reduce idleness through 'special measures.'[243] The Armaments Commando complained, however, that the high rate of absenteeism at Rzeszow was unacceptable and requested that the management establish a Labour Education Camp in order to reduce it.[244] Whether a camp attached specifically to the plant was ever established is unclear. That the company made regular use of such camps is, however, shown by the cases of workers who were caught falsifying their workcards to show that they had produced more than was the case, or who were discovered arranging for colleagues to stamp their 'clocking-on' cards when they were in fact absent. For these transgressions, at least two workers were sent to a camp. One was sentenced to transfer for making four cigarette lighters, another for making a food container, and two for writing songs rather than working during the night-shift. These four workers, however, had their sentences commuted to a lengthy withdrawal of rations.[245]

Despite the expansion of internal disciplinary measures and the regular

240 MBAG VO 175/39, Memorandum on the Meeting with the Heads of Department and Foremen, 26.6.1943.
241 MBAG VO 175/24, Agenda for the Meeting with the Manufacturers on 7.11.42. at the Armaments Commando Warsaw, 6.11.1942.
242 MBAG VO 175/24, Extract from Circular No. 236 of Armaments Commando Krakow, 16.11.1942.
243 MBAG VO 175/24, Flugmotorenwerk Reichshof to Armaments Commando Krakow, 18.2.1943.
244 MBAG VO 175/24, Armaments Commando Krakow to Flugmotorenwerk Reichshof, 19.2.1943.
245 MBAG VO 175/39, Memorandum of the Discussion on 11 May 1943.

resort to external terror, the company never managed to get on top of the situation. Given the chaotic circumstances at Rzeszow, it is unsurprising that the success in setting up a rational, effective production process was limited. As a spare parts producer, the plant not only had to re-tool each time a new engine model was introduced (while continuing to produce parts for the old model for some time), but also had to adapt to constantly fluctuating demand for different parts, depending on which were causing problems at any given time. This contributed further to the highly improvised character and low productivity of the production process. Only approximately half the machine-tools were arranged in any form of group production, the rest simply being producing individually, a measure of the low degree of rational serial production reached at the plant.[246]

Despite the measures introduced at Rzeszow to attempt to alleviate the situation, productivity remained low. A survey of the 436 machines in the spare parts workshops in September 1942 found that they were working at only 64 per cent of capacity, owing to a lack of skilled workers and technical problems caused by the nature of the parts the plant was required to produce. The assembly line was working at only 44 per cent of capacity, as 'the machine workshops deliver only enough parts to provide the assembly line with work for one shift.' This was similarly the case in the tool-assembly and tempering workshops, which were working at 50 and 52 per cent of capacity respectively.[247] A survey of one workshop in May 1944 suggests that improvements in the meantime had been limited. Of the 20 machines examined, only three were producing 100 per cent or more of their planned production; of the rest, 14 were producing at below 80 per cent of the rate required, with some as low as 16 and 29 per cent. The reasons for these low rates lay primarily in the poor physical state of the workers and in the fact that some machines were being operated by new female workers who were as yet unused to the work.[248]

The management was able, in reviewing production since its takeover of the plant, to point to a strong increase in output from January to June 1942, but this was the result of starting full production after the completion of the reorganization process of the previous two years. Increases in production of over 40 per cent from January to October 1942 were, if anything, a consequence of the increase in the number of productive working hours the management was able to extract from the workers, not of improvements in the production process. From February 1943 to June 1943 the company reduced production times by about 20 per cent.[249] This was followed by a further reduction of 38 per cent from March 1943 to March 1944.[250] These must be

246 MBAG VO 175/29–30, List of Machines transferred from Rzeszow to Untertürkheim (undated).
247 MBAG VO 175/24, Report on the Usage of Floor Space and Machinery, 28.9.1942.
248 MBAG VO 175/28, Extract from the Supervision Report for Department 107, 5/1944.
249 MBAG VO 174/28, Flugmotorenwerk Reichshof to Armaments Commando Krakow, 21.6.1943.
250 MBAG VO 175/42, Romstedt to Generalingenieur Mahnke, 20.3.1944.

seen against the background of a very low starting point, however, and a comparison with Genshagen shows how unproductive the plant remained. In March 1943, it took twice as long to produce the same part in Rzeszow as it did in Genshagen.[251] The work-rate of the Polish workers was estimated at approximately 70 per cent of that of the workforce at Genshagen – which itself contained a very high percentage of east European workers.[252] The substantial increases in output achieved by the management over the two and a half years of its work are clearly explicable not primarily in terms of a 'modernized' production process, but were rather the result of increases in the workforce, lengthening of working hours and, above all, brutal intensification of labour, reflecting a broader policy in the occupied east based on short-term exploitative plunder.

c) The Racial Hierarchy Completed: Daimler-Benz and Jewish Forced Labour 1942–4

A further source of labour brutally exploited by German industry during the occupation of Poland was that of the Polish Jews, who, in September 1939, had been ordered into forced labour by Reinhard Heydrich. Working mainly within the newly established ghettos or in labour camps attached to large-scale projects, many hundreds of thousands of Jews experienced a period of protracted suffering prior to deportation to the extermination camps – if they survived the forced labour itself. The Jews were put to work not only by the SS, but also in cooperation with the regular Wehrmacht, in large-scale armaments production or building projects with industry, or in 'public works' programmes involving civilian agencies. The deployment of Jews in large armaments plants actually reached a peak in 1942, at the very time when Operation Reinhard, the programme of destruction of the Jews of the Generalgouvernement, was at its height. The role of Jewish forced labour in the economic exploitation of Poland thus not only allows an examination of the collusion of broad sectors of the non-SS economic and functional elites in the barbarism of Nazi Jewish policy, but also shows in a particularly acute fashion how the attempts to exploit the Polish economy for war purposes foundered to a large degree on the pursuit of racial reordering and genocide. As the case of Rzeszow shows, the primacy of racial destruction, which was at the core of National Socialism, meant that all attempts by industry to exploit Jewish labour in the long term were doomed to inevitable failure. Nonetheless, once again, industry was not only able to instrumentalize this labour in its own interests, but also contributed, through its active fostering of a racist climate within the factory, to an intensification of the Jews' suffering prior to their deportation to the extermination camps.

At Rzeszow as elsewhere, the problems of maintaining a steady level of

251 MBAG VO 175/39, Program Discussion, 9.3.1943.
252 MBAG War Plants 27, Memorandum concerning Flugmotorenwerk Reichshof GmbH, 19.11.1943.

production were compounded by the continuous process of transferring Polish labour to work in factories in Germany. By the summer of 1942, the imperative to increase production in the face of the changed military context, combined with the expansion of labour transfer back to Germany under Sauckel, had caused an acute shortage of labour at the plant.[253] During June and July 1942, the problem of labour supply at Rzeszow was discussed intensively by the management and the Armaments Commando. From late June onwards, the possibility of supplying Jewish workers was debated with the Armaments Commando. The precise content of these negotiations is unknown, but it is clear that the management of the plant was keen to procure Jewish workers from the outset. Following these discussions, the management wrote to the Labour Office on 30 June informing it that the plant was about to set up a separate production line for small engine parts.[254] In doing so, it was satisfying a key precondition for the deployment of Jewish labour at the plant – namely deployment in a separate workshop – and it seems likely that this was carried out with the aim of increasing the likelihood of procuring the Jewish workers. In the letter, the management wrote of its new plans and its need for increased labour:

> Given the lack of suitable skilled labour please supply us with about 400 Jews, who we ask to be chosen from the available supply of Jewish skilled metal-workers. If the number of Jewish skilled metal-workers capable of work is insufficient, please allocate us suitable male Jewish workers, who, in the absence of skilled workers, we can train.

While attempting to secure this supply, the management continued to oppose the transfer of workers from Rzeszow. On 2 July the director involved refused again to accept the Armaments Commando's plans, stating that this would jeopardize production, and requesting for a second time that the OKW exempt Rzeszow from the process.[255] The management conceded, however, that should this exemption not be granted, it would be willing to give up 120 skilled and semi-skilled workers and 80 unskilled workers. The Labour Office promised that, in this event, it would 'as far as possible supply semi-skilled workers and Jews as replacements.' The question of deploying Jewish labour was then further discussed by the management, the Armaments Commando, and the SS representatives responsible for the execution of Jewish policy locally 'on the basis of the firm's request to the Labour Office to supply Jewish workers' at a meeting on 17 July.[256]

253 See Broszat, *Nationalsozialistische Polenpolitik*, pp. 99–105; Herbert, *Fremdarbeiter*, pp. 180–89.
254 MBAG VO 175/26, Flugmotorenwerk Reichshof to Labour Office Reichshof, 30.6.1942.
255 MBAG VO 175/24, Memorandum (Armaments Commando Krakow) concerning Transfer of Workers from Flugmotorenwerk Reichshof to the Old Reich, 4.7.1942.
256 MBAG VO 175/24, Memorandum, 20.7.1942.

It is clear that, although their initial availability was a product of policy formulated autonomously by the regime, the pressure to supply Jewish workers came from the company. The proposals met, in fact, with a lukewarm response from the SS, whose representative argued that those Jews who had just been deported from Rzeszow were of 'such low value with regard to their deployment as labour' (*arbeitseinsatzmäßig derart minderwertig*) that deployment at the Flugmotorenwerk Rzeszow was not possible. The remaining Jews in the area were also, according to the SS, 'only deployable to a limited extent . . . there is therefore no possibility of supplying Jews from the Rzeszow area.' However, the SS invited the firm to take part in the next combing-out operation in the neighbouring area of Debnica 'to make the necessary selection'. Even here, the SS argued that there were hardly any suitable Jewish workers to be had, and that it was having difficulty securing sufficient Jews for its own purposes, so that there was little chance of obtaining labour for the factory.

Despite these claims, the firm managed within a relatively short period of time to secure the Jewish workers required. When exactly they arrived is unclear. By 6 August, however, 450 Jewish workers had been supplied to Rzeszow.[257] Of these, only 390 had come from combing-out operations at Debnica and Przemysl, so that 60, despite the scepticism and opposition of the SS, must have been recruited from elsewhere – probably from the town of Rzeszow itself.

When the Jewish workers arrived, they had just been filtered off from the main rounding-up process by which the majority of Jews were being transported to the extermination camps.[258] They had been ordered by the SS to bring their own clothing, bedding and crockery for use in the barracks in which they were to live.[259] The majority, however, those from Debnica and Przemysl, had not been permitted to bring anything, so that the firm had to report to the SS that 'we have got into great difficulties on the issue of accommodating these 390 Jews in the barracks. We have neither blankets nor straw sacks, and in addition we have no supply of underclothes, which we desperately need if the Jews are not to become totally filthy.'[260]

By the end of August 1942, the number of Jewish workers had reached 600.[261] However, within a month of their arrival the Rzeszow management was informed during a visit of the combing-out commission that the deployment of Jewish workers was only possible until the winter of 1942–3,

---

257 MBAG VO 175/24, Flugmotorenwerk Reichshof to General Plenipotentiary for Building in the Generalgouvernement, 6.8.1942.

258 Hilberg notes that on 22 July 1942 5000 Jews were deported from Przemysl to Belzec (Hilberg, R., *Die Vernichtung der Europäischen Juden*, Frankfurt/M., 1982, p. 516).

259 MBAG VO 175/24, Armaments Commando Krakow to Flugmotorenwerk Reichshof, 7.8.1942.

260 MBAG VO 175/24, Flugmotorenwerk Reichshof to SS Krakow, 14.8.1942.

261 MBAG VO 175/24, Flugmotorenwerk Reichshof to to the Building Assessor of the RMfBuM, 29.8.1942.

and that all remaining Jews in the area were to be deported 'further east' in early 1943. The commission pointed out that there was 'little point in going to great costs to retrain these Jewish workers, as by the time they can be productively deployed they will have to be given up.'[262] This was confirmed on 5 September, when General Keitel, the head of the OKW, ordered that all Jews in armaments production were to be replaced by Poles. Thereafter, all the military commander of the Generalgouvernement could achieve was a concession that such Jews would only be 'released' by industry when Polish replacements had been trained.[263]

The management thus began to follow a dual policy of trying to retain the Jewish workers for as long as possible – despite clear pressure from the SS to release them – while trying to secure replacements from the Polish *Baudienst* or 'Building Service', a National Socialist forced labour organization which coordinated the exploitation of young Polish male workers. The deployment of slave labour formed no part of the company's long-term plans. Jewish workers were not procured out of a humanitarian desire to protect them (as was often claimed by industry after the war). It was rather the case that they were cynically instrumentalized in pursuit of short-term company interests in a specific context (acute short-term labour shortage, demands to raise production) and then abandoned once these interests had been achieved.[264] The Jews were deployed as a 'stop-gap' measure in the interests of securing a smooth continuity in labour supply, and thus of production, until better replacements had been found. Again, it is precisely the short-term nature of the company's intentions that accounts for much of the treatment of the workers. Further, as was the case in its German plants, the normalization of barbarism facilitated the uncritical establishment of a Nazi racial hierarchy within the plant, with Jews being treated even more badly than Poles. Functional exploitation combined with a culture of brutal and discriminatory racism on a daily basis to ensure that the experience of the Jewish workers was one of unspeakable suffering.

By October 1942 the Rzeszow management had secured the supply of 450 replacement workers from the Polish Building Service. It argued against the immediate deportation of the Jewish workers, demanding that the plant be allowed to retain them until the Polish workers had been trained:

'The training period will, according to the quality of the human material, take eight to 12 weeks. For this reason it is a matter of absolute importance to the war effort that the withdrawal of the Jews currently deployed in productive

262 MBAG VO 175/24, Flugmotorenwerk Reichshof to Armaments Commando Krakow, 23.8.1942.
263 Madjczyk, *Okkupationspolitik*, pp. 222–3.
264 On the attitude of German industry to National Socialist policy towards the Jews see Barkai, A., 'German Entrepreneurs and Jewish Policy in the Third Reich' in: *Yad Vashem Studies* 21 (1991) pp. 125–53.

labour be postponed under all circumstances until the completion of this training, i.e. until the end of March. Not until we are in a position to take the newly trained Building Service workers into the factory can we give up the Jews with a – under the circumstances – minimal disruption of production.'[265]

In other words, as soon as the company had trained their replacements, it was ready to release the Jews for deportation – in the full knowledge of what this meant for the Jews concerned. For Daimler-Benz, only the securing of a steady production was important. It even attempted to coordinate the arrival of the Polish replacements and the deportation of the Jewish workers in the interests of simplifying the question of accommodation. The barracks in which the Jewish workers slept were to be used to house the Polish workers after the Jews had been deported. The Armaments Commando wrote to the management to ask what barracks the firm already had and to know their 'current capacity for Jews, future capacity for Poles.'[266] A marginal note by the manager responsible – '500 Jews = 300 Poles!' – shows not only how the experience of the Jews was conditioned by the dictates of the National Socialist regime's racial policy but also how the management acted on and reinforced the same racist logic of the SS. The company informed the Armaments Commando accordingly that 'the barracks, which previously contained 500 Jews, can, after rebuilding and repair, accept about 300 Building Service workers. If the same number of Building Service workers are to be deployed as the current number of Jews, four more barracks for 50 men each will be needed.'[267] Whereas for the Polish workers the company insisted on 'at least to some extent tolerable housing' out of a need 'to persuade these people from the start to stay here as our permanent workforce', for the Jewish workers these considerations were irrelevant.[268]

From the beginning, the living conditions of the Jewish workers were barbaric. They were 'housed' in five barracks, in which there were 'long double-sided plank-beds, stacked on top of one another, so that in a 30-man barrack 100 Jews can be accommodated.'[269] Two naked flames were used as lighting, and in each barrack two 'ovens' made of building tiles were used for heating. For a planned 500 workers, the firm installed two transportable toilets, erected over holes in the ground. The whole barrack area was surrounded by a barbed-wire fence. The Jews were to be fed separately from the Polish workforce, and their march to and from the factory took place under police and factory security guard. The Armaments Commando also

265 MBAG VO 175/24, Flugmotorenwerk Reichshof to Armaments Commando Krakow, 25.10.1942.
266 MBAG VO 175/24, Armaments Commando Krakow to Flugmotorenwerk Reichshof, 16.11.1942.
267 MBAG VO 175/24, Flugmotorenwerk Reichshof to Armaments Commando Krakow, 18.11.1942.
268 MBAG VO 175/24, Flugmotorenwerk Reichshof to Director of the Oberfeldkommandatur, 19.10.1942.
269 MBAG VO 175/24, Memorandum/Buildings Description, 6.8.1942.

stipulated that 'the Jews receive 80 per cent of the wages paid to the Polish workers . . . the wages are to be paid to the police.'[270] In addition to the appalling conditions in which the Jews lived, they were perpetually subjected to a brutal and arbitrary regime of terror within the factory.[271] The slightest transgression could be used as the pretext for the most inhuman mistreatment, which in many cases culminated in summary shootings or in such brutality that the victim died as a direct result. Individual acts of mistreatment took place against a background of everyday racism within the factory. In line with SS policy, all contact with the Jewish workers was strictly forbidden to the German workers.[272] That the management actively participated in establishing racist practice within the plant is shown, for example, by the case of a German foreman who was sacked by the manager (without any pressure from outside) 'because he had lowered himself to greeting the Jews with a handshake and had swapped postage stamps with them.'[273] The climate of racism was further reinforced by exclusion of Jewish workers from receiving extra allocations of food or drink.[274]

The Jewish workers were to be deployed in a separate department to other workers. The available documentary material does not, however, allow a full insight into precisely how the Jewish workers were used or what role they played within the production process. It is also unclear how far the management was successful in its attempts to recruit primarily skilled workers. Most seem to have been given at least a minimal period of training. Given the appalling conditions, it is not, however, surprising that the labour of the Jewish workers was of poor quality. The management complained that the work of the Jews had 'considerable shortcomings, which, however, have to be put up with in view of the unhealthy circumstances in the General-gouvernement.'[275] The deployment of the Jews led, for example, to far higher wastage of material and of high-quality steel for tools, of which there was a great shortage.

Parallel to the process of attempting to raise the productivity of the Polish workforce, the management tried – purely by terror – to force a higher work-rate out of the Jews. In March 1943 the manager informed the Armaments Commando that he had started measuring the productivity of the Jews. Those whose work was considered satisfactory were allowed extra clothing 'and preferential treatment in other ways compared to the others'. At the same

270 MBAG VO 175/124, Memorandum Regarding Deployment of Jews, Rzeszow, 17.7.1942.
271 Examples of brutality are given in Bellon, *Mercedes in Peace and War*, p. 246. See also the cases examined by the Federal Justice Department, Ludwigsburg, ZSL II 206 AR-Z 2 14/77 and II 206 AR-Z 183/75. These give a clear impression of the nature of the regime and what it meant for the Jewish workers.
272 MBAG VO 175/39, Decree of the RFSS regarding Deployment of Jews as Labour 29.10.1943.
273 MBAG VO 175/39, Memorandum regarding the Discussion on 12.11.1943 with the German Foremen and Heads of Department.
274 MBAG VO 175/28, Memorandum, 11.2.1944.
275 MBAG VO 175/24, Flugmotorenwerk Reichshof to Armaments Commando Krakow, 25.10.1942.

time, they were informed that 'in future, those who are lazy or who work badly will be placed at the disposal of the authorities.'[276] The Armaments Commando noted that the work-rate of the Jews in its area had gradually improved, but it seems unlikely that this was the result of any improvement in conditions – a probable initial improvement is to be seen as the natural consequence of gradual familiarization with the labour process.[277] The rapid deterioration in the physical condition of the Jews ensured that productivity remained low, however.

Exactly how many of the Jewish workers died and under what circumstances is hard to ascertain. By January 1943, the number of Jews had fallen from 600 to 498 (16 per cent of the 'foreign' workforce).[278] By the next month, however, a further allocation of 107 Jews brought the number back to 605.[279] By the end of February, the figure had fallen dramatically to 248.[280] It seems likely that the health of the majority of these workers had declined so much that they were unable to work any more, and that they had been deported en masse. By 1 June, however, the figure had risen again to 334, of whom the vast majority were directly integrated into the production process.[281] At least three separate allocations – the initial one, one in February 1943, and a further one in the first half of 1943 – are discernible.

From mid-1943 the firm seems to have come under increasing pressure finally to release the Jews for deportation. In May 1943 – in a statement indicative of the management's changed attitude – the various foremen were informed that 'the exchange must be attempted as soon as possible.' A survey was to be made to discover which Jews were immediately disposable; these were then to be listed by the personnel department and the list was to be passed to the SS. The management stated further that 'a transfer of those Jews remaining in the factory must take place as soon as possible.'[282] The management nonetheless continued to attempt to coordinate the deportation process with the supply of replacements, insisting that the majority of the remaining 334 Jews in June 1943 could only be released 'at the same rate as trained workers can be supplied as replacements.'[283] In September 1943, however, the Armaments Commando finally informed the management that the 'Higher SS and Police Chief for the East has refused the exchange of the Jewish workers', indicating that the majority of Jews were finally transported away without replacement.[284] The figures for the total workforce of Rzeszow, which

276   MBAG VO 175/24, Flugmotorenwerk Reichshof to Armaments Commando Krakow, 8.3.1943.
277   BA-MA Freiburg RW 23–10, KTB War Diary of Armaments Commando Krakow, 3.Q.1942.
278   MBAG VO 175/42, Situation Report, January 1943.
279   MBAG VO 175/42, Situation Report, February 1943.
280   MBAG VO 175/31, Flugmotenwerk Reichshof to Haspel, 27.2.1943.
281   MBAG VO 175/24, Flugmotorenwerk Reichshof to Armaments Commando Krakow, 9.6.1943.
282   MBAG VO 175/39, Memorandum of the Discussion of 11 May 1943 Armaments Commando Krakow.
283   MBAG VO 175/24, Flugmotorenwerk Reichshof to Armaments Commando Krakow, 9.6.1943.
284   MBAG VO 175/24, Armaments Commando Krakow to Flugmotorenwerk Reichshof, 29.9.1943.

otherwise show a steady increase under the Daimler-Benz management, register a drop of over 400 during the summer of 1943, which is probably at least partly explained by the deportation of the remaining Jewish workers.[285] For those who remained, further suffering awaited in the form of forced labour at underground dispersal sites. At least some, however, survived the war.

The war witnessed a substantial deterioration in the working conditions of the German workforce. Working hours were lengthened, the labour process was intensified, and the management was able to use the dissolution of the core German male workforce, which occurred as a result of the influx of first women and then foreign workers to push through new techniques that further subjected the workers to managerial control. These new methods, backed up as they were by massive state terror, were used with great effect to integrate the new groups of workers into the factory and to exact punishing work-rates from the forced foreign workers in particular. The high degree of integration of the forced workers at Daimler-Benz, a product of the serial production methods in operation in the capital-intensive automotive engineering industry at this time, further facilitated the huge intensification of labour in the final third of the war, as the company opted to square the circle of raising armaments output without large-scale capital input by brutal exploitation of its defenceless workforce.

The resort to exploitation was not only a product of rational company choice. Unquestioning participation in the establishment of the National Socialist racial hierarchy reflected the extent to which the process of creeping barbarization in the 'Third Reich' had undermined any moral scruples within the economic and functional elites concerning the vicious racism of the regime. Undoubtedly, the fact that this moral erosion was gradual facilitated the transition to the situation as it stood in 1944 – the terrorization of German workers from 1933 onwards paved the way for the harsh treatment of west European workers; the brutal treatment of Soviet workers, and the normalization of this culture of barbarism, eased the way to the deployment of concentration camp inmates under even worse conditions. At no point, therefore, was the conventional industrialist confronted with a clear option of shifting from essentially acceptable to unspeakably inhumane behaviour.

This is not to say that it 'just happened'. Insofar as industrialists and managers did drift into barbarism, they did so in any case because they broadly accepted National Socialist ideology and had allowed it to permeate the culture of the company. Daimler-Benz's managers collaborated in the exploitation of forced foreign workers primarily because it was in the company's interests to do so. It is a mark of the extent of the erosion of moral norms in the Third Reich that the appalling suffering of the victims was not,

285   MBAG Haspel 19, Statistical Monthly Reports 1942–1944.

apparently, discussed once; it is a mark of the narrowness of the technocratic manager's field of vision that the only thing that seemed to matter was the interest of the company. Self-identification with the company took precedence over any self-identification with the real suffering of humans. The company was able to survive in a relatively healthy position down to the end of the war at least partly at the expense of the health, and indeed in many cases the lives, of these thousands of victims of forced labour.

VII. Business, Racial Barbarism and Self-Preservation: The Dispersal of Production 1943–5

1. Overview

The centralizing tendencies in the German war economy, resulting from Speer's rationalization drive in the second half of the war, were paralleled by an equally strong decentralizing tendency created by the need to safeguard the capacity of German industry from the impact of Allied bombing from 1943 onwards. As this intensified, the advantages of concentrating large-scale production in single plants had to be weighed more and more against the threat posed to output of a possibly crucial item if individual plants were heavily damaged by attacks. This placed strong limits on the desirability of over-concentration of production. Indeed, the need to have more than one production line of any item to minimize the impact of the temporary – or permanent – loss of output of any individual plant led to measures being introduced to set up parallel lines away from the major industrial centres. Increasingly, individual production lines were also moved out of major industrial plants to less threatened sites in rural or small town locations. In December 1942, Speer ordered the immediate dispersal of key 'unique' production lines away from those areas threatened by air raids together with the preparation for the dispersal of other important production lines in the event of bomb damage.[1] The RMfBuM – represented by the Armaments Inspectorate in each area – was to allocate dispersal capacity to major companies, which were to transfer production lines earmarked for relocation by the branches of the Wehrmacht and other purchasing agencies in conjunction with the industrialists themselves.[2]

Initially, like most other companies, Daimler-Benz was slow to respond to the idea of dispersing production to external locations. In January 1943, part of its aero-engine development was transferred to Backnang, in line with a

---

1 MBAG VO 175/14, Decree of the RMfRuK concerning Prevention of Disruption to Production through Air Raids, 21.12.1942.
2 MBAG VO 175/14, Implementation Decree concerning Prevention of Disruption to Production through Air Raids, 21.12.1942.

decision taken prior to Speer's dispersal decrees, but this is probably to be seen more in terms of an expansion into an overflow site than as a move to safe-guard facilities against bombing.[3] The attitude of the company underwent a clear change, however, after one of its factories had actually been bombed. In April 1943, the Mannheim plant was hit in an air raid, bringing home to the board in very concrete terms the potential threat represented by Allied bomb-ing.[4] Although this and other early air raids caused little disruption to pro-duction, they brought about a visible change in the company's attitude to the war, and above all, to the idea of decentralizing production. The enthusiastic participation of the company in the dispersal programme from this point onwards suggests, when taken together with the development of Daimler-Benz's investment strategy in the second half of the war, that the bombing of Germany had a more marked impact on the economy from an early stage than might be deduced from output figures. After all, the dispersal programme itself caused considerable disruptions which militated against further increases in output that might otherwise have been achieved. At any rate, the speed with which the company altered its attitude to dispersal shows that even if the early air-raids did not disrupt production unduly, they were instrumental in causing a reorientation of business attitudes towards the war.

During the first half of 1943, the Daimler-Benz board took initial measures to decentralize its production and administration and to secure the safety of its documentation, plans and other property. As part of the process of concen-trating the production of marine engines in Untertürkheim, for example, vari-ous departments were simultaneously transferred to locations outside Stuttgart, such as Wendlingen (repairs, cylinder production), Vaihingen/Enz (camshaft production), Heilbronn (valve production) and Bad Cannstatt.[5] During 1943, material and parts storage were also decentralized, both by dividing the storage of parts and materials among several stores within the plant, and by removing as much as possible to outlying workshops, guest houses, etc, in order to mini-mize the potential losses in an air raid.[6] The process underwent an initial inten-sification after the first significant damage was caused to a Daimler-Benz plant, in a raid on Marienfelde in August 1943. In the following period, a large num-ber of departments from the company's plants (initially, above all those engaged in aero-engine production) were dismantled and relocated in small factories or parts of factories in surrounding small town and rural areas, which thereafter delivered components for assembly at the main plants.[7]

3 Pohl et al., *Die Daimler-Benz AG*, p. 88.
4 Roth, 'Der Weg zum Guten Stern', p. 310.
5 MBAG Minutes of the Board Meetings of DBAG 1943–5, Minutes of the Board Meeting of DBAG on 12 and 13.4.1943.
6 MBAG Minutes of the Board Meetings of DBAG 1943–5, Minutes of the Board Meeting of DBAG on 14 and 15.9.43.
7 The relocation of departments from large industrial plants to smaller plants – some of which had already been shut down for the duration of the war, some of which were forced to close down specifically to make room for the dispersal of large plants – caused considerable friction in many

As the bombing began to intensify, however, the limits of the policy of dispersing production to small factories outside the main industrial centres started to show. Increasingly, all locations were endangered by air raids, and there was in addition a limit to how much capacity was available in small plants. Some large-scale industrial production could not be transferred to smaller plants without losing precisely the benefits that large-scale production was meant to bring. Finally, the disruption to the transport network caused by bombing and the lack of transport capacity meant that the fragmentation of production caused insoluble problems when it came to transporting the various components for assembly and delivery.

From late 1943 onwards, the RMfRuK, which gradually centralized juris-diction over the dispersal process under its control, attempted to relocate German industrial capacity and protect it from further bombing by trans-ferring major production lines to underground locations.[8] Above all, the production of air-force armaments was gradually moved to a range of underground sites, some of which were pre-existing tunnels or quarries, others of which were dug out of the ground during 1944.[9] This was coordinated from March 1944 onwards by the Fighter Staff, which was set up to oversee the process.[10] In conjunction with the SS, which provided hundreds of thousands of concentration camp inmates as labour for these projects, the Fighter Staff coordinated the allocation of a multitude of sites to the companies involved, which for their part competed fiercely with one another for the best sites and for labour and building materials. While the SS was, in formal legalistic terms, responsible for the deployment of the concentration camp inmates, not only was it always in practice the result of cooperative on-site discussions with Daimler-Benz, but the company actively pressed for the deployment of as

cases between the large companies, who wished under all circumstances to protect their machinery, and the small recipient companies who feared for the loss of their property. This friction was duplicated within the regime as those organs that tended to represent the interests of small-scale industry – including the Gauleiters – in many instances opposed the transfer of large industrial units to their areas, fearful that this could undermine civilian morale or focus bombing attacks on their areas. Daimler-Benz clearly attempted where possible to reach a mutually acceptable agreement with the owners of the recipient firms – some of whom were perfectly willing to comply. Where this was not possible, however, it was more than willing to achieve its aims by putting pressure on the Armaments Inspectorate or Armaments Commando to confiscate the relevant site and allocate it to Daimler-Benz against the wishes of its owners. This came to be the case more and more as the bombing intensified and Daimler-Benz's desire to safeguard its machinery became correspondingly greater. An example of this is contained in MBAG Haspel 10,93, Correspondence between DBAG Untertürkheim and Heinrich Otto u. Söhne, April/May 1943.

8   For to overview of the dispersal programme and the relationship between industry and the organizational apparatus involved see Perz, *Projekt Quarz*, pp. 129–53.

9   The USSBS estimated that by September 1944 50 per cent of all machine-tools in the aero-engine industry had been dispersed. (USSBS, *Finished Report No. 3. The Effects of Strategic Bombing on the German War Economy. Overall Economic Effects Division*, Washington D.C., 1947, p. 50.

10 MBAG Haspel 8,82, Decree of the Reich Marshall of the Greater German Reich and Deputy for the Four Year Plan, 4.3.1944.

many internees as possible. The rescuing of the company's capital goods was predicated on the mass deployment of forced labour, and Daimler-Benz participated in the full knowledge that the brutal exploitation of this labour was an integral and essential feature.[11]

As part of this process, major elements of Daimler-Benz's aero-engine production were also transplanted to a wide range of underground locations.[12] The core of Daimler-Benz's aero-engine production at Genshagen was transferred to three major sites – to 'Hochwalde', near Frankfurt/Oder, to 'Rote Erde', and to 'Goldfisch', in the Neckar Valley.[13] From mid-1944, other elements of Daimler-Benz's production were also earmarked for underground dispersal sites, some of which were completed, others never came to fruition for lack of labour, building materials and suitable sites.

While for the regime the dispersal programme was instituted with the aim of safeguarding – and where possible increasing – production, for industry it provided the possibility of protecting its machinery and plant with a view to surviving the war and securing a basis upon which to enter the post-war period. Haspel outlined his basic agenda for the company in the board meeting of 15–16 April 1944: 'Come what may, one thing is clear: whoever manages to manoeuvre his productive capacity beyond the end of the war will be in the strongest position.'[14] Although the relationship between the RMfRuK and the Fighter Staff on the one hand and industry on the other was not totally free from conflict on individual points, there was a basic community of interest – despite the fact that different agendas were being followed – between the regime's wish to safeguard armaments production and industry's desire to prepare for the post-war period by dispersing production facilities. In individual cases, tension could emerge, when, for example, companies were reluctant to install valuable machinery in damp locations where they could be harmed by rust or corrosion. In general, however, and without overestimating the range of choices or freedom of manoeuvre available to industrial companies in the final phase of the war, it can be said that Daimler-Benz was positively disposed towards the underground dispersal process and was able, within this process, to pursue an independent agenda focused on the post-war period.

---

11 For an example of the constant pressure applied by Daimler-Benz managers for SS labour see MBAG Haspel 8,82, Memorandum of Building Discussion with Engineer Ewald (Armaments Staff) 24.11.1944. An analysis of the appalling experience of the concentration camp inmates on one of Daimler-Benz's sites is provided by Schmid, M., 'Goldfisch, Gesellschaft mit beschränkter Haftung. Eine Lokalhistorie zum Umgang mit Menschen' in: HSG (ed.), *Das Daimler-Benz Buch*, pp. 482–513. For an analysis of a comparable project see Perz, *Projekt Quarz*, pp. 245–491.

12 See the (incomplete) table in Pohl et al., *Die Daimler-Benz AG*, pp. 91–2.

13 On the history of 'Goldfisch' see Fröbe, R., 'Wie bei den alten Ägyptern. Die Verlegung des Daimler-Benz-Flugmotorenwerks Genshagen nach Obrigheim am Neckar 1944/45' in: HSG (ed.), *Das Daimler-Benz Buch*, pp. 392–470.

14 MBAG Minutes of the Board Meetings of DBAG 1943–5, Minutes of the Board Meeting of DBAG on 15 and 16.1944.

The dispersal that took place in 1943 was carried out in a more or less planned and orderly manner, enabling a smooth transfer of production lines without disruption of output. In 1944, and especially from the summer onwards, the decentralization process increasingly took on the character of rushed improvization and crisis management. Especially after the destructive bombing of Daimler-Benz in September and October 1944, a wave of rushed relocations of machinery took place with a view to safeguarding it on an interim basis, before production was eventually reconstituted on a centralized basis at the envisaged underground sites.

Much of the documentary evidence allows no more than a limited reconstruction of the various stages of the dispersal process. Of the many locations involved, some are only mentioned once or twice, and many more are mentioned that obviously never came to fruition or that were begun but not completed. The available material allows, however, a relatively clear reconstruction of the dispersal of the Sindelfingen plant. In the following this forms the basis for a case study of an individual plant. After that, there is an examination of the dispersal of the Mannheim plant, which, as the key plant in Daimler-Benz's plans for the post-war period, allows an analysis of the company's agenda with regard to manoeuvring itself into the immediate post-war situation. Although in some respects the phases in the company's participation in the dispersal process would be easier to trace were one to follow the development of the various projects simultaneously, the underground dispersal sites discussed in the following are treated as independent units. This better reflects the roles the sites themselves came to occupy and the manner in which they came to operate as the Reich collapsed and the war drew to an end – fully functioning, self-contained worlds increasingly isolated from the main plants and from the other sites, a fact which is also undoubtedly important in explaining why they kept working and functioning as long as they did.

2. The dispersal of Sindelfingen

a) Surface Dispersal

The Sindelfingen management began to decentralize the storage of materials, tools and components within the plant, and to relocate some of it in the surrounding locality, in the summer of 1943.[15] In addition, it began to put pressure on the Armaments Commando to allow the transfer of its valuable bookkeeping machines out of Sindelfingen, arguing that it had a fully self-contained bookkeeping department with unique machines that were very liable to damage if bombed.[16] The pressure on the management to transfer

---

15 MBAG Huppenbauer 461, DBAG Sindelfingen to Factory Air Raid Protection Office Central Württemberg, 4.8.1943.
16 MBAG Huppenbauer 468, DBAG Sindelfingen to Armaments Commando Stuttgart I, 20.7.1943.

these machines from Sindelfingen was increased by the bombing of the Marienfelde plant in August 1943, during which the bookkeeping department there was destroyed. Haspel had thereupon intervened and demanded to know of the Sindelfingen management what steps it had taken to secure its own bookkeeping department.[17] The management, as a result, immediately renewed its pressure on the Armaments Commando, bombarding the officials with telephone calls and repeating its demands for the transfer to be facilitated.[18] As a result, it was offered the use of a carpentry firm in Holzgerlingen, to which the transfer finally took place.[19]

Parallel to this, the Sindelfingen management began making detailed and concrete plans for the relocation of substantial parts of its productive capacity in the summer of 1943. The plant listed its major production lines, the amount of floor space needed by each and the number of workers and machines involved in a letter to the Armaments Commando in July 1943, which became the basis for the subsequent planning of the dispersal process.[20] Lengthy negotiations then took place between the company, the Armaments Commando and other local authorities, and the owners of potential plants or sites. In August 1943, however, despite pressure from the Sindelfingen management to transfer more production out, it was decided initially to set up second production lines only for some of Daimler-Benz's aero-engine parts.[21] These production lines, excluding the presses, used a total of 26 machines (out of a total inventory of 850–900 machines) and needed a total floor space of 2800 square metres, thus representing only a very small part of Sindelfingen's total capacity.[22]

Following extensive examination of potential sites outside the Stuttgart conurbation, and, after negotiation with the Armaments Commando, the Gau Economic Chamber and the owners of the sites concerned, the Sindelfingen management was able to report that it had found a suitable site and that the Armaments Commando would agree to a decentralization to this factory.[23] Over the following four months, the necessary building work was carried out and the transfer to the plant – in Iselshausen, in the Black Forest – was planned. By January 1944, work in Iselshausen had been completed to the point where, should a disruption to production in the main plant occur, no loss to overall production would be caused.[24] By May 1944, the Iselshausen

17 MBAG Huppenbauer 468, Memorandum to Ing. Held/DBAG Sindelfingen, 24.8.1943.
18 MBAG Huppenbauer 468, DBAG Sindelfingen to Armaments Commando V (Stuttgart), 25.8.1943.
19 MBAG Huppenbauer 468, DBAG Sindelfingen to Armaments Commando Va (Stuttgart), 10.9.1943.
20 MBAG Huppenbauer 461, DBAG Sindelfingen to Armaments Commando Stuttgart, 15.7.1943.
21 MBAG Huppenbauer 461, Minutes of Negotiations regarding the Dispersal of Important Production Lines, 24.8.1943.
22 MBAG Huppenbauer 461, DBAG Sindelfingen to Armaments Commando Stuttgart, 15.7.1943.
23 MBAG Huppenbauer 461, Minutes of the Negotiations regarding the Dispersal of Important Production Lines 24.8.1943.
24 MBAG Huppenbauer 330, Minutes of the Departmental Meeting of 26.1.1944. In all 206 workers, including 60 IMIs, and an eventual total of 46 machines were transferred to Iselshausen,

site was producing as a fully self-contained unit.[25]

b) Underground Dispersal: Project 'Brasse'

In late February 1944 – prior to the formation of the Fighter Staff – the Sindelfingen management was ordered by the RMfRuK to prepare for the transfer of some of its production to a disused mine (the 'Friede' mine) near Obrigheim.[26] Initially it was planned to transfer production of DB 603 engine parts to this location, but this project fell through when the site was instead allocated to the Genshagen plant.[27] In the meantime, however, Jahr, the head of Daimler-Benz's dispersal unit (set up in January 1944 to coordinate the company's dispersal plans and liaise with the authorities), had ascertained that adjacent to the Friede mine were two others, 'Hochhausen' and 'Ernst'.[28] In March 1944, Jahr requested Kirmaier, Daimler-Benz's representative at the Fighter Staff, to engineer their confiscation for the company, underlining how it attempted to exert pressure via its deputies within the regime to secure private company interests.[29]

The 'Ernst' site, which assumed the codename 'Brasse', was informally promised to Sindelfingen by mid-May after an intervention by the Special Committee T2 and officially assigned by the end of the month.[30] In all, 12,000 square metres were allocated, and building work proper was set to begin on 1 July 1944. K. C. Müller reported that the site would take eight weeks to prepare.[31] Even assuming punctual completion of the building work – on a schedule that was proven by events to be wildly optimistic – the time wasted by first planning for a transfer to the Friede mine and by then securing Brasse meant that Sindelfingen in May had no underground sites that would be ready to receive production lines in the near future.[32] Brasse needed substantial work, as the caves were full of rocks and silt that had collected

which was the only major dispersal project completed prior to May 1944 by the Sindelfingen plant and which remained the only surface dispersal of a productive department to be carried out during the war (See MBAG Huppenbauer 461, Overview of Dispersal Planning for Daimler-Benz AG Werk Sindelfingen, 30.5.1944.

25   MBAG Huppenbauer 461, Overview of Dispersal Planning for Daimler-Benz AG Sindelfingen, 30.5.1944.
26   MBAG Huppenbauer 474, RMfRuK to DBAG Sindelfingen, 29.2.1944. The site eventually gained the codename 'Goldfisch'.
27   MBAG Huppenbauer 474, Special Committee T2 to DBAG Sindelfingen, 22.5.1944.
28   MBAG Huppenbauer 461, Administration Decree No. 1306 regarding Dispersal Measures, 13.1.1944.
29   MBAG Haspel 9,90, Jahr/DBAG Sindelfingen to Kirmaier/Fighter Staff, 24.3.1944.
30   MBAG Huppenbauer 474, Special Committee T2 to DBAG Sindelfingen, 22.5.1944; MBAG Haspel 9,90, Hörmann/Fighter Staff to DBAG Sindelfingen, 30.5.1944.
31   MBAG Huppenbauer 474, Memorandum, 23.5.1944.
32   Haspel's frustration with the lack of progress made in the initial phases of the underground dispersal programme was expressed in the board meeting of 15 and 16.4.1944, in which he complained that 'in the dispersal programme we have been treated miserably.' (MBAG Minutes of the Board Meetings of DBAG 1943–5, Minutes of the Board Meetings of DBAG on 15 and 16.1944.).

during 40 years of disuse. Some of the caves were structurally weak, and some parts had collapsed completely.[33]

The delays in procuring a site for Sindelfingen and the need to wait even longer for building to start meant that the management was forced to look for alternative solutions to the problem of safeguarding its production lines prior to the completion of Brasse. During May 1944, at a time when Allied air raids were already intensifying and when it was clear that the war was moving towards its closing stages, the decision was taken temporarily to move some of Sindelfingen's production to another underground location that had hitherto been earmarked for Daimler-Benz's Colmar plant. The transfer to a part of this site – a tunnel near Colmar codenamed 'Kranich', which had been prepared by the SS using the labour of concentration camp inmates – was intended as an interim dispersal enabling the company to move out some of its most important production immediately rather than have to leave it exposed to further air-raids. The plan was gradually to transfer a large proportion of Sindelfingen's aero-engine parts production, which would then operate at Kranich until the completion of Brasse, now set for the final quarter of 1944.[34]

The company attempted to plan the move, which was to begin in mid-June, in such a way as to facilitate a smooth transition without disruption to output, transferring one line at a time over a space of weeks. By late May, the main plant at Sindelfingen was ready to begin transferring machinery to Kranich and planned to start sending equipment immediately. However, delays were being caused by the continued failure to complete the supply of electricity, water, gas and accommodation for the workers, and, as a result, the date for commencement of production had to be put back by two weeks to 1 July 1944.[35] Finally, during July production lines were successively transferred.[36] Despite the delays in installation, the Sindelfingen management had thus by the end of the month managed to relocate a significant proportion of its capacity to Kranich and was able to report by August that, under the circumstances, production was going well.[37] On 18 July 1944, 468 workers (178 Germans, 175 Italian military internees and 115 Russian men and women) were deployed at Kranich, out of a total productive workforce of 5224.[38]

---

33 MBAG Huppenbauer 474, Memorandum concerning Visit to 'Brasse', 27.6.1944.
34 MBAG Huppenbauer 461, Overview of Dispersal Planning for Daimler-Benz AG Sindelfingen, 30.5.1944.
35 MBAG Huppenbauer 461, Overview of Dispersal Planning for Daimler-Benz AG Sindelfingen, 7.6.1944.
36 MBAG Huppenbauer 480, DBAG Sindelfingen to Haspel, 27.6.1944; DBAG Sindelfingen to Haspel, 18.7.1944; S 3 to Ing. Held/Sindelfingen, 25.7.1944.
37 MBAG Huppenbauer 476, DBAG Sindelfingen to Kirmaier/Fighter Staff, 8.8.1944.
38 MBAG Huppenbauer 480, DBAG Sindelfingen to Haspel, 18.7.1944. Once all the projected transfer of production had taken place, it was planned to have a total of 900 workers at Kranich (MBAG Haspel 9,90, Memorandum regarding State of Project A 10, 1.6.44). However, in response to the changing front situation the Sindelfingen management changed its mind about locating further production lines in Alsace-Lorraine.

The example of Kranich shows how it was feasible, up to the summer of 1944, to re-establish production lines at underground locations where sites already existed and while transportation links were still good enough to allow them to procure the materials and components necessary to function. This stood in marked contrast to the attempts to build production sites from scratch, which, as the Brasse site shows, were often excessively optimistic.

While the transfer to Kranich was taking place, work continued throughout the summer on the Brasse site and on the plans to install various production lines there. Progress remained slow – in June 1944 the Sindelfingen management was still complaining that 'Brasse 123 is in a very poor state' and via Kirmaier was putting pressure on the Fighter Staff to secure extra labour for the site.[39] At this point, the company was still in the process of carrying out the dredging work.[40] The launching of the second front and military developments in the east created further pressure on the company to intensify the work on Brasse and install machinery as soon as possible. With the landing of the Allied troops, the territorial integrity of the western part of Germany seemed under much more immediate threat, and the Kranich site in particular appeared greatly exposed. Not until Brasse was complete could production lines now at Kranich be brought back to Germany to a location much closer to Daimler-Benz's south German plants and out of immediate danger.

Faced with the need to accelerate the building process, the company intensified its contacts with the SS, with whom it was clearly attempting to establish and maintain a close working relationship and on whose cooperation it was reliant for the adequate supply of concentration camp inmates. During July and August 1944 there were discussions with the SS to concretize the details of the planned project, such as drainage, ventilation, supply of water, heat and energy, and questions of barrack and kitchen provision.[41] Nonetheless, on 6 August, three weeks before the site had originally intended to be ready, the company was only halfway to completing the drainage process. Despite the fact that it had managed to procure extra concentration camp workers from the SS, a month later building work was still progressing slowly.[42] It was commented that 'even with the greatest exertion, which would have to be applied immediately, it will barely be possible to begin setting up our machinery before the beginning of December this year.'[43] Yet another delay had been built into the timetable, with installation of machinery now planned for 15 December.[44] The building work was consistently hampered by

39 MBAG Huppenbauer 474, Kirmaier/Fighter Staff to Held/DBAG Sindelfingen, 10.6.1944.
40 MBAG Huppenbauer 474, DBAG Sindelfingen to Kirmaier/Fighter Staff, 15.6.1944.
41 MBAG Huppenbauer 474, DBAG Sindelfingen to SS-Special Inspectorate III, 15.7.1944; Minutes of Discussion with the Manufacturers on 14.8.1944; Minutes of the Meeting following On-Site Visit of 31.8.1944.
42 MBAG Huppenbauer 474, Memorandum concerning Visit to 'Brasse', 6.8.1944; Minutes of the Meeting Following On-Site Visit on 31.8.1944; to 'Brasse'.
43 MBAG Huppenbauer 474, DBAG Sindelfingen to Haspel, 28.9.1944.
44 MBAG Haspel 9,90, K. C. Müller to Haspel, 27.10.1944.

repeated decisions from the authorities to stop work on the site, which the company constantly had to struggle to reverse, and by continued lack of sufficient workers to be able to press ahead at a faster pace. Three hundred concentration camp inmates were transferred from Kranich to Brasse in October 1944, but only 150 arrived, as the rest were killed on the way during an Allied attack.[45] In addition, the site suffered from transportation problems, such as a lack of lorries to transport cement and a lack of petrol.[46]

The massive bombing of Daimler-Benz's plants in September and October 1944, which rendered large amounts of floor-space unusable, led to renewed pressure from the board on the Sindelfingen management to accelerate progress. The ability of Daimler-Benz to maintain production – and thus to guarantee its supply of raw materials, the retention of its labour and the safeguarding of its capacity – was henceforth dependent on the dispersal sites, and Haspel repeated his demand to push forward the building of Brasse with all means available. The management complained bitterly about the way in which the project had been handled: 'Work has in no way been pushed forward to the extent planned . . . it was planned to have the Ernst mine [Brasse] ready for installation by mid-October. The fact is this deadline has now arrived, and the floor is still being levelled and laid.' Further: 'Key issues are still undecided – e.g. the formation of the entrance, the ventilation of the mine, the underpinning of the damaged pillars, the heating question, etc.' It concluded that 'if work is to be carried out as planned, considerably more workers must be deployed' and that 'given the above points, it seems impossible that the Brasse mine will be ready for installation this year.'[47]

Despite the fact that the management, in recognition of the impossibility of the original project, had decided to slow down half of the building programme and devote all its energies to a speedy completion of the other half, the arrival of the December deadline saw the site still not ready for installation. Progress was being made to such an extent, however, that the company was able to begin concretizing plans for the transfer of labour and machinery from Sindelfingen to Brasse during the first half of 1945. In the first quarter of 1945, 600 productive workers were to be deployed in the complex, with a further 600 workers to be transferred in the second quarter, representing thus a quarter of Sindelfingen's total labour force.[48] At the beginning of January, work had finally reached the point where the management could have begun assembling the machinery immediately – if the entrance to the mine had been ready. Installation thus remained impossible, leading the company to gain a guarantee from the SS that extra

---

45   MBAG Haspel 9,90, Kiemle to Dir. Langheck/Sindelfingen, 17.10.1944.
46   MBAG Haspel 9,90, K. C. Müller to Haspel, 27.10.1944.
47   MBAG Huppenbauer 474, Memorandum regarding Visit of the 'Ernst' Mine ('Brasse'), 10.10.1944.
48   MBAG Huppenbauer 474, DBAG Sindelfingen to Armaments Commando Stuttgart, 13.12.1944.

labourers would be provided to work on the entrance, that nightshifts would be introduced for the labourers, and that 'on the part of the building management everything necessary is done.'[49]

In early January, barracks for the initial 600 workers had been procured, and the management began installing equipment on the part of the floor that had been cemented.[50] During February, machinery and goods finally began arriving at the site from Sindelfingen.[51] Even then, however, the Daimler-Benz representatives on-site had no means of getting the machinery from the railway to the mine. By mid-March, the site had still not begun producing.

The repeated failure to get production moving became the subject of a bitter dispute between the SS and the company in the last few weeks of the war. An SS representative complained that, although the site had been built in sections according to the wishes of Daimler-Benz to allow the assumption of production as quickly as possible, the company had failed to move any machinery in. It argued that since the end of January 7300 square metres of concreted floor space had been ready and that by mid-February 1945 the electricity supply had been installed, so that the mine had been ready for the installation of machinery for months and ready for production for three weeks. He finally threatened to transfer the site to another company, as 'at the current time, when the need for underground capacity is rising daily, it is unacceptable to leave such space unused, even for short periods of time.'[52]

The company, however, realized that the war was coming to a very rapid conclusion and was unwilling to install much of its machinery in a cold, damp location when it was obviously no longer useful, or indeed possible, to do so. Some machines were ultimately moved in, the company seemingly going through the motions to satisfy the SS, but it refused to install others owing to the 90 per cent relative humidity in the caves. Further, as it pointed out to the SS, it had insufficient facilities to allow the deployment of large numbers of workers, and some of the machinery necessary to set up production was still missing, the transport network having long since collapsed. While the management assured the SS that it was doing everything possible, it had clearly recognized the futility of the project and was concerned now only to avoid damaging its expensive machinery unnecessarily in the last weeks of the war.[53]

---

49 MBAG Huppenbauer 474, Minutes of the Discussion in 'Brasse' on 3.1.1945; DBAG Sindelfingen to Kiemle, 9.1.1945.
50 MBAG Huppenbauer 474, Memorandum regarding Visit of 'Brasse', 3.1.1945.
51 MBAG Huppenbauer 474, Memorandum regarding 'Brasse', 26.2.1945.
52 MBAG Huppenbauer 474, SS Command Mosbach to DBAG Sindelfingen, 15.3.1945.
53 MBAG Huppenbauer 474, DBAG Sindelfingen to SS Command Mosbach, 26.3.1945; Huppenbauer 474, Report on the Visit to 'Brasse' on 20.3.1945. The report of 20.3.1945 notes that the foreign workers from Sindelfingen were in a heavily loused state and that the health of all the workers was, as a result of the weather and food situation, very poor. There were only very primitive sanitary facilities available, and absolutely no facilities for washing clothing.

c) Underground Dispersal: Project 'Jaspis'

A central issue for the Sindelfingen plant, partly for its Fighter Staff production, but above all for its role as the main producer of car and lorry bodies within the post-war concern, was the need to transfer its huge presses to a safe location.[54] Brasse was, however, unsuitable for the presses. In the first place, it would be very difficult to transport them there. Furthermore, because the Brasse mine was structurally unsound, it would be too dangerous to install machines that caused such huge vibrations, as these might dislodge rock from the mine roof and cause accidents.[55] This led the Sindelfingen management to the conclusion that another site was needed, especially given that it was also keen to vacate Kranich as soon as possible and that substitute capacity in addition to Brasse had to be found for this too.[56]

In April 1944, preliminary examinations were made of the potential of a number of sites located in or near the quarries of a state prison (*Landes-strafanstalt* – LSA) in Rottenburg, near Tübingen.[57] The proximity of the location to Sindelfingen and Untertürkheim and the ready supply of building labour in the form of the inmates of the LSA, whom the Reich Justice Authorities were willing to place at Daimler-Benz's disposal and whom Daimler-Benz was more than willing to exploit, made it a very suitable site. It was therefore quickly decided to push ahead with a large-scale relocation of Sindelfingen's productive capacity there. Throughout May, the management began planning the preparation and utilization of the site – codenamed 'Jaspis' – which, once fully under way, was to be worked upon by up to 2000 inmates of the LSA, coordinated by three local building firms.[58] By the end of May, it was able to note that 'everything is ready for building work to begin immediately' and pressed the authorities to allocate extra building firms and personnel in order to force the process forward.[59]

The Jaspis project, the completion of which was planned for the end of 1944, became the focus of Daimler-Benz's long-term planning for the dispersal of the Sindelfingen plant. It was eventually decided to reconstitute all of Sindelfingen's underground production lines there, with Kranich and Brasse taking on the character of interim dispersals. At this point it was intended that Jaspis should consist of an initial 6300 square metres, rising to a huge 18000 square metres.[60] Of a total inventory of 888 machines in June 1944, the

---

54 MBAG Haspel 9,90, Memorandum on the Results of the Inspection of the Large Presses in Sindelfingen, 14.4.44.
55 MBAG Huppenbauer 474, Memorandum on the Visit to 'Brasse', 27.6.1944.
56 MBAG Huppenbauer 461, DBAG Sindelfingen to Kirmaier/Fighter Staff, 4.8.1944.
57 MBAG Huppenbauer 476, Reich Office for Geological Research to DBAG Sindelfingen, 21.4.1944; Huppenbauer 476, Memorandum regarding Rottenburg, 25.4.1944.
58 MBAG Huppenbauer 476, Minutes of the Meeting in the LSA Rottenburg on 4.5.1944; Minutes of the Meeting regarding Preliminary Work for S2 on 17.5.1944.
59 MBAG Huppenbauer 476, Memorandum regarding Underground DIspersal, 25.5.1944.
60 MBAG Huppenbauer 461, Overview of Dispersal Planning for Daimler-Benz AG Sindelfingen, 7.6.1944.

company planned to disperse a total of 423 – 46 at Iselshausen and 377 underground.[61] It was envisaged that all 377 of these machines, including the 96 presses, would eventually be assembled at Jaspis.

During the following two months, the company, clearly reacting to the intensification of the air raids and to the changes in the military situation on both the eastern and western fronts in the summer of 1944, revised its dispersal schemes further. In a new set of plans made in August 1944, Jaspis was envisaged as an initial project of 8380 square metres, rising to a final 21,720 square metres, to start production in the first quarter of 1945.[62] It was now decided to transfer 426 machines (including a new total of 107 presses) underground, in addition to the 46 at Iselshausen, leaving 429 – i.e. less than half of Sindelfingen's total inventory – at the main plant.[63] Significantly, the space needed for the press shop had increased, as a part that had previously worked in the vehicle sector had now been transferred to fighter production.[64] Clearly, the company was trying to have as many as possible of its key machines deployed at least nominally in fighter production, in order to facilitate their dispersal as quickly as possible within the Fighter Staff programme. Above all, as the Sindelfingen management stressed to Haspel, 'it is planned to build the press shop section with all means at our disposal as quickly as possible.'[65]

As with Brasse, from the outset Jaspis was beset by problems that rendered such planning redundant and that underline the lack of realism with which some of these projects were undertaken. They were partly caused by the increasing difficulty of procuring labour, materials and expertise against the background of a gradual descent into economic chaos, and partly a result of the innate lack of feasibility of a project which, like the underground dispersal programme as a whole, was based on assumptions which were initially at least optimistic and increasingly the product of fantasy.

The initial plans for the tunnel system at Jaspis entailed digging a series of parallel tunnels, each seven metres wide. This was deemed necessary to allow a satisfactory arrangement of the production process. However, even at this early stage, in recognition of the amount of work involved, the planning was scaled down, and it was decided to restrict the width of the basic tunnels to six metres, building seven-metre ones only where the size of the machinery demanded it.[66] Further, one month into the planning process, after a

61   MBAG Huppenbauer 461, Dispersal Overview 10.6.1944.
62   MBAG Huppenbauer 461, Overview of Dispersal Planning for Daimler-Benz AG Sindelfingen, 3.8.1944.
63   MBAG Huppenbauer 461, Dispersal Overviews, 2.8.44. Overall, the bulk of the productive departments were now to be relocated, while those remaining consisted largely of non-productive departments such as research and development and the tool-making workshops (MBAG Huppenbauer 461, Dispersal Planning DBAG Werk Sindelfingen, 3.8.1944).
64   MBAG Huppenbauer 461, DBAG Sindelfingen to Kirmaier/Fighter Staff, 4.8.1944.
65   MBAG Haspel 9,90, DBAG Sindelfingen to Haspel, 18.7.1944.
66   MBAG Huppenbauer 476, Memorandum regarding the Discussion on 30.5.1944.

substantial amount of preliminary work had already been carried out, the Sindelfingen management was informed by its site manager at Jaspis that the authorites in Berlin had refused permission for the project, as the current plan involved the construction of a huge vaulted structure for the presses which would have taken a year to build and would have required far too much labour and too many resources.[67] As a result of this false start, of further confusions regarding control of the site, and of difficulties in procuring skilled building labour as a result of competition from other firms equally desperate to rescue their capital goods, the project experienced endless delays. Two months after the initial project had been conceived, the site had thus in effect made no progress, and the presses were still not catered for in the company's dispersal plans.

The stopping of the initial project, which was by now key to the dispersal of Sindelfingen, threw the whole programme into crisis. It clearly caused confusion within the Fighter Staff too, as a Daimler-Benz representative there contacted the management in late June asking to know if the company still wanted the site. Despite the failure of the project thus far, the reply was unequivocal: it must 'by all means be secured for Sindelfingen.'[68]

Clearly, the Sindelfingen management was allowed to retain control, since work continued, though now according to a new plan, in the vicinity of the abandoned original project. Given the embryonic state of the project, however, the management continued to experience difficulties in ensuring that it was included in the minimum building programme of the RMfRuK. The increasing scarcity of building expertise and shortages of materials meant that inclusion was essential to give the project any chance of success at all. Without allocation to a priority category, building work could not even be started, and although the company put pressure on the authorities in Berlin to have the site included, it was initially unable to get any allocation of priority at all – this, as the management complained bitterly, despite the fact that all the necessary labourers, up to 1800 men, could immediately be placed at the project's disposal by the Reich Justice Ministry.[69]

At last, however, the Sindelfingen management was able to ensure the inclusion of Jaspis in the minimum building programme of the RMfRuK.[70] On 25 July, i.e. six weeks after the launching of the second front, the company representative on site finally reported that 'the building site has now been activated on a small scale.'[71] Thirty prisoners and eight German workers were deployed, working from 7 am to 7 pm in preparing the access road and beginning the digging of two of the planned nine tunnels.

67 MBAG Huppenbauer 476, Memorandum regarding Sindelfingen, 22.6.1944.
68 MBAG Huppenbauer 476, DBAG Sindelfingen to Hermann/Fighter Staff, 23.6.1944.
69 MBAG Huppenbauer 476, Memorandum regarding Discussion of S2 with General Plenipotentiary for Building 29.6.1944.
70 MBAG Haspel 9,90, Kirmaier/Fighter Staff to DBAG Sindelfingen, 15.7.1944.
71 MBAG Huppenbauer 476, Daily Note, 25.7.1944.

As with Brasse, progress was hampered from the start by shortages of materials and various utilities. Of the original four pneumatic drills supplied, only two could be used because of a lack of compressed air.[72] Then, only a week after building work had begun and despite the inclusion of Jaspis in the minimum building programme, the Organization Todt (OT), which was also involved in the dispersal process, particularly in supplying labour, ordered that the project be terminated.[73] It took the renewed intervention of Haspel in the Fighter Staff for the future of Jaspis to be secured. In the end, the company was able to pursuade the OT that at least the first section of the building work must be completed, and that 'the heavy, irreplaceable presses, which are used by the producer company in unique production lines and which have no adequate blast walls around them in the plant, absolutely must as soon as possible be transferred to a tunnel.'[74] As a result, the decision was negated and building work was resumed with the support of the OT, which was now to procure an additional building firm.[75]

Work finally gathered pace during August, using increasing numbers of LSA prisoners. The company attempted to force the pace by a variety of means, clearly keen to transfer production to the site as soon as possible. In August, the company representative reported that it was planned to introduce shift work within the next ten days to accelerate the building process.[76] As a result of slow progress in constructing the barrack complex, however, the number of prisoners deployed on the project was nowhere near the projected 2000 workers. In addition, the difficulty of procuring sufficient armed guards for the site to prevent the prisoners escaping limited the extent to which the numbers could be increased.[77]

Despite the proximity of the site to the LSA and thus to its major supply of forced labour, the very nature of the labour posed an additional threat to the ability of the company to bring the project to fruition as quickly as possible. The Daimler-Benz engineer at Jaspis noted with alarm: 'I have established that the prisoners deployed in the quarry, whether German or foreign workers, will, after completion of their sentence, be conscripted to another firm, or, in

72   MBAG Huppenbauer 476, Daily Note, 29.7.1944.
73   MBAG Haspel 9,90, Kiemle to Haspel, 31.7.1944.
74   MBAG Haspel 9,90, Memorandum (Kiemle), 31.7.1944.
75   MBAG Haspel 9,90, Memorandum regarding the Discussion on 1.8.1944 with OT-Squad Württemberg regarding 'Jaspis' 549.
76   MBAG Huppenbauer 476, Daily Note, 5.8.1944.
77   Even initially, when only 30 prisoners were deployed, the Daimler-Benz engineer overseeing the project complained that 'the biggest problem is the guarding of the prisoners' (MBAG Huppenbauer 476, Daily Note, 29.7.1944). The Sindelfingen management repeatedly requested more guards, arguing to the Fighter Staff that armed guards were essential to watch over what it described as 'dangerous criminals', while Kirmaier used his position within the Fighter Staff to attempt to procure guards from the SS, from the military, and even from the Gestapo (MBAG Huppenbauer 476, DBAG Sindelfingen to Kirmaier/Fighter Staff, 8.8.1944; MBAG Huppenbauer 476, Kirmaier/Fighter Staff to Held/DBAG Sindelfingen, 28.8.1944).

the case of foreigners – in one instance it concerns French prisoners – are to be released to France.' He argued: 'We must resist the withdrawal of these former prisoners, as we cannot afford to let prisoners who, for example, have been trained as explosives experts leave the building site after serving their sentence.'[78] In addition, there was the possibility that French prisoners would return to France and give away the location of the site. The Sindelfingen management, on the basis of this knowledge, expressed their fears to Kirmaier at the Armaments Staff (the renamed Fighter Staff), arguing: 'We must put an end to this situation, above all by getting the Armaments Staff to prevent the LSA from releasing prisoners. Civilian prisoners who have completed their sentences must be conscripted to the building firms.'[79]

As the site grew, the company attempted to improve the prospects of a speedy completion in other ways. By the end of August, work on four of the projected nine tunnels was in progress. Three building firms were working seven days a week, carrying out one explosion in each tunnel each day, after which the prisoners would spend the whole day labouring under dreadful conditions to clear the rubble away.[80] This was clearly not sufficient, however, for the Daimler-Benz engineer – as the company representative on site, he was one of the main sources of pressure to intensify the building process – who demanded that further tunnels be started to give the explosives experts sufficient work. This was communicated to the Daimler-Benz board, and Haspel was told about the site engineer's 'bitter complaints' about the poor progress of the building work.[81]

By the end of September, a total of 66 civilian building employees, 176 prisoners and 22 OT workers – 264 in total – were deployed on nine tunnels, building on the remaining five having begun.[82] With one exception, all tunnels had reached a depth of between 11 and 34 metres. Two months after building work had started, the two main tunnels envisaged for the press shop had reached depths of only 29 and 34 metres, although these were clearly being treated as the main priority. On 30 September, the nine tunnels had been dug to a combined depth of 166.50 metres. By 7 October, one week later, this total had reached only 185.90 metres, against a new planned total of 237.50 metres. Four of the nine tunnels had made no progress, and only three had made progress of five metres or more. Of a planned 71.00 metres, only 19.40 metres had been dug in one week, less than 30 per cent of the amount required.[83] The site continued to make only slow progress in the following

78 MBAG Huppenbauer 476, Daily Note, 29.7.1944.
79 MBAG Huppenbauer 476, DBAG Sindelfingen to Kirmaier/ Armaments Staff, 10.8.1944.
80 MBAG Huppenbauer 476, Hagmeier to Dir. Langheck/DBAG Sindelfingen, 23.8.1944.
81 MBAG Haspel 9,90, DBAG Sindelfingen to Haspel, 28.8.1944.
82 MBAG Huppenbauer 476, September Closing Report Site 'Jaspis' (undated, end of September 1944).
83 MBAG Huppenbauer 476, Weekly Report of 1.10.–7.10.1944, 'Jaspis'. (The document is clearly falsely dated.) The progress made thus far in fact corresponded to a maximum of four weeks' work, although work on the site had begun in July. See also MBAG Huppenbauer 476, Minutes of the Discussion of 7.10.44 on the Building Site regarding Progress of the 'Jaspis' Project.

period. From 8 to 13 October the total amount of tunnel dug rose from 185.90 metres to 212.70 metres, as opposed to a new projected total of 246.20 metres. Only 26.80 metres out of a planned 60.30 metres had been completed, with again only three tunnels making progress of more than five metres.[84] Similarly, in the following week, of a planned 87 metres, only 39 metres were dug, so that work was still only being completed at half the planned rate.[85]

In the following week, however, the rate of increase started to show substantial improvement. The number of workers, which had stood at 325 in the first week of October, had risen substantially by the end of the month. In addition, the introduction of shift work at about this point had contributed to an improvement in productivity. These two factors, especially the fact that explosions could now take place round the clock, meant that of the planned 95 metres for the week, 60 metres was achieved, i.e. almost two-thirds of the total.[86]

The introduction of shift work in winter conditions represented a further hardship for the LSA prisoners, who were already being forced to produce heavy physical labour under appalling conditions seven days a week. In the first shift, the OT and building company workers worked 8½ hours and the prisoners 9½ hours. In the second shift, while the OT and building workers similarly worked for 8½ hours, the prisoners were forced to work a huge 11½ shift. Prisoners working on the nightshift were thus subjected to a gruelling 80½ hours of work per week.[87]

By the beginning of November, the site was beginning to make faster progress, digging in the first week of November a total of 93 metres against a total target of 113 metres. The two main press tunnels had now reached depths of 60 metres and 47 metres. However, no sooner had the project begun to gather steam, than the effects of the collapsing German economy caused renewed difficulties and progress began to slow again. The following week, only 80 metres of tunnel were dug.[88] Although during the first week of November 16 train wagons full of presses arrived at Jaspis, nearly four months after building work had started the company was forced to inform Kirmaier that 'it is still impossible to say when the first machines can be installed.'[89] Not

---

84 MBAG Huppenbauer 476, Weekly Report, 8.–13.10.1944.
85 MBAG Huppenbauer 476, Weekly Report, 14.–20.10.1944.
86 MBAG Huppenbauer 476, Weekly Report, 20.10.–27.10.1944.
87 While the lengthening of the prisoners' work hours helped to some extent to accelerate the building work, this was not enough to satisfy the company engineer, who argued that for the civilian workers too, 'the working day can only, in the interests of the project, be extended.' The worktime of the civilian labourers had been cut from 10½ to 8½ hours, as the labour of the building workers was subject to regulations that did not apply to prison labourers, but the engineer proposed various legal loopholes to allow increases in the working hours of these labourers too (MBAG Huppenbauer 476, Weekly Report, 28.10.–3.11.1944).
88 MBAG Huppenbauer 476, Weekly Report of 3.11.–10.11.1944.
89 MBAG Huppenbauer 476, DBAG Sindelfingen to Kirmaier/Armaments Staff, 1.11.1944. The presses came from France, presumably from 'Kranich', rather than directly from Sindelfingen.

only was the site threatened by the lack of building materials and equipment, but there were renewed fears that the Armaments Staff was considering stopping the project. The company thereupon intervened with Kirmaier, expressing concern that 'it is repeatedly being mentioned that Jaspis is down for closure in Berlin, but no one knows anything definite.'

In a manner typical of the way in which influence was used in the war, Kirmaier was charged with finding out precisely what the situation was and 'to tell us by the quickest method possible, so that if necessary Dr Haspel can intervene.' In the event, it is unclear whether Haspel's intervention was necessary but the rumours of closure came to nothing and work continued.[90] As the procurement of the necessary building equipment became more and more difficult, the company intensified its efforts to compensate by increasing the number of prison inmates on the site. Of the projected 1800–2000 prisoners, only approximately 250 were deployed on the site, as the necessary barracks for the extra workers were still not ready. The site manager complained that that 'up until now only 247 prisoners have been deployed, although 400 prisoners for the building are already here. The OT building management must thus be made to demand the remaining 153 prisoners from the prison and deploy them in the building of the barracks.'

As building progress fell back to below 50 per cent of the required rate, the plans for the project were revised – the height of most of the tunnels was to be reduced from 6 to 4.50 metres, in the hope that this would accelerate completion. The Daimler-Benz representative simultaneously attempted to improve the chances of success by pressing to have machinery transferred to Jaspis, reminding the management of the possibility of having machinery confiscated from other sites, and again demanding the supply of more drilling hammers and steels.[91] By late November, however, the project was simultaneously suffering from a shortage of steels, wood, lorries and transport facilities.[92]

Furthermore, just three weeks after the rumours of closure had died down, there were renewed threats that all underground dispersal projects in southern Germany were to be stopped, and the decision was taken to withdraw the OT from Jaspis. This would mean that one of the building firms could not continue at the site as it was dependent on the OT for explosives experts, and the other firms would also slow down through having insufficient explosives to work the nightshift. Above all, the press tunnels would grind to a halt as these had been the responsibility of the OT. The Daimler-Benz engineer informed the Sindelfingen management, in somewhat understated fashion, that 'under the above circumstances we have strong doubts about the punctual continuation of progress on the building site.'[93]

90   MBAG Huppenbauer 476, Weekly Report of 3.11.–10.11.1944.
91   MBAG Huppenbauer 476, Weekly Report of 11.11.–17.11.1944.
92   MBAG Huppenbauer 476, Memorandum, 20.11.1944.
93   MBAG Huppenbauer 476, Hagmeier to Dir. Langheck, 23.11.1944.

For the moment, building work continued. By 22 December, the number of workers had reached 676 and the press tunnels had attained depths of 125 and 84 metres. A total of 692 metres had been dug in the nine tunnels, and the connecting cross-tunnels linking the main tunnels were now being channelled out. However, although the rate of progress had again improved and was now the best yet, since building had begun in July only 2140 square metres of floor space, or 28 per cent of the first phase (7750 square metres), was complete.[94] This was less than ten per cent of the originally planned 22,000 square metres – put another way, at current rate of progress, the site would be finished in late 1948.

The building work continued into 1945. In mid-January, against the background of an ever-nearing front, it was reduced to a single shift, the nightshift being abandoned owing to the transfer of prisoners to another project. The Sindelfingen management, in anticipation of this, again pressurised the Armaments Staff for substitute labour.[95] It sought to offset the losses primarily, however, by increasingly transferring foreign workers from the main plant into building work at the site. Of the 762 workers at the site in mid-February 1945, the number of prisoners from the LSA had fallen to 251, while the number of foreign workers had risen to 272, the vast majority of whom had arrived recently.[96] These had been directly transferred from the Sindelfingen plant to Jaspis.[97]

During January and February, as machinery was finally being transferred to Brasse, large volumes of machine-tools began to arrive from Sindelfingen. However, by the end of February, the site manager informed the Sindelfingen management that progress was grinding to a halt as no further explosives were being supplied.[98] The board – possibly lacking any sense of an alternative in the circumstances – still refused to give up. Haspel had clearly long since recognized the hopelessness of the situation, but argued nonetheless 'that now, and in the immediate future even more so, we will have so many labourers at our disposal that it must be attempted under all circumstances to push precisely this building project forward.'[99] While an intervention at a higher level was pointless, as no further official allocations of cement were available and the transportation network had anyway long since ceased to function as a unified system, Haspel suggested that 'as so often in the past years, if these things cannot be regulated via official channels, one has to try and look after oneself on a local level.'

Building seemingly continued until at least the end of March, although by this stage only one tunnel was being dug, the rest having ground to a halt.[100]

94   MBAG Huppenbauer 477, Report of 9.12.–22.12.1944.
95   MBAG Huppenbauer 477, DBAG Sindelfingen to Kirmaier/Armaments Staff, 12.1.1945.
96   MBAG Huppenbauer 477, Report of 16.1.–15.2.1945.
97   MBAG Huppenbauer 477, DBAG Sindelfingen to Haspel, 24.3.1945.
98   MBAG Haspel 9,90, Kiemle to DBAG Sindelfingen, 28.2.1945.
99   MBAG Haspel 9,90, Memorandum, 3.3.1945.
100 MBAG Huppenbauer 477, Report on the 'Jaspis' Project: State as of 23.3.1945.

The final report of the Sindelfingen management to Haspel on the Jaspis project reported that of the total floor space dug out, eight months after building had started and a year after the initial project had been conceived, 1000 square metres were ready to receive the machines – less than five per cent of the project had thus been fully completed.[101]

3. The Dispersal of Mannheim

As plants primarily producing under the Fighter Staff, Genshagen, Sindelfingen and Untertürkheim were the objects of substantial dispersal projects from a very early stage. From August 1944 onwards, as the Allied bombing intensified, the attention of the Daimler-Benz board increasingly focused on the issue of dispersing production from the Mannheim and Gaggenau plants. The programme for these plants, as lorry-producing factories, was in a far more direct way linked to plans for the transition to the post-war period, in which these production lines would be the focal point of the company's initial activity.

Plans to disperse lorry production were being formulated internally at least by May 1944.[102] However, compared to aero-engine production, the actual relocation began relatively late. In the period prior to August 1944, the Mannheim management moved only the lorry repair workshop and the generator repair and installation workshop, to Weinheim, on the Bergstrasse, where they functioned as a fully self-contained unit.[103] Apart from this, the production of fuel tanks had also been transferred to a site in Weinheim, involving a further 33 machines and 45 workers. Of a total of 1794 machine-tools on the Mannheim inventory engaged in lorry production, 78, or approximately five per cent, had thus been moved by the summer of 1944. In addition, at some stage, the production of tank components had also clearly been transferred to Weiler, in Alsace, involving 322 machines and 450 workers.[104] Including this production line, the proportion of dispersed machine-tools at this point can be taken as approximately 20 per cent.[105]

The process of re-tooling for the Opel 3-ton lorry, which at this point was nearly complete, was a key factor limiting the ability of the management to decentralize production effectively and smoothly. As with the company's aero-engine lines, the tooling process would be complicated by the demands of simultaneously relocating production, and priority was given to getting production going before considering relocating any part of it.[106] This became all the more

---

101 MBAG Huppenbauer 477, DBAG Sindelfingen to Haspel, 24.3.1945.
102 MBAG Haspel/'Arbeitskreis LKW', Minutes of the Lorry-Discussion on 31.5.1944.
103 BA (P) 46.03 Film 3380, Overview of Dispersal Projects for DBAG Mannheim (August 1944).
104 BA (P) 46.03 Film 3380, DBAG Mannheim to Armaments Staff, 10.9.1944.
105 Either way, it can be seen that, both for Sindelfingen and Mannheim at least, Roth's claim that by the winter of 1943–4 'most production lines' had been dispersed is an exaggeration (Roth, 'Der Weg zum guten Stern', p. 310).
106 BA (P) 46.03 Film 3380, DBAG Mannheim to Main Committee for Vehicle Production, 20.9.1944.

important from early August onwards after Opel's Brandenburg plant, the main producer of the 3-ton lorry, was bombed extensively, so that according to Opel, 'production at this plant [would] be interrupted for a very long time.'[107] Daimler-Benz thus became the sole functioning producer of the Opel 3-ton lorry. Both the interests of the military and those of Daimler-Benz, which now had an effective monopoly, demanded full-scale production as rapidly as possible. Haspel, in recognition of this, took the view that small-scale relocations to Alsace which had been offered should not be accepted and that 'production should stay in Mannheim if an underground dispersal is not possible.'[108]

During August 1944, however, the Mannheim management began to concretize extensive contingency plans for a possible large-scale decentralization of Mannheim's lorry production.[31] Of a total of 1794 machine-tools engaged in lorry production, the Mannheim management planned eventually to transfer 1619 (89 per cent) and 1544 out of a total of 3123 workers. During September, the management put pressure on the Main Committee for Vehicle Production to agree to a large scale decentralization. It argued that while up to this point the principle had been applied of only transferring fully operative production lines, it had been unable as a result of recent air raids to bring its production to this position, and that 'it must therefore be considered if the situation has not become so urgent, that in some cases we should deviate from this principle.'[110] In practice, the impact of the Allied bombing was in any case such that some components suppliers had already ceased supplying and the plant was being forced to improvise the production of various components itself at short notice.[111] The demands to ensure as efficient and rational as possible an implementation of the decentralization process were becoming correspondingly academic.

Parallel to the process of putting pressure on the Main Committee for official approval of the decentralization plans, the management conducted extensive negotiations with the owners of the various sites that the company had earmarked for the dispersal of its workshops. In addition, the front situation was now such that it was forced to find a new location in Germany for the tank gear production currently in Alsace. For this, a possible underground site, the 'Eschershausen' mine, in the locality of Holzminden, was considered. This, however, was nowhere near completion, so it was

107   BA (P) 46.03 Film 3380, Opel AG to DBAG, 7.8.1944.
108   MBAG Minutes of the Board Meetings of DBAG 1943–5, Minutes of the Board Meeting of DBAG on 18.8.44.
109   BA (P) 46.03 Film 3380, Overview of Dispersal Projects for DBAG Mannheim (August 1944).
110   BA (P) 46.03 Film 3380, DBAG Mannheim to Main Committee for Vehicle Production, 20.9.1944.
111   Thus, for example, the plant was forced to set up production of bearings for the drive shaft after its subcontractor failed, using tools and workers transferred to Mannheim from Untertürkheim (BA [P] 46.03 Film 3380, Memorandum of the Discussion of 28.9.1944. regarding Lorry Program and Underground Dispersal, 29.9.1944.

necessary to find an additional site to serve as an interim location for this production line too.[112]

As with all other dispersals of major production departments, the management demanded that 'it not be forgotten that the functioning of the dispersed department and its ability to ensure delivery must remain safeguarded.'[113] By the end of September, it had arranged sites for most of the workshops that it regarded as being in most urgent need of relocation. The tempering shop was to be transferred to Heidelberg, where 2000 square metres had been allocated to Daimler-Benz. A paper factory in Wiesloch was provided for the partial relocation of the tank parts production line, and a company in Buchen was forced to give up 2000 square metres for the production of engine casings. Space in two smaller factories in Limbach was allocated to the Mannheim plant for the production of tools and appliances.[114]

Despite considerable resistance from the owners of the companies whose premises Daimler-Benz was planning to use, the company was able, using its contacts with the powerful Armaments Inspectorate, to push through its interests in the majority of cases. The management noted the existence of the premises of a gelatine factory in Eberbach, in the Neckar valley, where 3600 square metres were potentially available. According to its own assessment, these halls would be eminently suitable for its heavy machinery and a large number of machine-tools for lorry production could be relocated there.[115] It elected to put pressure on the Armaments Staff to have the factory confiscated for the Mannheim plant, and, despite the fact that it had already been allocated to the Flugzeugwerke Speyer – as the Mannheim management was fully aware – Daimler-Benz was still able to use its influence to procure the site, and part of the tank components production line was transferred to this site in early October.[116] Over the course of October and November, those projects that had been allocated and finalized were carried through.[117]

The extent to which the intensification of the air raids and the damage to Daimler-Benz's plants in the autumn had changed the management's attitude is

---

112   BA (P) 46.03 Film 3380, DBAG Mannheim to Armaments Staff, 10.9.1944.
113   BA (P) 46.03 Film 3380, Factory Management to Dir. Werner, 28.8.1944.
114   BA (P) 46.03 Film 3380, Memorandum regarding Planned Dispersals, 22.9.1944.
115   BA (P) 46.03 Film 3380, Memorandum, 1.10.1944.
116   BA (P) 46.03 Film 3380, DBAG Mannheim to Armaments Inspectorate, 7.10.1944.
117   By mid-October, 405 workers (including 150 Russian men and 75 Russian women) were located at the sites in Eberbach and Buchen (BA [P] 46.03 Film 3380, Standards Department to Dir. Werner, 9.10.1944). Further, the management reported in its overview of its dispersal activities given to the Main Committee on 13 November that 47 more workers and to additional 77 machine-tools had been transported to Eberbach in the form of the tool-making department, and that the transfers to Heidelberg (40 workers and to increased total of 34 machines), Limbach (57 workers and 35 machine-tools) and Wiesloch (79 workers and 98 machine-tools) had either been carried out or were in the process of being carried out. In addition to this, three new locations for motor parts production, involving 90 machine-tools, had been planned, and the management was searching the Würzburg-Nürnberg area for suitable locations for most of its remaining production lines.

visible in its report to the Main Committee of 13 November. Surveying the previous months, it argued that 'it was originally planned to carry out the decentralization after production had fully started, as obviously the one suffers as a
result of the other . . . [but] the developments in the west have brought the
necessity of dispersal to the fore. We have therefore already for weeks been pushing through the decentralization process on our own initiative, insofar as we
could find remotely suitable locations.'[118] It noted, however, that of the 45,000
square metres needed by Mannheim to fulfil its plans, only 30,000 square metres
had been allocated by the Armaments Staff,and demanded 'that we [be] told as
soon as possible where these 30,000 square metres are available, so that we can
make progress without delay', and reaffirming its wish that 'all levers [be] set in
motion in order to carry out the decentralization as soon as possible.'

In mid-December, 711 machine-tools and 1057 workers out of a total of
2546 machine-tools and 4222 workers had been relocated or were about to be.
The new plans of the Mannheim management envisaged that when the
process was completed, 1997 machine-tools and 2645 workers would have
been transferred.[119] In late 1944, however, there was a clash of opinion
between the Daimler-Benz board and the management of the Mannheim
plant over the strategy to be pursued with regard to the dispersal of
Mannheim. As the issue of transportation began to reduce the ability of the
individual dispersed plants to coordinate their production and transfer parts
between themselves and the main plant, the advantages of the dispersal
strategy hitherto pursued began to diminish. While the Mannheim management was motivated primarily by the desire to save its machinery from the
immediate threat of bombing as an end in itself, the Daimler-Benz board was,
as argued above, increasingly preoccupied with the development of an overall
strategy for the immediate post-war period in which Mannheim, as the main
intact producer of lorries within the concern, would play a pivotal role.[120]

With the primarily military production of Genshagen, Untertürkheim,
Sindelfingen and Marienfelde, the need to continue beyond the end of the war
was unimportant, as the plants would have to re-tool completely for civilian

118 BA(P) 46.03 film 3380, DBAG Mannheim to Main Committee Vehicles Production,
     13.11.1944.
119 BA (P) 46.03 Film 3380, Overview of Surface Disposals, 15.12.1944. The difference in the total
     number of machine-tools at Mannheim in August 1944 (1794) and December 1944 (2546) is
     owing to the fact that machines were arriving in large numbers in the latter stages of the tooling
     process for production of the 3-ton Opel.
120 The Gaggenau plant had also been the object of extensive decentralization measures, with a
     large number of projects, both overground and underground, being carried out (see the list of
     major dispersal sites in National Archives, Washington D.C. RG 243 USSBS Docs 77a3,
     Dispersals in the German Vehicle Industry). The Armaments Staff had ordered the dispersal of
     Gaggenau in October 1944 (MBAG Haspel 9,84, DBAG/Hörmann to Kiemle, 14.10.1944). By
     this point, however, production at Gaggenau had come to a standstill as a result of intensive
     bombing in September–October 1944 (USSBS, *Finished Report No. 2. Overall Report, European
     War*, Washington D.C., 1947, p. 65). Mannheim thus remained the only functioning plant with
     a core production readily adaptable to post-war markets.

production once the war was over. It was thus acceptable from a company point of view, in the last three months of the war, to disperse production in a way that would mean that it would eventually collapse for reasons of transportation, as long as the prime aim of saving the substance of the company was achieved. The attitude of the board to the Mannheim plant, on the other hand, was conditioned not only by a wish to avoid the threat of bombing, but also by the need to decentralize production in such a way as to safeguard the continuation of production, with as little disruption as possible, into the immediate post-war period. As it became clear that the war was not only lost, but that its end was imminent, the need to avoid any (even temporary) dismantling of production lines that would leave the company in a position where it would be unable to produce immediately the war was finished became a key consideration.

This point was underlined unambiguously in a series of letters from Haspel to Werner, one of the directors of the Mannheim plant, in late 1944 and early 1945. Werner, informing Haspel of the measures currently being undertaken at Mannheim, explained that the management was examining a range of locations, such as Gera, Schwabach and Bamberg, with a view to carrying out further individual relocations of various departments.[121] These were clearly envisaged as interim sites pending completion of an underground project that the management began integrating into its concrete plans in December 1944. Haspel's reply gives an excellent insight into both the constraints upon the management at this stage of the war and the strategy that the Daimler-Benz board, above all Haspel, was trying to implement within these constraints.

Given the overall context as regards lorry production at this stage, Haspel was aware that Mannheim as a whole could not be dispersed until Opel had begun producing again, unless the military situation was such that the plant was in immediate danger – and once this was the case, 'we all know that a complete clear-out could no longer be carried out, purely for reasons of air attacks and lack of transport.' Further, he argued:

'If we carry out a large-scale dispersal of Mannheim, production will cease for many weeks. The biggest problem for you will then be transplanting your workforce to the new dispersal locations. You cannot remotely expect to transfer the families with them, and would thus experience great difficulties when the men all have to leave but are forced to leave their families behind in the danger zone. This has been the general experience in recent times and its importance cannot be underestimated.'

He then outlined his attitude to Werner's plans to seek out further small locations in central Germany:

---

121 BA (P) 46.03 Film 3380, DBAG Mannheim/Werner to Haspel, 15.12.1944.

All I can say is that this will create problems of transportation which, as things stand, and unless the situation radically alters, will not be overcome. For me, a dispersal only really has any point if the core of the production process is transferred underground. Only in the form of an underground project does the dispersal have any sensible meaning.

Daimler-Benz's plans for the post-war period aside, the situation as regards overall production of the 3-ton lorry demanded that decentralization of the plant had to be carried out in such a way as to allow the continuation of production. This was no longer proving possible with numerous small-scale projects: 'We have experienced with so many plants that have been relocated that they have moved from one air threat to another for six or eight months and have not been able to produce any more . . . if production is split up in this way, you will no longer have any control over it.'

In order to combine the continuation of production with some measures to minimize potential bomb damage in the event of air raids, Haspel suggested an alternative strategy. While he argued that the Main Committee or Special Committee for 3-ton lorry production would not agree to a full decentralization of Mannheim, he proposed that Mannheim's production lines be spread out more within the plant by moving out a single more or less self-contained production line and allowing the rest to expand into the available space, which in the event of air-raid damage could then be moved together again.[122] The long-term aim remained, however, an underground relocation, which Haspel demanded be pushed through 'with all means at our disposal'.

Daimler-Benz had begun looking for an underground site for the Mannheim plant in August 1944.[123] A potential location, which was already being built by the Armaments Staff, had been examined by Decker, one of Mannheim's directors, in November 1944. At this project, situated near Vaihingen/Enz and codenamed 'Gallenit', 9000 square metres of space was provisionally allocated to Mannheim on 18 November, with an option on a possible further 12,000 square metres that might be built later.[124] It was at that point being worked on by 600 concentration camp inmates, with the possibility of 200 to 300 further labourers being deployed; but a shortage of barracks and a lack of transportation meant that the rate of progress was incredibly slow. Work on the second 12,000 square metres had not even begun, and the whole project was not likely to be completed until the end of April 1945, although Decker remarked that with pressure this could be accelerated.[125]

122   BA (P) 46.03 Film 3380, Haspel to Werner, 19.12.1944.
123   MBAG Minutes of the Board Meetings of DBAG 1943–45, Minutes of the Board Meetings of DBAG on 18.8.44.
124   MBAG Haspel 9,91, Memorandum regarding the Visit to the Underground Dispersal Site 'Gallenit', 21.11.1944. 'Gallenit' was built using concentration camp labour primarily from Natzweiler.
125   MBAG Haspel 9,91, Memorandum, 21.11.1944.

The Mannheim management immediately began planning for the utilization of Gallenit. It aimed to install its machinery gradually in the completed tunnels while the other tunnels were still being built, 'so that a perpetual expansion of the Gallenit site can take place while simultaneously keeping production going.'[126] It simultaneously sought to accelerate the building work by transferring 200 of its 1060 concentration camp inmates hitherto deployed on the assembly lines in Mannheim to the building site.[127]

The success of the Gallenit project was, however, jeopardized by continued uncertainty over whether the site had actually been allocated to Daimler-Benz. Throughout December 1944 and January 1945 Haspel repeatedly had to intervene to ascertain that Gallenit was definitely reserved for Mannheim's production, clearly anxious to ensure that Daimler-Benz would be able to continue with its own separate production of the 3-ton lorry and thus avoid the possibility of Mannheim's machinery being requisitioned by the Armaments Staff and allocated elsewhere.[128] As late as 10 January 1945, he complained to Kirmaier at the Armaments Staff that 'Gallenit has not yet been finally allocated to Mannheim. We are in danger of a possible underground location being set up in which a motor production line consisting of Opel and Daimler-Benz will be formed. This would, in practise, mean the dissolution of our 3-ton production . . .'[129] He sought to justify opposition to this on the grounds that it would have a negative impact on production of the 3-ton lorry from a military point of view. It is clear, however, that the continuation of a separate production line was, in a context where there was increasing competition between companies for control of machinery and goods, crucial so that Daimler-Benz could maintain control over its machinery and ensure the existence of an independent line for the transition into the post-war period.[130]

---

126 MBAG Haspel 9,91, Report regarding the Visit to the Building Management for 'Gallenit', 8.12.1944.
127 BA (P) 46.03 Film 3380, Werner to Haspel, 22.12.1944.
128 MBAG Haspel 9,91, Haspel to K. C. Müller, 19.12.44; Haspel 9,91, DBAG Mannheim to K. C. Müller, 4.1.45.
129 MBAG Haspel 9,91, Haspel to Kirmaier/Armaments Staff, 10.1.45.
130 The extent to which companies attempted to use and influence developments with regard to the allocation of dispersal capacity in order to disadvantage other firms' decentralization activities and thus gain a competitive advantage for the immediate post-war period is shown by Daimler-Benz's strategy with regard to the 'Häverstedter Tunnel' in Westphalia. The Mannheim management informed board member K. C. Müller on 4 January 1945 that 5000 sq metres of this site had been confiscated for Daimler-Benz, but noted that in view of its poor location it was not really suitable for the company's needs (MBAG Haspel 9,91, DBAG Mannheim to K. C. Müller, 4.1.1945.). Müller replied that 'the allocation of the Häverstedter tunnel is naturally nonsense' (MBAG Haspel 9,91, K. C. Müller to DBAG Mannheim, 7.1.1945). Eight days later, however, although it had been internally agreed that the site was of no use to it, the company continued consciously to delay telling the Main Committee for Vehicle Production, to whom this tunnel had been allocated. The obvious intention was to prevent the Main Committee from allocating it to another firm and thus to disrupt other firms' ability to utilize the site (MBAG Haspel 9,91, DBAG Gaggenau to Haspel, 15.1.1945).

As with the other sites, the shortage of transportation and building materials meant that nothing approaching the necessary progress was being made, so that the original planned completion date here also had to be put back, in this case from 1 April 1945 to mid-June.[131] In view of the failure to push the Gallenit project forward to the stage where production transfer could be started – by 15 January only 3000 square metres were complete – much of Mannheim's productive capacity (which had since virtually ground to a halt) remained at the main plant.[132] The imminence of the end of the war, however, led Haspel, now totally focused on the short-term transitional phase into the post-war scenario, to reiterate even more strongly his opposition to a dismantling of Mannheim's production lines, repeating his 'refusal to allow a quasi-planless fragmentation of Mannheim just for the sake of getting out of Mannheim' and his demand that the functioning of Mannheim as an independent unit be maintained at all costs.[133] The result of this was that, apart from the dispersals carried out up to November 1944, the bulk of Mannheim's productive capacity remained intact, essentially undamaged by bombing, and able to resume production, under occupation, by the end of March 1945.[134]

4. Total Destruction and 'Zero Hour'? The Success of the Dispersal Programme

Exactly what proportion of the company's machinery was destroyed as a result of bombing is impossible to ascertain. Figures are only available for some of the plants, and these give no indication as to what machine-tools were lost, their value, or their importance. Given that the figures only relate to machinery lost from the total inventories as of 1944, it is also impossible to assess the impact of bombing on the one hand against the expansion of capacity during the war period or the acquisition of machinery plundered from the occupied east and west.

In the cases of Sindelfingen and Mannheim it is clear that, even where production was not actually resumed in the dispersal sites, the vast majority of productive capacity remained intact. This is especially the case for Mannheim, which survived essentially unscathed.

131 MBAG Haspel 9,91, Report regarding 'Gallenit', 20.1.1945.
132 MBAG Haspel 9,91, DBAG Gaggenau to Haspel, 15.1.1945. Work on 'Gallenit' eventually ceased in the first week of February 1945 owing to lack of building materials (MBAG Haspel 9,91, OT to DBAG Mannheim, 7.2.45). The Mannheim management requested that Haspel intervene with the authorities in Berlin to try to reverse the decision, but was informed by the board that, according to Haspel's inquiries, all building work had stopped – 'The way things stand, intervention stands no chance of success either' (MBAG Haspel, 9,91, DBAG Mannheim to Haspel, 8.2.45; DBAG to DBAG Mannheim, 13.2.45).
133 BA (P) 46.03 Film 3380, Haspel to Werner, 15.1.1945.
134 Joachim Jungbeck, 'Zerstörung und Wiederaufbau' in: HSG (ed.), Das Daimler-Benz Buch, pp. 375–82.

Figures available for the Gaggenau and Untertürkheim plants confirm the experiences of Sindelfingen and Mannheim as having been reasonably representative.[135] In the two raids on Gaggenau in 1944, only 408 out of a total 2500 machine-tools, or 16.5 per cent, were destroyed or heavily damaged.[136] For the Untertürkheim plant, which was the object of repeated raids, the USSBS calculated that in attacks on the plant on 26 and 27 November 1943, 3.2 per cent of machine-tools were destroyed and 4.8 per cent were damaged. In attacks on 21 February and 2 March 1944, a further six per cent were destroyed and 5.8 per cent were damaged.[137] In the major attack on 5 September 1944, it calculated that 12 per cent were destroyed and a massive 43 per cent damaged. This last figure needs qualifying, however, in that the statistics refer only to the number of machines damaged as a proportion of those still actually in the plant. Of the 4554 machine-tools on Untertürkheim's inventory, 1964 had already been dispersed and only 2590 remained.[138] Of these, 1448 were damaged, but only 568 were heavily damaged or destroyed. While in total 60 per cent of all floor space at Untertürkheim had been rendered unusable, only approximately 22 per cent of its machine-tools were destroyed. Untertürkheim was the plant that, of all Daimler-Benz's south German plants i.e. those plants that formed the core of the post-war concern, suffered the most damage.

While it is clear that saving machinery and manoeuvring the company through to the post-war period was the primary aim, and that as such the company's motives can be analysed to a large extent on the basis of a means–ends basis, it is easy to over-stress the rationality of the whole dispersal process and the extent to which it was purely focused on a clearly discernible long-term scenario. The fact that the company intensified its attempts to carry through the projects in almost direct proportion to the growing impossibility of them ever coming to fruition suggests that its motivation was more complex and is partly to be sought in the specific end-of-war context. In the extremely uncertain situation of January or February 1945, there was still no knowing when the war would actually end. In this context, keeping production going in the short term, at least in some form, was as important to the company as simply removing the machines from the immediate danger-zone. This was especially important when one considers that the cessation of production could have led to the conscription of the company's labour force and the confiscation of its machinery and thus to a *de facto* dissolution of the company. Participation in the dispersal process was essential to maintaining the

---

135 Figures for Genshagen and Marienfelde are not available. Genshagen's experience was in any case different in that it fell into the Soviet zone of occupation and was largely dismantled.
136 USSBS, *Finished Report No. 2. Daimler-Benz Gaggenau*, Washington D.C., 1947, p. 8.
137 USSBS, *Finished Report No. 79. Daimler-Benz AG Stuttgart-Untertürkheim*, Washington D.C., 1947. Table 9 Summary of machine-tool damage.
138 MBAG Haspel 2,16, Machine Tool Inventory for Untertürkheim/Effects of the Air Raid of 5.9.1944.

substance of the company in the short as well as the long term.

The limits of the extent to which the dispersal process was driven by rational long-term considerations and a perspective that went beyond the end of the war can be seen especially when one considers the pressure that came from the managers or engineers on the ground to intensify the process. In many cases it was precisely those on the ground in each individual case, rather than the board, who were creating the pressure to force the pace of the various projects. One can speculate that this is partly explicable by reference to the need of individuals to justify themselves and their activity in the face of pressure from the SS. Alternatively, continuing to work 'purposefully' could serve to avoid a call-up. Retaining a position in a small dispersal plant in February 1945 was as good a way of staying in one piece as any.

Nonetheless, the fact that, right up to the final weeks of the war, engineers in the various sites were circulating accident prevention regulations or studying the best way to set up machinery in the plant suggests that, as communications with the rest of the company, and indeed with society at large, were weakening, the dispersal sites came increasingly to function almost as self-contained worlds of their own. As at the main plants, where other aspects of daily normality – above all family and social life – had dissolved or ceased to function, continuation in even the most objectively hopeless of cases can arguably be explained by the need of those on the ground to retain the workplace as a 'normal' functioning sphere in which the illusion of structured existence against the background of a collapsing society could be maintained. Whatever the truth may be, when the economy gradually reconstituted itself after the war Daimler-Benz was able, as a result of the dispersal programme, to resume production largely intact.

VIII. Conclusions

Clearly, the post-war recovery of German industry depended primarily upon developments that occurred after 1945. If nothing else, the argument that suggests that post-war prosperity was mainly a product of the allegedly 'modernizing' impact of National Socialism rests on a very western perspective on recent German history, ignoring the fact that two Germanies emerged in the post-war period with two very different trajectories of economic and political development. Nonetheless, an examination of the history of Daimler-Benz AG in the Second World War, and specifically of company strategy as reflected through its rationalization policy, reveals four main factors that provided the preconditions for recovery.

The huge expansion of production in the 1930s, in an economic and political climate much more favourable to industry, created a context for the formulation of rationalization policy that was, in many ways, quite different from that of the initial post-fusion restructuring in the late 1920s. However, throughout the 1930s the company – like most other companies – continued to invest primarily in the flexible multi-purpose machine-tools traditionally preferred by German industry. The war greatly limited the capacity of manufacturers to do otherwise, as a large proportion of special-purpose machine tools were traditionally imported. However, it is clear that the specific conditions of the German war economy encouraged the continued investment in multi-purpose machine-tools anyway. The lack of clear orders from the procurement agencies (a reflection of the polycratic structure of the regime) and the regular changes in production programme and in product design made it difficult for the company to plan in advance. This occasioned, if anything, an even greater need for flexibility than usual, despite the ostensibly guaranteed market created by the demand for maximum armaments output. The improvised response to successive demands was also in significant measure a product of the innate uncertainty of the war situation – throughout the war, the company's investment strategy was generally characterized by a high degree of caution, by the need to adapt long-term decisions to constantly changing military and economic situations, and by a clear desire not to disadvantage itself in the long term for short-term gains. This cautious investment strategy manifested itself most clearly in the company's attitude to the occupied east.

As a first thesis it can therefore be suggested that the key to the rapid recovery of West German industry after the war – assuming Daimler-Benz to be representative – lies in the fact that its conversion to armaments production was characterized by a high degree of improvization and by the need to retain exceptional flexibility, which later facilitated a rapid reconversion to peacetime production. Partly because of the specific conditions of the German war economy, also undoubtedly as part of a conscious managerial strategy, the company did not convert capacity to armaments production in such a way as to undermine its ability to reconvert to peacetime production after the war. This was not a product of opposition to the war or a sign of unwillingness to produce armaments – the company was happy to participate in and profited greatly from war production – but reflected the centrality of the period beyond the war to company strategy.

A second aspect of the development of the company during the war that contributed to a rapid post-war recovery – and that is definitely to be seen as part of a conscious strategy – lies in its attempts to retain a core of consumer-orientated production lines during the war, which it would be able to carry straight through into the post-war period. Not only was the company aware that the war would be over at some point, but, seen from the German perspective, it was widely believed at most points that the war would be over soon. A return to peacetime consumer conditions thus seemed imminent. While it knew that in the war aero-engines and tanks would be its main areas of activity, the company was thus keen to continue producing cars and lorries for the military too, as both could easily be converted from existing peacetime models. In the first half of the war, it maintained large-scale production of cars – even converting one of its car engines into a spotlight motor in order to have an excuse to carry on producing it. After being forced to give up car production, it switched its strategy to lorries, which, as a result of the 3-ton Opel licence project, it carried on producing until 1945 and almost uninterruptedly into the post-war period. It also continued throughout the war to develop new models for peacetime, despite the fact that this was strictly banned.

Third, a very clear strategic shift took place in early 1944 back towards lorry production, as it became obvious that the war would soon be over. Even if it had not initially disrupted production much, the onset of Allied bombing had already occasioned a marked change in the company's attitude, which had greatly influenced its investment strategy from the middle of the war onwards, and from early 1944 the company began consciously to plan for a resumption of peacetime production. Whereas car production had largely been abandoned, lorry production remained intact; and whereas it was assumed that demand for cars would be weak in the post-war period, the need to rebuild bombed cities would create a strong stimulus for the building industry and with it strong demand for lorries. This shift manifested itself in a variety of ways – for example, in the process of shifting tools from the tank to the lorry sector, and in the setting-up of an internal working party on lorry production to discuss ways of rationalizing that sector and improving the company's competitive position.

Finally, although all plants had suffered bomb damage, in many cases severe, and although production at the main plants had come to a virtual standstill by October 1944, the impact of Allied bombing was more limited than this would suggest. From the summer of 1943 to the beginning of 1945 most of the company's productive capacity was relocated away from its factories, initially to smaller factory sites, then increasingly to huge underground caves that were dug out over the course of 1944 using tens of thousands of concentration camp inmates as forced labourers. The safeguarding of the bulk of Daimler-Benz's productive capacity was thus directly dependent on the brutal physical exploitation of thousands of concentration camp inmates. How many of Daimler-Benz's machine-tools were in fact destroyed is impossible to say for sure, but a reasonable estimate would be 15 per cent. Although some key machine-tools were undoubtedly destroyed, causing bottlenecks in key production lines after the war, the essential substance of the company remained intact in 1945.

In the light of these points, it seems clear that the preconditions for a rapid resumption of production were in many ways satisfied in 1945 – the company entered the post-war period with a largely intact inventory suited to peacetime production, a set of production lines orientated to peacetime and a clear strategy.

Clearly, an examination of one company can only allow firm conclusions to be drawn about that company itself, and there are limits to how far one can generalize about the nature of the war economy on the basis of the experience of one firm operating in specific branches. However, recognition of the extent to which uncertainty was the dominant element in the company's strategy in the war offers a new way of approaching some of the more general questions concerning the mobilization of the war economy itself. The expectation of an imminent return to peacetime and the concomitant fear of over-expansion led the company to adopt a cautious response to the outbreak of war. As suggested, the failure of the regime initially to mobilize the economy effectively for war can be explained not only simply by reference to either the strategy ('Blitzkrieg' economics) or the structure (polycratic inefficiency) of the regime itself, but also by recognizing the extent to which industry's perspectives at this point were focused beyond the war, resulting in a reluctance to expand and rationalize war production in what was regarded as an anomalous situation. One can nonetheless agree with Corelli Barnett's assessment that inadequacies in the performance of the German armaments industries, in the first half of the war at least, were to a great extent a product of the mismanagement of the regime, and not a reflection of the innate inefficiency of German manufacturing industry. This again underlines the point that German industry was in a fundamentally healthy condition and was well placed to recover and capture markets after the war.[1]

As far as the radical expansion of production in the second half of the war is concerned, a further four main points emerge:

First, it is clear that the subdivision of the war into two simple halves is an oversimplification as far as the development of the economy and its mobilization for war is concerned. In different sectors, different factors combined at different junctures to produce varying phases of expansion and stagnation. In key sectors such as aero-engine and tank production, the lift-off period occurred prior to the appointment of Speer and the centralization of jurisdiction under the RMfBuM, and much of the expansion of output in the aero-engine sector from 1942 onwards was a product of efforts to mobilize and expand capacity going back 12 or 18 months before Speer's appointment.

However, the winter of 1941–2 marked a clear turning point, both because the post-war period faded rapidly into the background, thus creating a radically different scenario for industry, and because it ushered in the radical reform of the regime's administrative structures, above all the emergence of Speer and the marginalization of the military in the management of the war economy. The second half of the war witnessed considerable internal reorganization at Daimler-Benz which led to significant increases in output. Nevertheless, the long-term benefits to German industry of a process that was still characterized by a great deal of improvization should not be exaggerated. Again, the expansion of output was the result of a variety of factors. Individual internal reorganization often brought greater results than attempts at industry-wide macro-rationalization, as the case of the 3-ton Opel licence shows. Overall, however, the reform of the regime's administration of the war economy was probably more important than radical restructuring of production at shop-floor level.

Third, the winter of 1941–2 represented a radical change in direction with regard to the labour supply situation. The huge influx of forced foreign workers greatly altered the conditions under which production had to be organized and maintained. However, while the accelerated dissolution of the core German male labour force facilitated the restructuring of production in some areas – above all aero-engine production – the deployment of forced labour did not, in general, have a radical long-term impact upon the nature of production at Daimler-Benz's core plants, which remained orientated towards a high-skilled workforce. The extent to which this was the case is underlined by the extensive training given to foreign workers. Where an extensive subdivision of labour was carried out, this did not represent a phase of accelerated 'modernization' of production processes in the sense that it

1   Barnett, C., *The Audit of War*, London, 1987, pp. 60–2.

provided a positive basis for the expansion of output in the 1950s, but is to be seen as the product of crisis management and improvization in a short-term and anomalous situation. It is worth recalling the comment of the Mannheim management on such developments in late 1941: 'It is much less an issue of production in volume than one of production at all.'

Fourth, the war witnessed the accelerated introduction of new pay and incentive structures at Daimler-Benz. Some of these reflected the ongoing evolution of secular trends in factory management, others – specifically the non-financial incentives – were peculiar to the war situation. These were a major means of intensifying the work-rate and achieving gains in output, especially in the last third of the war, when the company viewed investment and long-term rationalization as a means of raising output with growing caution. Again, the increasing proportion of foreign workers, their growing integration into the production process and, with it, their integration into the pay and incentive systems facilitated a reversion to short-term physical exploitation through intensification of labour, of which the foreign workers were the major victims. The social policy and productivity-related pay structures developed in the war were part of longer-term secular trends in German industrial management, adapted to the conditions of the National Socialist regime and the war, rather than specifically National Socialist initiatives implemented as a part of the DAF's 'modernizing' function. In most aspects of factory management, personnel management and 'social rationalization' generally, the company was able to retain a substantial degree of autonomy.

The partial independence enjoyed by industry within the regime was essential in enabling the company to pursue its own interests, within a situation whose development was conditioned by decisions and policies made on the political plane. The willing collaboration of industry in the exploitation of the occupied territories and of prisoners of war, foreign workers and concentration camp inmates is also to be understood in terms of the brutal pursuit of short-term rather than long-term (i.e. expansionist) business interests in the situation presented by the war – company behaviour was dominated by the need to exploit whatever market, labour and resources were available in the given context. In the last third of the war especially, the company was willing to collaborate in the escalation of short-term exploitation as a substitute for the increase of output through long-term investments that might damage the company's prospects for the post-war period.

That the company was able to make the transition to the eventual post-war period occurred in spite of, not because of, Nazi policy. Suggesting that the preconditions for a resumption of production were basically in place is quite different from suggesting that the German economy underwent a 'modernizing' transformation during the war as a result of specifically Nazi policies. However one defines it, the short-term improvization, chaos and crisis management of the war economy are hard to analyse usefully using the term. To do so would be to impose a model of constructive development on a regime that was singular in its destructiveness. The myth of the West German economic miracle should be relativized, but it should not be replaced with far more dangerous myths about the Third Reich.

Bibliography

A. Primary Sources

1. Archiv der Mercedes-Benz AG, Stuttgart – MBAG

   Bestand Kissel   Bestand Vertrieb
   Bestand Haspel   Bestand DBAG
   Bestand Huppenbauer   Bestand Ausbildung
   Bestand Werlin   Goldene Fahne
   Bestand Forstmeier   Geschäftsberichte
   Bestand Kriegswerke

2. Bundesarchiv, Koblenz – BA(K)

   NS 4 Na Natzweiler
   NS 19 Reichsführer SS Persönlicher Stab
   R 3 Reichsministerium für Rüstung und Kriegsproduktion
   R 7 Reichswirtschaftsministerium
   R 13 IV Wirtschaftsgruppe Fahrzeugindustrie
   R 41 Reichsarbeitsministerium

3. Bundesarchiv, Abteilung Potsdam – BA(P)

   31.01 Reichswirtschaftsministerium
   46.03 Reichsministerium für Rüstung und Kriegsproduktion
   62 DAF 1 Deutsche Arbeitsfront/Zentralbüro
   80 Ba2 Deutsche Bank
   80 Ba6 Bank der Deutschen Luftfahrt

4. Bundesarchiv-Militärarchiv, Freiburg – BA-MA (Freiburg)

   RL 3 Generalluftzeugmeister
   RW 20 Rüstungsinspektionen
   RW 21 Rüstungskommandos

5. Hauptstaatsarchiv Stuttgart

   E 397 Landesernährungsamt
   E 151/03 Innenministerium – Polizeiabteilung

6. Stadtarchiv Stuttgart

   363 Ernährungsamt

7. Stadtarchiv Mannheim

   Bestand Zweiter Weltkrieg

8. Zentrale Stelle der Landesjustizverwaltungen, Ludwigsburg

   419 AR-Z 176/69 Natzweiler/NL Mannheim-Sandhofen
   AR-Z 177/1969 Natzweiler/NL Wesserling-Urbis
   II 206 AR-Z 2 14/77 Judenghetto Rzeszow
   II 206 AR-Z 183/75 Flugmotorenwerk Rzeszow
   IV/406 AR-Z 21/1971 Genshagen

9. National Archives, Washington D.C.

   RG 243 United States Strategic Bombing Survey

10. Imperial War Museum, London

FD 2228/45	FD 4889/45
FD 3200/45	FD 5507/45
FD 4872/45	FD 361/45

B. Published Literature

'Arbeitsphysiologie in der Kriegswirtschaft' in: *Der Vierjahresplan* (1940), pp. 191–3
'Arbeitsstudien fördern die Leistung' in: *Der Vierjahresplan* (1939), pp. 880–1
Arbeitswissenschaftliche Institut der DAF, 'Betriebliche Sozialleistungen in der Kriegswirtschaft' in: *Jahrbuch* (1939), I, pp. 415–27
———, 'Rasse und Leistung' in: *Jahrbuch* (1939), I, pp. 415–27
———, 'Die Einsatzfähigkeit von Arbeitskräften für Fließbandarbeiten. Auszug aus einer gutachtlichen Stellungnahme' in: *Jahrbuch* (1939), I, pp. 441–53
———, 'Zur Frage der Ungelernten' in: *Jahrbuch* (1940–1), I, pp. 309–59
———, 'Zum Einsatz der Frau in Industrie und Handwerk' in: *Jahrbuch* (1940–1), pp. 373–419
———, *Der Ausländer-Einsatz in der Deutschen Wirtschaft*, Berlin, March 1942
———, *Arbeitseinsatz der Ostarbeiter in Deutschland*, Berlin, March 1943

———— (ed.), *Die Leistungsfähigkeit von Ostarbeiter in Deutschland im Vergleich zur Leistung Deutscher Arbeiter an Hand von Akkordunterlagen*, Berlin, 1943

————, *Arbeitseignung und Leistungsfähigkeit der Ostarbeiter in Deutschland*, Berlin, March 1944

Arnhold, Karl, *Der Deutsche Betrieb. Aufgaben und Ziele Nationalsozialistischer Betriebsführung*, Leipzig, 1939

'Der Aufschwung der Automobilwirtschaft' in: *Die Deutsche Volkswirtschaft* (1934), pp. 240–3

Axmann, Artur, *Der Reichsberufswettkampf*, Berlin, 1938

Backes, Uwe, Jesse, Eckhard, and Zitelmann Rainer (eds.), *Die Schatten der Vergangenheit. Impulse zur Historisierung des Nationalsozialismus*, Frankfurt, 1991

Barkai, Avraham, 'German Entrepreneurs and Jewish Policy in the Third Reich' in: *Yad Vashem Studies* 21 (1991), pp. 125–53

Bartsch, Heinrich, 'Deutsche Sozialpolitik im Kriege' in *Die Deutsche Volkswirtschaft* (1939), pp. 999–1000

Behnken, Klaus (ed.), *Deutschland-Berichte der Sozialdemokratischen Partei Deutschlands*, Salzhausen/Frankfurt, 1980.

Bellon, Bernard, *Mercedes in Peace and War*, New York, 1990

Benkert, Hans, *Gefolgschaft und Leistungssteigerung*, Berlin, 1940

————, 'Wege der Rationalisierung im Industriebetrieb' in: *Zeitschrift des Vereines Deutscher Ingenieure* (1939), pp. 1314–23

————, 'Die Werkzeugmaschine in der Massenfertigung' in: *Der Vierjahresplan* (1939), pp. 1135–7

'Die Berufsausbildung der Erwachsenen im Kriege' in: *Der Vierjahresplan* (1940), pp. 609–10

Bickel, E., 'Rationalisierung der Arbeitsvorbereitung für die Werkstatt' in: *Automobiltechnische Zeitschrift (ATZ)* (1930), pp. 771–6.

B.I.O.S. (ed.), *Investigation of Production Control and Organization in German Factories*, London, 1946

————, *Report on Visit to Daimler-Benz AG at Stuttgart-Untertürkheim*, London, n.d.

Birk, Gerhard, *Ein Düsteres Kapitel Ludwigsfelder Geschichte 1936–1945. Enstehung und Untergang der Daimler-Benz-Flugmotorenwerke Genshagen/Ludwigsfelde*, Ludwigsfelde, 1986.

Blaich, Fritz, *Wirtschaft und Rüstung im Dritten Reich*, Düsseldorf, 1987

————, 'Die 'Fehlrationalisierung' in der Deutschen Automobilindustrie 1924 bis 1929' in: *Tradition* 18 (1973), pp. 18–33

Bock, Gisela, *Zwangssterilization im Nationalsozialismus. Studien zur Rassenpolitik und Frauenpolitik*, Opladen, 1986

Böckler, Stefan, *Kapitalismus und Moderne. Zur Theorie Kapitalistischer Modernisierung*, Opladen, 1991

Boelcke, Willi, *Die Deutsche Wirtschaft 1930–1945: Interna des*

Reichswirtschaftsministeriums, Düsseldorf, 1983

Böhrs, Hermann, 'Leistungssteigerung durch richtige Organisation der Arbeit' in: *Zeitschrift des Vereines Deutscher Ingenieure* (1943), pp. 233–8

Borst, K., 'Betriebsführer und Gefolgschaft im Kriege' in: *Die Deutsche Volkswirtschaft* (1939), pp. 617–19

Brady, Robert A., *The Spirit and Structure of German Fascism*, London, 1937

———, *The Rationalization Movement in German Industry*, New York, 1933

Broszat, Martin, *Nationalsozialistische Polenpolitik 1939–1945*, Stuttgart, 1961

———, *The Hitler State*, London, 1981

———, 'Plädoyer für eine Historisierung des Nationalsozialismus' in: *Nach Hitler. Der Schwierige Umgang mit unserer Geschichte. Beiträge von Martin Broszat*, Munich, 1986, pp. 159–73

Bunk, Gerhard, *Erziehung und Industriearbeit*, Weinheim/Basel, 1972

Burkhardt, Lothar, 'Technischer Fortschritt und Sozialer Wandel. Das Beispiel der Taylorismus-Rezeption' in: Treue, W. (ed.), *Deutsche Technikgeschichte*, Göttingen, 1977, pp. 52–98

Burleigh, M. and Wippermann, W., *The Racial State. Germany 1933–45*, London, 1991

Büttner, H.W., *Das Rationalisierungskuratorium der Deutschen Wirtschaft*, Düsseldorf, 1973

Campbell, Joan, *Joy in Work, German Work*, Princeton, 1989

Carroll, Berenice, *Design for Total War. Arms and Economics in the Third Reich*, The Hague, 1968

Castorp, Cornelius, 'Der Deutsche Kraftfahrzeugabsatz 1935' in: ATZ (1936), pp. 72–6

Conrad, Christoph, *Erfolgsbeteiligung und Vermögensbildung der Arbeitnehmer bei Siemens 1847–1945*, Stuttgart, 1986

Cuntz, H., 'Planvolle Umschulung. Grundsätzliches und Praktische Erfahrungen eines Industriellen Großbetriebes' in: *Der Vierjahresplan* (1939), pp. 868–70

Czichon, Eberhard, 'Der Primat der Industrie im Kartell der Nationalsozialistischen Macht' in: *Das Argument* 10/47 (1968), pp. 168–92

Daimler-Benz AG Werk Sindelfingen (ed.), *Unser Werk in den Kriegsjahren 1939–1944*, Sindelfingen, 1944

Däubler, Wolfgang, 'Arbeitsrechtsideologie im Deutschen Faschismus – einige Thesen' in: Rottleitner, Hubert (ed.), *Recht, Rechtsphilosophie und Nationalsozialismus*, Wiesbaden, 1983, pp. 120–7

Diner, Dan (ed.), *Ist der Nationalsozialismus Geschichte? Zur Historisierung und Historikerstreit*, Frankfurt, 1987

Dlugborski, W. (ed.), *Zweiter Weltkrieg und Sozialer Wandel. Achsenmächte und besetzte Länder*, Göttingen, 1981

Dülffer, Jost, *Deutsche Geschichte 1933–1945. Führerglaube und Vernichtungskrieg*, Stuttgart, 1987

Edelmann, Heidrun, *Vom Luxusgut zum Gebrauchsgegenstand. Die Geschichte der Verbreitung von Personenkraftwagen in Deutschland*, Frankfurt, 1989

Eichholtz, Dietrich, *Geschichte der Deutschen Kriegswirtschaft*, (East) Berlin, 1971

——, and Gossweiler, Kurt, 'Noch einmal. Politik und Wirtschaft 1933–1945' in: *Das Argument* 10 (1968), pp. 210–27

——, and Schumann, Wolfgang (eds.), *Anatomie des Krieges. Neue Dokumente über die Rolle des Deutschen Monopolkapitals bei der Vorbereitung und Durchführung des Zweiten Weltkrieges*, (East) Berlin, 1969

Esenwein-Rothe, Ingeborg, *Die Wirtschaftsverbände von 1933 bis 1945*, Berlin, 1965

Evans, Richard J., *In Hitler's Shadow. West German Historians and the Attempt to Escape from the Nazi Past*, London, 1989

'Fabrikations- und Terminkontrolle in der Karosseriefabrikation' in: ATZ (1933), pp. 18–19

Fließende Fertigung im Deutschen Maschinenfabriken, (ed.) Hauptausschuß Maschinen beim Reichsminister für Bewaffnung und Munition, Essen, 1943

Forstmeier, Friedrich and Volkmann, Hans Erich (eds.), *Wirtschaft und Rüstung am Vorabend des Zweiten Weltkrieges*, Düsseldorf, 1975

——, *Kriegswirtschaft und Rüstung*, Düsseldorf, 1977

'Fortschreitende Normung und Typisierung' in: *Der Vierjahresplan* (1940), pp. 12–13

'Frauenarbeit im Betrieb' in: *Der Vierjahresplan* (1940), pp. 378–9

'Frauenarbeit in der Industrie' in: *Der Vierjahresplan* (1941), pp. 932–3

Frei, Norbert, *Der Führerstaat. Nationalsozialistische Herrschaft 1933 bis 1945*, Nördlingen, 1987

——, 'Wie Modern war der Nationalsozialismus?' in: *Geschichte und Gesellschaft* 19 (1993), pp. 367–87

'Freiwillige Sozialleistungen der Industrie' in: *Die Deutsche Volkswirtschaft* (1940), p. 613

Frese, Matthias, 'Von NS-Musterbetrieb zum Kriegsmusterbetrieb. Zum Verhältnis von DAF und Großindustrie 1936–44' in: Michalka, W. (ed.), *Der Zweite Weltkrieg*, Munich, 1989, pp. 382–401

——, *Betriebspolitik im Dritten Reich. Deutsche Arbeitsfront, Unternehmer und Staatsbürokratie in der Westdeutschen Großindustrie 1933–1939*, Paderborn, 1991

Freyberg, Thomas von, *Industrielle Rationalisierung in der Weimarer Republik*, Frankfurt, 1989

——, and Siegel, Tilla *Industrielle Rationalisierung unter dem Nationalsozialismus*, Frankfurt, 1991

Friesecke, Hans, 'Innerbetrieblicher Einsatz der Unternehmerinitiative' in: *Der Vierjahresplan* (1937), pp. 591–4

Funke, J.W., 'Vom Betrieblichen Vorschlagswesen' in: *Der Vierjahresplan* (1942), pp. 569–72

Gartman, D., *Auto Slavery. The Labor Process in the American Automobile Industry 1897–1950*, New Brunswick, 1986

Geary, D., 'Employers, Workers and the Collapse of the Weimar Republic' in: Kershaw, Ian (ed.), *Weimar: Why Did German Democracy Fail?*, London, 1991

'Gefolgschaft und Leistungssteigerung' in: *Der Vierjahresplan* (1939), pp. 1147–8

'Geordnete Rationalisierung' in: *Die Deutsche Volkswirtschaft* (1939), p. 1053

Gillingham, John, *Industry and Politics in the Third Reich*, London, 1985

———, 'The Deproletarianization of German Society: Vocational Training in the Third Reich' in: *Journal of Social History* 19 No.1 (1986), pp. 423–32

Graben, Heinz von, *Die Werkszeitschrift als Mittel der Betrieblichen Sozialpolitik*, Munich, 1957

Gramsci, Antonio, 'Americanism and Fordism' in: Hoare, Quintin and Smith, Geoffrey Nowell (eds.), *Selections from Prison Notebooks*, London, 1971, pp. 277–318

Gross, J.T., *Polish Society under German Occupation. The Generalgouvernement 1939–1944*, New Jersey, 1979

Gründger, Erich, 'Kraftfahrzeugfertigung im Lichte der Rohstofffreiheit' in: ATZ (1935), pp. 293–7

Gurland, A.R.L., 'Technologische Entwicklung und Wirtschaftsstruktur im Nationalsozialismus' (1942) in: Alfons Söllner (ed.), *Wirtschaft, Recht und Staat im Nationalsozialismus. Analysen des Instituts für Sozialforschung 1939–42*, Frankfurt, 1984, pp. 235–83

Hachtmann, Rüdiger, *Industriearbeit im Dritten Reich. Untersuchungen zu den Lohn- und Arbeitsbedingungen in Deutschland 1933–1945*, Göttingen, 1989

———, 'Arbeitsmarkt und Arbeitszeit in der Deutschen Industrie 1929–1939' in: *Archiv für Sozialgeschichte* 27 (1987)

Hamburger, Ernest, 'The German Labor Front' in: *Monthly Labor Review* 59 (1944), pp. 932–44

Hamburger Stiftung für Sozialgeschichte (HSG) (ed.), *Das Daimler-Benz Buch. Ein Rüstungskonzern im Tausendjährigen Reich*, Nördlingen, 1987

Hamburger Stiftung zur Förderung von Wissenschaft und Kultur (HSzFWK) (ed.), *Deutsche Wirtschaft. Zwangsarbeit von KZ-Häftlingen für Industrie und Behörden*, Hamburg, 1991

Hansen, Eckhard, *Reichswehr und Industrie. Rüstungswirtschaftliche Zusammenarbeit und Wirtschaftliche Mobilmachungsvorbereitungen 1923–1932*, Boppard/Rhein, 1978

———, *Wohlfahrtspolitik im NS–Staat. Motivation, Konflikte und Machtstrukturen im 'Sozialismus der Tat' des Dritten Reiches*, Augsburg, 1991

Hasse, Albrecht, 'Arbeitsschutz im Kriege mit besonderer Berücksichtigung des Arbeitszeitschutzes' in: *Der Vierjahresplan* (1940), pp. 92–5

Haverbeck, Edgar, 'Werkzeugmaschinen für die spanlose Formung' in: *Der Vierjahresplan* (1939), pp. 1145–6

Hayes, Peter, *Industry and Ideology. IG Farben in the Nazi Era*, Cambridge, 1987

Heidebroek, E., 'Betriebsingenieure und Betriebsorganization' in: *Der Betrieb* (1931), pp. 1–4

Helms, Alfred 'Sozialistische Leistungssteigerung' in: *Der Vierjahresplan* (1944), pp. 75–6

Hentschel, Völker, 'Wirtschafts- und Sozialhistorische Brüche und Kontinuitäten zwischen Weimarer Republik und Drittem Reich' in: *Zeitschrift für Unternehmensgeschichte* 28 (1983), pp. 39–80

————, 'Daimler-Benz im 3. Reich. Zu Inhalt und Methode zweier Bücher zum gleichen Thema' in: *Vierteljahresheft für Sozial- und Wirtschaftsgeschichte* 75 (1988), pp. 74–100.

Herbert, Ulrich, *Fremdarbeiter. Politik und Praxis des Ausländer-Einsatzes in der Kriegswirtschaft des Dritten Reiches*, Berlin/Bonn, 1985

————, 'Arbeit und Vernichtung. Ökonomisches Interesse und Primat der Weltanschauung im Nationalsozialismus' in Diner, Dan (ed.), *Ist der Nationalsozialismus Geschichte?*, pp. 198–236.

————, 'Arbeiterschaft im Dritten Reich. Zwischenbilanz und Offene Fragen' in: *Geschichte und Gesellschaft* 15 (1989), pp. 320–60

Herbst, Ludolf, *Der Totale Krieg und die Ordnung der Wirtschaft. Die Kriegswirtschaft im Spannungsfeld von Politik, Ideologie und Propaganda*, Stuttgart, 1982

————, 'Kontinuität und Diskontinuität in den Deutschen Nachkriegsplanungen 1943 bis 1946/7' in: *Bulletin des Arbeitskreises 2. Weltkrieg* (1985), pp. 49–69.

Herttrich, 'Zur Entwicklung des Metalleinsatzes im Automobilbau' in: ATZ (1940), pp. 609–11

Hilberg, Raul, *Die Vernichtung der Europäischen Juden*, Frankfurt/M., 1982

Hildebrand, Klaus, *Das Dritte Reich*, 4. edn., 1991

Hildebrandt, H. (ed.), *Beiträge zur Metallfacharbeiterfrage. Die Streuung der Facharbeiteranteile in den Betrieben der Eisen- und Metallwirtschaft*, Sonderveröffentlichung des RABls, Berlin, 1942

Hinrichs, Peter, *Um die Seele des Arbeiters. Arbeitspsychologie, Industrie und Betriebssoziologie in Deutschland*, Cologne, 1981

Homburg, Heidrun, *Rationalisierung und Industriearbeit. Das Beispiel des Siemens-Konzerns Berlin 1900–39*, Berlin, 1991

Homze, Edward L., *Foreign Labor in Nazi Germany*, Princeton, 1967

Hoppmann, Barbara et al., *Zwangsarbeit bei Daimler-Benz*, Stuttgart, 1994

Hupfauer, Theo, 'Richtige Menschenführung steigert die Leistung' in: *Der Vierjahresplan* (1939), p. 606

————, 'Im neuen Leistungskampf der Betriebe' in: *Der Vierjahresplan* (1939), p. 866

Huth, Hermann, *Wirtschaftliche Fabrikbetrieb*, Berlin, 1938

Ingenlauf, Peter, *Probleme der Rationalisierung im Rahmen nationalsozialistischer Wirtschaftsauffassung*, Würzburg, 1938

'Innerbetrieblicher Leistungssteigerung' in: *Der Vierjahresplan* (1939), pp. 734–5

James, Harold, *The German Slump. Politics and Economics 1924–1936*, Oxford, 1986

Janssen, Gregor, *Das Ministerium Speer. Deutschlands Rüstung im 2. Weltkrieg*, Frankfurt/M., 1968

Jungbeck, Joachim, 'Zerstörung und Wiederaufbau' in: HSG (ed.), *Das Daimler-Benz Buch*, pp. 375–82

Kehrl, Hans, *Krisenmanager im Dritten Reich*, Düsseldorf, 1973

Kershaw, Ian, *Hitler*, London, 1991

————, *The Nazi Dictatorship. Problems and Perspectives of Interpretation*, London, 3rd edn., 1993

Kirchberg, Peter, 'Typisierung in der Deutschen Kraftfahrzeugindustrie und der Generalbevollmächtigte für das Kraftfahrwesen' in: *Jahrbuch für Wirtschaftsgeschichte* 10 (1969), pp. 117–142

Kirstein, Wolfgang, *Das Konzentrationslager als Institution des Totalen Terrors*, Pfaffenweiler, 1992

Knoop, Oscar, 'Industrielle Gesichtspunkte bei der Typenwahl von Personenkraftwagen' in: ATZ (1930), pp. 85–7

'Konzentration in der Berufserziehung' in: *Der Vierjahresplan* (1943), p. 419

Koppenhöfer, P., 'Erste Wahl für Daimler-Benz: Erinnerungen von KZ-Häftlingen an die Arbeit im Daimler-Benz Werk Mannheim' in: *Mitteilungen der Dokumentationsstelle zur Nationalsozialistischen Sozialpolitik* 15–16 (1986), pp. 5–30

————, 'In Buchenwald war die Verpflegung Besser. KZ-Häftlinge bei Daimler-Benz Mannheim' in: HSG (ed.), *Das Daimler-Benz Buch*, pp. 514–42

Kranig, Andreas, *Lockung und Zwang. Zur Arbeitsverfassung im Dritten Reich*, Stuttgart, 1983

Kratzsch, Gerhard, *Der Gauwirtschaftsapparat der NSDAP*, Münster, 1989

'Kriegsarbeit der Frau' in: *Der Vierjahresplan* (1943), pp. 116–17

'Der Kriegsberufswettkampf der Deutschen Jugend 1943–1944' in: *Der Vierjahresplan* (1943), pp. 404–8

Kroener, B., 'Der Kampf um den Sparstoff Mensch. Forschungskontroversen über die Mobilisierung der Deutschen Kriegswirtschaft 1939–1942' in: Michalka, W. (ed.), *Der Zweite Weltkrieg*, pp. 402–17

————, 'Die Personelle Resourcen des Dritten Reiches im Spannungsfeld zwischen Wehrmacht, Bürokratie und Kriegswirtschaft 1939–1942' in: MGFA (ed.), *Das Deutsche Reich und der Zweite Weltkrieg*, Band 5/1,

Stuttgart, 1988

Kruk, Max and Lingau, Gerald, *100 Jahre Daimler-Benz. Das Unternehmen*, Mainz, 1986

Kugler, Anita, *Arbeitsorganisation und Produktionstechnologie bei der Adam Opel Werke (von 1900 bis 1929)*, Berlin, 1985

———, 'Von der Werkstatt zum Fließband. Etappen der frühen Automobilproduktion in Deutschland' in: *Geschichte und Gesellschaft* 13 (1987), pp. 304–39

———, 'Die Behandlung des Feindlichen Vermögens in Deutschland und die Selbstverantwortung der Rüstungsindustrie. Dargestellt am Beispiel der Adam Opel AG von 1941 bis Anfang 1943' in: *1999. Zeitschrift für Sozialgeschichte des 20. und 21. Jahrhunderts* 2 (1988)

Kupke, E., *Jeder Denkt Mit!*, Berlin, 1939

'Kurzfristige Umschulung in der Kriegswirtschaft' in: *Der Vierjahresplan* (1939), pp. 1291–2

Lange, Karl, 'Werkzeugmaschinen als Grundlage der Produktionssteigerung' in: *Der Vierjahresplan* (1939), pp. 1133–4

Langelütke, H., 'Der Aufschwung der Automobilindustrie' in: *Die Deutsche Volkswirtschaft* (1935), pp. 831–2

———, 'Stand und Aussichten der Automobilkonjunktur' in: *Die Deutsche Volkswirtschaft* (1936), pp. 143–5

Leifer, G., 'Der Einfluß des planmäßigen Arbeitseinsatzes auf die Leistung der Betriebe' in: *Der Vierjahresplan* (1936), pp. 666–70

'Leistung ist alles' in: *Die Deutsche Volkswirtschaft* (1942), pp. 457–8

'Leistungsteigerung auch im Kriege' in: *Die Deutsche Volkswirtschaft* (1940), pp. 609–10

Ley, Robert, 'Ertüchtigung durch Berufserziehung – eine Nationalsozialistische Verpflichtung' in: *Der Vierjahresplan* (1937), pp. 74–7

———, 'Sozialismus und Leistung' in: *Der Vierjahresplan* (1942), pp. 410–11

Ludwig, Karl-Heinz, *Technik und Ingenieure im Dritten Reich*, Düsseldorf, 1979

Mai, Gunther, 'Die Nationalsozialistische Betriebszellenorganization (NSBO) von der Gründung bis zur Röhm-Affäre (1928–1934)' in: *Vierteljahresheft für Zeitgeschichte* 31 (1983), pp. 571–613

———, 'Warum steht der Deutsche Arbeiter zu Hitler – zur Rolle der Deutschen Arbeitsfront im Herrschaftssystem des Dritten Reiches' in: *Geschichte und Gesellschaft* 12 (1986), pp. 212–34

———, 'Arbeiterschaft Zwischen Sozialismus, Nationalismus, und Nationalsozialismus. Wider Gängige Stereotypen' in: Backes et al. (ed.), *Die Schatten der Vergangenheit* pp. 195–217

Maier, C.S., 'Between Taylorism and Technocracy. European Ideologies and the Vision of Industrial Production in the 1920s' in: *Journal of Contemporary History* 5 (1970), pp. 27–61

———, 'The Factory as Society' in: R.J.Bullen (ed.), *Ideas into Politics*, London, 1984, pp. 147–163

Mansfeld, Werner, 'Leistungssteigerung und Sozialpolitik' in: *Der Vierjahresplan* 1939, pp. 656–9

——, et al., *Das Gesetz zur Ordnung der Nationalen Arbeit. Kommentar*, Berlin, 1940

Marcuse, H., 'Some Social Implications of Modern Technology' in: *Zeitschrift für Sozialforschung* 9 (1941), pp. 414–39

Marrenbach, Otto, *Fundamente des Sieges. Die Gesamtarbeit der Deutschen Arbeitsfront 1933–1939*, Berlin, 1940

——, 'Großkampf der Fabriken' in: *Der Vierjahresplan* (1942), pp. 74–5

Mason, Timothy W., 'Der Primat der Politik – Politik und Wirtschaft im Nationalsozialismus' in: *Das Argument* 8 (1966) pp. 473–94

——, 'Primat der Industrie? – Eine Erwiderung' in: *Das Argument* 10 (1968), pp. 193–209

——, 'Zur Entstehung des Gesetzes zur Ordnung der Nationalen Arbeit vom 20. Januar 1934' in: Mommsen, Hans et al. (eds.), *Industrielles System und Politische Entwicklung in der Weimarer Republik*, Düsseldorf, 1974, pp. 322–51

——, *Arbeiterklasse und Volksgemeinschaft*, Opladen 1975

——, *Sozialpolitik im Dritten Reich*, Opladen, 1977

——, 'Die Bändigung der Arbeiterklasse im Nationalsozialistischen Deutschland. Eine Einleitung' in Sachse et al., *Angst, Belohnung*, pp. 11–53

Mende, Franz, 'Menschenführung und Betreuung im Ausländereinsatz' in: *Neue Internationale Rundschau der Arbeit* (1943), pp. 227–32

Messarius, Gustav, 'Das Leistungsertüchtigungswerk und seine Übungsleiter' in: *Der Vierjahresplan* (1944), pp. 40–2

Meyer, S., *The Five Dollar Day. Labour Management and Social Control in the Ford Motor Company*, New York, 1981

Meyer-Berkhout, B., *Typenbeschränkung und Rationalisierung der Deutschen Kraftfahrzeugindustrie*, Dresden, 1942

Michalka, W. (ed.), *Der Zweite Weltkrieg. Analysen, Grundzüge, Forschungsbilanz*, Munich, 1989

Michel, E., 'Fließarbeit und ihre Entwicklungsmöglichkeiten' in: *Maschinenbau* (1925), pp. 416–17

Militärgeschichtliches Forschungsamt (MGFA) (ed.), *Das Deutsche Reich und der Zweite Weltkrieg*, Band 5/1, *Organization und Mobilisierung des Deutschen Machtbereichs. Kriegsverwaltung, Wirtschaft und Personelle Resourcen 1939–41*, Stuttgart, 1988

Milward, Alan S., *The German Economy at War*, London, 1965

——, *War, Economy and Society 1939–1945*, London, 1975

——, 'Arbeitspolitik und Produktivität in der Deutschen Kriegswirtschaft unter Vergleichendem Aspekt' in: Forstmeier and Volkmann (eds.) *Kriegswirtschaft und Rüstung 1939–1945*

Mollin, Gregor, *Montankonzern und Drittes Reich. Der Gegensatz Zwischen*

Monopolindustrie und Befehlswirtschaft 1936–44, Göttingen, 1988

Mommsen, Hans, 'Nationalsozialismus als vorgetäuschte Modernisierung' in Pehle (ed.), *Der Historische Ort des Nationalsozialismus* pp. 31–46

———, 'Aufarbeitung und Verdrängung. Das Dritte Reich im Westdeutschen Geschichtsbewußtsein' in: Diner, (ed.), *Ist der Nationalsozialismus Geschichte?* pp. 74–88

———, 'Zwangsarbeit und Konzentrationslager bei den Volkswagenwerken' in: HSzFWK (ed.), *Deutsche Wirtschaft*, pp. 221–25

Mulert, Jürgen, 'Der Arbeitnehmer bei der Firma Robert Bosch zwischen 1886 und 1945' in: *Zeitschrift für Unternehmensgeschichte* 32 (1987), pp. 1–29

Müller, R.-D., 'Die Mobilisierung der Deutschen Wirtschaft für Hitlers Kriegsführung' in: MGFA (ed.), *Das Deutsche Reich und der Zweite Weltkrieg*, Band 5/1, pp. 347–689

———, 'Die Mobilisierung der Wirtschaft für den Krieg – Eine Aufgabe der Armee?' in: Michalka (ed.), *Der Zweite Weltkrieg* pp. 349–62

Musewald, Dora, 'Berufserziehungsmaßnahmen für Metallarbeiterinnen' in: Fachamt Eisen und Metall der DAF (ed.), *Die Frau in der Eisen und Metall-Industrie. Steigerung der Nationalen Produktionskraft. 3. Reichstagung in Stuttgart*, Stuttgart/Berlin, 1939

Naasner, W., *Neue Machtzentren in der Deutschen Kriegswirtschaft 1942–1945. Die Wirtschaftsorganisation der SS, das Amt des Generalbevollmächtigten für den Arbeitseinsatz und das Reichsministerium für Bewaffnung und Munition/Reichsministerium für Rüstung und Kriegsproduktion im Nationalsozialistischen Herrschaftssystem*, Boppard am Rhein, 1994

Neitzel, Gustav, 'Arbeitsschutz im Kriege mit besonderer Berücksichtigung des Betriebsschutzes' in: *Der Vierjahresplan* (1940), pp. 92–5

Neumann, Franz, *Behemoth. Struktur und Praxis des Nationalsozialismus 1933–1944*, Frankfurt, 1984

'Neuzeitliche Werkzeugmaschinen im Automobilbau' in *Automobiltechnische Zeitschrift* (1936), pp. 561–73

Nevins, A., *Ford. The Times, the Man, the Company*, New York, 1989

Noakes, Jeremy (ed.), *The Civilian in War*, Exeter, 1992

———, and Pridham, G. (eds.) *Documents on Nazism 1919–1945*, London, 1974

———, (eds.) *Nazism 1919–1945. A Documentary Reader*, 3. vols, Exeter, 1983–8

'Normung und Leistungssteigerung' in: *Der Vierjahresplan* (1939), pp. 674–6

Overy, R.J., 'Cars, Roads, and Economic Recovery in Germany 1932–8' in: *English Historical Review* 28 (1975) pp. 466–83

———, *Goering. The Iron Man*, London, 1984

———, 'Blitzkriegswirtschaft? Finanzpolitik, Lebensstandard und Arbeitseinsatz in Deutschland 1939–1942' in: *Vierteljahresheft für Zeitgeschichte* 36 (1988), pp. 379–435

———, 'Mobilization for Total War in Germany 1939–1941' in: *English*

Historical Review 103 (1988), pp. 613–39

———, War and Economy in the Third Reich, Oxford, 1994

———, 'Rationalization and the Production Miracle in Germany during the Second World War' in: War and Economy in the Third Reich pp. 343–75

———, 'Heavy Industry and the Third Reich: The Reichswerke Crisis' in: War and Economy in the Third Reich pp. 93–118

Pehle, Walter (ed.), Der Historische Ort des Nationalsozialismus, Frankfurt, 1990

Perz, Bertrand, Projekt Quarz. Steyr-Daimler-Puch und das Konzentrationslager Melk, Vienna, 1991

Petzina, Dieter, Autarkiepolitik im Dritten Reich. Der Nationalsozialistische Vierjahresplan, Stuttgart, 1968

Peukert, D. and Reulecke, J., Die Reihen fast Geschlossen. Beiträge zur Geschichte des Alltags unter dem Nationalsozialismus, Wuppertal, 1981

———, Inside Nazi Germany. Conformity, Opposition and Racism in Everyday Life, London, 1987

———, The Weimar Republic, London, 1991

Pingel, Falk, Häftlinge unter NS-Herrschaft, Hamburg, 1978

———, 'KZ-Häftlinge zwischen Vernichtung und Arbeitseinsatz' in: Michalka (ed.), Der Zweite Weltkrieg, pp. 784–97

Piskol, J., 'Zur Entwicklung der Aussenpolitischen Nachkriegskonzeptionen der Deutschen Monopolbourgeoisie 1943 bis 1945' in: Jahrbuch für Wirtschaftsgeschichte, (1969), II, pp. 329–45

Pohl, Hans et al., Die Daimler-Benz AG in den Jahren 1933–45. Eine Dokumentation, Wiesbaden, 1986

Preller, Ludwig, 'Das Zwiefache Profil Betrieblicher Sozialpolitik' in: Der Vierjahresplan (1942), pp. 321–4

Prinz, M., Vom Neuen Mittelstand zur Volksgenossen. Die Entwicklung des Sozialen Status der Angestellten von der Weimarer Republik bis zum Ende der NS-Zeit, Munich, 1986

Prinz, Michael and Zitelmann, Rainer (eds.), Nationalsozialismus und Modernisierung, Darmstadt, 1991

Propagandaamt der DAF, Die Kriegsarbeit der DAF, Berlin, 1944

Quadflieg, F., 'Rationalisierung und organisches Prinzip' in: Die Deutsche Volkswirtschaft (1939), pp. 143–6

'Rationalisierung der Lackierverfahren des Automobilbaues der Adlerwerke' in: ATZ (1931), pp. 601–4

Rebentisch, D. and Teppe, K. (eds.), Verwaltung Contra Menschenführung im Staat Hitlers, Göttingen, 1986

Rebentisch, D., Führerstaat und Verwaltung im Zweiten Weltkrieg, Stuttgart, 1989

Recker, Marie Luise, Nationalsozialistische Sozialpolitik im Zweiten Weltkrieg, Munich, 1985

Reich, Simon, The Fruits of Fascism, New York, 1991

Reichskuratorium für Wirtschaftlichkeit (RKW) (ed.), *Handbuch der Rationalisierung*, Berlin, 1930

————, *Der Mensch und die Rationalisierung*, Band 1, Jena, 1931

————, *Der Mensch und die Rationalisierung. Mensch und Arbeitsgerät*, Jena, 1933

————, *Der Mensch und die Rationalisierung. Eignung und Qualitätsarbeit*, Jena, 1933

Reiniger, H., 'Neuzeitliche Glühofen für fließende Fertigung in Motorfahrzeugfabriken' in: ATZ (1929), pp. 506–9

'Reparatur Moderner Serienwagen' in: ATZ (1930), pp. 799–800

Reulecke, J., 'Die Fahne mit dem Goldenen Zahnrad: Der Leistungskampf der Deutschen Betriebe 1937–1939' in: Peukert und Reulecke (eds.), *Die Reihen Fast Geschlossen*, pp. 245–92

Rohde, Horst, 'Das Eisenbahnverkehrswesen in der Deutschen Kriegswirtschaft 1939–1945' in: Forstmeier and Volkmann (eds.), *Kriegswirtschaft*, pp. 134–174

Rohwer, Götz, 'Die Lohnentwicklung bei Daimler-Benz Untertürkheim 1925–1940' in: 1999. *Zeitschrift für Sozialgeschichte des 20. und 21. Jahrhunderts* 4 (1989), 1, pp. 52–83

Roth, Karl-Heinz, 'Der Weg zum guten Stern des Dritten Reiches: Schlaglichter auf die Geschichte der Daimler-Benz AG und ihrer Vorläufer 1890–1945' in: HSG (ed.), *Das Daimler-Benz Buch*, pp. 27–382

————, 'Nazismus gleich Fordismus? Die Deutsche Autoindustrie in den Dreißiger Jahren' in: 1999. *Zeitschrift für Sozialgeschichte des 20. und 21. Jahrhunderts* 5 (1990) 4, pp. 82–9

————, 'Die Daimler-Benz AG. Ein Rüstungskonzern im Tausendjährigen Reich. Forschungsstand, Kontroversen, Kritik' in: 1999. *Zeitschrift für Sozialgeschichte des 20. und 21. Jahrhunderts* 8 (1993) 1, pp. 40–64

————, and Schmid, M. *Die Daimler-Benz AG 1918–1948. Schlüsseldokumente zur Konzerngeschichte*, Nördlingen, 1987

Rüther, Martin, 'Zur Sozialpolitik bei Klöckner-Humboldt-Deutz während des Nationalsozialismus. Die Masse der Arbeiterschaft muß aufgespalten werden' in: *Zeitschrift für Unternehmensgeschichte* 33 (1988), pp. 81–117

Sachse, Carola, *Betriebliche Sozialpolitik als Familienpolitik in der Weimarer Republik und im Nationalsozialismus. Mit einer Fallstudie über die Firma Siemens*, Berlin, 1987

————, *Siemens, der Nationalsozialismus und die Moderne Familie. Eine Untersuchung zur Sozialen Rationalisierung in Deutschland im 20. Jahrhundert*, Hamburg, 1990

————, 'Zwangsarbeit Jüdischer und Nichtjüdischer Frauen und Männer bei der Fa. Siemens 1940–45' in: Internationale Wissenschaftliche Korrespondenz zur Geschichte de deutschen Arbeitbewegung (IWK) 27 (1991), 1, pp. 1–11

————, et al., *Angst, Belohnung, Zucht und Ordnung. Herrschaftsmechanismen* im Nationalsozialismus, Opladen, 1982

Salter, Stephen, 'The Mobilization of German Labour 1939–1945', unpublished D.Phil., Oxford, 1983

Schell, Adolf von, 'Neue Wege der Deutschen Motorisierung' in: Der Vierjahresplan (1939,) pp. 362–4

——, 'Nationalsozialistische Wirtschaftsformen und Kraftfahrzeug-industrie' in: Der Vierjahresplan (1939), pp. 1010–12

Scheunemann, Werner, 'Konzentration auf den Sieg' in: Der Vierjahresplan (1942), pp. 88–90

——, 'Der Schaffende Mensch im Kriegsjahr 1941' in: Der Vierjahresplan (1942), pp. 140–1

Schley, Edgar, 'Vier Jahre – das Wunder Deutscher Motorisierung' in: ATZ (1937), pp. 53–9

Schmeer, R., 'Verpflichtung zur Berufsausbildung' in: Der Vierjahresplan (1939), pp. 660–1

Schmid, M., 'Unsere Ausländische Arbeitskräfte. Zwangsarbeiter in den Werken und Barackenlagern des DB–Konzerns' in: HSG (ed.), Das Daimler-Benz Buch, pp. 559–591

Schmidt, K.H., 'Betriebswissenschaftliche Grundlagen für die Einführung der Fließarbeit' in: Maschinenbau (1925), pp. 409–15

Schmiede, Rudi and Schudlich, Edwin, Die Entwicklung der Leistungs-entlohnung in Deutschland, Frankfurt/M., 1976

Schmitt, A., 'Die Geschichte des Konzentrationslagers Mannheim-Sandhofen. Ein Beitrag zur Zeitgeschichte im Regionalen Bereich', Zulassungsarbeit, Ludwigsburg, 1976

Schoenbaum, David, Hitler's Social Revolution, London, 1967

Schomerus, Heilweg, Die Arbeiter der Maschinenfabrik Esslingen, Stuttgart, 1977

Schumann, Hans-Gerd, Nationalsozialismus und Gewerkschaftsbewegung. Die Vernichtung der Deutschen Gewerkschaften und der Aufbau der Deutschen Arbeitsfront, Hannover, 1958

Schumann, W., 'Nachkriegsplanung der Reichsgruppe Industrie im Herbst 1944' in: Jahrbuch für Wirtschaftsgeschichte 3 (1972), pp. 259–95

——, 'Die Wirtschaftspolitische Überlebensstrategie des Deutschen Imperialismus in der Endphase des Zweiten Weltkrieges' in: Zeitschrift für Geschichtswissenschaft 27 (1979), pp. 499–513

Seebauer, Georg, 'Leistungssteigerung durch Rationalisierung' in: Der Vierjahresplan (1938), pp. 523–5

——, 'Leistungssteigerung als Kampfmittel' in: Der Vierjahresplan (1939), pp. 1064–7

——, 'Bewährte Gemeinschaftsarbeit an der Rationalisierung' in: Der Vierjahresplan (1943), pp. 105–7

Seebold, Gustav-Hermann, Ein Stahlkonzern im Dritten Reich. Der Bochumer Verein 1927–45, Wuppertal, 1981

Seidler, F.W., *Fritz Todt. Baumeister des Dritten Reiches*, Berlin, 1988

Seubert, Rolf, *Berufserziehung und Nationalsozialismus. Berufliche Bildung und Berufspolitik Bd. 1*, Weinheim/Basel, 1977

Siebel, Fritz, 'Der Unternehmer und Betriebsführer in der Luftfahrtindustrie' in: *Der Vierjahreplan* (1937), 648–52

Siegel, Tilla, 'Lohnpolitik im Nationalsozialistischen Deutschland' in: Sachse et al., *Angst, Belohnung*, pp. 11–139

———, 'Rationalisierung statt Klassenkampf. Zur Rolle der Deutschen Arbeitsfront in der Nationalsozialistischen Ordnung der Arbeit' in: Mommsen, Hans (ed.), *Herrschaftsalltag im Dritten Reich. Studien und Texte*, Düsseldorf, 1988

———, *Leistung und Lohn in der Nationalsozialistischen Ordnung der Arbeit*, Opladen, 1989

———, 'Der Doppelte Rationalisierung des Ausländereinsatzes bei Siemens' in: *IWK* 27 (1991) 1, pp. 12–24

Siegfried, K.-J., *Rüstungsproduktion und Zwangsarbeit 1939–1945*, Frankfurt/M., 1987

Sklavenarbeit im KZ, Dachauer Hefte Nr. 2, Dachau, 1986

Smelser, Ronald, *Robert Ley. Hitler's Labor Front Leader*, Oxford, 1988

———, 'Die Sozialplanung der Deutschen Arbeitsfront' in: Prinz and Zitelmann (eds.) *Nationalsozialismus und Modernisierung*, pp. 71–92

———, 'How Modern Were the Nazis?' in: *German Studies Review* 13 (1990), pp. 285–302

Speer, Albert, 'Selbstverantwortung in der Rüstungsindustrie' in: *Der Vierjahresplan* (1943), pp. 242–3

———, *Inside the Third Reich*, London, 1971

Sperling, H., 'Der verstärkte Arbeitseinsatz der Frau' in: *Die Deutsche Volkswirtschaft* (1940), pp. 790–2

Spohn, Wolfgang, *Betriebsgemeinschaft und Volksgemeinschaft. Die Rechtliche und Institutionelle Regelung der Arbeitsbeziehungen im NS-Staat*, Berlin, 1987

Stahlmann, Michael, 'Management, Modernisierungs- und Arbeitspolitik bei der Daimler-Benz AG und ihrer Vorläuferunternehmen von der Jahrhundertwende bis zum Zweiten Weltkrieg' in: *Zeitschrift für Unternehmensgeschichte* 3, (1992), pp. 147–80

———, *Die Erste Revolution in der Autoindustrie. Management und Arbeitspolitik von 1900–1940*, Frankfurt, 1993

Starcke, Gerhard, *Die Deutsche Arbeitsfront. Eine Darstellung über Zweck, Leistung und Ziele*, Berlin, 1940

Stegmann, D., 'Zum Verhältnis von Grossindustrie und Nationalsozialismus 1930–1933' in: *Archiv für Sozialgeschichte* 13 (1973), pp. 399–482

Stein, Helmut, 'Aufgaben des Vorrichtungsbaues bei der Leistungssteigerung' in: *Zeitschrift des Vereines Deutscher Ingenieure* (1942), pp. 697–702

Streit, C., 'Sowjetische Kriegsgefangene – Massendeportation –

Zwangsarbeiter' in: Michalka (ed.), *Der Zweite Weltkrieg*, pp. 747–60

Strohmeyer, H.C., 'Die Deutsche Automobilindustrie im Jahre 1934' in: *Die Deutsche Volkswirtschaft* (1935), pp. 147–50

———, 'Strukturwandel in der Automobilwirtschaft' in: *Die Deutsche Volkswirtschaft* (1936), pp. 180–1

Studders, Herbert, *Die Facharbeiterfrage in der Kriegswirtschaft*, Hamburg, 1938

Thomas, Georg, *Geschichte der Deutschen Wehr- und Kriegswirtschaft 1918–1943/45*, Boppard am Rhein, 1966

Tröger, Annemarie, 'Die Frau im Wesensgemäßen Einsatz' in: Frauengruppe Faschismusforschung (ed.), *Mutterkreuz und Arbeitsbuch*, Frankfurt, 1981

———, 'Die Planung des Rationalisierungsproletariats. Zur Entwicklung der Geschlechtsspezifischen Arbeitsteilung und des weiblichen Arbeitsmarkts im Nationalsozialismus' in: Kuhn, Annette and Jörn Rüsen, (eds.) *Frauen in der Geschichte Bd.* 2 Düsseldorf, 1982, pp. 245–313

Tolliday, Stephen and Zeitlin, Jonathon (eds.), *Between Fordism and Flexibility*, Oxford, 1986

'Die Typenbegrenzung in der Kraftfahrzeugindustrie' in: *Der Vierjahresplan* (1939), pp. 530–1

Turner, H.A., *German Big Business and the Rise of Hitler*, Oxford, 1985

Umbreit, H., 'Auf dem Weg zur Kontinentalherrschaft' in: MGFA (ed.), *Das Deutsche Reich und der Zweite Weltkrieg*, Band 5/1

United States Strategic Bombing Survey (USSBS) (ed.), *Finished Report No. 2. The United States Strategic Bombing Survey. Overall Report (European War)*, Washington D.C., 1947

———, (ed.), *Finished Report No. 3. The Effects of Stragic Bombing on the German War Economy*, Washington D.C., 1947

———, (ed.), *Finished Report No. 53. The German Anti-Friction Bearings Industry*, Washington D.C., 1947

———, (ed.), *Finished Report No. 54. Machine Tools and Machinery as Capital Equipment*, Washington D.C., 1947

———, (ed.), *Finished Report No. 77. German Motor Vehicles Industry Report*, Washington D.C., 1947

———, (ed.), *Finished Report No. 79. Daimler-Benz AG, Untertürkheim, Germany*, Washington D.C., 1947

———, (ed.), *Finished Report No. 82. Daimler-Benz, Gaggenau Works, Gaggenau, Germany*, Washington D.C., 1947

'Voraussetzungen der Leistungssteigerung' in: *Der Vierjahresplan* (1942), pp. 186–7

Vorländer, H. (ed.), *Nationalsozialistische Konzentrationslager im Dienst der Totalen Kriegsführung. Sieben Württembergische Aussenkommandos des KZ Natzweiler-Elsass*, Stuttgart, 1978

Wagenführ, Rolf, *Die Deutsche Industrie im Kriege 1939 bis 1945*, Berlin, 1963

Warlimont, P., 'Aufgabe der Fördertechnik bei der Einfuhrung von Fließarbeit' in: (*Maschinenbau*) 1925, pp. 430–1

'Der Weg der Rationalisierung' in: *Der Vierjahresplan* (1941), pp. 657–8

'Werkzeitung im Kriege' in: *Der Vierjahresplan* (1943), pp. 419–20

Werk Sindelfingen, Stuttgart, 1990

Werk Untertürkheim. Stammwerk der Daimler-Benz Aktiengesellschaft. Ein Historischer Überblick, Stuttgart, 1983

Werlin, Jakob, 'Vier Jahre Aufbau in der Motorisierung' in: *Der Vierjahresplan* (1937), pp. 87–8

———, 'Fünf Jahre Motorisierung im Nationalsozialistischen Deutschland' in: *Der Vierjahresplan* (1938), pp. 79–80

———, 'Fortschritte der Motorisierung' in: *Der Vierjahresplan* (1939), pp. 70–3

———, 'Acht Jahre Motorisierung – Acht Jahre Vorsprung' in: *Der Vierjahresplan* (1941), pp. 315–17

Werner, Wolfgang Franz, *Bleib übrig! Deutsche Arbeiter in der Nationalsozialistischen Kriegswirtschaft*, Düsseldorf, 1983

'Wichtige Mitarbeiter an der Motorisierung' in: *Der Vierjahresplan* (1941), pp. 318–19

Wiedemann, W., 'Die Anwendung der Fließarbeit in Amerika und in England' in: *Maschinenbau* (1925), pp. 430–1

Winkler, Dörte, *Frauenarbeit im Dritten Reich*, Hamburg, 1977

Wisotsky, Klaus, *Der Ruhrbergbau im Dritten Reich*, Düsseldorf, 1983

Wolsing, Theo, *Untersuchungen zur Berufsausbildung im Dritten Reich*, Kastellaun, 1977

Wysocki, Gerd, *Arbeit für den Krieg*, Braunschweig, 1992

Zangen, Wilhelm, 'Die Reichsgruppe Industrie im Kriege' in: *Der Vierjahresplan* (1940), pp. 4–5

Ziegler, Jürgen, *Mitten unter Uns. Natzweiler-Struthof: Auf den Spuren eines Konzentrationslager*, Hamburg, 1986

Zitelmann, Rainer, *Hitler. Selbstverständnis eines Revolutionärs*, 2. Edn., Stuttgart, 1989

Zmarzlik, H., 'Berufsnachwuchslenkung auch im Kriege' in: *Die Deutsche Volkswirtschaft* (1939), pp. 1056–8

Zollitsch, Wolfgang, *Arbeiter zwischen Weltwirtschaftskrise und Nationalsozialismus*, Göttingen, 1990

Zumpe, Lotte, *Wirtschaft und Staat in Deutschland 1933 bis 1945*, (East) Berlin, 1980

Index